ten·der ténder/ **adj** soft enough for the teeth to go through easily; the point at which something is ready to eat: the leaves of a bunch of spinach, a ripe fig. **Soft or delicate in substance**. Not hard or tough. **Ripe**. Ripe and ready to eat. Yielding readily to pressure. **Fragile**. Of a delicate nature; so soft as to be hurt, crushed, or broken easily. Requiring careful handling: a tender subject. **Affectionate**. Benevolent; compassionate; careful. **With gentle feeling**. Showing care, gentleness, sensitivity, and feeling.

   Botanical. Needing protection from harsh weather, especially frost and cold.

[**13th century. Via French** *tendre* **from Latin** *tener* **"delicate, tender" (source also of English tendril).**]

For Allan Jenkins

To Louise Haines, for her tireless encouragement, support, and patience. I can never, ever thank you enough. To Jonnie for his pictures and friendship, to Sam Wolfson for her brilliance, and to Jiri Merka for all his hard work.

To the wiser and more experienced gardeners whose words I turn to for enlightenment: Beth Chatto, Joy Larkcom, Carol Klein, Jekka McVicar, Sarah Raven, Chris Young, Charles Dowding, Christopher Stocks. To Monty Don and Dan Pearson, without whom this garden would still be a backyard. And thank you too to Huw Morgan; Katie Findlay; and to everyone at The Royal Horticultural Society and *The Garden*.

To Jane Scotter, who knows more about growing vegetables than I ever will. Thank you for your beautiful produce, much of which is pictured here in these pages and has become so much a part of my cooking life. Thank you too to everyone at the magical place that is Fern Verrow.

Gratitude is also due to: Jane Middleton, Araminta Whitley, Rosemary Scoular, Victoria Barnsley, John Bond, Julian Humphries, Michelle Kane, Graham Cook, Elizabeth Woabank, Sarah Randell, Mark Adderley, Nadia Sawalha, Tim d'Offay, and to Allan Jenkins, Nicola Jeal, Caroline Boucher, and everyone at *The Observer*. To Franco Chung and Rob Watson for their technical expertise and to Dalton Wong and James Duigan for helping me feel better than I have ever done in my life. And an enormous shout to all those kind, generous, and communicative readers whose thoughtful words keep me going.

This book is what it is because of you all.

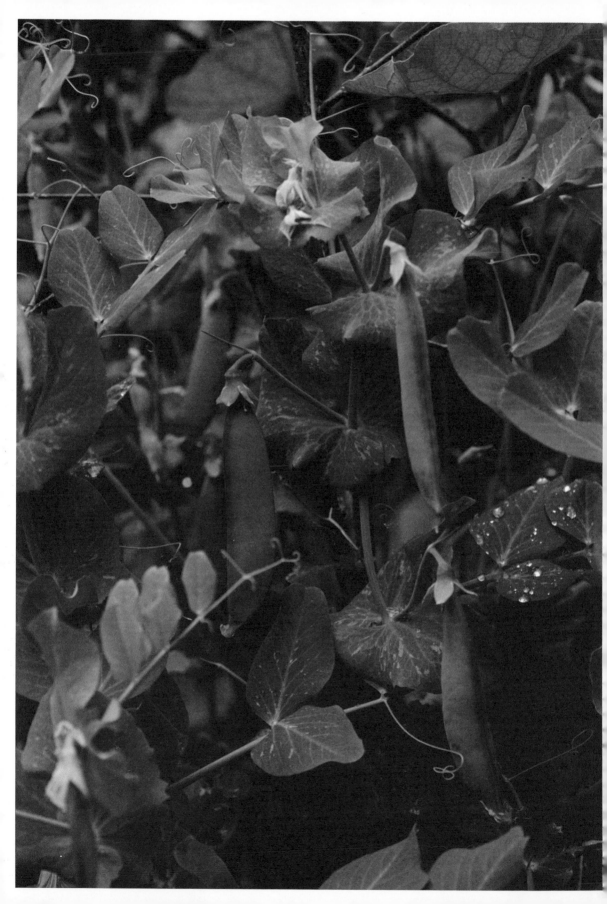

Tender

A cook and his vegetable patch

NIGEL SLATER

Photographs by Jonathan Lovekin

TEN SPEED PRESS
Berkeley

Published in the United States by Ten Speed Press,
an imprint of the Crown Publishing Group, a division
of Random House, Inc., New York.
www.crownpublishing.com
www.tenspeed.com

Ten Speed Press and the Ten Speed Press colophon are
registered trademarks of Random House, Inc.

Originally published in hardcover in Great Britain by
Fourth Estate, a division of HarperCollins Publishers,
London, in 2009

Library of Congress Cataloging-in-Publication Data
is on file with the publisher.

ISBN 978-1-60774-037-7

Printed in China

Interior design by BLOK
Cover design by Colleen Cain

10 9 8 7 6 5 4 3 2 1

First U.S. Edition

Introduction

I keep lists. Some copied into notebooks in neat italic script in blue-black ink, others scribbled almost illegibly in soft pencil on the back of an old envelope. Most remain in my head. There is the usual inventory of things I need to do, of course, but also less urgent lists, those of books to read or read again, music to find, plants to secure for the garden, and letters to be written (few of which will ever see the light of day). One list that has remained in my head is that of favorite scents, the catalogue of smells I find particularly evocative or uplifting. Snow (yes, I believe it has a smell), dim sum, old books, cardamom, beeswax, moss, warm pancakes, a freshly snapped runner bean, a roasting chicken, a fleeting whiff of white narcissi on a freezing winter's day.

High on that list comes cress seeds sprouting on wet blotting paper. It is a smell I first encountered in childhood, a classroom project that became a hobby. Cool and watery, fresh yet curiously ancient, as you might expect from a mixture of green shoots and damp parchment, it has notes of both nostalgia and new growth about it. Sometimes, when I have watered my vegetable patch late on a spring evening, I get a fleeting hint of that scent. A ghostlike reminder of how this whole thing started.

I guess I have always grown something to eat: that cress on a blotter when I was still in short pants; beans in a jam jar; carrots and candytuft in a forlorn strip of my parents' garden. There were the tomato plants precariously balanced on the window ledge of my student digs, orange and lemon seeds and other unmentionable plants nurtured under grow lights, salad sprouters, a bucket garden on a balcony. Then there were the herbs in pots that lethally adorned the fire escape of my first apartment and its communal garden. That I would one day turn my own lawn into a vegetable patch was, I suppose, inevitable.

Perhaps because I was brought up on frozen peas—they were virtually the only vegetable that passed my lips until I was in double figures—I now have a curiosity and an appetite for vegetables that extends far beyond any other ingredient. Shopping at the market on a Saturday morning, I will spend four or five times as long choosing my beans, tomatoes, or lettuces than I will buying anything else. Vegetables beckon and intrigue in a way no fish or piece of meat ever could.

The beauty of a single lettuce, its inner leaves tight and crisp, the outer ones opened up like those of a cottage garden rose; the glowing saffron flesh of a cracked pumpkin; the curling tendrils of a pea plant; a bunch of long, white-tipped radishes; a bag of assorted tomatoes in shades of scarlet, green, and orange is something I like to take time over. And not only is it the look of them that is beguiling. The rough feel of a runner bean between the fingers, the childish pop of a pea pod, the inside of a fur-lined fava bean case, the cool vellumlike skin of a freshly dug potato are all reason to linger. And all this even before we have turned the oven on.

Their beauty and tactile qualities aside, what you do with them is loaded with even greater sensual pleasure. Just listen to this: a supper of golden pumpkin with a crisp crumb-crust flecked with parsley and garlic; a dish of emerald cabbage leaves with shards of sizzling ginger; a crumbling soft-pastried tart of leeks, cream, and cheese; a bright carrot chutney on a mound of ivory-colored rice to make your lips prickle. Soporific risottos of asparagus; gratins of potato, garlic, and cream; yellow tomatoes with a sauce the color of terra-cotta that makes your mouth tingle with chile, lemongrass, and fresh mint. None of this is difficult, time-consuming, or expensive. It is straightforward, approachable cooking for eating either for its own sake or on the same plate as a piece of meat or fish.

While still enjoying my crackling pork roasts and grilled lamb, my baked mackerel and crab salad, I have become more interested than ever in the effect of a diet higher in "greens" than it is in meat—both in terms of my own well-being and, more recently, those implications that go beyond me and those for whom I cook. As Michael Pollan, author of *In Defense of Food* (The Penguin Press, 2008), says: "In all my interviews with nutrition experts, the benefits of a plant-based diet provided the only point of universal consensus." On a personal note, I would simply say that I feel much better for a diet that is predominantly vegetable based.

Every little bit helps

We have damaged this planet. We have plundered its natural resources, emptied its seas, scorched its earth, turned its beating heart into a toxic rubbish dump. There have been decades, if not centuries, of take rather than give. I do not wish to relinquish entirely the deep sense of fulfillment I get from eating meat and fish, but I now place less importance on them in my diet than I did. It is the meat and the crackling rather than the vegetables

that are now on the side. When you lift the lid of my casseroles, peer into my pots, or read my plate, it is the veggies that play the starring role.

And yes, it is worth "reading" our plate before we dig in. Where did that food come from? Does it sit comfortably with our conscience and what we believe good food to be? What, other than our immediate appetite, does it benefit, and crucially, what damage is that plate of food doing?

If digging up our gardens, getting an allotment, shopping at farmers' markets, growing organically, and eating sustainably is seen as a sign of our collective guilt for what we have done to the planet, then so be it. We can never totally undo what has been done. But there are some of us, hopeful, deluded, possibly a wee bit mad, who are happy to try to put in more than we take out. One of the ways we can do that is to eat a greener diet.

Swapping my lawn for leeks and lettuces has a lot to do with wanting to know as much as possible about what I am eating. It is, I suppose, my way of making a deeper connection with my food, a desire to know the whole story rather than just what it says on the label. More than anything, the move is about a desire for simplicity. Our food production has become so complicated, with its air miles, pesticides, extended shelf life, marketing, and packaging. I hanker after something simpler, more honest and direct. More holistic, if you like. The idea of planting a seed, watching it grow, then eating the result instantly does away with much of the baggage that goes hand in hand with our modern food supply.

I don't have to grow or cook. There is enough good food out there for a life free of both garden and stove. But in much the same way as I cook partly for the gratification of watching a potato turn from ivory to gold in the pan, for a taste of the sticky stuff on the surface of meat as you turn it in the roasting pan, for the feel of a ripe peach and its blessed juice trickling down my stubbly chin, I grow for the joy it brings. I like getting my hands in the soil as much as I like rubbing butter into flour to make pastry. Sometimes there's bread dough under my fingernails, sometimes manure. Sometimes, truth be told, there's a bit of both.

I plant seeds because I get a buzz from watching green shoots poke through the soil, from looking after them as something precious and vital, protecting them from the pigeons and foxes and clumsy feet that roam the modern city garden, from feeding them and watching them bloom. Cooking with vegetables you have grown gives not only an extraordinary sense of completeness and a simplifying of the food chain, but also the chance to experience a profound respect for an ingredient—something we are unlikely to feel for an item picked up in a "two for the price of one" promotion in a supermarket. It helps us to understand our food and to appreciate its value, I might even suggest to develop a certain reverence.

I don't own acres of land and probably never will. The bulk of my fruit and vegetables still come from market stalls, shops, and a weekly organic box delivery. I still go to the produce market and the supermarket for much of my fruit. What I grow is simply the icing on the cake. If it seems as if I'm playing at it, then fine, I will wear whatever label you want to hang round my neck, but all I know is that I am having fun with the space I have and eating some great food.

Right now, as I write, my little urban garden is home to three varieties of zucchini; two of fava beans; pole beans; runner beans; borlotti; ruby, white, and yellow chard; peas—both snow and purple podded; spinach; five varieties of tomatoes; three of potatoes; summer squash; pumpkin; and beets. I have seven varieties of lettuce, plus arugula, cabbage, cavolo nero, Brussels sprouts, globe and Jerusalem artichokes, carrots, leeks, red cabbage, and more herbs than you can shake a *mezzaluna* at. I'm not sure the cauliflower will survive, though—you need to know what you are doing with that one.

And to think I could have had a piece of grass on which to kick a ball around instead.

Moving in

I moved into this house on a scruffy London terrace on the eve of the new millennium—the date chosen not for the possibility of harnessing any beneficial cosmic energy abroad on that auspicious point in the calendar but simply because I knew it would be the only day of the year the Aussie movers could block the exceptionally narrow lane with a van and get away with it. As revelers' fireworks lit up the night sky and the whole world partied, I released three elderly and somewhat bewildered cats into their new and laughably empty home, upended a bottle of not very cold champagne into the only glass I could find, and toasted the echoey old house and its long, thin, and abandoned garden.

The house had previously been home to a celebrated collection of Italian art, a Victorian slum so grim it had a closing order slapped on it, and a hospice run by Catholic nuns (one of whom appears not to have quite departed). It had also had one of its front windows blown out during the Second World War. It holds mysteries, too. Why is there a false wall in the scullery and what does it hide? The attached garden has the elongated, rectangular proportions typical of many terraces all over England but has the advantage of being west facing and a good bit longer than usual. Curiously, it looks much (much) larger in photographs, particularly those taken from the chimney stacks, than it really is. At only 40 feet (12 meters) long, we are hardly talking about much more space than the average allotment.

The land on which the house sits had, until the early 1800s, been pasture for the local dairy farms. The remains of dairies are scattered all over this part of London. There has been a cheesemonger, in various guises, farther along the terrace since Victorian times. Mostly laid to lawn that had

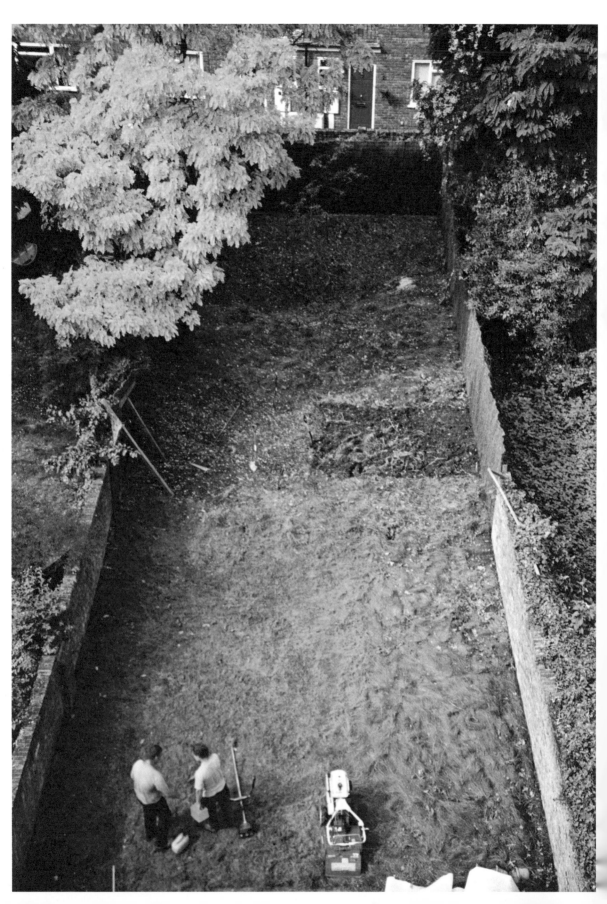

gone to seed, the garden had but a single fig tree, its gray branches stretched out like spindly, adolescent arms across the brown grass, and an old and graceful golden robinia. The space was basically a clean slate.

At the stroke of midnight, I sat down on the back steps and vowed to dig up my lawn and grow at least some of my own vegetables and fruit.

In a city garden as small as this, I could only dream of any idea of self sufficiency (this is hardly the lost gardens of Heligan), but over the next few years I would go on to grow dark, smoky-leaved cabbages, violet carrots, Turkish Orange eggplants, eight varieties of potato, speckled pole beans, and gnarled and exquisitely flavored heirloom tomatoes. I would experience the pleasure of growing food from seed, to complement the food I trudged home with from the shops; vegetables and fruit that have become the new backbone of my daily cooking and eating and have signaled an important, life-enhancing new order in my kitchen.

The site

A friend, perhaps after one glass of rosé too many, once referred to the space as having a cloisterlike quality to it. True, its high hedges and tall gates make for a feeling of solitude. You do indeed feel hidden. And yes, there is shade and a corridor around the perimeter, and the vegetable patch is laid out in a series of six small beds similar to those of early monastery gardens. At night you can hear your footsteps on the deep gravel paths and the stone terrace. In winter you can see fox prints in the snow. At dusk in midsummer the garden is heavy with the scent of white jasmine and crimson sweet peas. There are bees, butterflies, squirrels, foxes, and, two gardens away, a resident woodpecker. But in reality, it is nothing more than just the back garden to a London terraced house. And a shabby one at that.

The garden's feeling of enclosure and protection—of a secret space— exists partly because of the trellis mounted on top of the old brick walls and the thick growth of ivy that has formed a solid, tangled mass around it. In places, I need to climb a ladder to trim the top and use a machete to beat it into submission. At the far end is a row of tall hornbeams, chosen for the piercing green of their young leaves in spring and the fact that their bright leaves offer reflected light to the neighboring houses, rather than blocking it as would leylandii.

Small though it is, the garden is split into three distinct enclosures: an old York stone terrace that is home to the rickety, recycled dining table; the diminutive vegetable patch of which I now write; and a tiny, gated section of tranquil, fragrant green-and-white shrubs. My sanctuary. I should also include the wide garden steps that are currently home to pots of everything, from Tradescant roses and lemon thyme to purple sage, runner beans, and wild strawberries. Getting much afternoon sunshine, this space is useful

for ripening tomatoes and even, in a good year, eggplants. It is an absurd amount to cram into a tiny city garden, but I like the fact that every inch is put to good use.

There is also a large, deep lightwell, to which I have never really given a name. "Terrace" would imply endless sunshine, "patio" makes me cringe, and "basement" just sounds plain depressing. Whatever you call it, the space is sheltered, warm, and enjoys the afternoon sun. Lined with tiny, French wire-cut bricks rescued from the restoration of St. Pancras station, it is home to a large and much used cold frame (the best money I have ever spent), terra-cotta pots of tomatoes and zucchini and, in deepest summer, an eight-foot tepee of green beans. It is where I plant all my seeds, pot up seedlings, and overwinter the pelargoniums and the more fragile of the potted herbs. A Petite Negra fig tree has made its home here too, its branches dripping with almost-black fruit in late summer. A billowing rose—Souvenir de Madame Léonie Viennot—clambers up the sunny side, hiding a dodgy wall that desperately needs attending to. It is dark and a little damp in the way that basements often are, and is very much a silk purse made from a sow's ear, but an invaluable little space nevertheless. It often makes me feel I could have made more of "basements gone by."

Every wall is used: an espaliered Doyenne du Comice pear on the south-facing wall, a fig in the basement, a Fragola grapevine framing the kitchen doors. I would put something up the kitchen walls if it didn't mean removing the headily fragrant Chinese jasmine that frames the scullery window.

I realize I have created what is effectively an allotment to which I don't have to travel. But then, the waiting list for an allotment in my part of the world runs into years. When I look at the garden now, with its ivy-clad walls, its rows of radishes, its quinces and espaliered pears, not to mention the bed of Arran Victory potatoes and "dinner-plate" dahlias, it is hard to picture it nine years previously, when it was just a patch of ill-mown grass.

By default, the space has become a haven to butterflies, bees, and ladybugs, and amid its low box hedges, rambling nasturtiums, and small fruit bushes lives a family of cute but not totally welcome urban foxes.

Self-sufficiency—dream on

There is no possible way I could be self-sufficient in vegetables and fruit with a garden of this size. Most friends with allotments treat what they pick as a bonus rather than expecting it to meet all their vegetable needs. That is not the point. I grow simply for the pleasure of growing; for the joy of watching seeds turn into plants and seeing them—sometimes—come to fruition. Failures? Listen, there's been more than a few. But the surprising successes, such as the eighty bunches of Fragola grapes that hung like fairy lights from the two tiny vines in the (appallingly wet) summer of 2008, the endless tomatoes, or the glowing yellow zucchini flowers that greet me each autumn morning, are worth the occasional row of lettuce seedlings disappearing overnight or the Florence strawberries that were eaten by everything in the garden except me.

I have sown somewhat more than I have reaped. But as somewhere to watch things grow, a place to tend and nurture, to sit and eat, to drink and think, to taste and smell, and most importantly to understand the unity of growing, cooking, and eating, it is a monumental success. At least it is to me.

The soil

I garden on clay and I cannot tell you how much hard work has gone into getting the soil right. A few weeks after I moved in, Montague Don, friend and at that time stablemate at *The Observer*, stuck his spade into the parched soil and declared it "typical London clay. It's going to need a lot, and I mean a lot, of organic matter."

And organic matter it has had. Bucketfuls of compost made from my own vegetable peelings, bag after bag of well-rotted horse manure, bracken and sheep's wool from a traditional hill farm in the Lake District, and much from my local council's green waste system (it collects our garden trimmings, even our old Christmas trees, turns them into compost, then offers the sweet, tobacco-textured results back to the community). The garden's soil is now as rich and sweet as Sachertorte.

The ground has seen no chemicals and no peat since the day I picked up my spade. Every cell in my body believes in organic gardening, even if it does mean the odd heartache when a row of fava beans is munched by slugs overnight because (whisper it) the organic slug pellets don't work as well as the nonorganic ones.

Once the lawn was dug up and recycled, the ground dug first mechanically, then by hand, the real work of getting the soil "right" started. Many are the days I could barely straighten my back from carrying bags of manure from the pavement through to the garden. Like many typical terraced homes, we have no back entrance, so there is no alternative but to carry eighty bags of steaming horseshit through the house. I have learned to pick a dry day.

My soil is now what I hope Monty might call "in good heart." If I have one piece of advice for anyone "growing their own," it is to get this right before you plant a single seed. Even if it means missing a season while you plant green manure such as red clover or trefoil. The soil is like a bank account. We should put in more than we take out.

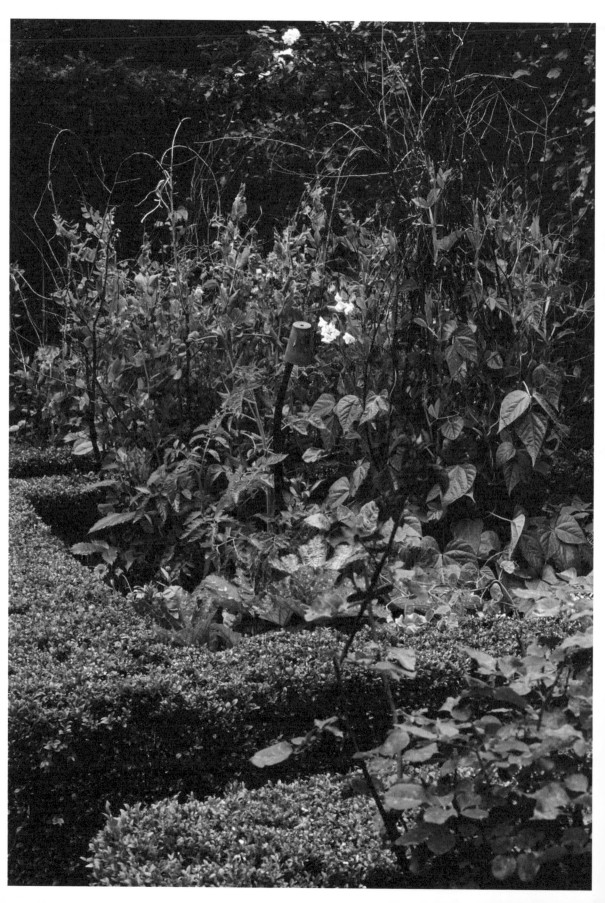

The seeds

I get my seeds from friends, seed catalogues, and specialty nurseries. I have always preferred the artisan and the cottage industry to big business, and tend to take that approach with seeds too. It's not that there is anything wrong with the big seed companies, far from it; it is just the way I like to do things. The choice of organically grown seeds is getting wider by the year. It is a mistake to turn our noses up at the more pricey seeds, which can often turn out to be better value. I have found that you generally get what you pay for, and bargain-basement seeds often mean a poor germination rate.

Wherever your seeds come from, they need some form of organization. An old shoebox, constantly in a state of suppressed chaos, sufficed for several years. When it finally fell to pieces, I found opened packets five years past their pull date. Then someone gave me an old church collection box, much polished, with spookily creaking hinges and two compartments just the right size for seed packets. What used to hold the harvest festival coins now holds a harvest festival of its own. The important thing is that your seeds have somewhere dark, dry, and cool to wait. Heat, moisture, and light will render them impotent in no time.

The seed catalogues have become an annual source of inspiration, information, and temptation. Winter afternoons are often spent thumbing through seed pamphlets and trawling Internet sites before putting in my order for violet-colored beans and firecracker-red chiles. It is almost impossible not to get carried away. You could do worse than follow my habit of writing out your wants list in the late afternoon, then taking a red pencil to it the next day. A night's sleep can often induce a reality check.

I struggle for outdoor space to grow, but more crucially for space indoors to germinate. This old house has just two tiny windowsills. Both are filled to bursting with little coir pots, toilet paper roll middles, and seed trays, all filled with seed compost by the first week in March. Sprouting seed by the window is fine for the initial germination but can produce spindly plants unless the room is cool. As luck will have it, this house is almost permanently cool, even in deepest summer. Friends have been known to wear a fleece to dinner.

It was with great relief that I discovered the joy of the garden-ready plug plant—a bag of plump little seedlings delivered to your door all ready to pot up. What seems expensive at first glance turns out to be a saving, in that I treasure each little plant even more. I use this system for things I find tricky to germinate, which includes the brassica family and tomatoes. Everything else I grow from seed.

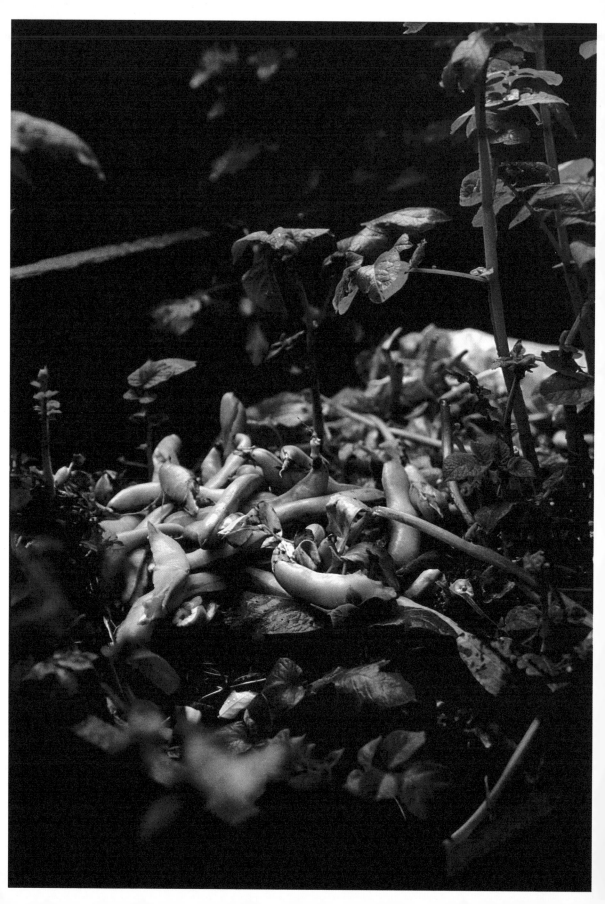

Into the garden

The decision to surround each of the six beds with box hedging is an attractive one, but to be honest, I wouldn't do it again. Raised beds would be my recommendation to anyone setting up a vegetable garden from scratch. Hedges, however neatly they frame your peas, beans, and swaying sunflowers, are also snail hotels, providing a home for hundreds of gastropods who come out at night, drink from your beer traps, then go on a drunken rampage. So, unlike the average allotment holder, I cannot plant directly into the soil. I have to germinate my seeds in pots, then transfer them when they are big enough to put up with losing the odd leaf or two to munching snails. Too many have partied on my carefully nurtured seedlings. I sometimes think the hedges would have gone long ago if it wasn't for the achingly beautiful sight of them covered in snow.

Compost

At the very back of the garden, hidden in the last of the small enclosures and shaded by the branches of a damson tree, is the compost heap. A mixture of prunings, annual weeds, vegetable peelings, and the odd bit of cardboard, this source of horticultural treasure has at last done well. After a tricky start, I now have a deep store of black, moist, homemade compost.

Despite being properly constructed of heavy, untreated wooden slats with air holes and a strong cover of old carpet, the compost heap at first refused to work. Nothing seemed to rot down; the prunings and peelings remained in much the same state for months on end. Visiting the Fern Verrow biodynamic farm in Herefordshire and admiring their several heaps at various stages of production, I could see straightaway that mine was too dry. The pile had too many twigs and not enough moist green stuff. It needed a drink. Watered regularly, topped up with every bit of soft, green leaf or vegetable peeling I could muster, the decomposition process soon started and the heat built up.

Turning the compost is something that serious gardeners tend to get almost emotional about. Not me. I often fail to remember to turn the contents over for weeks on end, forget to cover it in winter, and allow six-foot-high (two-meter-high) potato plants to take root in it. Yet now it has got going, it seems to cope with my neglect just fine. Ideally, I should go in there with the pitchfork once every two weeks and lift the bottom to the top. At the very least I should push the garden hose down into its depths in dry weather. But invariably I just leave it to sort itself out. Which it now does. Just remember to keep your heap moist and give it more green stuff than brown.

Slugs, snails, and other buggerances

I am troubled by slimy creatures more than most because of the box hedging around the veg beds and the ivy covering the walls. I use a twice-annual application of nematodes to fight off the slugs. The snails meet a quicker end.

Having been through the lexicon of slug and snail protection methods, I have settled on the following: Young plants get a deep copper ring placed around them that gives any approaching snails a mild electric shock. Tender plants are also protected by wicker cloches, which, though not entirely slug-proof, do help a bit. I sometimes resort to environmentally friendly slug pellets. The most successful deterrent of all is "the gardener's shadow." One trip into the garden after a rainfall and I can collect a hundred of them in just a few minutes. Another good way is to upturn stones, bricks, and old pots in winter. You will find them clustered together, spending the winter in little communes.

The urban fox is a problem, and none more than the ones who live under next door's robinia tree. They look cute enough sunbathing on their lawn in the afternoon, sometimes six at a time, and they spend time in my garden, curled up in a flower bed three feet from where I am digging, but they also cause untold damage. They dig up plants, excavate vast holes under the compost, and loosen the boards. I have found nothing that will deter them (infuriatingly, the cubs sleep next to the expensive electronic fox-scarers). Worst of all is when they go shopping, bringing other people's carelessly stored rubbish bags into my garden. Yes, there are times when I could happily shoot them myself, but they remain part of this garden, and I feel it is as much their space as mine. Probably more so.

I resort to organic sprays for serious attacks of white, green, and black fly, but also plant chives, garlic, and masses of marigolds to deter them. And even if the pyrethrum they contain doesn't do the trick, nothing looks prettier than a marigold in a vegetable patch.

Tools, and why they matter

My gardening tools mean as much to me as my kitchen equipment. Yes, every trowel, plant label, and piece of string is beautiful and with good reason. Just as carpenters take care of chisels, just as architects care about what pen they use for their drawings (believe me, they do), then I care about my kitchen and gardening equipment. It matters to me that something feels good in the hand, that it has a certain patina, and that it does the job well. Most of my stuff is secondhand and much loved. Yes, my copper spade and Japanese pruning shears cost a bit of money, but, like a decent kitchen knife, they make each job all the more pleasurable.

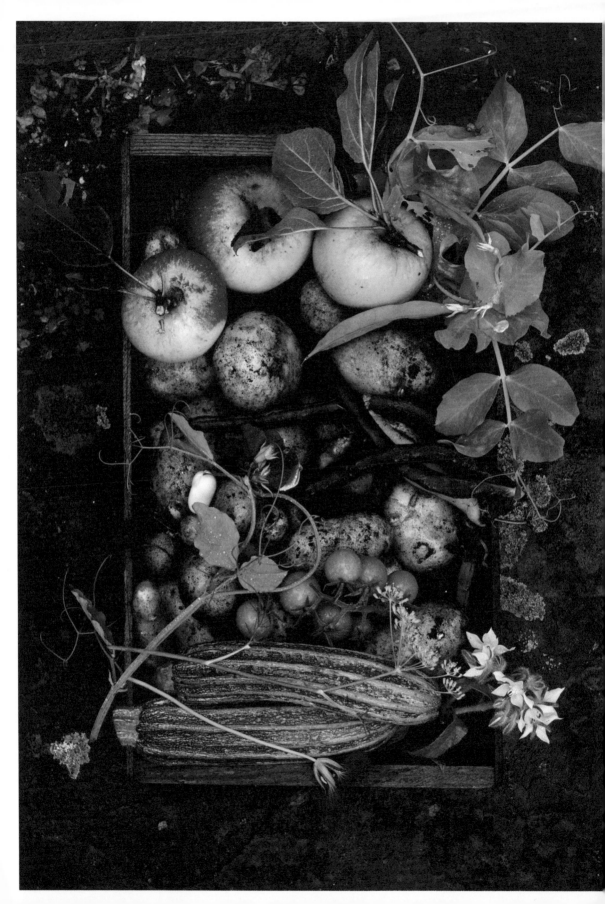

The payoff

There are two ways to put up a set of shelves. There are those who buy them flat-packed and put them up as quickly as they can. Job done. Something to hold the books and DVDs while they watch television. Then there is the sort of person who makes them from scratch, choosing the wood, feeling the grain, taking time over every detail, and enjoying the process. The shelves become more than just something to hold books.

It's the same with cooks. There is the "do-it-and-dust-it" cook, who does it purely to get something on the table with which to fill the belly, and then there is the one who takes delight in unfolding a cabbage leaf by leaf, rubbing his or her hands over the rough skin of a russet apple, or sniffing a freshly cut lemon. The person who finds satisfaction in choosing the right knife and picking the right pot, who enjoys the scent of ingredients and the feel of food in his or her hands. Chopping, slicing, stirring, tasting, seasoning all become acts of contentment rather than chores to be hurried through. Although there is something in this book for both sorts of cook, it is this second person who I suspect and hope will get the most out of it.

Watching someone you love eat a tomato you have grown yourself makes it more than just a tomato. It becomes a source of glorious, yet strangely humbling, pleasure.

In the kitchen

I am a gentle cook, and one who believes that there is delight in food far beyond what is on the plate. Choosing a seed from a catalogue (who could resist a squash named Amish Pie or an apple called Cornish Gillyflower?), planting it, nurturing it to harvest, then picking it and taking it into the kitchen adds more to the satisfaction of a supper than any amount of flashy presentation. Even a vegetable or fruit chosen with care at the market, brought home in its paper bag, and treated with respect can bring a certain fulfillment.

There is little point in taking the trouble to grow our own vegetables unless we can find an adequate technique to get to the heart of the ingredient. With a sweet potato, that technique would involve using dry heat such as baking or roasting to unleash its melting sweetness. An onion is cooked slowly in olive oil, duck fat, or butter to tease out its hidden sugars. A head of fennel is sliced as thin as parchment to temper its unrelenting aniseed notes. A pumpkin is left to mellow, a Brussels sprout to freeze. That is why it is often fascinating and sometimes difficult to cook something you don't know very well, working out the best way to get it to show you its reason for being.

Sometimes, capturing the energy that emanates from that vegetable or fruit is straightforward. A bright, vivid green spinach leaf might need nothing other than a little steam and lemon juice to do it justice; a fat, starchy parsnip might ask for little more than a good roasting to prove to us its worth. Other vegetables are more complex and difficult to get to know (I am still trying to discover what makes kohlrabi tick).

I would like to think I know more now than I did before I picked up my trowel and dug that first furrow for red and white radishes. How to get the best out of a vegetable, yes, but also the different ways to treat it in the kitchen, which seasonings will make it sing, what other ingredients it is most comfortable or most exciting with. What are the classic recipes not to be missed by a newcomer and what new ways are there that might be of interest to an old hand?

Right now, I have come in from the vegetable patch—a romantic mingling of vegetables, fruit, herbs, and flowers—and feel elated. There is an unusual abundance, even for midsummer, and a sense of energy in the garden. I have just picked the first tomatoes of the year. Tiny, green-shouldered Sungold, no bigger than a malted milk ball. They are sweet-sharp and burst refreshingly in my mouth. Almost best of all is the deep, herbal scent of tomato leaves on my fingers. Another one for my list.

A note on the US edition

In editing this book for an American audience, we sought to do two things: one, to make it as much a treasure trove of information, inspiration, and solid cooking advice for Americans as it is for its original British audience; and two, to retain the book's engaging style and tone. To that end, the recipes and cooking instructions have been Americanized, so that ingredients, terminology, and measurements are familiar to US readers. Any errors or omissions are that of the American publisher, Ten Speed Press.

The allotments referred to throughout this book are small parcels of land leased to private citizens in England (and Europe) by local government entities for the purpose of growing food crops. Allotments differ from community gardens in that they are not worked by a group of people, but by the individual to whom the land is leased.

The organic-box program in the UK is equivalent to the US system known as Community Supported Agriculture, or CSA, in which farmers deliver their locally grown produce directly to consumers in a weekly box throughout the farming season. In this program, farmers offer a certain number of "shares" to the public; consumers purchase a share and in return receive a weekly produce delivery.

The vegetable diaries and growing seasons reflect the experiences in the particular climate of a London garden. In the vegetable varieties sections, US-friendly cultivars are denoted with asterisks.

Asparagus

There is a moment in late April, somewhere between the end of the plum blossom and the height of the apple, just as the Holly Blue butterflies start to appear in the garden, that the early asparagus turns up at the farmers' market. Tied in bunches of just six or ten, these first green and mauve spears of *Asparagus officinalis* are sometimes presented in a burlap-lined wicker basket, as if to endorse their fragility and their expense. Their points tightly closed, a faint, gray bloom of youth still apparent on their stems, it would take a will stronger than mine not to buy.

The older I get, the more interested I become in the shoots that the Persians called *asparag*, and in Pershore, the heart of the old British asparagus trade, they still call "sparrow-grass." The farms around Kent and Suffolk sell it from open sheds an egg's throw from the field in which it has been grown, and where I have been known to bring it back by the armful when it's cheap enough. You see the occasional row on an allotment, but the plants take up the most space of any vegetable and require vigilant picking and careful transport home. "Grass," as it is so often known by greengrocers and farmers alike, remains expensive for a reason.

Life is full of small rituals, and never more so than in my kitchen. The first asparagus of the year is boiled within minutes of my walking through the door with it, butter is carefully melted so that it is soft and formless but not yet liquid, then I eat it with the sort of reverence I usually reserve for mulberries or a piece of exquisite sashimi. It is almost impossible not to respect those first spears of the year.

The short, six-week season starts in late April, and once it is up and running, the price drops and the bundles get fatter. I could have it every day—in a salad with cold salmon, stirred into a frugal rice pilaf, chopped and stirred into the custard filling of a tart, or grilled and served with lemon juice and grated pecorino. I might get tired of its side effects—it contains methyl mercaptan, which makes most people's pee stink—but its flavor is the strongest sign yet that summer has started.

By mid-June all but a few stragglers have gone, and the farmers rest their ancient plants till next spring.

Asparagus in the garden

There are days when I covet my neighbors' untended, overgrown garden. It's a haven for the foxes whose earth stretches far under the "lawn," on which they lie sprawled in the sun, six at a time. The land would make a much-needed overflow for my own vegetable patch.

In celebration of the luxury of more space, my first planting would be asparagus, one of the few vegetables I have yet to grow for myself. The crowns, as the root-balls are known, take up a considerable amount of room, far more than I can afford to offer them in my own tiny garden. You can raise plants from seed, if you are capable of waiting three years for them to gather strength before your first pick. Most people buy two- or even three-year-old crowns instead. They are usually delivered in late spring, wrapped in newspaper, a mass of dangling, spiderlike roots sporting a short stalk or two. You dig them in—they thrive on sandy soil and sunshine—planting them in deep, manure-lined trenches under a generous 4 inches (10cm) of soil, and then you must pamper them with seaweed and more manure and ply them generously with drink.

As a thank you, they will send up occasional spears from late April to midsummer. Picking stimulates growth, but it is unwise to pick for too long. The farmers around my childhood home in Worcestershire would never harvest for more than six weeks for fear of exhausting the plants. Leaving a few late arrivals to develop into feathery fronds—the sort a bridegroom attaches to a buttonhole carnation—will help to restore the crown. Resting fields in growing areas can be spotted in late summer by tall fronds dotted with carmine berries, waving in the breeze.

Asparagus needs to be cut, never pulled, and you should slice as near to the crown as possible. The temptation to pick every last spear should be avoided. I have seen growers lowering their bundles into buckets of water after cutting to keep the ends moist. Dried up, they will find few takers.

Asparagus in the kitchen

There are two types of asparagus of interest, three if you count the fat "jumbo" spears, whose flavor is rarely as impressive as their size: the thin "sprue," finer than a pencil, and the thicker spears for picking up with our fingers. Sprue is my favorite size for working into a salad with samphire, melted butter, and grated lemon. Being supple, it tangles elegantly round your fork.

The thicker spears are most tender at their flowering point, less so at the thick end where the stalk has been cut from the plant. You can often eat the entire spear, and a tough end is no real hardship—it acts as something to hold while we suck butter off the tastiest bits. Some people prefer to trim their "grass," whittling the white end to a point with a paring knife or peeler.

Get the spears to the pot as quickly as you can. They lose their moisture and sweetness by the hour. If you have to store them (I often buy three bunches at once at the Sunday farmers' market), stand them in a bowl of water like a bunch of flowers.

We can safely ignore the more far-fetched ways to boil asparagus, which range, in case you have a fancy to try, from standing them upright in a pan with their feet supported by new potatoes to cradling them over the water in a kitchen towel like a baby in swaddling clothes. Well intentioned, but unnecessary. Just lower the bundle of stalks tenderly into a shallow pan of merrily boiling water. If they are too long, let the points rest on the edge of the pan, where they will steam while the thicker ends tenderize in the water. They are good grilled over charcoal too, where the smokiness they take on makes up for the very slight lessening in juiciness. And they can be baked in aluminum foil or parchment paper with butter, a few sprigs of tarragon or chervil, and some moisture in the form of white wine or water so that they effectively steam in the sealed parcel.

Once we have tired of boiled asparagus and melted butter, the spears make a deeply herbaceous soup or a mild, rather soporific tart and marry well with pancetta or soft-boiled eggs. A few in a salad will make it feel extravagant, even if the only other ingredients are new potatoes, oil, lemon juice, and parsley. My all-time favorite asparagus lunch is one where a small, parchment-colored soft cheese is allowed to melt lazily over freshly boiled spears. The warm cheese oozing from its bloomy crust makes an impromptu sauce.

Seasoning your asparagus

Butter Melted, for dressing lightly cooked spears.

Lemon juice An underused seasoning for buttered asparagus. Particularly good where Parmesan is involved.

Tomato A fresh tomato sauce, made by roasting small tomatoes, crushing them with a fork, then stirring in olive oil, crushed garlic, and a splash of red wine vinegar.

Parmesan Finely grated over buttered spears or used to form a crust on a gratin of asparagus and cream.

Bacon Toss a pan of bacon or pancetta snippets and its hot fat over freshly cooked spears.

Cheese Soft, grassy cheeses, especially the richer cow's milk varieties.

Eggs As a filling for a tart, or simply soft boiled, as a natural cup of golden sauce in which to dip lightly cooked spears.

And...

* Weed your asparagus bed by hand. A hoe may damage emerging shoots.
* Despite not providing a harvest for the first three years, a crown can remain prolific for twenty years or more. I have heard of them even older.
* I was taught how to pick asparagus by a grower in Evesham. He showed me how to push the soil gently away from the lower part of the stalk with your fingers to reveal the end, which you then cut as close as possible to the crown, taking care not to cut into it.
* This vegetable loses its sweetness by the hour. Anything that has traveled from overseas is likely to disappoint.
* Avoid cooking asparagus in aluminium pans. It can taint the spears.
* Roll lightly cooked spears in thinly sliced ham, lay them in a shallow dish, cover with a cheese sauce, and a heavy dusting of Parmesan and bake until bubbling.

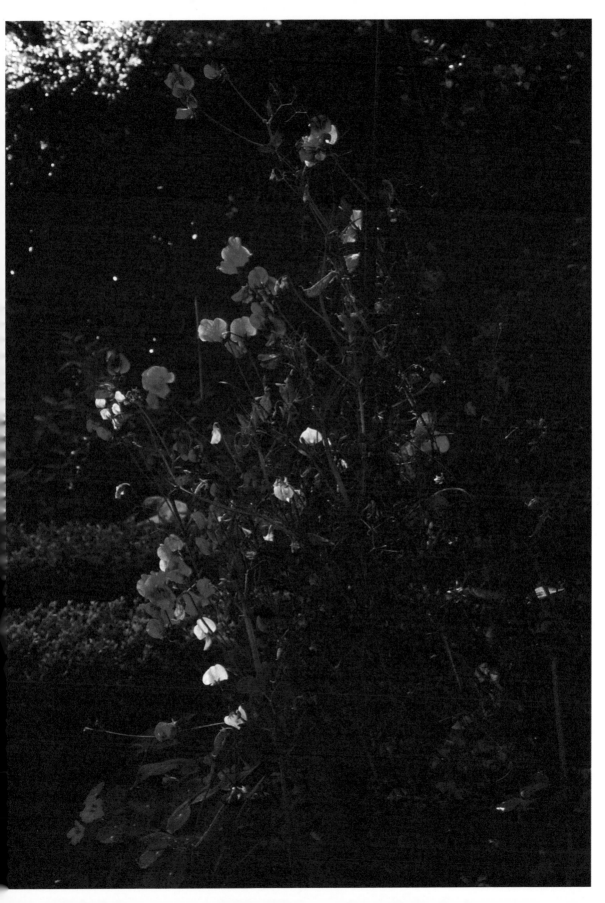

A pilaf of asparagus, fava beans, and mint

Asparagus is something you feel the need to gorge on, rather than finding the odd bit lurking almost apologetically in a salad or main course. The exceptions are a risotto—for which you will find a recipe in *Appetite*—and a simple rice pilaf. The gentle flavor of asparagus doesn't take well to spices, but a little cinnamon or cardamom used in a buttery pilaf offers a mild, though warmly seasoned base for when we have only a small number of spears at our disposal.

enough for 2
fava beans, shelled – a couple of handfuls
thin asparagus spears – 12
white basmati rice – ⅔ cup (120g)
butter – 4 tablespoons (50g)
bay leaves – 3
green cardamom pods – 6, very lightly crushed
black peppercorns – 6
a cinnamon stick
cloves – 2 or 3, but no more
cumin seeds – a small pinch
thyme – a couple of sprigs
green onions – 4 thin ones
parsley – 3 or 4 sprigs

to accompany the pilaf
chopped mint – 2 tablespoons
olive oil – 2 tablespoons
yogurt – ¾ cup (200g)

Cook the fava beans in deep, lightly salted boiling water for four minutes, until almost tender, then drain. Trim the asparagus and cut it into short lengths. Boil or steam for three minutes, then drain. Wash the rice three times in cold water, moving the grains around with your fingers. Cover with warm water, add a teaspoon of salt, and set aside for a good hour.

Melt the butter in a saucepan, then add the bay leaves, cardamom pods, peppercorns, cinnamon stick, cloves, cumin seeds, and sprigs of thyme. Stir them in the butter for a minute or two, until the fragrance wafts up. Drain the rice and add it to the warmed spices. Cover with about ¼ inch (1cm) of water and bring to a boil. Season with salt, cover, and decrease the heat to simmer. Finely slice the green onions. Chop the parsley.

After five minutes, remove the lid and gently fold in the asparagus, fava beans, green onions, and parsley. Replace the lid and continue cooking for five or six minutes, until the rice is tender but has some bite

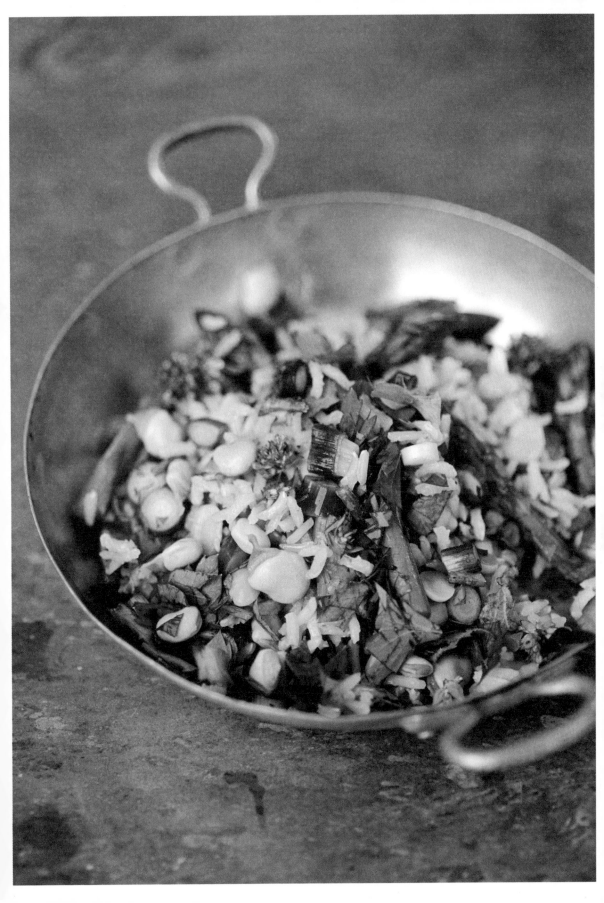

to it. All the water should have been absorbed. Leave, with the lid on but the heat off, for two or three minutes. Remove the lid, add a tablespoon of butter if you wish, check the seasoning, and fluff gently with a fork. Serve with the yogurt sauce below.

To accompany the pilaf
Stir 2 tablespoons of chopped mint, a little salt, and 2 tablespoons of olive oil into ¾ cup (200g) thick, but not strained, yogurt. You could add a small clove of crushed garlic too. Spoon over the pilaf at the table.

Warm asparagus, melted cheese

I have used Taleggio, Camembert, and English Tunworth from Hampshire as an impromptu "sauce" for warm asparagus with great success. A very soft blue would work as well.

> *enough for 2*
> thick, juicy asparagus spears – 24
> a little olive oil or melted butter
> soft, ripe cheeses such as St. Marcellin or any of the above – 2

Bring a deep pan of lightly salted water to a boil. Trim any woody ends from the asparagus and lower the spears gently into the water as soon as it is boiling. Cook for four or five minutes, until tender enough to bend. Lift the spears out with a slotted spoon and lower them into a shallow baking dish. Brush them lightly with olive oil or melted butter.

Preheat the broiler. Slice the cheese thickly—smaller whole cheeses can simply be sliced in half horizontally—and lay them over the top of the spears. Place under a hot broiler for four or five minutes till the cheese melts. Eat immediately, while the cheese is still runny.

A tart of asparagus and tarragon

I retain a soft spot for canned asparagus. Not as something to eat with my fingers (it is considerably softer than fresh asparagus, and rather too giving), but as something with which to flavor a quiche. The canned stuff seems to permeate the custard more effectively than the fresh. This may belong to the law that makes canned apricots better in a frangipane tart than fresh ones, or simply be misplaced nostalgia. I once made a living from making asparagus quiche, it's something very dear to my heart. Still, fresh is good too.

enough for 6

for the pastry
butter – 7 tablespoons (90g)
all-purpose flour – 1¼ cups (150g)
an egg yolk

for the filling
medium-thick asparagus spears – 12
heavy cream – 1¼ cups (284ml)
eggs – 2
tarragon – the leaves of 4 or 5 bushy sprigs
grated pecorino or Parmesan – 3 tablespoons

Cut the butter into small chunks and rub it into the flour with your fingertips until it resembles coarse breadcrumbs. Mix in the egg yolk and enough water to make a firm dough. You will find you need about a tablespoon of water or even less.

Roll the dough out to fit a 9-inch (22cm) tart pan (life will be easier when you come to cut the tart if you have a pan with a removable bottom), pressing the pastry right into the corners. Prick the pastry base with a fork, then refrigerate it for a good twenty minutes. Don't be tempted to miss out this step; the chilling will stop the pastry shrinking in the oven. Meanwhile, preheat the oven to 400°F (200°C). Bake blind for twelve to fifteen minutes, until the pastry is pale golden and dry to the touch.

Decrease the oven temperature to 350°F (180°C). Bring a large pan of water to a boil, drop in the asparagus, and let it simmer for seven or eight minutes or so, until it is quite tender. It will receive more cooking later but you want it to be thoroughly soft after its time in the oven, as its texture will barely change later under the custard.

Put the cream in a pitcher or bowl and beat in the eggs gently with a fork. Coarsely chop the tarragon and add that to the cream with a seasoning of salt and black pepper. Slice the asparagus into short lengths, removing any tough ends. Scatter it over the partly baked pastry shell, then pour in the cream and egg mixture and scatter the cheese over the surface. Bake for about forty minutes, until the filling is golden and set. Serve warm.

Roast asparagus

There is no joy in undercooked asparagus. Neither, curiously, is there much flavor. It must be soft and juicy, otherwise it loses much of its magic. Baking the spears in an aluminum foil parcel in the oven will suit those who don't like messing around with boiling water and steam, and keeps the asparagus surprisingly succulent.

> *enough for 2*
> thin asparagus spears – 1 pound (450g)
> light, mild olive oil – 2 tablespoons
> the juice of a lemon

Preheat the oven to 350°F (180°C). Place the spears on a large sheet of aluminum foil. Drizzle over the oil and lemon juice and then scatter over a seasoning of salt. Bring the edges of the foil up and seal them tightly (you want the asparagus to cook in its own steam). Bake for fifteen to twenty minutes, until the spears are tender.

Asparagus with pancetta

Cured pork products get on well with our beloved spears, bacon and pancetta especially. Although it is not especially easy to eat, requiring fingers and forks, a rubble of cooked, chopped pancetta, and especially its melted fat, makes a gorgeous seasoning for a fat bunch of spears.

Boil a bundle of asparagus until it is just tender. Drain it carefully, then lay the spears in a shallow baking dish. Preheat the oven to 400°F (200°C).

Melt a generous slice of butter in a shallow pan and fry a handful of diced pancetta, or mildly smoked bacon if that is what you have, until its fat is golden. Spoon it, and the butter, over the asparagus, then sprinkle with a little grated Parmesan. Bake for ten minutes, until the cheese has melted.

Beets

I have a weakness for a beet in all its guises: sliced in a sweet-sharp salad, slowly baked with cream, grated in a mustardy rémoulade, pickled in a lip-smarting vinegar, and as an ingredient in contemporary meat patties. Newly harvested and pushed through the mill of a juicer, a fresh beet can sometimes taste as if you are biting into clean, sweet earth.

The earthiness is not to everyone's taste. Neither is the sugar quotient that can make beets difficult to marry with other ingredients. The intensely savory qualities of beef and its roasted fat contrast well, as do the knife-edge notes of marinated herring or mackerel. Anything exceptionally acidic or high in umami—an aged Parmesan, perhaps, or some thin slices of dark rye bread—is worth a try. Soy sauce can be a strangely good partner too, but the two are difficult to bring together in a recipe without upsetting purists.

Beet's concentrated jewel-like color is both its joy and its downfall. It is Murphy's law that it should marry so happily with the virginal white of goat cheeses, mascarpone, and thick puddles of crème fraîche, none of whose looks are improved by a pink stain curdling the outer edge. Unable to take baby-pink food to heart, I make a habit of mixing the scarlet roots with dairy ingredients or mayonnaise only at the last minute, often passing a bowl of sour cream and chopped dill around for diners to anoint their own salad at the table. The exception being beet "dauphinoise," an extraordinarily successful, if luridly colored, accompaniment to a beef rib roast or a bowl of brown basmati.

The organic vegetable box has introduced many of us to the opportunity that is a bunch of beets. It was initially the inclusion of beets in my weekly delivery that caused the most angst in my house. To waste an old rutabaga for want of inspiration was one thing; to fail to cook a bunch of garnet bulbs and their blood-veined plumes of green leaves quite another.

At first, I returned the tops to the fridge with a promise to use them tomorrow (then forgetting). It took a while to learn that I needed to pounce upon them the moment the box arrives. Once they have even slightly wilted, they are as good as compost.

In deepest summer I have taken to buying a bunch of golden beets— much used in Victorian kitchens but all too rare now—whenever I see them, if only for the interest they arouse. Steamed, sliced, and tossed with walnut oil, white wine vinegar, and a pinch of grated orange zest, they glow on the plate. They bleed less dramatically than their bloody soul mates, yet possess the same earthy qualities. Elegant and cheering on a gray summer's day with rounds of chalky sheep's cheese and slices of tobacco-brown bread.

The red-black globes we know so well are the domesticated form of wild sea beet, which grew around the coastlines of the Mediterranean. Cultivated by the Greeks and the Romans, their leaves were used as potherbs, while the swollen roots were used medicinally rather than in the kitchen. Stephen Nottingham, whose worship of all things beet has provided a fascinating and exhaustive Internet study, points out that the Romans used the roots to produce a curative broth. To this day, beet juice is drunk to "stimulate and cleanse the kidneys." But we can thank the Victorians for giving it the prominence it has in our kitchens today.

A beet in the garden

I grow beets two ways: first, a single row planted in the same sunny bed as the summer squash, and secondly as salad leaves in seed trays, to be picked long before they get the chance to form a bulbous root. The large beet leaves I cook instead of spinach tend to come as a gift with those bunches of deep-red roots I buy at the market, the large leaves from my garden-grown roots being too tatty to serve as a vegetable.

Bolthardy is the variety I have grown most successfully. It is reliable and has no inclination to bolt (though its leaves could be more prolific). The golden beets in my patch have so far stayed on the small side, but were nevertheless worth the space.

Most people sow in April and I usually follow suit, but it is a mistake to plant too early. If spring is cold, then wait awhile, otherwise things tend to sulk. Those wanting to keep themselves in beets through to the autumn might like to sow in June, too. Sow the seeds in clusters, then thin to 2¾ inches (7cm) apart, chucking the thinnings into the salad bowl. Seeds take approximately twelve weeks to mature, though some of mine have taken considerably longer. April sowings should be just about large enough in August. June plantings will keep you going through to early winter. Keeping the snails away from their tuft of leaves is a problem. I resort to eco-friendly slug pellets.

Varieties

Bolthardy* Self-explanatory really. It's hardy and bolt resistant.
Bull's Blood* An eighteenth-century variety with exceptionally
dark red leaves.
Chioggia Barbietola* A sweet variety with red and white rings inside.
Cooks to a slightly disappointing pink.
Cheltenham Green Top Elongated, tapering root, dull green leaves.
Burpee's Golden* A round root of saffron gold and green leaves with
yellow veins. Turns a deep orange-yellow when cooked.
Egyptian Turnip-Rooted A slightly flattened, deep-red root, much
of which grows out of the ground. Good for those with shallow soils.
Blankoma* A large, white variety I can get less than excited about.

*Available from US seed sources.

A beet in the kitchen

If you boil a bunch of small summer beets they will be ready in twenty
minutes. Their skins should come off with a brush of the thumb—a
soothing job if you don't mind carmine fingers. The wiry tuft of stem can
be pushed out easily enough too. Cut the warm beets into quarters and
toss with a fruit vinegar such as raspberry, a splash from the walnut or
hazelnut oil bottle, and perhaps some fresh dill. A sweet salad such as this is
particularly good with oily fish fillets grilled until their skin crisps.

Older specimens whose circumference is approaching that of an orange
can take up to forty-five minutes to reach tenderness but are still rarely less
than delicious. There is likely to be a more obvious earthiness in older roots,
but the inherent sweetness will still be there. Dressing them with something
sharp while they are still warm will balance the sugar level. Try a shake-up
of cider vinegar, walnut oil, and a pinch of warm, musky caraway seeds that
you have briefly toasted in a shallow pan.

If the oven is on anyway, I sometimes bake my beets, each one wrapped
in loosely crumpled foil so they partially steam as they bake. It's a good use
for those bits of used-but-clean aluminum foil you keep for recyling yet
rarely do anything with. A little water in each will stop them scorching. The
flavor and indeed the sweetness seem particularly intense. They take longer
to cook this way—much longer, a good hour for a small one—but the cost is
negligible if there's a slow roast in the oven anyway. They are ready when you
can pierce them through the heart with a skewer. As you might a vampire.

The all-staining juice that seeps from a cut beet will leave its print on
anything it touches, and you will be lucky not to color at least your fingers,
if not your shirt. Much of the leakage can be avoided by keeping the beet's

skin intact and the plug of stem in place throughout the cooking process. Cut either one beforehand and the juice will seep into the cooking water, leaving you with Barbie-pink beets and a pan of blood-red water. The only time I peel at the outset is when I'm using one raw.

A raw beet has much going for it. I toss the coarsely grated roots into a carrot salad (dressed with lemon and mint leaves); fold them into yogurt with a hint of crushed garlic to make a beet tzatsiki to accompany falafel; introduce them into a celery root rémoulade; and occasionally toss them through a salad of winter leaves. The trick is not to overmix or prepare too early. A light, last-minute stirring of grated roots through the yogurt or mayonnaise is all that is needed. Any earlier or more thoroughly and you have got a marshmallow-pink lunch.

Oily fish love a beet at their side. I often include them, boiled and thinly sliced, in a herring salad (both ingredients enjoy being partnered with dill) and have served a salad of yellow beets with grilled sardines before now. I also like a pile of it, grated raw, on the same plate as gravlax. It is a sensation with the traditional accompanying mustard sauce.

Perhaps unsurprisingly, this vegetable is good in sweet things. I use it in a cake whose crumb is also freckled with blue-gray poppy seeds, where its inclusion keeps the cake moist. I rarely mention the addition of the vegetable until everyone reaches for a second slice.

And then there are the leaves. Many produce markets, farmers' markets, and vegetable boxes supply their *Betula vulgaris* with its plume of leaves intact. It is a reliable sign of freshness, as they wilt after only a day or two. They are good to eat, but are less tender and more robustly flavored than those members of the beet family grown for their leaves alone, such as chard.

My own beet leaves have never been particularly plentiful, possibly because I grow a relatively new variety that was developed for its bulbous root rather than its leaves. Heirloom seeds may give a more plentiful crop.

The early leaves that appear three or four weeks after planting are fine in a salad. To prevent them softening too much, dress them only minutes before eating. The older leaves can be steamed in a finger's depth of water. Cover with the lid and they will steam themselves to tenderness in a minute or two. Stir-frying with garlic and green onion is an instant vegetable dish, though they do tend to disappear in the pan the way spinach does.

Seasoning your beets

Dill Scatter chopped fronds over a beet salad.
Rye bread Dark bread, cream cheese, sliced beets. A sandwich of great sophistication.
Gherkins The sour note is a balance for the sweetness.
Onion A savory base for any warm beet dish.

Sour cream, fromage frais, crème fraîche Piquant dairy produce, including buttermilk and yogurt, provides an uplifting note that is exciting with the sweet earthiness.

Vinegar Almost any vinegar works well, including the more mellow versions such as balsamic and those made with soft fruit.

Cumin The dusty, almost fetid notes of toasted cumin seeds can be included in any beet dish, but particularly when it is served as a soup.

Apple juice Apples can always be worked into a beet salad, but the juice can be included in a refreshing dressing too.

Horseradish Freshly grated in a salad, stirred into crème fraîche as an accompaniment, scattered over a beet purée.

Walnut oil The most appropriate oil for dressing the warm roots.

Mustard A sound choice for seasoning a salad.

Capers A sharp shock to make the sugary roots sing.

Chocolate File under strange but true. Better still, make the moist beet cake (page 054).

And...

* While walnut oil is probably the most appropriate dressing for a beet salad, the most suitable cooking medium is a flavorless oil such as peanut or vegetable.

* The pink-and-white striped Chioggia variety doesn't bleed as dramatically as the red varieties. The yellow ones don't seem to bleed at all.

* Oily fish, sardines, mackerel, and herring, are a safe bet for a beet-type accompaniment. Grilled or marinated fish are particularly fine.

* Beet risotto is often cited as worth eating. Use a strongly flavored stock and be generous with the Parmesan.

* Try adding grated raw roots with chopped dill to an omelette.

* Roast, peel, cube, and dress with walnut oil and lemon juice as a side dish to cold roast pork.

* Shred raw and mix with mustard mayonnaise to make a pink-freckled rémoulade, as an accompaniment to thinly carved air-dried ham.

* Steam and mash to eat alongside boiled ham and parsley sauce. A pretty plateful.

* Use as a substitute for carrots in a traditional carrot cake.

* Partner with pickled fish such as rolled herring fillets in a salad with spinach leaves.

* Thinly slice roasted or steamed golden beets, then dress with a vinaigrette of olive oil, balsamic vinegar, a dab of Dijon mustard, and the zest and juice of an orange. A few rings of paper-thin onion, raw and sweet, wouldn't go amiss. Call it a carpaccio if you must.

* I once made a beet quiche. As it came from the oven, it looked like a huge, round bruise.

A light touch for meatballs

Late spring, 2007. Six small beets, round as golf balls and not much bigger, arrive in a thick brown paper bag, its edges sewn together with string. The air of moist Riverford soil and sweet roots wafts up as the bag is torn open, but the day is leaden with damp and cold and I have rarely felt less like eating a beet salad.

Supper is going to be meatballs: fat, crumbly patties of ground lamb with garlic, dill, and parsley. It crosses my mind that a handful of grated beets might sweeten the ground meat and lighten the texture.

What we end up eating on the coldest spring day for years is plump rounds of sweet and spicy meat, crunchy with cracked wheat and crimson with the vivid flesh of finely grated beets. The inclusion of the roots has broken up the solid lump of ground meat and married well with the garlic and clean-tasting herbs. We dip the sizzling patties into a slush of shredded cucumber, yogurt, and mint, given a snap of piquancy (to balance the beets) with a spoonful of capers.

> *makes 12 to 16, enough for 4 or more*
> fine or medium cracked wheat – ½ cup (75g)
> raw beets – 9 ounces (250g)
> a small to medium onion
> ground lamb – 14 ounces (400g)
> garlic – 2 large cloves, or even 3, crushed
> chopped dill – 2 heaping tablespoons
> parsley – a small handful, chopped
> a little peanut oil
>
> **for the dressing**
> cucumber – about a third of a medium one
> mint – the leaves from 4 or 5 sprigs, chopped
> capers – a tablespoon
> yogurt – ¾ cup (200g)

Put the cracked wheat in a bowl, pour over enough boiling water to cover, then set aside to swell.

Peel the beets and onion and grate them coarsely into a large bowl. Add the ground lamb, garlic, dill, parsley, and a generous grinding of salt and black pepper.

Squeeze any water from the cracked wheat with your hands and add to the meat. Mix everything together thoroughly, then squish the mixture into little patties about the size of a flattened golf ball. Cover with plastic wrap (I do this tightly because the chopped garlic will taint everything in the fridge), then chill for at least an hour.

Preheat the oven to 350°F (180°C). Make the dressing by grating the cucumber coarsely and leaving it in a colander, lightly sprinkled with salt, for half an hour. Squeeze it dry, then mix it with the chopped mint, capers, and yogurt. Season with salt and black pepper.

Heat a nonstick pan, brush the patties with a little peanut oil, and fry until golden on both sides. Try not to move the meatballs very much when they are cooking; you risk them falling apart. Once they are lightly browned on both sides, carefully lift them into a baking dish and finish in a hot oven for fifteen to twenty minutes (incidentally, you can only tell if they are done by tasting one, as the beets give them a rich red color, making it impossible to gauge by sight whether they are cooked).

Drizzle with the cucumber dressing and eat.

Chickpea patties, beet tzatsiki

The chickpea possesses a dry, earthy quality and a knobbly texture that I find endlessly useful and pleasing to eat. No other member of the legume family has quite the same mealy, warm nuttiness.

This is the bean I want bubbling on the stove when there is pouring rain outside, filling the kitchen with its curiously homey steam as it slowly simmers its way to tenderness. Unlike its more svelte cousins, the flageolet and the cannellini, the chickpea is almost impossible to overcook. The length of time it takes to soften rules it out of weekday cooking for me, so I sometimes resort to opening a can. Chickpeas, often labeled *ceci* or *garbanzo*, leave their can relatively unharmed, which is more than you can say for a flageolet. They make good patties that you can season with cumin, chile, garlic, sesame, or coriander and fry until lightly crisp on the outside.

Chickpea patties need a little texture if they are to be of interest. I process them only so far, leaving them with a texture that is partly as smooth as hummus with, here and there, a little crunchiness.

The patty mixture needs a good ten minutes to rest before cooking. To calm the garlic notes, I spoon over a sauce of yogurt, grated cucumber, and mint or a similar one of shredded beets, taking care not to overmix it to a lurid pink.

makes 6 small patties, enough for 2
chickpeas – a 14-ounce (400g) can
garlic – 2 cloves
ground cumin – a teaspoon
ground coriander – a heaping teaspoon
hot paprika – a scant half teaspoon
an egg
flat-leaf parsley – a small bunch
mint – a small bunch
olive oil
lemon wedges, to serve

for the tzatsiki
beet – a large raw one
plain yogurt – ¾ cup (200g)
garlic – a single juicy clove, well crushed
mint leaves – a few

Drain and rinse the chickpeas. Put them in a food processor with the garlic, cumin, coriander, paprika, egg, and a generous grinding of salt and black pepper. Chop the parsley and mint leaves coarsely (I use a couple of tablespoons of each), add to the processor, then blitz until smooth, but still with some small pieces of chickpea detectable. It is much more interesting with a slightly lumpy texture than a totally smooth one. Leave to firm up for a few minutes while you make the tzatsiki (your first thought may be that the mixture is too soft to make patties).

Grate the beet finely. Stir in the yogurt, a little salt and black pepper, the garlic, and a few chopped mint leaves.

Warm a very shallow layer of olive oil in a nonstick frying pan. Take heaped tablespoons of the mixture out of the bowl and place them in the hot oil, pressing down lightly to smooth the top. Leave them be until the underside is golden. I avoid any temptation to prod and poke; they must be allowed to form a thin crust. Flip over confidently but tenderly with a spatula to cook the other side. They are done in three or four minutes, when the outside is faintly crisp and golden and the inside is soft and creamy. Serve with the beet tzatsiki and the lemon wedges.

Goat cheese and beet salad with toasted hemp and poppy seeds

A good contrast here between the sweetly warm beets, nutty hemp, and tangy goat cheese. Any crisp, slightly bitter salad leaf will work. The English-grown ivory and crimson chicory, crunchy, juicy, and appealing to the eye, works well but the classic white would be just as welcome.

enough for 4

for the salad
small to medium beets – 8
hemp seeds – 2 teaspoons
chicory – 7 ounces (200g)
goat cheese – 12 to 16 slices
a small basket of mustard and cress
poppy seeds – 2 teaspoons

for the dressing
red wine vinegar – a tablespoon
Dijon mustard – a tablespoon
hemp seed oil – a tablespoon
olive oil – 3 tablespoons
coarsely chopped parsley – 2 tablespoons

Bring a deep pan of water to a boil. Make the dressing by mixing the vinegar and mustard together and then adding the oils. Stir the parsley into the dressing with a grinding of salt and black pepper.

Trim the leaves from the beets (save them for cooking like spinach), taking care not to cut the skin. Wipe the beets clean of any mud or sand. Put them into the boiling water and decrease the heat to an energetic simmer. Test the beets occasionally for tenderness, either by lifting them from the water and rubbing the skin—it will peel off easily if the beet is ready—or by testing with a skewer. They should be ready in about thirty minutes, depending on their size and age.

Drain the beets and, when they are cool enough to handle, remove their skins. Cut each one into six wedges from stalk to root. Toss gently in some of the dressing and set aside.

Toast the hemp seeds in a nonstick pan for a minute or two, until they smell warm and nutty. Separate the chicory leaves and toss gently with some of the dressing. Divide them among four plates. Add the goat cheese, mustard, and cress and tuck in the beets. Scatter the poppy seeds and toasted hemp over the salad.

Marinated mackerel with dill and beets

Clean flavors here, a delightful main-course salad for a summer's day. You could use other fish, such as red mullet, if you prefer, but the richness of mackerel's flesh goes well with the sweet beets and tart marinade. Some watercress would be good with this, and maybe a few slices of dark bread and butter.

enough for 4
medium beets (golden or otherwise) – 4
a little olive oil
mackerel – 4, filleted

for the marinade
cider vinegar – 3½ tablespoons (50ml)
lemon juice – ½ cup (120ml)
bay leaves – 2
a small carrot
an onion
garlic – a small clove
sugar – a teaspoon
coriander seeds – a teaspoon
juniper berries – about 12
white peppercorns – 5
black peppercorns – 5
olive oil – ⅓ cup (80ml)
a little fresh dill – finely chopped

Preheat the oven to 400°F (200°C). Wash the beets and wrap them in foil, then bake for fifty minutes or so, until tender—or, if you prefer, boil them in deep, unsalted water for about thirty minutes, until tender when pierced with the tip of a knife. Remove and discard their skins. Slice into thick rounds and set aside.

For the marinade, pour the vinegar and lemon juice into a stainless-steel saucepan with ⅔ cup (150ml) water. Add the bay leaves. Scrub the carrot and slice it finely. Peel the onion and slice that similarly. Peel and squash the garlic and add it to the pan, together with the carrot and onion, sugar, coriander seeds, and juniper berries. Bring all to a boil, then add a teaspoon of salt and the peppercorns. Pour in the olive oil and let the mixture simmer for a minute or two, until the onion has softened slightly. Turn off the heat.

Warm a little olive oil in a nonstick frying pan. Season the fish fillets and lay them, skin side down, in the oil. Let them color, then turn them over. Lift them from the pan and place in a shallow dish.

Add the dill and beets to the marinade. Pour over the fish and let cool. Lift the fish onto plates and spoon over the vegetables and juices.

A chilled soup of goat cheese and beets

In the 1980s, puréed beets, snipped chives, and swirls of sour cream made a startling chilled soup that became an almost permanent fixture at the café in which I cooked for much of the decade. The most outrageous Schiaparelli pink, it was a picture in its deep white-porcelain tureen. I wish now I had had the nerve to include the finely chopped gherkins whose sweet-sour pickle notes could have lifted the soup from its candy-cane sweetness. One glance at a Russian or Swedish cookbook would have been enough.

enough for 4
raw beets – 1 pound (500g)
peanut or vegetable oil – 2 tablespoons
green onions – 4 to 6
vegetable or light chicken stock – 3 cups (750ml)

for the goat cheese cream
softish goat cheese – 3½ ounces (100g)
thick yogurt – 3 tablespoons
mixed chopped chives and mint – 2 tablespoons

Preheat the oven to 400°F (200°C). Cut the leaves from the beets (cook them later, treating them as you might spinach) and scrub the beets well. Put them in a roasting pan with a tablespoon of oil and three of water and cover tightly with aluminum foil. Roast for forty-five minutes to an hour, until dark and almost tender.

Warm the second tablespoon of oil in a shallow pan. Chop the green onions and let them soften for five minutes or so in the oil. Set aside.

Peel the beets and chop the flesh coarsely. Put them in the pan with the onions, pour over the stock, and bring to a boil. Simmer for seven or eight minutes, cool slightly, then purée in a blender until smooth. Check the seasoning. It will need salt and black pepper. Pour into a pitcher and chill in the refrigerator.

To make the cream, remove the skin from the goat cheese and mash the flesh with a fork. Stir in the yogurt and chopped herbs. Serve the soup when it is thoroughly chilled, adding spoonfuls of the herb cream at the table.

Beet seed cake

This tastes no more of beets than a carrot cake tastes of carrots, yet it has
a similar warm earthiness to it. It is less sugary than most cakes, and the
scented icing I drizzle over it is purely optional. The first time I made it, I
used half sunflower and half Brazil nut oil, but only because the Brazil nut
oil was new and I wanted to try it. Very successful it was too, not to mention
boosting everyone's zinc levels.

enough for 8 to 10
self-rising flour – 1¾ cups (225g)
baking soda – half a teaspoon
baking powder – a scant teaspoon
ground cinnamon – half a teaspoon
sunflower or Brazil nut oil – ¾ cup (180ml)
light muscovado sugar – 1 cup (225g)
eggs – 3, separated
raw beets – 5 ounces (150g)
juice of half a lemon
golden raisins or raisins – ½ cup (75g)
mixed seeds (sunflower, pumpkin, flax) – ½ cup (75g)

for the icing
confectioners' sugar – ½ cup (50g)
lemon juice or orange blossom water
poppy seeds

Preheat the oven to 350°F (180°C). Lightly butter a rectangular loaf pan
(8 x 4 inches [20 x 9cm], measured across the bottom, and 2¾ inches [7cm]
deep), then line the bottom with parchment paper.

Sift together the flour, baking soda, baking powder, and cinnamon. Beat
the oil and sugar in a stand mixer until well blended, then mix in the egg
yolks one at a time. Grate the beets coarsely and fold into the mixture, then
add the lemon juice, golden raisins, and the seeds.

Fold the flour, baking soda, and baking powder into the beet mixture
and combine at low speed.

In a separate clean bowl, beat the egg whites until light and almost stiff.
Fold gently but thoroughly into the beet mixture, using a large metal spoon
(a wooden one will knock the air out). Pour the mixture into the prepared
pan and bake for fifty to fifty-five minutes, covering the top with a piece
of aluminum foil after thirty minutes. Test with a skewer for doneness.
The cake should be moist inside but not sticky. Let the cake rest for a good
twenty minutes before turning it out of its pan onto a wire cooling rack.

Make the icing. Sift the confectioners' sugar into a bowl and add enough lemon juice or orange blossom water to achieve a consistency where the icing will run over the top of the cake and drizzle slowly down the sides (about three teaspoonfuls), stirring to remove any lumps. Drizzle it over the cake and scatter with poppy seeds. Rest for a bit to set before eating.

An extremely moist chocolate-beet cake with crème fraîche and poppy seeds

I have lost count of the number of appreciative emails and blog mentions about the brownies and the chocolate almond cake in *The Kitchen Diaries*. They are received gratefully. It is true that I am rarely happier than when making chocolate cake. I especially like baking those that manage to be cakelike on the outside and almost molten within. Keeping a cake's heart on the verge of oozing is down partly to timing and partly to the ingredients— ground almonds and very good-quality chocolate will help enormously. But there are other ways to moisten a cake, such as introducing grated carrots or, in this case, crushed beets.

The beets are subtle here, some might say elusive, but using them is a lot cheaper than ground almonds, and they blend perfectly with dark chocolate. This is a seductive cake, deeply moist and tempting. The serving suggestion of crème fraîche is not just a nod to the sour cream so close to beets' Eastern European heart, it is an important part of the cake.

> *enough for 8 as a dessert*
> beets – 8 ounces (250g)
> fine dark chocolate (70 percent cocoa solids) – 7 ounces (200g)
> hot espresso – 4 tablespoons
> butter – ¾ cup plus 2 tablespoons (200g)
> all-purpose flour – 1 cup plus 2 tablespoons (135g)
> baking powder – a heaping teaspoon
> good-quality cocoa powder – 3 tablespoons
> eggs – 5
> superfine sugar – scant 1 cup (190g)
> crème fraîche and poppy seeds, to serve

Lightly butter an 8-inch (20cm) springform cake pan and line the bottom with a round of parchment paper. Preheat the oven to 350°F (180°C).

Cook the beets, whole and unpeeled, in boiling unsalted water. Depending on their size, they will be tender when pierced with the tip of a knife within thirty to forty minutes. Young ones may take slightly less. Drain them, let them cool under running water, then peel them, slice off their stem and root, and process in a blender or food processor until a coarse purée.

Melt the chocolate, broken into small pieces, in a small bowl set over a pot of simmering water. Don't stir.

When the chocolate looks almost melted, pour the hot espresso over it and stir once. Cut the butter into small pieces—the smaller the better—and add to the melted chocolate. Push the butter down under the surface of the chocolate with a spoon (as best you can) and let soften.

Sift together the flour, baking powder, and cocoa. Separate the eggs, putting the whites in a large mixing bowl. Stir the yolks together.

Now, working quickly but gently, remove the bowl of chocolate from the heat and stir until the butter has melted into the chocolate. Let sit for a few minutes, then stir in the egg yolks. Do this quickly, mixing firmly and evenly so the eggs blend into the mixture. Fold in the beets. Whisk the egg whites until stiff, then fold in the sugar. Firmly but gently, fold the beaten egg whites and sugar into the chocolate mixture. A large metal spoon is what you want here; work in a deep, figure-eight movement but take care not to overmix. Lastly, fold in the flour and cocoa.

Transfer quickly to the prepared cake pan and put in the oven, decreasing the heat immediately to 325°F (160°C). Bake for forty minutes. The rim of the cake will feel spongy, the inner part should still wobble a little when the pan is gently shaken.

Set the cake aside to cool (it will sink a tad in the center), loosening it around the edges with a thin icing spatula after half an hour or so. It is not a good idea to remove the cake from its pan until it is completely cold. Serve in thick slices, with crème fraîche and poppy seeds.

Broccoli and the sprouting greens

And then, just as I feel the days of darkness and parsnips will never end, I spot the first spears of sprouting broccoli at the market. Early-season sightings are not something that usually excites me unless they are in my own garden. The blurring of the seasons put paid to that sentiment long ago. The first rhubarb, asparagus, even red currants barely get me to raise an eyebrow now (though catch-us-if-you-can gooseberries and damsons still set my heart pumping), but spotting the first homegrown sprouting at the end of a long winter feels as if someone is throwing you a life raft.

Broccoli, both the fat, cloudlike bunches we get all year (officially "calabrese") and the longer, slimmer stems of "sprouting" around in the earliest days of spring, are made up of masses of tight flower buds. Buds that, left unharvested, will open into simple, nectar-heavy, yellow flowers that are adored by bees. We pick them long before the buds burst, in order to catch the shoots at the most sweet and tender.

The members of the brassica family that form a head kindle greater respect than the leafier varieties such as kale and cabbage. The long-stemmed heads are so fine, so elegant, so beautiful on the plate that you wonder, briefly, why they aren't considered the most precious vegetables in the world. In our house, they are.

Tough in the garden or the field, where they will shrug off the hardest frosts, "heading" greens need a tender touch in the kitchen. Although I should, as a nod to some sort of botanical correctness, include cauliflower here, it behaves very differently in the kitchen and so gets its own chapter.

Green, white, or purple sprouting, with its long stems and shadowy heads, marks a turning point in the year in much the same way as spying the first pumpkin, only with a lighter heart. You know that spring and its pulse-quickening air is not far behind. You have crossed a line—a line that you can often smell and feel even before you can see it. Sprouting is the proof.

The first British-grown shoots of sprouting broccoli usually appear in the shops in late February and early March, though I have seen them earlier. They will be with us until May, by which time I will have had my fill and be keen to get to the asparagus and the first peas.

The broccoli family in the garden

You can grow both the plump everyday calabrese and the slimmer-stemmed sprouting broccoli from seed, sowing the latter in mid- to late spring in drills ⅜ inch (1cm) deep and a foot (30cm) apart. Most find it easier to sow in pots or seed trays and then transplant when the plantlets are a finger or so high. Harvest in late winter and early spring by snapping off the shoots, leaving the large leaves in place, as these will protect the next batch of shoots.

I have yet to grow either from seed, preferring to buy them as young plants ready for the garden. Sometimes I pick up a tray at the farmers' market, other times I order them online.

A broccoli diary

January Order seeds.
April Realize I am never going to get round to sowing them, so order "plug plants" online instead.
June I am concerned when a newspaper parcel of Red Spear sprouting broccoli and large, domed Marathon arrives with what I consider a worrying amount of yellowing leaves. "Stress," I mutter, and give them an hour or two's soak in a bucket of rainwater while I give the bed a final going over with the rake to remove any leaves and break up large clods.

The plants, with their neat plug of sticky soil around the roots, go into holes deep enough to reach just below the lowest of their leaves. I firm them in with a carefully placed foot—they hate to wobble around—spray them with liquid soap, and place an organic "brassica collar" around each stem to ward off the cabbage root fly that is so fond of laying its eggs where stem meets soil. They come in packets of thirty from gardening suppliers.

All this is done on a Saturday morning in pouring rain. I like the refreshing prickle of drizzle on my skin, but there comes a point when your clothes becomes heavy with water, rain drips down your neck, and the soil becomes too damp to step on without risk of compacting it. I stop when my socks feel wet. The plants look happier now they are trimmed of their weaker leaves and have their feet in good-hearted soil.
August After a few weeks of sulking, the sprouting has got a spurt on, the stems have straightened, and the plants appear in a good state of health. Over the next few weeks I pay very little attention to them.

January A warm Christmas, followed by a freezing New Year. The garden is dark almost as soon as lunchtime soup is finished and the bread and cheese packed away. Creep out with a shining flashlight and the leaves and heads glisten in the frosty air, standing happily until we are ready to bring them in. Few vegetables, or plants of any sort, thrive so positively in minus temperatures. I can hardly wait to tuck them under a blanket of blisteringly hot cheese sauce.

Varieties

Calabrese
The ubiquitous, cloudlike heads of bluish green that are as easy to find as frozen peas. No supermarket, however small, is without its box of plastic-wrapped, usually Spanish supply of what we have come to know as "broccoli." The British crop, like plump, green clouds, is generally sown in spring and can be harvested from June to November.

Fiesta* Horrid name for heavy heads of a reliable and vigorous variety.
Trixie Even worse name, like something you might call a toy poodle, for what is one of the only varieties to be resistant to the dreaded club root.
Belstar* Handsome, blue-green domes with tight, small beads. Does well for organic growers and has an exceptionally fine flavor.

Purple sprouting
Bordeaux Summer and autumn cropping variety. Won't survive the cold. Sow in April.
Red Spear* Cold, hardy, small, deep-purple spears of great tenderness and flavor. Will stand happily through the coldest nights. Sow in late summer for February-to-March picking.
Rudolph* Pick early, from midwinter.
Early Purple Sprouting* Tall, fast growing, and colorful, with many sprouts.

White sprouting
The white varieties are finer and (I find) more fragile in both garden and kitchen. They are less happy with serious cold than the purple forms and they tend to break up more easily in the pot. Their flavor is more delicate too. White Eye and White Star* are currently the two that are easiest to find. Sow indoors during April and May.

*Available from US seed sources.

Calabrese and purple sprouting in the kitchen

My early attempts to understand this family of top-notch vegetables failed on two counts. First I overcooked it, massively, and then, wastefully, failed to realize the delicious potential of its stems. The overcooking was almost certainly due to not having seen the vegetable anywhere but in the supermarket. Once you see the stems and their tight heads growing, as they are in my vegetable patch as I write, it is easier to understand what you are dealing with: in this case exceptionally young, tender shoots, their leaves barely unfurled, that will require little cooking time.

Then, I cut them too short, as if it was all about the heads, discarding far too much of the toothsome stalk. Picked young enough, the stems are the best bit—a mouthful of lightly crunchy, vivid green vegetable that is immediately sweet and juicy. Anyone who eats at a good Chinese or Vietnamese restaurant soon understands the pleasure of the stems, especially once they meet the holy trinity of ginger, garlic, and soy.

Some shoots are deepest purple. We can cheerfully take no notice of the seed catalogues and cookbooks that tell you purple sprouting broccoli always turns green when cooked. Many varieties will stay darkly purple unless you insist on cooking them to death.

My organic box company sends a plastic bag of purple sprouting, its flower heads tightly closed, its stems still moist from being recently cut. They once delivered exceptionally late in the day (I thought I had been forgotten), by which time the pork chops were almost on the plate. It turned out to be the point at which I finally understood the treasure I had before me. By leaving myself no time in which to cook them, I used just a shallow depth of water and, with the chops rapidly cooling on their plates, whipped the spears out before they were fully cooked. Brilliant purple and green, the stems al dente and still with some crunch, it turned out to be the best thing that could have happened.

That said, you can successfully slow-cook the sprouting version. Rather than steam, you bring it to tenderness (and beyond) with olive oil, lemon, a scattering of dried chiles, garlic, and water, then dress it with more olive oil and chopped anchovies. Dust it with heroic quantities of Parmesan. Yes, it ends up the color of a frog, but the flavor is extraordinary. The stems are sweeter and milder, the texture almost buttery. A relaxing change from the usual uptight al dente treatment.

The large, clustered heads of calabrese need breaking up into more manageable florets, where they will cook more quickly and evenly. Otherwise, the outer florets will be overcooked by the time the heat has penetrated those hiding near the stalk. The stems, though short and thick, are surprisingly tender and shouldn't be discarded.

Sprouting needs no such preparation. The whole, lightly trimmed stems can be dropped into boiling water, steamed, or pampered like asparagus with the tips slightly out of the water, so that the buds steam while the stems boil. Whichever way you go, the stems are ready when the tip of a knife inserted into their thickest part goes in without pressure.

I must put in a word for the leaves. I never discard them. Slender, quietly flavored, elegantly fringed, they cook in seconds. It would break my heart to see them sent to the compost.

Only the very thickest stems will prove unpleasantly tough. The ideal seems to be roughly the thickness of an asparagus spear. I leave the gently curling leaves on. The fragile bracts can occasionally hold caterpillars that you really won't want to eat. Wash them gently in a bowl of cool water, as if you were rinsing dirt from a child's hand. Try not to break them up. Once a floret has broken away from its stem, it tends to get lost in the cooking water.

I rarely boil the stems now, preferring to let them steam in a large shallow pan in a finger's depth of water. Get the water boiling first. Lay the stems in a single layer, with most of the stems and heads lying proud of the water; covered with a lid, they will steam rather than boil. Rolling around in deep boiling water like washing in the machine, the florets are easily damaged. The difference between a serving of sprouting that has been treated with respect and one that arrives on the plate in a broken heap is astonishing.

For the tubbier calabrese, I have had much success with one of those collapsible, flat "water-lily"-style steamers that sit in a shallow pan. Bamboo Chinese steamers are efficient too.

If I am cooking them for lunch, a matter of just three or four minutes in the steamer, I lower the heads into a bowl and scatter them with a mixture of toasted pine nuts; dark, smoky raisins; and a drizzle of olive oil. On this occasion, drizzle means exactly what it says.

Broccoli seems to go cold quicker than any other vegetable (this could, of course, be my imagination, but it explains why cauliflower is usually served under a duvet of blistering cheese sauce). A hot plate is more important than usual, and will keep your calabrese warm for a little longer.

Seasoning the broccoli family

Butter A simple way to start and where, I guess, many would be tempted to leave it.

Hollandaise There is no other sauce that can do for this vegetable what a pitcher of hollandaise can.

Anchovies Chop them finely, let them soften in a little butter over medium heat, then pour them over freshly steamed spears. A squeeze of lemon will add much excitement.

Mustard Either in a dressing with olive oil and lemon juice, stirred into a runny hollandaise-type sauce, or as a seasoning for cheese sauce to cover your lightly cooked heads.

Ginger Shredded and frizzled and tipped over the top with browned garlic.

Soy The salty notes of soy work particularly well with calabrese. Even a few drops of dark soy added at the table will make it sing.

And...

* There is much confusion over the term broccoli. Many—including most supermarkets—use it to refer to the plump, short-stemmed heads of green calabrese. Others use it purely for purple sprouting. Officially, it is used as a catchall term for members of the family that includes stubby calabrese and the longer shoots of purple and white sprouting.

* Calabrese can mean different things in different parts of the UK. When I lived in Cornwall, we used it to refer to cauliflower.

* Raw-food lovers often find this family hard going, but the smaller shoots eat well enough if you leave them in a dressing of oil, lemon, and balsamic vinegar for twenty minutes before adding them to your bowl of leaves.

* Served as an accompaniment, broccoli introduces a flash of brilliant green to our supper, and isn't fussy about what it shares a plate with. That said, it seems particularly suited to any form of cured pork. It is in hog heaven with boiled ham, speck, or those plate-sized bacon steaks. Bring meat and vegetable together with some parsley sauce and you have one of the great culinary threesomes of all time.

* The rather old-fashioned habit of surrounding cauliflower cheese with triangles of toast, very *à la mode* in 1950, is an idea worth updating with broccoli and cheese sauce. I use a seeded loaf, one of those whose crust is speckled with pumpkin and sesame seeds, toasted and tucked on the side. It makes a perfectly honorable main course.

* Slow-cooked sprouting, baked with garlic, lemon juice, and Parmesan, is something to serve with a pork chop, but it is also excellent as a dinner in its own right. I spoon the deliciously disintegrating heads and their cooking juices over brown rice or cracked wheat for a cheap and homey supper.

Sprouting and blood oranges on a frosty March day

The market: stumpy carrots, the prickle of frost, dark greens, the scent of wet soil. Here and there among the trestle tables are shallow baskets: Russian kale, tips of cavolo nero with their infant leaves, broccoli heads the size of a mushroom, and sprigs of purple and white sprouting so small you can hold ten in the palm of your hand.

Each sprig of vegetable is so precious, so diminutive, as timid as a chanterelle. I pick them up with finger and thumb, which seems the way they must have been picked from their stems. These are shoots plucked from the stem after the growing heart of the plant has been removed. No smothering of cheese sauce, just a three-minute trip in the steamer and a classic hollandaise to dip them in, let down with a dash of cream and a grating of zest from a blood orange.

> *enough for 3*
> purple sprouting – 4 large handfuls, steamed
> egg yolks – 3
> melted butter – ¾ cup plus 2 tablespoons (200g)
> lemon juice
> the finely grated zest of a blood orange
> heavy cream or crème fraîche – 3 tablespoons

Bring a pan of water to a boil and find a heatproof glass or ceramic bowl that will fit neatly into it without actually touching the water. Drop the yolks—large, deep orange ones if you have them—into the bowl and then a splash of water. Whisk, pouring in almost all the melted butter, slowly at first as if you were making mayonnaise, then as the sauce thickens up, a little faster. The water in the pan should be simmering rather than boiling and if you stop whisking your sauce will fail (though I have occasionally brought it back to life with a splash of simmering water from the pan).

Once it is thick and creamy, squeeze in a little lemon juice and stir in a good pinch of salt. No pepper. The sauce can be used as it is.

One late-spring day last year, I got this far, then decided to add the finely grated zest of a blood orange and three tablespoons of thick cream, whisked in at the end. The idea of bright green vegetables and vivid blood oranges seemed right for a day that saw the garden freckled white with frost and the sky clear and pale gray. I spooned thick lines of the orange hollandaise over the tiny stems of steamed sprouting and ate it with rounds of grilled ciabatta.

A soup of broccoli and bacon

A good use for the older, tougher specimens. I have made this with those plastic-entombed bunches from the late-night corner market and you would never have known it.

enough for 6
a medium onion
butter – 2 tablespoons (30g)
smoked bacon – 7 ounces (200g)
potatoes – 3 smallish
chicken or ham stock – 6½ cups (1.5 liters)
broccoli, purple sprouting or other dark calabrese – 10½ ounces (300g)
milk – ⅔ cup (150ml)

Peel the onion, chop it coarsely, and soften it in the butter in a deep pan. I never let it color, preferring to keep it pale and translucent. Stir in half the bacon, snipped into short lengths (keep six short pieces for later), then the potatoes, scrubbed and cut into small pieces. Let the ingredients marry with as little color as possible, then pour in the stock and bring to a boil, adding salt and pepper as you go. Decrease the heat so that the mixture simmers gently for fifteen to twenty minutes or so, until the potatoes collapse against slight pressure from the back of a spoon.

Introduce the greens, trimmed of any exceptionally tough stems, and simmer for ten minutes. The greens should still live up to their name. Pour in the milk, simmer briefly, then process the mixture in a blender until smooth, checking the seasoning as you do so. Broil the remaining bacon until crisp, then serve the soup in warm bowls, each with a piece of crisp bacon on its surface.

Pasta with sprouting and cream

Pasta sends me to sleep. Actually, it always has. It's just that for years I failed to make the connection between my postprandial tiredness and what had been on my plate. I now take my dough of flour, eggs, and water in much smaller quantities, using it as the supporting actor rather than the lead. The result is a fresher, less heavy plate, yet somehow just as comforting. In many cases the pasta is padded out with vegetables: spinach, mushrooms, tomatoes, eggplants, peas, cavolo nero, or broccoli.

Members of the broccoli family work rather well with pasta, the folds and hollows of the cooked dough neatly holding onto crumbs of green vegetable. In what follows, we get a lot of pleasure for very little work: a plateful of soothing carbs with a creamy, cheesy sauce and masses of lightly cooked green vegetables. In short, a cheap, quick weekday supper.

> *enough for 2*
> purple sprouting broccoli or other young greens – 9 ounces (250g)
> orecchiette – 9 ounces (250g)
> butter – 2 tablespoons (30g)
> garlic – 2 cloves, thinly sliced
> anchovy fillets – 4, rinsed and chopped
> crème fraîche – 1 heaping cup (250ml)
> Gorgonzola cheese – 6 ounces (170g), crumbled

Bring two deep pans of water to a boil. Trim the purple sprouting, keeping the leaves intact and discarding any dry ends or tough stems. Generously salt the water in one of the pans and drop in the pasta.

Lightly salt the water in the other pan and add the purple sprouting. As soon as it is tender, a matter of three or four minutes, drain it and wipe out the pan, returning the pan to the heat with the butter, garlic, and anchovies. Let the garlic and anchovies cook slowly for a minute or two—the anchovies will almost dissolve—then spoon in the crème fraîche and crumbled cheese and bring to a boil, stirring and immediately decreasing the heat to a slow bubble. Chop the purple sprouting coarsely, then add it to the sauce and season with black pepper.

Drain the pasta lightly (a few tablespoons of the cooking water will help thin the sauce to the right consistency) and add it to the broccoli sauce.

A stir-fry of broccoli and lamb

Broccoli doesn't stir-fry well from raw. The beaded crown—the tight flower buds—tends to burn before the stem even approaches tenderness. Heads that have been briefly blanched in boiling water will, however, stir-fry deliciously, soaking up the ginger and soy or whatever other seasoning you might throw at them. In the last year or two I have taken to adding them to stir-fries of ground lamb or pork, letting the meat thoroughly caramelize in the thin pan before adding the greens.

It's a very quick, bright-tasting supper, invigorating and toothsome. But you do need to be brave with the meat, letting it glisten and almost crisp before you add the rest of the ingredients.

enough for 2
broccoli – a large handful of florets
green onions – 3
garlic – 3 plump cloves
hot red chiles – 2
peanut oil – 3 tablespoons
ground lamb – 10½ ounces (300g)
a lime
nam pla (Thai fish sauce) – 1 tablespoon
sugar – a teaspoon
cilantro leaves – a small handful

Blanch the florets of broccoli in boiling water for one minute. Drain and set aside. Chop the green onions, removing the darkest green leaves as you go. Peel the garlic and chop it finely, then seed and chop the chiles. Get the oil really hot in a shallow pan or wok, then cook the onions, garlic, and chiles until soft but not colored, moving them quickly round the pan as you go. It will appear there is too much oil, but bear with me.

Add the ground lamb and let it color appetizingly. It should go a rich golden color. Add the drained broccoli. In a small bowl, mix the juice of the lime with the nam pla and sugar. Add to the hot pan and let sizzle briefly, scraping at the gooey stickings on the bottom of the pan and stirring them in as you go. Check the seasoning—you may need a little salt—and stir in the cilantro.

Brussels sprouts

This garden is at its most magical when deep in snow. The branches of the fig tree stretch out across the vegetable patch like witches' fingers. A Winter Nellis pear hangs from the little tree by the kitchen door, frozen on its stem. The purple sprouting, red cabbage, artichokes, and kale lie under a thick snowflake mantle.

February 2, 2009. I wake to a deep, eerie silence, the vegetables sleeping under layers of heavy snowfall, my yew hedges and climbing roses turned into a scene from Narnia. It's the rosehips that make my heart melt, plump amber and scarlet baubles still visible beneath the powdery snow. That and the fox tracks leading from the compost heap, whose carpet covering he often curls up on, to the kitchen door. A walk of hope if ever there was one.

Brussels sprouts are the only vegetable I cannot eat unless the weather is cold. No frost, no sprouts. I am not alone. The Brussels sprout, a cabbage leaf in bud, has never been part of the cooking of the Mediterranean or Asia, and barely left Belgium and northern France before the late nineteenth century. Frost makes the sprout. It takes the bitterness out and gives us an appetite for strong flavors. Lightly cooked, so its color is bright and there is still crispness at its heart, the Brussels has much going for it. Eaten at the wrong time of year, cooked too long, or served with too much else on the plate, the sprout is hard going. At least it was for me, and for many years, too.

A sprout in the garden

The joy of growing from seed is that you can nurture old varieties of Brussels sprout, such as Bedford Fillbasket or Evesham Special from the 1920s. Both conjure up the thought of sepia photographs of farm laborers and wicker hampers laden ready for market. The pleasure of picking up a net bag of ready-prepared sprouts from the supermarket is that you don't have to grow them, let alone consider the variety.

Somewhere in between these two extremes of getting vegetables into your kitchen lies the plug plant. These ready-grown young plantlets, usually 3 to 4 inches (8 to 10cm) high, provide the possibility of growing your own for those disinclined or unable to plant seed or who think of the supermarket as the devil's own child.

Brussels sprouts are easy to grow from seed. You need light potting compost and module trays. Sow in April. They benefit from a rich soil, but too much nitrogen will make them bushy rather than productive. Transfer the plants to prepared beds when they have four true leaves above their seedling leaves. You will need a good 20 inches (50cm) between them, and they will take up a lot of your growing space all summer and autumn. A stick up each one is essential. It will support the stems so the plant can concentrate on being productive.

A Brussels diary

Mid-August A bundle of small plants the length of a pencil arrives in the mail. Previously I have bought them from the farmers' market, where they often have boxes of young plants in June and July, but I wanted to be specific about the variety, so mail order works better for me. So no Bedford Fillbasket, but a modern variety called Maximus, described by the National Vegetable Society as "superbly flavored, smooth, tight buttons that hold well on the plant for picking from late September to Christmas." I plant them early in the evening when the day has cooled and water them well.

August 25 I put in cane sticks to support the stems, tying them loosely with string. Even in a wet summer, they appear to need a good soaking at least twice a week. Keeping the pigeons away is an endless task. Tired of running up the garden waving a tea towel at them, I place a sheet of plastic net over the plants (and spend the remainder of the summer detaching snails and leaves from its clutches).

October 1 The plants are now a good eighteen inches high, jade green and dusky mauve. As beautiful a vegetable as you could ever imagine. I worry that their stems are not as thick as I would wish.

December I have rather ignored all the brassicas for the last few weeks. They are at the stage where they must get on with things unattended.

A slightly disappointing number of actual sprouts this year, but the "tops" are glorious, especially those that I pick from the snow after Christmas. For all the space they take up, a row of Brussels is a beautiful sight in a garden or allotment. Standing blue and green against the winter's sky, like something from a fairy story, they are worth every inch of space they consume.

Varieties

As vegetables go, I feel that sprouts show less of a difference between varieties than most. We don't exactly get a choice at the produce market or the supermarket, but my own pick for the garden was Maximus. I was guided purely by what I had been told about its flavor, but yield is a consideration for many, as is the stems' ability to stand in the vegetable patch through winter wind and frost. Fortress comes highly recommended. Incidentally, the young stems are crisp and will snap if handled unsympathetically.

Maximus I have done well with this autumn variety, even if I have found their color a little pale in the pot. If I am going to eat sprouts, then they must be zinging with color.
Evesham Special* A hardy one this, and a heavy cropper too. Will overwinter in the snow.
Bedford Fillbasket Large sprouts of a very old variety, named after England's commercial growing center.
Bosworth A popular choice for many allotment holders, known for its ability to stand well throughout the coldest winter.
Red Rubine A red variety, small and mildly flavored. I have grown these with mixed success, but their purple veins do look very beautiful on a frosty morning.
Revenge Very hardy, though the name might be more appropriate for a Jerusalem artichoke. Mid- to late winter.
Churchill* Big, smooth sprouts from a hardy, easy-to-grow variety; very early harvest.
Bubbles* Dark green, tasty, perfectly spherical sprouts; tolerant of warm weather.
Long Island Improved* Good flavor and high yield; a popular commercial variety before hybrids took its place.

*Available from US seed sources.

A sprout in the kitchen

There are two forms of interest here: the buttonlike sprouts and the bushy heads from the top of the stalk.

If you haven't bought your sprouts in a net from the supermarket or a paper bag from the produce market, then pull them from the stalk, working from the bottom up. There may be a few tatty outer leaves that need trimming away. I suggest you don't cut a cross in the bottom like my Granny did. It makes for a soggy sprout. If you worry about the outer leaves overcooking, cut each sprout clean in half. They will cook in a minute or two that way. Small sprouts are prized for their mild flavor.

Sprouts like to dance around in lots of rapidly boiling water with a very little salt. Too much salt will make them mushy, as will any attempt to keep them waiting. Serve them up immediately they are tender.

The pong of sprouts—fetid, stale, institutional—takes on a considerably more welcome note if there is a turkey roasting nearby. The two are virtually inseparable after the winter solstice on December 21. After that, the smell of the cabbage's particularly pungent little brother needs something else if your kitchen isn't to suffer a whiff of sulfur. Cheese will do the job, either blue or hard and savory, such as Parmesan or Spenwood; bacon, especially the tarry smoked versions; or the old-as-time smell of soy, ginger, and anise, redolent of Chinese cooking.

There is no classic sprout recipe to match asparagus hollandaise, pommes dauphinoise, choucroute garnie, or stuffed zucchini flowers. The *petit chou* has never been a star and we do the best we can to make it palatable. I recommend nut or seed oils as a cooking medium, walnut oil for dressing, warm butter as a simple sauce, and bacon fat to refry them the next day. Olive oil seems awkward in their presence. A pan of Brussels sprouts, trimmed and halved and tossed in duck fat, has a mellowness to it unachievable with any other fat.

I'm not sure anything will come from slow cooking these little buttons. A quick flash in a pan with snippets of pancetta, smoked bacon, or shredded salami is a sound idea, as is a squeeze of orange juice in a dish of briefly boiled sprouts with a little butter and crushed juniper berry. Chestnuts tossed among this vegetable suffer from the Marmite effect. One either loves or hates it.

I eat the Brussels sprout as a main dish under a blanket of cheese sauce. On a cold night in February, after a walk round the garden lighting candle lanterns in the snow as we went, we wolfed down a supper of sprouts with a sauce made from blue cheese from Randolph Hodgson and Joe Schneider's Stichelton Dairy. Robust, slightly salty, a little too rich: just the food for the coldest day of the year.

I wouldn't want to curry them (or be downwind of anyone who had), or throw them into the stockpot, where they risk adding a cabbagey note.

But they can make a surprisingly delicate soup, even an exciting one if you add a little Roquefort or crisp bacon. It's the sort of soup I want to eat when my socks have pulled down inside my Wellingtons after a long, slushy walk. I probably don't need to mention that they make a stirring bubble and squeak, but will in case you find yourself staring uninspired at a bowl of cold cooked sprouts on a Monday.

On a more original note, they are a revelation served raw. Try them with a dressing of whole-grain mustard, lemon zest, and walnut oil. They work if shredded finely (when they curiously resemble crepe paper), and like a good half hour's soaking in their dressing. Something with crème fraîche, sour cream, or thick yogurt would be sublime.

The heads of the stalks, sold as "sprout tops," come as loose rosettes of leaves, often with immature "sproutlets" attached. Treat them as you would cabbage, but with an even shorter cooking time.

To rid the kitchen of the scent of sprouts, try a candle or, better still, my trick of lighting a strip of *papier d'arménie*, the ancient French booklets of scented paper whose pages you tear out, fold like origami, then light with a match. Their heady smell of incense and old bookshops works on anything.

Seasoning your sprouts

All of the flavors that flatter other members of the brassica family apply to the sprout. Butter, bacon, cream, juniper, caraway, apple, lemon, pork all work their magic, and we should add chestnuts and almonds (sliced, toasted and scattered over your buttered sprouts), too.

And...

* I do think sprouts at Christmas are nonnegotiable. The family, all seventeen of them, expects them, and whether they love the flatulence-producing little things or feel distinctly noncommittal, they will be secretly disappointed if they don't get them. And we are not here to do that.
* If you turn a sprout top over, you will find several immature sprouts hiding under the open rosette of leaves. A treat.
* Sprouts, boiled ham, and parsley sauce. A forkful of calm and good taste if ever there was one.

A rich dish of sprouts and cheese
for a very cold night

Any blue cheese will melt into the sauce for these sprouts, but I have been
using a lot of Stichelton recently, a relatively new, gratifyingly buttery cheese
made from unpasteurized milk. A main course with rice or plainly cooked
pasta, and a particularly satisfying side dish for boiled ham.

enough for 4 as an accompaniment
Brussels sprouts – 1½ pounds (750g)
a little butter
Stichelton or other blue cheese – 6½ ounces (180g)
whole-grain mustard – a tablespoon
cream – 1¾ cups (400ml)
milk – 6½ tablespoons (100ml)
finely grated Parmesan – a handful

Preheat the oven to 350°F (180°C). Bring a large pot of water to a boil.
Remove any tatty leaves from the Brussels sprouts and cut each sprout in
half. When the water is boiling furiously, lightly salt it, then lower in the
sprouts. Let them come back to a boil, then boil for three minutes. Drain
thoroughly and put them in a lightly buttered shallow dish.

Crumble the cheese over the sprouts. Put the mustard in a bowl and
stir in the cream and milk and a grinding of black pepper. Pour the
seasoned cream over the sprouts and cheese, then scatter over the grated
Parmesan. Bake until the crust is lightly colored and the cream is bubbling.

Brussels with bacon and juniper

I often serve this as a main course, but it is in its element as a side dish.
Its bright green and smoky-bacon notes would be interesting with grilled
mackerel, or perhaps with thinly sliced cold meat such as roast pork or beef.
This is essentially a cheap dish, robust and earthy, to which you could add
caraway seeds if juniper isn't your thing, or shreds of fat-speckled salami in
place of the bacon, or a few croutons to make it more substantial.

> *enough for 4 as a side dish*
> Brussels sprouts – 14 ounces (400g)
> smoked bacon – 9 ounces (250g), the fattier the better
> juniper berries – 20

Bring a pan of water to a boil. Remove any tatty outer leaves from the
sprouts, then drop them into the boiling water. Return to a boil and
simmer for three or four minutes, until they are bright and crisp. Drain in
a colander.

Fry the bacon in a nonstick pan until crisp and golden. Meanwhile,
slice the sprouts in half. Once the bacon is ready, remove and drain on paper
towels. Add the sprouts to the pan—they will pick up all the crusty bits left
in the pan by the bacon.

Crush the juniper berries with the side of a knife blade or a pestle—you
only need flatten them. Add them to the sprouts, along with a light grinding
of salt and some black pepper.

Meanwhile, cut the bacon into pieces no smaller than a postage stamp.
When the sprouts are starting to soften but are still bright in color, return
the bacon to the pan for a few minutes. Serve sizzling hot.

A salad of sprouts, bacon, and pecans

Raw cabbage, especially the tight, white variety, would be good here if the idea of raw sprouts doesn't grab you.

enough for 2 as a light lunch dish

for the salad
smoked bacon – 5 slices
Brussels sprouts – 7 ounces (200g)
a large carrot
green onions – 2
shelled pecans – 2 tablespoons

for the dressing
plain yogurt – ¾ cup (200g)
peanut oil – 2 tablespoons
walnut oil – a tablespoon
parsley – a small bunch

Preheat the broiler. Broil the bacon until lightly crisp. Drain on paper towels, then cut into wide strips. Trim the sprouts and slice them very thinly. Scrub the carrot and peel it into long shavings with a vegetable peeler. Finely slice the green onions. Toast the pecans in a dry, nonstick pan for a couple of minutes until warm and fragrant.

Put the yogurt into a bowl, beat in the oils with a small whisk or fork, and season with salt and black pepper. Chop the parsley leaves, discarding the stalks, and stir in. Toss the sprouts, carrot, green onions, bacon, pecans, and dressing together. Check the seasoning and serve.

Sprouts, sprout tops, lentils, and endive

enough for 2
French or similar small lentils – ⅔ cup (125g)
red Belgian endive – 2 long ears
sprout tops – 2 heads
small Brussels sprouts – a handful

for the dressing
sherry vinegar – 2 tablespoons
walnut oil – 2 tablespoons
sunflower or peanut oil – 2 tablespoons
sugar – a pinch
Dijon mustard – 2 teaspoons

Rinse the lentils and add them to a pot of boiling water. They should be ready in fifteen to twenty-five minutes, depending on their age. Drain them in a colander.

While they are cooking, make the dressing. Dissolve a tiny pinch of salt in the vinegar, then beat in the oils, sugar, and mustard. As soon as the lentils are drained, toss them in the dressing.

Slice the endive into thin rounds. Shred the sprout tops (I like to make them about the width of pappardelle), then blanch them in lightly salted boiling water. Remove after a few seconds and flash under cold running water. Do the same with the sprouts, blanching them for a little longer.

Toss the greens, endive, and lentils together.

Some good things to add

* Cubes of feta cheese.
* Crumbled blue cheese, such as Roquefort or Cashel blue.
* Paper-thin slices of coppa, speck, or salami.
* Chunks of fried apple (toss cubes of peeled apple in hot butter until golden).
* Slices of raw pear.
* Sprouted mung beans.
* Slices of hot butcher shop sausage or blood sausage.
* Slices of crisp bacon (of course, but I can never resist them with anything from the cabbage family).

Sprout tops with sesame seeds and oyster sauce

Sprout tops share a luxury of growth and strong flavor with many of the Asian greens. One cold day in November I married them to an impromptu sauce of essentially Chinese ingredients. It worked. The tricky bit was working out what, in future, they needed to share a plate with. A slice of ham steak; a piece of lamb's liver; a fillet of mackerel, its skin crisped on the grill; a pile of sticky rice with some finely sliced air-dried sausages; a grilled mushroom the size of a saucer. All will work. Eminently.

enough for 4 as a side dish
garlic – 2 cloves
ginger – a 2-ounce (60g) knob
peanut oil – 2 tablespoons
oyster sauce – 3 tablespoons
rice wine – 3 tablespoons
soy sauce – 1 tablespoon
sugar – a pinch
sprout tops – a large handful
sesame seeds – 1 teaspoon

Peel the garlic, then slice it very thinly; I try to get it as thin as paper. Peel the ginger and slice thinly, then cut each slice into fine matchsticks. Warm the oil in a small pan, stir in the garlic and ginger, and let soften for a couple of minutes. They should color lightly.

Stir in the oyster sauce, rice wine, soy sauce, and the pinch of sugar. Make it a big one. Decrease the heat to low, so that the mixture bubbles only very gently for about five minutes.

Meanwhile, wash the sprout tops thoroughly, then put into a deep pan, the water still clinging to their leaves. Cover tightly with a lid and let steam for two or three minutes, until bright and wilted. Toast the sesame seeds in a nonstick pan till they smell warm and nutty.

Drain any liquid from the pan of sprout tops, then pour in the sauce. Toss the greens around gently until they are glossy, scatter with the toasted sesame seeds, and serve immediately. This is one of those dishes that needs to be served as hot as you can.

Mashed Brussels with Parmesan and cream

One of the gifts of the *nouvelle cuisine* movement was the puréed vegetable. At its worst, a sad puddle of unidentifiable beige gunk; at its most successful, a moreish pool of intensely flavored, silk-textured essence. Sprouts, which marry so happily with cream, tend to look like baby food when given this treatment, so I keep them coarsely chopped instead of whizzed to a pulp. I am exceptionally fond of this little side dish.

enough for 4
Brussels sprouts – 1¼ pounds (600g)
a little grated nutmeg
heavy cream – 1 cup (250ml)
Parmesan – scant 1 cup (100g) grated

Preheat the oven to 325°F (160°C). Remove any tatty leaves from the sprouts. Cook the sprouts in rapidly boiling unsalted water for four minutes. Drain, then put them in a food processor, along with some salt and pepper. Process briefly, till no more than coarsely chopped, then season with a very small pinch of nutmeg. Stir in the cream and most of the cheese. Scoop into a baking dish. Scatter with the reserved Parmesan and bake for twenty-five minutes or so, until golden.

Cabbage

The dead of winter, all is silent, the world hushed by a thick covering of snow. The point in the year when strident flavors are needed: game birds, smoked bacon, and dank mushrooms that have waited patiently in the fridge. It is the time for blood sausage, crisp white goose fat, red wine stews, pudding. It is now I reach for the winter spices: cinnamon, cloves, ginger, cardamom— and juniper, the dusky black berries with notes as clean and bright as a gin and tonic.

The cabbage family is suddenly allowed back into the kitchen. Each dark-green leaf somehow seems as if it will fend off our winter ills. Elephant ears of crinkled green, sparkling with dew; black plumes of cavolo nero like the feathers on a funeral horse, and the dense, ice-crisp flesh of red cabbage. Strong flavors indeed.

The brassica family is large. I think of it in two quite separate forms: those we eat as leaves—the cabbages, kales, and sprouts—and those we grow for their flowering heads, like broccoli, cauliflower, and white and purple sprouting. The most revered is the heading side of the family, but I have much respect for the leafier greens too, and admire the quiet grace of their jade, red, and dusk-blue leaves. Seen in the field under a flint-colored sky, they are as beautiful as any rose, as complex and mysterious as any peony.

I escaped cabbage until I was in my late teens, when it came, in gently sulfurous wafts, up the stairs of my college digs. A Saturday stew pressure-cooked to within an inch of its life. Pale cabbage, mild and almost timid, cabbage without the strength to offend. It sat in shallow pools of broth with lamb's vertebrae and thick carrots, and white potatoes full of steam.

Later, a winter spent in Cornwall, sitting round pub tables for want of work, formed an introduction, a wake-up call as it turned out, to vegetables other than zucchini and peas. We bought from trestles at the farm gate, leaving our money in an honesty box and taking away turnips, rutabagas, and cabbages. In January there were sprouts, and parsnips for mashing with butter and pepper. My sister-in-law taught me to cook a cabbage. A little water in the bottom of the pan, the leaves left large and dipped into the merrily boiling water only until their colors shone and their stalks became translucent. Seconds, not minutes.

Cabbages, round heads, pointed, red leaved, and green, smooth or blistered, tight or loose-leaf, are there for us when all the other leaves are out of season or come with an unfashionable seasoning of air miles.

The first primitive cabbages were bitter, their leaves loose and few. The mildness of flavor and the tight heads have come with domestication. In Gerard's 1633 *Herbal*, cabbages with "leaves wrapped together into a round head or globe" are mentioned, but it appears they were still unusual. Having gained and lost varieties through the centuries that followed, we now have a choice between the soft-leaved spring greens, pointed summer varieties, Christmas drumheads such as the crinkly Savoys, and the hard white types that store so well through the winter. Anyone with an organic-box delivery will see the styles of cabbage change as the year progresses, from soft, loosely packed heads of silky leaves in spring to the darker, coarser leaves of winter. They all have their merits.

A cabbage in the garden

Few sights in the garden are as beautiful as that of members of the cabbage family on a winter's morning, the frilled edges of their leaves encrusted with frost. Deep sea greens and misty blues, the January Kings fringed with madder rose, add a somber, curiously Venetian note to a garden whose only other color comes from the occasional rosehip.

I plant young seedlings rather than growing my drumheads and loose-leafs from seed, partly for want of space. They arrive, in neat bundles and trays, from a farm on Cornwall's Roseland Peninsula. The big-name mail-order companies can send out plantlets too, and this is often the most practical way for those of us without greenhouses or much space for germinating seeds.

Those with a little room outdoors can sow their winter cabbage seeds in March and April and spring greens in July and August. There are well-known seeds, such as January King and Primo, but specialty seed lists, such as those of Thomas Etty, tempt with less obvious varieties: Mr. Ellam's Early Dwarf, noted for its failure to bolt; Filderkraut for spring sowing; or Christmas Drumhead, whose modest size makes it suitable for small gardens. Scatter your seeds about a finger's width apart in fine compost in shallow seed trays. Cover with a thin layer of compost, water well, and keep the compost moist. They should be up in about two weeks.

Winter cabbage seedlings will need to go out into the garden in July; spring cabbage in September and October. I put mine in about 12 to 16 inches (30 to 40cm) apart, giving them room to heart up but also giving myself the space to weed around them. There is nothing quite so irritating as snapping the brittle stem of a healthy plant before its prime. They will tolerate a stony soil.

Little brassica collars that sit around the base of the stem are available from garden centers, and prevent the cabbage root fly laying its eggs. I regularly see allotments where cabbages stand firm and tall all winter, keeping families in greens until late spring. Mine grow shorter than most, I know not why, but often heart up better than I deserve. A net over them in late summer is not too much of an eyesore, especially if it is dark green, and will keep off the worst of the cabbage white butterfly.

A dozen cabbage plants will keep most families going throughout the major part of the winter. And that is probably what most of us end up with after the pigeons have had their fill. Pick them when their hearts are firm and before the outer leaves get too ragged.

Varieties

Choosing carefully, you could keep yourself in cabbage all year—from the soft-leaved summer varieties through to the strident flavors and thicker leaves of the winter ones. I tend not to plant any that will be ready for picking in summer, when my beds are too full of beans and squashes, and a brassica would strike too strong a note.

Spring Greens (to sow in July and August)
Duncan A small, pointed variety.
Wheelers Imperial Mr. Wheeler's compact variety has been an allotment favorite since 1840. Dark green outer leaves and thick veining.
Offenham Flower of Spring A delicate flavor from medium-sized leaves.
Gonzales* Small, dense, perfectly round heads.

Summer Cabbage (to sow in February and March)
Hispi Tight, pointed, pale green heads with a gentle flavor. A supermarket favorite because of its neat size.
Durham Reliable, popular variety with small heads that come to a point.
Blue Lagoon* Good-sized blue-green heads on compact plants.

Winter Cabbage (to sow from March to July for harvesting from December to February) Allow thirty weeks from sowing to maturity.
Christmas Drumhead An old-fashioned variety of small, tight heads and frilly open leaves. Popular since the 1920s.
January King* Large leaved, deeply veined, and often tinged with pink. Happy to stand in the freezing cold in the garden.
Protovoy Heavily blistered leaves that hold melted butter like a crumpet, dark-green outer leaves protect a paler heart; softer than January King.

*Available from US seed sources.

A cabbage in the kitchen

From September to April, my week isn't complete without some form of *chou* on my plate. They come into the kitchen with the new school term, Michaelmas daisies, and pumpkins, and go out when I dig out my short-sleeved shirts. During that time, they will appear briefly steamed and buttered; tossed with ginger, oyster sauce, and soy; wrapped around sausage stuffing; and shredded in knife-sharp salads with winter roots and yogurt.

In summer I occasionally turn to their bright emerald leaves—so much softer and smoother in the summer varieties—to accompany a piece of warm poached salmon (though I would rather have peas).

The leaves keep better as a whole head than they do once separated. Wrap the entire head in damp newspaper and store in the vegetable crisper of the fridge or in a plastic bag somewhere really cold. It will be fine for several days.

A stalk has to be really tough before I can be persuaded to remove it. I love its juicy crunch and rarely follow written instructions to discard it. The contrast of soft leaves and crisp stalk is part of the vegetable's appeal. Generally, the leaves behave better on the plate if cut up a little. I keep them as large as I sensibly can, though will sometimes make them more acceptable to polite eaters by rolling several leaves together tightly, then shredding them finely with a heavy cook's knife. The more demure of my friends can then twiddle them round their fork like fettuccine.

Seasoning your cabbage

I sometimes don't season my greens at all, taking them from their steam and squeezing a lemon over them instead. The juice brings all their sweetness to the fore.

Cream Has a calming effect on the more strident flavors, working especially well with nutmeg.

Juniper The vegetable's most appropriate seasoning, the bitter, gin-flavored spice teasing out all the leaves' sweetness. A must with red cabbage.

Caraway A very Germanic tone and one that is too often neglected here; the warm, musty notes lend an ancient, almost medieval character to the white variety. Toast the seeds first. Your kitchen will smell like a Berlin baker's.

Ginger Use freshly grated.

Gin Steam the shredded leaves, covered in aluminum foil, in a roasting pan with a little butter, water, crushed juniper berries, shredded dill, and a shake of the gin bottle.

Mushrooms Use as a stuffing, or as partners in a stir-fry.

Soy Dark soy, added late to a stir-fry, lends a mellow saltiness to any brassica. Even better with broccoli than with cabbage.

Vinegar White wine vinegar gives a sourness that is acutely refreshing with the white varieties. A good vinegary slaw can be a perfect thing on a piercingly cold winter's day. I tend to use red wine vinegar with red cabbage but I'm not entirely sure why.

Dill Finely chopped dill fronds bring a northern European tone to the leaves. Works best with white, rounded varieties.

Anchovies Finely chopped, melted into hot oil over medium heat, then use to dress dark green winter leaves.

Mustard Include mild versions in a cream sauce for a gratin and in dressings with walnut oil for a salad.

And...

* Any part of the pig works neatly with this group. A quick lunch of mine when I am at my desk is broiled bacon, blanched greens, toasted unsalted cashews, sprouted seeds, and a dressing of oil and vinegar.

* Slow-cooked Chinese pork dishes, the sort you simmer with onions, garlic, soy, and rice wine, always benefit from a pile of blanched leaves on the side, even if they aren't Chinese.

* Cabbage, simply steamed, has a lasting affinity with gravy. The two perform a perfect piece of chemistry—particularly when the gravy is exceptionally hot and sits in the craters and dimples of the cabbage leaves.

* Cabbage soup has been the last resort of crash dieters for decades. It works. But it works even better as a restorative after a cold or when you are generally in need of something both cleansing and soul enriching. I make a bowl of stock (homemade if I have it, powdered bouillon if not), then add a chopped tomato or two, a spoonful of canned (rinsed) flageolet or haricot beans, some finely shredded cabbage, crushed garlic, and masses of cilantro leaves and fresh mint.

* A good cabbage will squeak with freshness. To keep it that way for as long as possible, I wrap it in newspaper or I stuff it into a plastic bag—the type that seals when you press the edges together—spray water from a spray bottle in the bag and keep it in the vegetable crisper section of the fridge. I have had small cabbages keep in perfect condition for a week that way.

Simple steamed cabbage

Wash the leaves thoroughly in cold water, then tear them into manageable pieces. Bring a finger's depth of water to the boil in a large pan. Fill a steamer basket with the cabbage and then, when the water is boiling angrily, decrease the heat, and cover with a lid. It will cook in the steam in three or four minutes.

Boiled cabbage

The words hang heavy, wretched with disappointment. In reality, few things edible cheer me up more than a plate of cabbage freshly lifted from the steam, the colors clear and bright, the leaves singing with life. I add nothing save lemon and sometimes black pepper, coarse from the grinder. As a rule, my cabbage isn't boiled or even steamed, only blanched. Dipped briefly into boiling water, the leaves cook more quickly, and seem to stay a livelier color than when they are steamed. The water must be deep and at a rollicking boil. A little salt can go in, though I often forget, and then the leaves. No lid. I leave them for a minute or two. They won't look ready but they will be by the time you have grabbed the oven mitts with which to lift the pot to sink and drained them. Vibrant, exhilarating even, when placed on a stark white plate.

   If naked vegetables don't stir your juices, then a drizzle of balsamic vinegar, a dusting of grated Parmesan, a puddle of almost-melted butter, or a coating of mustardy French dressing just might.

White cabbage with oyster sauce

The brassicas are much revered in Chinese cooking, and dealt with elsewhere in this book, but the white cabbage, with its waxy leaves and crisp stalks, makes an excellent candidate for seasoning with the saltier accompaniments. On cold, rather gray days, the sort of day when nothing much happens, I often crave robust, dominating flavors—perhaps in a quest to inject some vigor into the occasion. Strident greens tossed in lip-tingling oyster sauce can be such a dish.

   In the last four or five years, this has become one of those recipes I use as a "knee-jerk" accompaniment—an alternative to opening a bag of frozen peas. It is excellent with grilled pork chops, though I have also eaten it atop a bowl of steamed rice before now.

   half a medium-sized cabbage
   peanut oil – a tablespoon
   oyster sauce – 2 tablespoons

Pull the cabbage leaves apart and wash them well. Taking two or three at a time, pile them one on top of another, roll them up, then cut into thin shreds with a large chef's knife. The width of the strips is a personal choice but I tend to slice mine about the same width as pappardelle, the widest of the ribbon pastas.

Bring a pan of water to the boil, salt it generously, then drop in the shredded cabbage. Leave at a galloping boil for a full minute. Drain and return the leaves to the empty pan. Immediately stir in the oil and the oyster sauce. Toss and serve straight away.

A crisp, sweet-sharp relish for Christmas

The sour crispness of red cabbage makes it a good ingredient for a relish. Something stirring—hot, sharp, sour, bright—to introduce to a gamey pâté or a wedge of pork pie with softly collapsing pastry. Not normally given to making pickles and chutneys, I find this startling relish manageable without feeling I am going too far down the preserving route.

> boiling water – 4 tablespoons
> tamarind pulp – 2 tablespoons
> carrots – 9 ounces (250g)
> red cabbage – 9 ounces (250g)
> fresh ginger – 2½ ounces (75g)
> sea salt – 4 teaspoons
> palm sugar (jaggery) or brown sugar – 2 teaspoons
> hot chiles – 2, shredded
> nam pla (Thai fish sauce) – a tablespoon
> rice vinegar – ⅔ cup (150ml)
> water – ⅔ cup (150ml)

Pour the boiling water over the tamarind pulp (you can find it at Asian markets and some supermarkets). Let sit a few minutes, then strain through a fine-mesh strainer. Discard the pulp and keep the tamarind water.

Finely shred the carrots, red cabbage, and ginger. Put them in a bowl with 2 teaspoons of the sea salt and the reserved tamarind water and let sit overnight. Drain off the liquid and add the palm sugar, the shredded hot chiles, the remaining salt, the Thai fish sauce, rice vinegar, and water. Mix thoroughly. Store in an airtight jar in the fridge. You can use it within a day or two, though it will keep for up to a week; just keep turning the jar over from time to time.

A cabbage soup

The frugality implied in the words "cabbage soup" appeals to me just as much as the fanciful descriptions of Michelin-starred menus. The words evoke a rich simplicity where nothing unnecessary intrudes. This is indeed a soup of extraordinary solace, gratifying in its purity. The stark fact that this was a meal formed in poverty is there for all to see.

Portugal has a cabbage soup, perhaps the best known of all, *caldo verde*. It is made with *couve gallego*, a yellow-flowered kale, whose leaves are flatter and less plumelike than the kale we generally buy in the market. The other ingredients are from the pantry, but should include a few slices of chorizo if the soup is to have any authenticity. This soup works with any coarse-textured greens and eminently, I think, with Savoy cabbage.

enough for 4
a large onion
garlic – 2 or 3 cloves
olive oil
potatoes – 3 medium, a waxy variety
bay leaves – 2
chorizo – a large piece (about 7 ounces [200g])
cabbage or kale leaves – 3 or 4 handfuls

Peel the onion and garlic and slice them thinly. Warm a glug or two of olive oil in a large, deep saucepan, then let the onion and garlic soften in it over low heat.

Peel the potatoes—I sometimes don't—then cut them into medium-sized pieces. Combine with the onion and let cook for five minutes before adding about 4 cups (a liter) of water. Season with salt, black pepper, and the bay leaves and let simmer for about twenty-five minutes, until the potatoes are ready to collapse.

With a fork or a potato masher, crush the potatoes so that they thicken the soup but remain quite lumpy here and there. Cut the chorizo into thick chunks and fry in a nonstick pan until the fat runs.

Shred the cabbage finely, then stir it into the soup and simmer for three or four minutes, until tender. Stir in the fried chorizo. I like to pass this soup round in rough, earthenware bowls.

Cabbage with beans, coconut, and coriander

Early January 2008 and I am having my annual tidy up of the pantry. The "lentil shuffle" as I call it, as that is basically what the job entails. Sorting out the pantry always results in my making something bean or lentil oriented. I think it must remind me of just how many I have. What follows is a rather hot bean curry. You could cool its ardor by skipping a chile or two. The greens offer a hit of cool freshness on top of the substantial and deeply spiced beans.

A speedier version, suitable for a midweek supper, can be made with canned beans. There is no real reason why you shouldn't use any dried or canned beans you wish here. Chickpeas will work well too. If I do decide to open a can instead, then I use three 14-ounce (400g) cans.

enough for 4 to 6
dried haricot beans – 1 pound (500g)
onions – 2 medium
vegetable or peanut oil – 2 tablespoons
garlic – 3 cloves
green cardamom pods – 8
coriander seeds – 2 teaspoons
mustard seeds – a teaspoon
cumin seeds – a teaspoon
ground turmeric – 2 teaspoons
chiles – 3 small, hot
chopped plum tomatoes – two 14-ounce (400g) cans
a pinch of sugar
coconut milk – 1 cup (250ml)
fresh cilantro – a large handful
a lime, maybe 2

for the greens
leafy soft green cabbage, such as spring greens –
  a good handful or more per person

Soak the dried beans in cold water overnight. The next day, boil the beans until tender in deep unsalted water. Drain and set aside. (If you are using canned beans, rinse them under cold running water, then set aside.)

Peel the onions, cut them in half and slice them thinly. Add them to the oil in a large, deep pan and let them soften, coloring lightly, over moderate heat. This often takes longer than you might imagine, a good fifteen minutes at least. Peel and chop the garlic and add to the onions.

Crack the cardamom pods open and extract the tiny seeds. Crush these coarsely, using a pestle and mortar or a very heavy rolling pin, then stir them into the softening onions. Crush the coriander seeds and then the mustard, and add them to the onions with the whole cumin seeds, ground turmeric, a generous seasoning of salt, and black pepper. Cook, stirring regularly, for at least five minutes, so that the spices toast in the heat.

Meanwhile, seed and finely chop the chiles and add, with the chopped tomatoes, 1¾ cups (400ml) of water and a pinch of sugar, followed by the cooked beans. Simmer gently over low heat, with the occasional stir, partially covered with a lid, for about thirty-five to forty minutes.

Mix the coconut milk into the sauce, simmer for a further five minutes, then add the cilantro leaves and the lime juice. When the curry is almost ready, make a tight fist of the greens and shred them quite finely. Steam or blanch briefly, then add to the curry.

A quick cabbage supper with duck legs

A preserved duck leg from the deli has saved my supper more times than I can count. Cased in its own white fat and crisped up in the oven or in a sauté pan, these "duck confit" are as near as I get to eating ready-made food. One January, arriving home cold and less than 100 percent, I stripped the meat from a couple of duck legs and used it to add protein to an express version of one of those lovingly tended cabbage and bean soups. The result was a slightly chaotic bowlful of food that felt as if it should be eaten from a scrubbed pine table in a French cave house. An extraordinarily heart-warming supper, immensely satisfying. An edible version of the sort of people one refers to as "the salt of the earth." I am certain no one would have guessed it hadn't spent the entire afternoon puttering away in a cast-iron pot.

enough for 4 as a main course
haricot beans – two 14-ounce (400g) cans
a leek – a large, thick one
smoked bacon – 6 slices
duck fat, peanut oil, or butter – a tablespoon
garlic – 2 cloves
a large carrot
potatoes – 4 small (about 9 ounces [250g] in total)
vegetable stock (or whatever there is on hand) – 2½ cups (600ml)
confit duck legs – 2
cabbage – a quarter, or a similar volume of spring greens
coarse-textured country-style bread – 4 slices

Empty the beans into a colander and rinse them under cold running water.

Halve the leek lengthwise and chop it coarsely, then rinse very thoroughly to remove any trapped grit. Slice the bacon into thick strips and warm it in a deep, heavy-bottomed pan with the fat or butter. Add the chopped leek and let it soften. Neither leek nor bacon should be allowed to color.

Peel and slice the garlic, scrub the carrot and chop it into small dice, scrub the potatoes and cut them into large chunks, then add all to the softening leek. Pour over the stock and bring to a boil. Decrease the heat so that the liquid simmers gently and leave until the potatoes are tender—a matter of twenty minutes or so.

Meanwhile, put the duck legs in a shallow pan with a lid and let them cook over medium heat until nicely warmed, about fifteen minutes. Strip the meat and skin from the duck and tear it into long shreds, but don't wipe off the fat; it will add warmth and a silky fattiness to the soup. Shred the cabbage leaves and stir, together with the duck meat, into the soup. Simmer for five or six minutes.

Toast the bread, tear into large pieces, and put a handful in the bottom of each bowl. Ladle the broth and meat into the bowls.

Winter cabbage, juniper, and cream

February 2008. The garden is all frost and cabbages. Here and there the occasional fat seed head, some purple sprouts on bending stalks, and piles of sticks that I have pulled off the trees that overhang the vegetable patch. The earth is crisp underfoot. Soup days.

The winter cabbages, especially Savoy and Protovoy, are blistered with webs and hollows that seem made to hold a sauce of some sort. At its simplest, this could be melted butter or hot bacon fat, but a cream sauce seems an especially attractive idea on a cold day, adding suavity to a coarse flavor and at a stroke tempering the leaves' stridency. The juniper in the spiced cream that follows makes this a perfect accompaniment to ham or roast pork, though I have been known to eat it with brown rice as a main dish in itself.

enough for 4 as a side dish
cabbage – 14 ounces (400g)
black peppercorns – 2 teaspoons
juniper berries – 2 teaspoons
butter – 2 tablespoons (25g)
heavy cream – ¾ cup (200ml)

Separate the leaves of the cabbage and shred them into finger-thick strips. I find the easiest way to do this is to pile the leaves on top of one another, then roll them up and shred them with a large knife.

Bring a pan of water to a boil, salt it lightly, and add the cabbage. Let it boil for barely a couple of minutes. You want the leaves to be tender enough to eat but still bright green and perky.

Meanwhile, crush the peppercorns and juniper berries lightly with a pestle and mortar, or with a heavy object on a chopping board. Drain the cabbage, return the empty pan to the heat, and melt the butter in it. Toast the crushed spices in the butter for a minute or two until fragrant, then pour in the cream. Let bubble for a minute or so, until it starts to thicken slightly, then season with a very little salt and add the drained greens. Toss them in the spiced cream until lightly coated. Serve immediately, while the sauce is still piping hot and creamy.

A winter slaw

There is much that appeals about the crude crunch of a winter slaw—white, purple, and moss green—eaten under a gray and watery sky. The snap of raw cabbage under the teeth can be exhilarating, especially when there is some sharpness in the dressing. I use yogurt sometimes, or a vinaigrette with lemon instead of vinegar, and occasionally introduce a fiery flash of blood orange or even grapefruit. The pink variety works particularly well. The crucial point is that this salad has a clean bite to it. The idea of gummy mayonnaise and the traditional coleslaw doesn't really enter into my head any more.

White cabbage, or maybe a slice across the brainlike interior of the red version, shreds of celery root, long gratings of carrot, and the occasional ice-white chevron of fennel regularly appear in my recipe. Several times each winter I find myself tossing in a ribbon of grated beet, added at the last moment so it fails to send its trail of blood through the ivory-white celery root. A little bleeding of the ingredients can be quite beautiful, but it is best not to mix too much, unless pink is your thing.

To the raw vegetable base, I will often add a caper or two, a handful of toasted almonds, a pinch of poppy seeds the color of torrential rain. I might add sesame or pumpkin seeds or jewels from a pomegranate. If an herb is included, it is most likely whatever happens to be at hand, but preferably dill, echoing the chill of Scandinavia, or flat-leaf parsley torn from its stem but not chopped. If luxury is wanted, then a little crème fraîche can be stirred in with the yogurt and olive oil that I use as a quick, light, and ultimately flattering dressing.

If protein is needed, I edge the plate with cuts of salami, coppa, or prosciutto straight from the deli slicing machine (my local deli cuts it thin enough to read a book through, then rolls it in cellophane so that each piece has a distinct curl to it, like an almond tuile). On a whim, I flick crisp gherkins, the tiny ones, in with the shredded roots, or fat, tadpolelike caper berries. Adding such piquant ingredients is a good wheeze with cabbage, to the point where I occasionally include some blue cheese too, such as Spanish Picos or Beenleigh Blue. They work in a similar way to the sourness that makes sauerkraut so tantalizing on the tongue.

The exact contents will depend on the roots and brassicas I use as the backbone. There may be walnuts or pecans, particularly if I have included celery root; almonds, sometimes smoked or salted, especially with red cabbage; sprouted azuki or lentils, though never alfalfa, which forms soggy nests among the layers of crisp cabbage. Cavolo nero, blanched for twenty seconds in boiling water, then dunked into iced water and shaken dry, is a regular once the frosts have set its flavor.

The dressing is invariably a 7-ounce (200g) tub of goat or sheep's yogurt stirred through with three or four tablespoons of olive oil, a scattering of chopped dill or parsley, and maybe the grated zest of a blood orange or perhaps a Sicilian lemon. Freshness and a snap of acidity are vital with a salad of roots and cabbage.

A slaw of red cabbage, blue cheese, and walnuts

The dressing is enough for four and will keep in the fridge for several days.

per person
a quarter of a red cabbage
half a medium bulb of fennel
a russet apple
a little lemon juice
a medium carrot
blue cheese, such as Harborne, Cashel, or Beenleigh – 5 ounces (150g)
walnuts – a handful
a rib of celery

for the dressing
mild red wine vinegar – 2 tablespoons
smooth Dijon mustard – 2 teaspoons
peanut oil – 3 tablespoons
walnut oil – 2 tablespoons
a pinch of superfine sugar

Shred the cabbage and fennel. Cut the apple into quarters, discarding the core, then slice finely. Toss the apple slices immediately in a little lemon juice to stop them from discoloring. Shred the carrot into matchsticks (or grate it very coarsely). Slice the cheese thinly. Toast the walnuts in a nonstick pan until they smell warm and nutty. Thinly slice the celery.

Make the dressing by mixing the vinegar and mustard with a little salt and black pepper. Beat in the peanut and walnut oils, then taste and add a little sugar if necessary.

Toss the salad ingredients together gently, so you don't break up the cheese too much. Divide among plates and drizzle over the dressing.

A word about red cabbage

Red cabbage owes its lack of popularity to its hatred of boiling water. It bucks the cooking method so dear to the British heart. It pickles nicely with allspice and malt vinegar and is the one member of this family that will wait for you once it has been cooked.

There is little wrong with the age-old method of cooking it, finely shredded, in a pan with a little flavorless oil, plus some juniper, wine vinegar, and perhaps some cubes of apple. The flavors go rather well with pork and the milder game, and the color is always cheering. As a larder staple, it keeps well too, staying in good shape in the fridge for a week or three.

I can't say I have ever grown this one, preferring to take my chances at the produce market. Though I do make a smart pickle with carrots and red cabbage for goosing up a coarse pâté (see page 097). I also serve the vegetable hot, with shards of smoked bacon and a Russet apple in the center. So good-natured to store, simple to prepare, crisp to eat, and colorful to look at. Its lack of popularity is a puzzle to me.

Red cabbage with cider vinegar

There will be quite a bit of this left over for the next day. Lovely reheated with cold ham.

enough for 4
a small red cabbage
a little olive or peanut oil
juniper berries – 8 to 10
cider vinegar – 3 tablespoons

Shred the cabbage finely, cutting away and discarding the hard core, rinse thoroughly, then drain. Heat a couple of tablespoons of oil in a wok or deep saucepan and add the red cabbage. Turn it in the oil, increasing the heat if nothing much is happening, until the color is bright—a matter of a minute or two.

Squash the juniper berries roughly, maybe with the flat side of a heavy knife blade or a pestle. You don't want them so much a powder, simply well bruised. Add them to the cabbage with most of the cider vinegar and a seasoning of salt and pepper. Cook the cabbage, covered, tossing occasionally. It will take seven to ten minutes to become tender but with some crunch left to it. Give it another five to ten minutes if you prefer it soft, which is actually when it is at its best. Freshen the taste if necessary with the last of the vinegar.

Turkey breast steaks, prune gravy, red cabbage

As cuts of meat go, the turkey breast steak is a relatively new one and will please those who like their protein neat, mild, and fat free. This addition to the meat counter has its advantages for a quick supper. It can be sizzled in butter with a few aromatics (bay, black pepper, thyme sprigs, and a curl of orange rind tend to cheer it up). Turkey still reeks of Christmas, but the white meat less so than the legs, which always smell like a roasting Christmas lunch.

Red cabbage makes a satisfactory accompaniment. Go further, with a few prunes and a bottle of Marsala, and you have something approaching a joyful Sunday lunch, though without a bone to pick.

enough for 2

for the gravy
an onion
a thick slice of butter
a small carrot
a rib of celery
all-purpose flour – 2 tablespoons
soft, pitted prunes – 7 ounces (200g)
a few sprig of thyme
bay leaves – 2
dry Marsala –scant 1 cup (200ml)
light stock or, at a push, water – 2 cups (500ml)

for the turkey steaks
a little butter
turkey steaks – 4, about 4 ounces (125g) each
a few leaves of thyme

Peel and coarsely chop the onion. Put it in a pan with the butter over medium heat and let it soften. Scrub and dice the carrot and celery and add to the onion. Let the vegetables cook until soft and lightly colored. Stir in the flour and let it turn pale golden, then chop the prunes and add them with the thyme and the bay leaves. Immediately pour in the Marsala and stock. Decrease the heat to a simmer and let bubble quietly for twenty minutes.

To prepare the turkey steaks, melt the butter in a large, shallow pan. Season the steaks with salt, black pepper, and the thyme leaves (don't skip the thyme). When the butter sizzles, lay the steaks in the pan and let them color on the underside before turning them over and continuing over gentle heat until tender. They should take about eight minutes, depending on their thickness. Remove to warm plates and serve with the hot prune sauce and the red cabbage that precedes.

A gratin of white cabbage, cheese, and mustard

All of the brassica family have an affinity with cream and cheese, yet it is those grown for their heads rather than their leaves that seem to get the comfort of dairy produce. Cauliflower and broccoli have long been served under a blanket of cheese and cream, but less so cabbage and the leafier greens. The reason, I have always assumed, is that the cabbage would be overcooked by the time the sauce has formed a crust in the hot oven. In practice, the "white" cabbages that sit on supermarket shelves like rock-hard footballs can be put to good use in a gratin. Their leaves and stalks are juicy when blanched in boiling water and the thicker leaves hold up very well under a sharp cheese sauce, flecked with nutmeg and hot white pepper.

I mostly use a cabbage gratin as a friend for a piece of boiled ham or bacon, especially one that has been simmered in apple juice with juniper berries and onion, but sometimes we eat it as it comes, as a TV dinner, like cauliflower cheese. My suggestion of Cornish Yarg is only because I have used it here to good effect. Any briskly flavored cheese is suitable.

enough for 4 as a side dish
milk – 2 cups (500ml)
cloves – 2
a couple of bay leaves
butter – 2 tablespoons (30g)
all-purpose flour – ¼ cup (30g)
a little nutmeg
heavy cream – scant ½ cup (100ml)
Cornish Yarg cheese – 1 cup (100g), grated
a medium-sized white cabbage
breadcrumbs – a large handful, maybe two

Bring the milk, cloves, and bay almost to a boil, then turn off the heat. Preheat the oven to 350°F (180°C).

Melt the butter in a saucepan and stir in the flour. Let it cook for a minute or two over medium heat, until it smells nutty. Pour in the milk and stir until it has thickened and any lumps have dissolved. If it remains stubbornly lumpy, then you had better get out the whisk. Season with salt, pepper (white would be a nice touch), and a grating of nutmeg. Stir in the heavy cream and the grated cheese.

Bring a generous pan of salted water to a boil. Cut the cabbage in half and then into thick slices, like wedges of cake. Dunk the cabbage into the boiling water for a minute or two and then drain.

Lay the cabbage pieces in a shallow ovenproof dish. Pour over the sauce, then scatter over the breadcrumbs. Bake for roughly forty-five minutes, until the crust is patchily golden, the edges bubbling enticingly.

Carrots

Not for me the pile of buttered carrots on the plate. Too sweet, too orange (too bloody cheerful more like it). But the carrot's place is assured in my kitchen as the bringer of earthy sweetness, a backbone vegetable on which to build layers of flavor.

The heirloom cultivars so popular in the Middle Ages are more my style: more earthy, I suppose, and their colors—white, yellow, purple-black, violet, burgundy, and plum—are softer. The colors of bruised flesh. But early carrots were, like the wild ones, thin affairs until the early 1600s, when Flemish gardeners finally produced a fatter, brighter carrot. The sandy soils of Belgium and Holland are much appreciated by this vegetable; indeed, most modern cultivars probably originate from the Dutch Long Orange. Now the varieties of antiquity are in demand again, their colors are intriguing in a salad with brown mustard seed, lemon juice, and much, much parsley.

India provides a good hunting ground for recipes (though the vegetable is said to have been domesticated first in Afghanistan). Grated with toasted cumin seeds, stir-fried with red chiles and turmeric, a bright pickle spiky with ginger and softened with garam masala, the grated roots stirred through a brown rice pilaf with the rich warmth of ground cardamom. Indian cooks understand how to tame the monotone sweetness of the carrot (the Italians once ate it as a dessert, with honey) while making it sing with vitality and freshness.

After peas, carrots were the only truly acceptable vegetable to me as an eight-year-old. But even then there were rules. If they were to pass my lips, they had to be cut into small dice, the same size as peas, and preferably appear at the same time, so they could share a fork. The frozen mixture of the two by Bird's Eye must have been manna from heaven for my mother. If they appeared whole, or even the size of a cork, the offending vegetable would be guaranteed to set off a quivering lower lip.

When I was thirteen, my father gave me a strip of ground to work for myself, complete with a painted sign bearing the legend, "Nigel's Garden." I planted carrots, cosmos, and candytuft. In contrast to the rich, fecund soil adjacent, where he grew strawberries and wigwams of scarlet runners, mine was stony and dry, partly shaded by an ancient pear tree, its fruit too high to reach. In July the ground became hot enough to fry eggs.

The carrots were thin, and many broke off as I pulled them. Their fragile flowers trembled in the wind. In winter, they were too firmly rooted to pull and the size of parsnips. My dad had to pry them out with the garden fork, while my stepmother poked them around the chicken that she would boil and plate up with mashed potatoes and parsley sauce.

None of the restaurants I ever worked in served carrots. They were backroom boys (to my eyes, carrots are unquestionably male), there to provide a balance for the piquant, gherkin-flecked sauce that accompanied paupiettes of veal, or in heroic chunks in a casserole of young lamb with needles of rosemary and curls of orange peel. But they were never stars.

I arrived at a Lake District hotel one spring, one of a ring of country-house hotels that had sprung up around the lakes in the 1980s. Daffodils shone through the rough grass that led down to the lake and I was taught to make pastry by the open window, so I could smell the green prickle of spring as I rubbed the butter into the flour. (Despite the obvious preciousness, this was the point at which I discovered that cooking can be so much more than just a way to make a living.)

The draw here was not so much the rooms, which were more luxurious elsewhere, or the formal garden, whose tubby stone putti looked ill at ease with the surrounding meadows, but the view across to Langdale Pike, which provided a suitably theatrical backdrop to the six-course, no-choice dinners. It seems crazy now to have offered a main course (roast beef, lamb in hay, local duck) surrounded by never less than six differently cooked vegetables (cabbage with gin and juniper, parsnip purée with pine nuts, red cabbage with apple, deep-fried cauliflower, zucchini with toasted almonds, straw potatoes), but they were assembled with care and thought and were rarely less than delicious. I make the parsnip purée to this day.

Carrots were much in evidence. Their sweetness no doubt went with the gilded cherubs that hung from the ceiling and the primroses that adorned the plates. If one could ever love the sugariness of a carrot, surely it would be here. The roots shone like stained-glass windows on the overcrowded plates: a cake of carrot and potato slices baked with fresh herbs; a purée of carrots with toasted cumin seed; grated carrots with walnut oil and orange zest; soups of carrot and orange, carrot and apple, carrot and beets; and a much copied one of carrots and cilantro leaf became trademarks. Good ideas all, but now I look for ways to temper their excessive sweetness. I could live without the carrot as a vegetable. But I very much value it, with onions, celery, and bay, as an earthy aromatic.

A carrot in the garden

Carrot leaves and flowers have an almost fairylike delicacy to them, belonging to the same family as lovage, fennel, and angelica. I allow a few to blossom in the garden simply for the fine beauty of their lace umbrella of flowers.

This garden's soil was initially too heavy for a carrot crop, which would be happier on the sandy soils farther south. Five years of digging in a compost of bracken and horse manure has now lightened it to the point where I feel a row or two of roots might survive. They dislike lumpy soil too, which makes them fork, so I break up the soil into a fine tilth, like that of a crumble topping, a week or so before planting the tiny seeds. For a spring crop, you should sow outside in late autumn, then cover with horticultural fleece. For early summer pickings, sow in early spring, as soon as the ground has warmed up a little. It needs to be about 44°F (7°C).

Few seeds are more diminutive than that those of the carrot family and they tend to grow in close tufts, which need thinning if the roots are to fatten properly. I find thinning tedious—I'd rather do almost anything else in the garden—but there is little choice. They need to end up about 4 inches (10cm) apart. Thinning in showery weather will prevent any passing carrot fly taking interest, as will discarding any thinnings rather than leaving them lying around. The second batch and their miniscule roots can be eaten as a treat.

Carrot fly is a problem on allotments and gardens alike, but my box hedges and a simple plastic tunnel seem to disguise the leaves from the fly's sharp eyes (the insects fly very close to the ground).

A carrot diary

April Carrot seed likes warm soil, so I wait until the weeds start to sprout before sowing. This year I plant the Early Nantes variety close to a row of onions in the hope that the alliums' smell will deter the carrot fly. More experienced gardeners say it works a treat. Two weeks after germination, when the fronds are just showing above the soil, a fox cub climbs into the tunnel for a snooze and squashes them flat. I start again.

This time two rows each of three varieties go in, each covered with a cane cloche secured to the ground by an iron spike or two. Three weeks later and the delicate fronds are up, already sporting tufts of the familiar bushy leaf. Throughout the early summer, small carrots, perfect for a salad or eating as a vegetable accompaniment, less so for a stew, are there for the picking.

Late July and early August The plumes of leaves are coming thick and fast. The painstaking job of removing every second or third carrot continues until they are 4 inches (10cm) apart. There is no alternative but to get down on hands and knees for this.

September 24 Some small but pleasingly formed specimens coming out now. The violet carrots are larger than the others—about the size of a small finger—but tougher and less sweet. The fact that they appear more "carroty" than even the organic ones may well be because they are rushed to the pot within the hour. Sometimes less. I continue picking right the way through the early winter and past Christmas, despite having the first October snow (2008) for seventy years.

Varieties

I am not fond of the modern, blunt-ended Amsterdam carrot. It is what I call a supermarket vegetable. I much prefer the traditional tapered main-crop varieties, such as Autumn King, even though the pointed end will be almost inevitably trimmed off. Modern cultivars often seem sweeter and less earthy too. I grow the older varieties, introduced in the 1800s.

James Scarlet Intermediate* Dates from 1870, a long main-crop variety with a good girth and earthy flavor. Sow in May, use by Christmas.
St. Valery* A medium-sized, particularly sweet root of exceptional length (though not on my soil) and slightly paler than most.
Chantenay* Short, cylindrical, and fast growing, a very sweet variety. The nonbrittle stems make these well suited to selling in bunches with their stalks intact.
Early Nantes* Yes, a bit of a stumpy end rather than an elegant point, but as rich in flavor as an early carrot can get. I plant this virtually coreless variety in April.
Purple Dragon* Purple skin and golden flesh. A tough chew, but heartbreakingly beautiful. Cut into rounds, they resemble sweeties, with a ring of papal purple around an orangey-yellow core.
Paris Round A sound choice for an early crop if your soil is lumpy or stony.
Autumn King* Main crop, a good choice if you have sandy soil, so its long taproot can go down unhindered by stones and clay.
De Djerba A root from Tunisia in shades of violet, black, and orange.
Violet Scarlet flesh with a violet skin.

*Available from US seed sources.

A carrot in the kitchen

The fat main-crop carrot is probably at its most useful as the sweetening element in a composite dish—a stew, soup, or "many layered" thing. Along with onions, leeks, and bay leaves, carrots often form the backbone of a recipe, exchanging flavors and introducing a firm ground on which to build. A small piece is good on the fork with boiled beef, and wonderful against the sharp edge of a marinated herring. Young spring carrots lack earthiness and are probably best crunched raw in lieu of a cookie, or included, thinly sliced, in a salad. They grate to a slush.

My weekly supply of carrots arrives in a sealed plastic bag, caked in wet Devonian mud, where they would, if necessary, stay crisp and juicy for a week. Each Friday afternoon, I split the newly arrived bag, rub off the mud with a scrubbing brush (they make a terrible muddy mess of the sink), then place the clean, wet roots in the vegetable crisper at the bottom of the fridge, lined with wet kitchen paper. Throughout the coming week, I pick at them, dipping them into tubs of store-bought hummus or grating their flesh into a salad with lemon juice, dill, or torn parsley.

Seasoning your carrots

Carrots appreciate being matched with members of their own family, working well with a little caraway, chervil, cumin, parsley, cilantro, or dill.

Chervil The leaves, like wisps of lace petticoat, are effective when stirred through a bowl of grated carrot dressed with lemon juice and black pepper.
Cilantro The carrot's best friend, in salad, in soup, and in a stir-fry with green onion and matchsticks of ginger.
Caraway Adds a musky note to a carrot loaf or a bowl of soup to eat with dark rye bread.
Cumin Toss the steamed roots with toasted cumin seeds or add them to a soup on a winter night.
Lemon juice A startling addition to a carrot salad that will also quell the excessive sweetness. Lime works well too, especially when you introduce chiles and fresh cilantro.
Mustard seeds The heat and sweetness make exciting bedmates.
Sugar Absurd, but in reality a pinch seems to bring the earthy flavor, often lost to the sugary notes, to the fore.
Orange Zest, juice, even cut into chunks and roasted, the vibrant parts of the orange marry neatly with our favorite root, working in harmony with its sweetness and lifting its earthiness in the same way it does with beets. The vivid orange of both fruit and vegetable is not for the fainthearted, but there is no better way to cheer up a plate of grilled lamb's liver and onions.

And...

* If you cut the stems of carrots and leave the roots in the soil, they keep very well for weeks. You can leave them there until you need them unless you live in an exceptionally cold part of the country.
* Keep the ground around homegrown carrots well weeded. They dislike competition.
* Manure will cause the roots to fork. I tend to add it the season before I sow. Keeping growing carrots moist will help keep their scent down, confusing the carrot fly. As will planting onions or garlic nearby.
* The stems and leaves are of no interest in the kitchen but of great value to the shopper. You can tell how fresh your bunch is by the fronds' state of health.
* Spring carrots seem to stay crisper without their plume of leaves. Snip them off when you get them home.
* I like to store main-crop roots with their soil on. They keep better that way, ideally in the vegetable crisper of the fridge—if not, in a paper sack in the shed. Ready-scrubbed carrots turn slimy if stored in the plastic bags they are sold in. I avoid them.
* Although long, thick main-crop carrots are available all year in the shops, they are most useful in autumn and winter, when their earthy density is particularly suited to slow cooking.
* Carrots, simply steamed, are happiest with braised or boiled beef, roast lamb, and unsmoked bacon joints. Main-crop carrots, mashed with butter, make excellent partners for broth-based stews of chicken or rabbit. The smallest spring carrots seem particularly at home with the mildest meats: young lamb, poussin, and rabbit.
* Carrot fritters (see page 130), if not being eaten as a main dish, make a charming side dish for roast chicken.

A salad of carrot thinnings

Carrots have been one of my quiet successes. The carrot thinning salad has become a regular weekly addition throughout the summer. Root vegetables no bigger than your little finger have a charm to them that insists you leave them whole. Cooking them, in shallow water so that they steam rather than boil, takes barely a minute or two. I dress them as soon as they are out of the pan, sometimes with a light, lemony dressing, other times with cilantro.

To turn this into a main-course salad, add spoonfuls of ricotta or cottage cheese to which you have added pepper and some of the dressing.

enough for 4
carrot thinnings – 6 handfuls, no thicker than your little finger,
    or 2 bunches of baby carrots
small beets – 6
red wine vinegar – 1 tablespoon
a clove of garlic, chopped
lemon juice – a tablespoon
olive oil – 4 tablespoons
cilantro leaves – a good handful (about 4 tablespoons)

Wipe the carrots and remove their stems. Don't peel the beets, but cut off any thick stems or tails. Put a shallow layer of water in a large, wide pan, add the beets, cover, and steam for ten minutes, then add the carrots. Remove the beets and carrots when they are tender. Peel the beets and cut into thin strips, somewhat similar in thickness to the carrots.

Make the dressing by dissolving a good pinch of sea salt in the red wine vinegar, then whisking in the chopped garlic, lemon juice, and olive oil. Add black pepper and toss gently with the beet strips and carrots. Add the cilantro leaves and toss again. Serve warm or at room temperature.

A soup the color of marigolds

It was a simple soup, ten minutes' hands-on work and barely half an hour on the stove. An onion, coarsely chopped, softened in a little olive oil in a deep and heavy pan. An equal amount of carrots and yellow tomatoes (I used 1 pound [450g] of each to make enough for four), chopped and stirred into the soft, translucent onion. About 4 cups (a liter) of water (I could have used stock), and some salt, pepper, and a couple of bay leaves. It simmered for half an hour, then I puréed it to a thick, pulpy broth in the blender. We ended up with four big bowls of coarse-textured soup, as bright and cheerful as a pitcher of June flowers, a few chives stirred in at the table. As we licked our spoons, someone mentioned it would have been good to have it chilled. But by that time it was too late to try.

A couple of carrot salads

Slices of soft, rare lamb or beef left from the Sunday roast, their pink flesh framed with crisp, yellow fat, need a bright, fresh-tasting salad to go with them: coarsely grated carrots stirred through with a sharply citrus dressing made from equal quantities of olive oil and lemon juice, seasoned with toasted cumin seeds, roughly torn parsley leaves, and glistening flakes of sea salt.

I sometimes make a knife-sharp, shockingly refreshing salad with carrots sliced wafer thin, tossed with a dressing of lime juice, pink grapefruit juice, finely chopped red chiles, torn cilantro leaves, and olive oil. I stir in a teaspoon or so of Thai fish sauce, other times salt. Occasionally I add a grilled pork steak to it, cut into thick fingers. The best bit is when the hot, lightly charred meat encounters the stinging dressing.

A simple "boiled" carrot

Brush the carrots clean under running water and chop them coarsely the size of a cork. Put them into a medium pan—they need to be in a single layer—with two tablespoons of water and a thick slice of butter, about 2 tablespoons (30g). Bring to a boil, cover with a tightly fitting lid, then let them cook at a moderate pace for seven or eight minutes. You need no salt, pepper, or sugar.

Remove the lid and check for tenderness. The idea is that they are tender but still retain a modicum of bite. Drain and serve.

A side dish of spiced and creamed carrots

Perhaps it was the carrot loaf of the 1970s, slimmers' soups, or the post–Second World War carrot cake recipes without the promise of walnuts and cream cheese frosting, but carrots rarely offer us a taste of luxury.

Fiddling around—there is no other word—with grated carrots one day, I wondered if there would be any mileage in a dish similar to creamed corn, where the sweet vegetables are stewed with cream to give a deliciously sloppy side dish. There wasn't. Until I worked backward and added spices to the carrots before enriching them with both cream (for richness) and strained yogurt (for freshness). The result is one of those suave, mildly spiced side dishes that can be used alongside almost anything. In our house it has nestled up to brown rice, grilled lamb steaks, and, most successful of all, sautéed rabbit.

enough for 4
carrots – 14 ounces (400g)
garlic – 2 cloves
ginger – a thumb-sized piece
green chiles – 3 or 4 small, hot ones
butter – a thick slice
yellow mustard seeds – a teaspoon
cashew nuts – 2 tablespoons
heavy cream – 4 tablespoons
plain yogurt – 4 heaping tablespoons
cilantro leaves – a good handful
lime juice – a generous squeeze

Shred or grate the carrots coarsely. Peel and crush the garlic, then peel and finely shred the ginger, and finely chop the chiles.

Heat the butter in a frying pan and add the garlic, ginger, and mustard seeds, holding a lid over them to stop them spluttering. Add the chiles and then, as everything becomes fragrant, the grated carrots. Let them cook, with the occasional toss, for three or four minutes.

Coarsely chop the cashews, toast them in a nonstick frying pan until golden, then set aside. Stir the cream and yogurt together and fold them into the hot carrots. Immediately spoon into a serving dish and top with the toasted cashews, cilantro leaves, and the lime juice.

Carrot and cilantro fritters

Vegetable fritters, given a savory edge with a flavorsome farmhouse cheese, are just the job for a quick lunch. Cheap eating, too. Grate the carrots as finely or as coarsely as you like, but you can expect them to be more fragile in the pan when finely grated. A watercress salad, washed, dried, and dressed with olive oil and lemon juice, would be refreshing and appropriate in every possible way.

makes 6 to 8, enough for 2 to 3
main-crop carrots – 11 ounces (325g)
a medium onion
a clove of garlic, crushed
heavy cream – ⅔ cup (150ml)
an egg, beaten
grated cheese, such as a good strong Cheddar – 3 heaping tablespoons
cilantro leaves – a handful, coarsely chopped
all-purpose flour – a heaping tablespoon
olive oil for shallow-frying

Scrub the carrots and push them through a food processor fitted with a grater attachment. If you prefer, grate them by hand using the coarse side of the grater. Either way, you are after long, thin shreds rather than mush. Transfer them to a bowl.

Peel the onion, finely slice or grate it, and stir it into the carrots along with the garlic and a seasoning of salt and black pepper. Stir in the heavy cream, beaten egg, grated cheese, coarsely chopped cilantro, and the flour.

Warm a shallow layer of olive oil in a nonstick frying pan. Drop large dollops of the mixture into the pan, a couple at a time, and fry until lightly cooked on the bottom. Turn with a spatula and let the other side color. They should take three or four minutes per side. The cakes are ready as soon as they are dark gold. Remove to a warm plate. A sheet of paper towel will remove any oil. Eat immediately.

Roast lamb with mint, cumin, and roast carrots

Young carrots, no thicker than a finger and often not much longer, appear in the shops in late spring, their bushy leaves intact. Often, they have a just-picked air about them, their tiny side roots, as fine as hair, still fresh and crisp. At this stage they lack the fiber needed to grate well, and boiling does them few favors. They roast sweetly, especially when tucked under the roast. The savory meat juices form a glossy coat that turns the carrot into a delectable little morsel.

I have used a leg of lamb here but in fact any cut would work—a shoulder or loin, for instance. The spice rub also works for chicken.

enough for 4 to 6
leg of lamb – 3 pounds (1.5kg)
garlic – 4 cloves
cumin seeds – 3 large pinches
mint leaves – a large handful
juice of 2 lemons
olive oil
finger carrots – 12
baby beets – 4
white wine or stock – a large glass

Put the lamb in a roasting pan. Peel the garlic and put it into a food processor with the cumin seeds, mint leaves, and lemon juice. Add a generous grinding of salt and some black pepper. Process to a coarse paste, adding enough olive oil to make a spreadable slush, thick enough to cling to the lamb.

Massage the roast well with the spice paste, spreading it over the skin and into the cut sides of the flesh. Set aside in a cool place (preferably not the fridge) for an hour, basting occasionally with any of the paste that has run off.

Preheat the oven to 400°F (200°C). Scrub the carrots and beets. If they are small, you can probably get away with a rinse. Either way, be careful with their skins, which are tender at this point in their life. Put the meat in the oven and roast for forty-five minutes to an hour, tucking the vegetables in around it after twenty minutes. The cooking time for the lamb will depend on how you like it done; forty-five minutes should give you a roast that is still pink and juicy inside. Remove from the oven and rest the meat for a good ten to fifteen minutes before carving and serving with the mint béarnaise below.

If you want to make a gravy, transfer the meat and carrots to a warm place, put the roasting pan over medium heat, then pour in a large glass of wine or stock, or even water, and bring it to a boil. Stir with a wooden spoon, scraping away at the pan to dissolve any stuck-on meat juices. Let the gravy bubble a little, check it for seasoning (it may need salt and pepper), then keep it warm while you carve the lamb.

Mint béarnaise sauce

a small shallot
white wine vinegar – 3 tablespoons
black peppercorns – 6
mint leaves – 2 tablespoons, stems reserved
egg yolks – 2
butter – 10 tablespoons (150g), soft, almost melted

Peel and finely chop the shallot, then put it in a small saucepan with the vinegar, peppercorns, and the stems from the mint leaves. Bring to a boil and watch it while it reduces to a tablespoon or so. Put the egg yolks into a heatproof bowl and place it over a pan of very lightly boiling water. The bowl should sit snugly in the top of the pan. Whisk the reduced vinegar into the egg yolks, holding back the debris in the pan, then slowly add the butter a little at a time, whisking almost constantly until it is thick and velvety.

Coarsely chop the mint leaves and stir them in, then taste for salt and pepper. Check that the sauce doesn't get too hot. It will keep warm until the lamb is cooked, with the occasional whisk, over the pan of water with the heat off.

A bright-tasting chutney of carrot and tomato

I tend to use this chutney as a relish, stirring it into the accompanying rice of a main course. It is slightly sweet, as you might expect, but tantalizingly hot and sour too. Scoop it up with a pappadam or a doughy, freckled paratha (I have been known to use a pita bread in times of desperation). On Mondays I sometimes put a spoonful on the side of the plate with cold meats. Palm sugar (also known as jaggery) is used in Indian cooking and is available in Indian markets.

makes 1 large jar
tamarind pulp (available from health-food shops and Indian markets) –
    2 tablespoons
carrots – 4 good-sized, scrubbed or peeled
vegetable oil – 2 tablespoons
garlic – 2 cloves, crushed
black mustard seeds – half a teaspoon
hot red or green chiles – 2 small, finely chopped
tomatoes – 6 small-medium, cut into quarters
palm sugar (jaggery) or brown sugar – 2 tablespoons
spirit vinegar (at least 5 percent acidity) – a tablespoon
green cardamom pods – 6

Cover the tamarind pulp with a scant ½ cup (100ml) boiling water, smash the brown, datelike goo into the water with a fork or spoon and leave it for twenty minutes. Push the softened paste and its liquid through a small sieve (I use a tea strainer) with the back of a spoon. Discard the seeds and solids.

Cut the carrots into thin, almost hairlike strips. The simplest way to do this is with an attachment disk of a food processor (the one you might use for coleslaw, say).

Warm the vegetable oil in a saucepan, then add the garlic. Add the mustard seeds and let them cook for a minute or two until they pop, then add the chiles. Once the chiles have started to soften, a matter of a minute or two, stir in the carrots and continue to cook for three or four minutes. Add the tomatoes; palm sugar; tamarind liquid; the vinegar; the whole cardamoms, lightly crushed (you just want the pods to open and the seeds to be revealed); and a grinding of salt. Continue cooking gently for ten minutes, until the carrots are showing signs of tenderness; I think they should be still a little crunchy. The chutney will keep in the fridge, sealed in a canning jar, for a few days.

A carrot cake with a frosting of mascarpone and orange

You could measure my life in health-food shops. It is to them I turn for the bulk of my pantry shopping, from parchment-colored figs and organic almonds to sea salt and cubes of fresh yeast. Their shelves are a constant source of inspiration and reassurance. It is also where I first came across organic vegetables, long before the supermarkets saw them as a moneymaker or the organic-box schemes would turn up at your door. It was these pine-clad shops, with their lingering scent of patchouli, that introduced me to the joys of the organic rutabaga.

To this day I wouldn't go anywhere else for my lentils and beans, though I can live without the crystals and self-help manuals. There is something endlessly reassuring about their rows of cellophane-encased dates and haricot beans, their dried nuggets of cranberry, and jars of organic peanut butter. And where else can you get a incense stick when you need one?

Health-food shops rarely used to be without a carrot cake on the salad counter, usually next to the black-currant cheesecake and the deep whole-wheat quiche. Good they were, too, with thick cream cheese icing and shot through with walnuts. I never scorned them the way others did, finding much pleasure in the deep, soggy layers of cake and frosting. This was first published in *The Observer* five or six years ago, and rarely does a week go by without an email asking for a copy to replace one that has fallen apart or stuck to the bottom of a pan. Few things make a cook happier than someone asking for one of your recipes.

enough for 8 to 10
eggs – 3
self-rising flour – 2 cups (250g)
baking soda – half a teaspoon
baking powder – a teaspoon
ground cinnamon – a teaspoon
salt – a pinch
sunflower oil – ¾ cup plus 2 tablespoons (200ml)
light muscovado sugar – scant 1 cup (250g)
carrots – 5 ounces (150g)
juice of half a lemon
walnuts – 1¼ cups (150g)

for the frosting
mascarpone cheese – 9 ounces (250g)
cream cheese – 7 ounces (200g)
unsifted confectioners' sugar – 1½ cups (150g)
the grated zest of a medium orange
walnut halves – a handful

Set the oven at 350°F (180°C). Lightly butter two 9-inch (22cm) cake pans, then line each with a round of parchment paper.

Separate the eggs. Sift together the flour, baking soda, baking powder, cinnamon, and salt. Beat the oil and sugar in a stand mixer until well beaten, then add the egg yolks one by one. Grate the carrots into the mixture, then add the lemon juice. Coarsely chop the walnuts and add them too.

Fold the flour into the mixture with the mixer on low speed. Beat the egg whites until light and stiff, then fold gently into the mixture using a large metal spoon (a wooden one will knock the air out).

Divide the mixture between the two prepared cake pans, smooth the top gently, and bake for forty to forty-five minutes. Test with a skewer for doneness. The cakes should be moist but not sticky. Remove from the oven and let rest for a good ten minutes before turning the cakes out of their pans onto a wire cooling rack.

To make the frosting, put the mascarpone, cream cheese, and confectioners' sugar into an electric mixer and beat until smooth and creamy. It should have no lumps. Mix in the orange zest.

When the cake is cool, sandwich the halves together with about a third of the frosting. Use the rest to cover the top and sides of the cake. I don't think you need be too painstaking; a rough finish will look more appropriate here. Cover the top with walnut halves.

Cauliflower

If any vegetable was made to sit under a blanket of smooth cheese sauce, then this is it. As you pour your creamy béchamel, mornay, or hollandaise over its chaste white curds it will stay there, caught among the gentle bumps, clouds, and hollows of this, the pinnacle of the brassica family. You know, for once, that this is a recipe that was always meant to be.

The perfect cauliflower (a cauli somehow just has to be perfect; there is no excuse for one of second rank) has a snow-white head, unblemished, its florets so closely packed that you can barely separate them. These curds, as they are known, should be hard, tight, and milky white. Even before you swaddle it in white sauce, it is a vegetable of peace and quiet beauty. A cauliflower's leaves, long and soft like the ears of a hare, curl over as if to protect its shy, white head from fierce sun or a hoar frost. The longest leaves are often cut off for practicality's sake, but there should be some still present when we buy, if only so we can gauge its freshness.

If I am being honest, the cauliflower is far from my favorite vegetable. Sometimes I think it wouldn't bother me if I never saw one again. Yet I occasionally long for a simple white bowl of cauliflower cheese on a frosty day, especially when it has been made with love, and the sauce has been improved with bay and clove and the cheese is of the robust sort that makes the veins on the roof of your mouth stand out. If there is snow on the ground, then even better.

Cauliflowers, white, ivory, cream, green, or violet, are available for most of the year. The extraordinary Romanesco, a variety turreted like a fairy castle, is there much of the time, too. As well as the summer and winter types, there are intermediate ones that keep the shops supplied without so much as a blip. But I don't want any sort of flowering cabbage in the summer. Later on, this is a vegetable that I am happy to turn into a gratin for the last outdoor lunch of the year, a pale soup for a snowy winter's day, or a crisp salad with sour cream and poppy seeds. All-year-rounder it may be, but for me it's a going-back-to-school type of ingredient.

Some historians put the home of this difficult-to-grow member of the cabbage family as Cyprus. Whatever, it came to us toward the end of the sixteenth century, possibly via Italy and Spain. Christopher Stocks, author of *Forgotten Fruits* (Random House, 2008), suspects it could have "quietly crept in" some time between the publication of Thomas Hill's *Gardener's Labyrinth* in 1577 (where it isn't mentioned) and Gerard's *Herbal* in 1597 (where it is).

Yes, I think the cauliflower would creep quietly in. Its chaste, slightly coy presence makes this a vegetable that would never shout its qualities. At its heart is a gentle cabbage flavor, mild and sweet when young, when you can also cook it without a smell lingering in the kitchen. Aged caulis are rather sad. The curd darkens to the color of old piano keys, the texture becomes grainy (Alice Waters calls it "ricey") and the florets spring apart. You can still use such a specimen for soup. There's a good one below with mustard and strong cheese to give it some bite.

A cauliflower in the garden

The cauliflower is regarded as a bugger to grow, or at least to grow well. Carol Klein calls it sensitive. It likes sun and a deep, moisture-retentive soil with a pH between 6.5 and 7.5. The soil should never dry out. The fuss continues with demands for a bed manured the autumn before sowing; an insistence on not growing your crop in the same spot two years running; the need to shield its curds from bright light by folding the larger leaves over the top, and even then you may well have to net them from the pigeons. This is indeed a vegetable for the committed gardener.

So, a challenge. Those who rise to it, rather than running off to the supermarket, will need to get the seed for summer varieties sown after Christmas in a greenhouse. If you are pretty much slug and pigeon free, you can plant winter and summer varieties in the spring directly where they are to grow or in modules, transplanting them when they are large enough to deal with without risk of damage to their delicate young leaves. They will need a good 2 feet (60cm) between plants. Both sun and intense cold will darken the heads, so keep them covered by the plumes of leaves that tower over the curds. You may need to break one in order to bend it over the modest white heart.

With luck and a fair wind, you could have a vegetable to be truly proud of. I have never grown one good enough for a soup, let alone a show. But I will keep trying.

Varieties

Well-organized growers manage to keep themselves in cauliflower all year round, following early summer types with autumn and winter heading varieties.

All Year Round* A variety that lives up to its name. Slow to mature and will stand happily in the cold.
Summer Heading Sow in a greenhouse any time from Christmas until February or directly into the soil in April and May. Transplant to their final position in early summer, harvest in late summer and early autumn.
Beauty A good long season.
Nautilus Reliable, and tolerant of less-than-perfect conditions.
Snowball* Small head of curds with long, pert ears of beautiful blue-gray. A little delicate, but has a good reputation as a fine early-season variety.
Igloo* (how could you resist?) Good for use as a mini-cauliflower, planted closer than usual, and will head up in July.
Autumn Heading Sow in modules in April and May, transplant in midsummer, harvest in late autumn.
Skywalker* A true autumn cauliflower. Vigorous, with tall leaves to protect the white curds.
Graffiti* Violet curds that are sweeter than most. Might win over cauli-phobes.
Kestel Very white curds appearing late summer to early autumn.
Winter Heading Sow in May or June for harvesting in November and December.
Cendis The variety I know best. A reliable choice for the organic gardener.
White Dove Sow in May and June for a late winter crop. You could be picking in February. Good, dark green leaves to protect against frost.

*Available from US seed sources.

A cauli in the kitchen

Yes, cauliflower cheese, but so, so much more. A cauli, snapped cleanly into florets, briefly steamed, then lightly battered and deep-fried is pleasing enough, but quite sensational when you dip the sizzling dumplings into a heart-pumping accompaniment of red chiles and lime juice, or spoon over a lemon-spiked green sauce.

Cauliflower's mild, almost creamy quality is what makes it such a successful contender for the spice treatment. Coriander seed, cumin, green chiles, paprika, and fresh ginger complement rather than mask this brassica's natural blandness. Throw garlic, onion, even curry spices, and garam masala at it and its flavor will still shine through.

We have our cheese sauce, the Indians have their aloo gobhi, the Spanish their fried florets scattered with paprika, capers, and vinegar. All of which are worth eating. Yet this vegetable has lost out in recent years to the more cheerful-colored broccolis and sprouting brassicas. There was even a recent media campaign to halt its decline. My own take is that we now like our vegetables to shriek their healthy credentials in green, orange, and red.

There was a vogue for cooking cauliflower whole. Yes, an entire head, coated in a pale cheese sauce, its saw-edged leaves poking up around the edge, is a quietly beautiful sight. But I would rather break mine up a bit, making it easier to cook more evenly and less of a trial to serve. Or could it just be that you get more sauce doing it my way?

There is very little to preparing this one for cooking. Just snap the white head into florets, rinse as you think fit, and it is ready for the steamer or a deep pan of hot water. Once inside, there is barely time to blink before its ivory stems soften. Few things in our shopping cart are easier to overcook.

The idea of raw cauliflower tends to polarize opinion, but it is worth trying the florets, crisp, mild, and white, tossed with a dressing of sour cream or yogurt mixed with chopped herbs such as parsley and tarragon. A scattering of steel-blue poppy seeds is rather beautiful against the white curds.

Seasoning your cauliflower

Cream Few vegetables, save possibly spinach, take to cream so well.
Nutmeg Cut the nut-shaped spice in half and grate it finely and abstemiously over warm cauliflower, or add it to a sauce. Easy to overdo, nutmeg needs using with caution.
Cheese The stronger cheeses marry well and the Cheddars especially. Parmesan was made for this brassica. Blue cheeses are worth trying too, especially the shyer ones like Stilton. Roquefort types are a tad too bold for such a subtle partner.
Sour cream You can make the salad mentioned above with raw florets tossed in sour cream and poppy seeds as an accompaniment to smoked salmon. It has the clean snap of a winter's day about it.
Parsley A lovely, peaceful herb with which to season the white curds. But do try dill and tarragon too.
Anchovies Chop them into an olive oil dip for raw florets.
Olives Green especially, scattered among a salad of lightly cooked cauliflower, lemon juice, olive oil, and capers.

And...

* The white curd of a growing cauliflower is very sensitive to weather conditions. Although protected by the leaves, it can suffer discoloration when it finds itself in stressful situations. Blazing sun and heavy rain will take their toll on the quality of the florets, as will constant touching by the proud gardener. Best keep our hands off until cutting time.
* You can store a cauli for up to a week in the fridge. Wrapping the head in plastic will prevent it drying out.
* Wash a cauliflower briefly, then shake it gently dry. It doesn't like to be left soaking.
* The leaves are not to be despised. I leave the smaller ones attached.
* A squeeze of lemon in the cooking water will keep a cauli white.
* In the sixteenth century, this vegetable was known as "Cyprus cabbage." Its smell when cooking can be surprisingly pungent. I find a drop of olive oil and a bay leaf in the water produce an aroma both savory and enticingly vegetal, while being distinctly less cabbagey.
* As a vegetable accompaniment, simply boiled and rolled in soft, salted butter, cauliflower is a perfectly charming partner for white fish, lamb, ham, and roast or boiled beef. It has a certain calm purity to it.

A luxury cauliflower cheese

I enjoy making a bit of a fuss about cheese sauce. The difference between a carelessly put together sauce and one made with care and love is astounding. Taking the trouble to flavor the milk with bay, clove, and onion, allowing the sauce to come together slowly to give its ingredients time to get know one another, and enriching it with a little cream will result in a sauce of twice the standing of one seasoned only with speed and sloppiness. There is much humble satisfaction in a simple dish, carefully made.

enough for 4 as a side dish, 2 to 3 as a main
milk – 4 cups (a liter)
a bay leaf
a small onion
cloves – 2
butter – 4 tablespoons (50g)
all-purpose flour – 6 tablespoons (50g)
heavy cream – 4 tablespoons
good, strong farmhouse Cheddar – ⅔ cup (100g) grated
a large cauliflower
finely grated Spenwood or Parmesan – 4 tablespoons

Pour the milk into a saucepan and drop in the bay leaf. Peel the onion, spike it with the cloves, and add to the pan. Bring to a boil. As soon as the milk starts to rise in the pan, turn it off and let sit for ten minutes to allow the bay and cloves to work their subtle magic. Set the oven at 425°F (220°C).

Melt the butter in a heavy-bottomed saucepan, stir in the flour, and let the mixture cook, stirring regularly, until it is golden and smells warm and nutty. Pour in the warm milk (leaving behind the onion while taking the bay leaf with you) and let it come almost to a boil. Stir as it thickens, seasoning with salt and pepper, and resorting to a whisk if you need to beat out any lumps. It is less trouble than a spoon. Turn down the heat and let the sauce simmer peacefully for a good fifteen to twenty minutes. Stir in the cream and the grated Cheddar, then correct the seasoning with more salt and pepper.

Break the cauliflower into large florets. Bring a pan of water to a boil, salt it lightly, then drop in the florets. Leave at a merry boil for three or four minutes, until they can be easily pierced with the tip of a knife. Drain them carefully so they don't break up, then put them in an ovenproof dish. Pour over the cheese sauce, fishing the bay leaf out or not as you wish, then scatter the surface with the grated Spenwood or Parmesan. Bake for twenty minutes or so, until the sauce has formed a patchily golden crust and is bubbling languidly around the edge.

A soup of cauliflower and cheese

You could measure my life in bowls of soup. Each New Year's Day brings a pot of lentil soup (a good-luck symbol throughout much of Europe); pea and mint soup is to celebrate early summer; cabbage soup for colds and crash diets; parsnip soup for frosty weekends; chicken broth to cleanse my soul. You probably don't want to know about the parsimonious soup-stew I put together from the weekly fridge cleanup.

I do believe in the power of soup to restore our spirits and to strengthen and protect us. Steaming, frugal, yet curiously luxurious, soup replaces many a meal in this house. With a good loaf on the bread board and fresh salad in the bowl, I have no shame in serving soup to visitors (only amusement in watching them looking round in vain for a main course). I first came up with the idea of this soup years ago, and have watched it do the rounds, yet it has never made it into any of my own books until now. It has something of the Welsh rarebit about it.

enough for 4 to 6
butter – 4 tablespoons (50g)
an onion, coarsely chopped
garlic – 2 cloves, crushed
a cauliflower – broken into florets
bay leaves – 2
crème fraîche – ¾ cup (200ml)
whole-grain mustard – 1 heaping tablespoon
Gruyère, Cantal, or strong Cheddar – about ¾ cup (120g) coarsely grated

to finish
dark rye bread – 2 slices
grated Gruyère – 1 heaping tablespoon

Melt the butter in a large, deep pan. Add the onion and garlic and fry until soft, but don't let them color. Boil the cauliflower in about 3½ cups (850ml) water until tender (about eight to ten minutes). Add the bay leaves to the onion, then add the cauliflower and its cooking water. Bring to a boil and add sea salt and black pepper. Cover and simmer for fifteen minutes, until the vegetables are truly soft. Remove the pan from the heat, discard the bay leaves, and let the soup cool slightly. Then, in two batches, purée the soup in a blender. Pour the mixture back into the pan and stir in the crème fraîche, mustard, and grated cheese. Bring the soup slowly back to a simmer.

To finish, preheat the broiler. Toast the bread on both sides, cover with the grated cheese, and let it melt under the hot broiler. Cut into triangles and float them on the soup.

Another fried cauliflower

enough for 2 as a principal dish
a medium cauliflower
sunflower or peanut oil for deep-frying
garbanzo bean flour – 3 tablespoons
paprika – half a teaspoon

for the salsa verde
parsley leaves – a generous handful
mint – 6 bushy sprigs
basil leaves – a handful
garlic – 2 cloves, crushed
Dijon mustard – a tablespoon
capers – 2 tablespoons, rinsed
olive oil – 6 tablespoons
lemon juice – 2 tablespoons

Break the cauliflower into florets. Boil in deep, salted water for a couple of minutes, then drain thoroughly.

To make the sauce, chop the herbs quite finely, but not so small they look like tea leaves, then stir in the garlic, mustard, and capers. Pour in the olive oil slowly, beating with a fork. Stir in the lemon juice and season with sea salt and black pepper. Be generous with the seasoning, tasting as you go. The sauce should be bright tasting and piquant.

Get the oil hot in a deep pan. Toss the cauliflower with the garbanzo bean flour, a little salt and pepper, and the paprika. When the cauliflower is coated, fry in the hot oil until crisp—a matter of three or four minutes or so. Drain on paper towels before serving with the sauce.

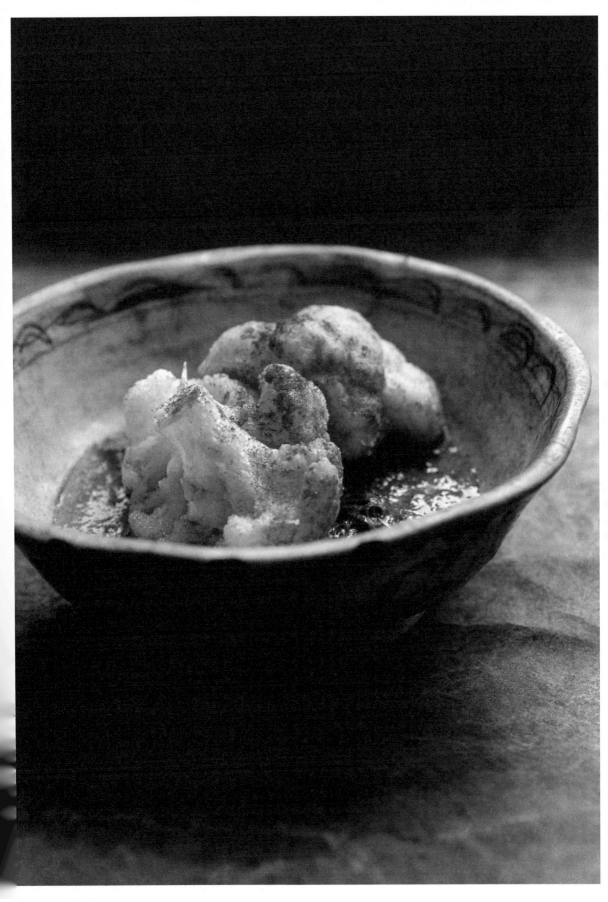

A mildly spiced supper of cauliflower and potatoes

If a cauliflower is happiest under a comfort blanket of cream and cheese, we can run with the idea, dropping the cheese and introducing some of the milder, more fragrant spices such as coriander and cardamom into the cream instead. With its toasted cashews and crisp finish of spiced fried onions, this is a mild dish, so I see no reason to soften the blow with steamed rice, preferring instead to eat it with a crunchy salad of Belgian endive and watercress (or some such crisp, hot leaf), using it to wipe the sauce from my plate.

enough for 4
onions – 3 large
peanut, vegetable, or sunflower oil
garlic – 4 cloves
ginger – a thumb-sized lump
ground coriander – a tablespoon
ground cumin – 2 teaspoons
cayenne – half a teaspoon
ground turmeric – half a teaspoon
tomatoes – 3 medium
water – 2½ cups (600ml)
potatoes – 3 medium
a large cauliflower
unroasted cashews – a good handful
green cardamom pods – 6
garam masala – a tablespoon
crème fraîche– ⅔ to ¾ cup (150 to 200ml)
cilantro – a small bunch

Peel the onions, chop one of them coarsely, then let it soften with a tablespoon or two of oil in a deep pan over medium heat. Halve and thinly slice the others and set aside. Peel the garlic cloves, slice them thinly, then stir into the softening onion. Continue cooking, without browning either the onion or the garlic. Peel the ginger, cut it into fine matchsticks, then add to the onion and garlic.

Stir the ground coriander, cumin, cayenne, and turmeric into the onion. Let them fry for a minute or two, then coarsely chop the tomatoes and add them to the pan. Add the water and bring to a boil. Season with salt and a generous grinding of black pepper. Cut the potatoes into large pieces (as if for boiling) and add them to the pan. Decrease the heat and let simmer for fifteen minutes before breaking the cauliflower into large florets and adding to the sauce. Quickly toast the cashews in a small, nonstick frying pan until golden. Add them to the pot, cover, and continue to simmer for fifteen to twenty minutes.

Meanwhile, fry the reserved onions in a little oil in a shallow pan until deep, nutty gold. While they are cooking, crack the cardamom pods, scrape out the seeds, crush lightly, and add to the onions. Continue cooking for five minutes or so, then, when all is gold and fragrant, remove and place on paper towels.

When the cauliflower and potatoes are tender when pierced with the tip of a knife, stir in the garam masala (the spices in it are already roasted, so it needs very little cooking) and the crème fraîche. Simmer for a minute, then serve topped with the reserved cardamom onions and the coarsely chopped or torn cilantro leaves.

Celery

More than any other, celery is the vegetable I associate with Christmas. The Fenland-grown white stalks are at their peak then, with more earthy, mineral notes than the green celery we see for the rest for the year. They possess more of a crunch too, and less water. Balance a crumb of Stilton on a single stalk and you have the essence of the season on your tongue.

I am thankful enough for the green stuff. Translucent, juicy, commonplace, its fresh-tasting ribs make a cool contrast to a musky hummus or a smoky *moutabal*. I use a stalk as one might a spoon, in place of hot pita, to scoop up the sloppy, garlicky sauces.

Celery comes to us from the wild "smallage," a thin, tough, and stringy member of the carrot family that was used as both a herb and a medicine. The flowers are tiny and white, like fairy parasols, their scent strong and unmistakable. The Italians look the most likely to have bred the thicker, milder-tasting stalks we know now, some time around the sixteenth century. They appeared in Britain a century later.

Christmas celery, with its flatter, ice-white stalks, was something we put on the table in a pitcher of cold water at home, which had the effect of crisping it up nicely. A trick I use to this day. White celery comes with strings, which perversely I like, but which puts many people off. It is rare to find green celery with strings and when you do, they are less tough and tend to snap rather than sticking in your teeth.

It has to be said that of all the vegetables I have grown, cooked with, or talked about, celery is the most unpopular. For every person I have met who turns their nose up at rutabaga or claims not to think much of parsnips, I must have come across twenty who reckon they "hate" celery. A lifelong fan, I almost feel like starting an appreciation society. I like vegetables that remind you that they come from the soil, and few do that as uncompromisingly as this one. At least, the white stalks do; I'm not sure some of the imported green stuff has ever been near real earth.

A well-made celery soup is the voice of calm. I stir in blue cheese to give it some bite. Having once been virtually the only soup offered on hotel lunch menus, it has now almost disappeared. I still make it though, and there is a good working recipe on page 158. You can bake the stalks too, and serve them with pot-roast pheasant, the recipe for which is in *Appetite*.

Celery in the garden

I have no doubt that a standing trench of celery is a beautiful sight on an allotment, an achievement to make any grower puff out his chest, but such an undertaking would defeat even the most enthusiastic home-grower. I have never grown celery, and what is more I probably never will. Celery is a crop for only the most committed of gardeners. Even the modern "self-blanching" varieties such as Loretta and Celebrity, for which there is no need to dig a trench, are beyond this gardener-cook.

Celery's copious demands mean that growing a row is either a nonstarter or an obsession—unlike everything else in this book, there is nothing in between. Your seed will need both warmth and light, and may be slow to germinate. Seedlings must be grown at a minimum of 50°F (10°C) and young plants will need protecting with fleece. You will be required to dig a trench, cosset your young plants with plenty of water, and keep on almost permanent slug patrol, as they find the fleshy stalks as irresistible as a delphinium. There is midseason mulching to do and the late-season earthing up—the notorious blanching—that will keep your stalks pale and crisp. And don't even ask about the celery fly. When the great Alan Titchmarsh refers to growing celery as "decidedly challenging," I think one gets the message. I regard growing it as beyond the simple realms of this book, written for the enthusiastic amateur. But don't let me put you off. If you fancy trench warfare, go for it.

Celery in the kitchen

Celery is the place where vegetables and aromatics meet. Its principal use in my kitchen is as a way to get hummus into my mouth if I am not in the mood for bread (or more likely, there simply isn't any) but a close second is when it joins bay leaves and onion as the aromatic foundation of a stew or a soup. For this alone, it is worth its place in the shopping bag.

In a stew, braise, sauce, or soup, celery is often used as part of the base, with onion, garlic, carrot, bay leaves, and sometimes thyme sweated in butter, to produce a backbone on which to build up flavor. These base notes will vary according to which country you are cooking in—the Spanish will add tomato, the Italians more garlic—but a small amount of celery, perhaps a single stalk in a recipe for six, is usually present. The stalks can turn bitter when they color, so it is best to keep the heat moderate, and add them after the onion and garlic have started to soften.

Heads of celery are rarely used as a vegetable in their own right. A shame, because they can be made into a particularly juicy and sweet main course when baked in a cheese or herb-flecked sauce or poached in stock. Like Belgian endive, celery doesn't conform to the boiled-and-buttered knee-jerk treatment so beloved of the British cook, so it needs a little more thought. I make a good celery soup, and a warming gratin too, but I know I am unusual in giving this vegetable so much of a starring role.

Elizabeth David was fond of celery, pointing us in the direction of a dip of mashed anchovies, olive oil, and vinegar and toward a slightly more interesting idea with a garlicky version of hollandaise sauce, both for raw stalks. I think we have all moved on a bit now, but her idea of stewing the roughly chopped ribs in a shallow pan of butter and oil for fifteen minutes and finishing them with a spoonful of good chicken stock is still valid. A lovely dish with pheasant or other game, or pork chops.

Seasoning your celery

Anise Any of the anise herbs—tarragon, dill, chervil, and fennel—has the effect of bringing out the stalks' better points.

Anchovy Difficult to use the two together, but an anchovy mayonnaise for a celery-based salad is a possibility, as is adding a crushed fillet or two to an oil and vinegar dressing.

Parsley A lovely combination with celery.

Mushrooms A good friend.

Walnuts There is a lot of crunch going on when the two are combined, but nevertheless their flavors are more than happy together.

Cheese Use for a marriage made in heaven. Any cheese is a worthy suitor, but especially the soft, Brie-like varieties and most of all the blues.

Celery salt Made from crushing sea salt with celery seeds, this is a faintly bitter aromatic to enhance any celery-based dish and also a worthwhile seasoning for other vegetable-based recipes. It is the principal seasoning for a Bloody Mary.

And...

* Celery is good with game in any form: stuffed around the bird in a pot roast, included in a salad of cold pheasant and apple, or served as a vegetable beside roast venison or a casserole of squab.
* White celery often has strings running down the length of its ribs. Remove them by grabbing them at the root end between thumb and knife blade and pulling down.
* Celery provides the earthy note in the base for a stew, marrying perfectly with the sweet notes of the carrot and the savory ones of the onion, but adding a few dill seeds will make it more prominent. A good one for true celery lovers.
* Cooking the heads whole is not really an option, as soil gets trapped at the root end of each stalk. Slicing them in half lengthwise lets you rinse out any grains of soil before cooking. The green ones are easier to deal with than the white.
* Celery is one of the few vegetables to emerge from the canning process virtually unscathed. Though only from the cook's point of view rather than the cheese eater's.
* Most of Britain's commercial white celery is grown on the Fens, where the plants love the deep, black soil and moist climate. This is the Rolls-Royce of celery and worth looking out for from October until the New Year.
* The leaves cut from the top of the stalks make an interesting addition to a salad, particularly ones containing apples or cheese. I tend to munch them while I'm chopping the rest.
* Rather than serving celery snapped off into stalks, it is an idea to cut the entire head, still joined at the root, in half lengthwise, then again into three, so that you get a long "wedge" rather than a single stalk. This way, you get the crisp outer ribs and the tender inner ones all at once.
* Adding a lump of celery root to a celery soup will intensify the flavor and add body.

A dish of baked celery and its sauce

When making a sauce to blanket a dish of boiled celery ribs, I like to harness the mineral quality by using the celery's cooking water in with the milk. It deepens the flavor and, together with parsley, establishes the vegetable's earthy flavor. Celery blanched in deep water, smothered with a duvet of slightly bland and salty sauce, and given a crust of breadcrumbs and cheese is certainly worth eating. I have suggested making a crust for the celery and its sauce with Parmesan and breadcrumbs, but there is much success to be had with Berkswell, the sheep's milk cheese from the Midlands. Despite being a rather different cheese from Parmesan, it has a similar fruitiness.

enough for 6
celery – 2 plump heads
a small onion
bay leaves – a couple
milk – 1 cup (250ml)
butter – 4 tablespoons (45g)
all-purpose flour – ⅓ cup (40g)
Parmesan – a couple of handfuls, freshly grated
flat-leaf parsley – a small bunch
fresh breadcrumbs – a large handful

Snap the heads of celery into individual ribs (a strangely satisfying task), then wash, trim, and neaten them where necessary. Lay the ribs in a large, ovenproof baking dish or saucepan and pour in enough water barely to cover them. Peel and thinly slice the onion, then add to the dish with the bay leaves, a little salt, and some black pepper. Poach over low heat, with the water at a gentle bubble, till the celery is tender to the point of a knife.

Preheat the oven to 350°F (180°C). Remove the celery, onion, and bay with a slotted spoon and lay them in a large, shallow ovenproof baking dish or roasting pan, leaving the hot cooking liquor behind. Warm the milk in a small pan. In a separate pan, melt the butter over medium heat and stir in the flour. Continue cooking, stirring pretty much continuously, until you have a pale, golden paste—it will smell warm and slightly nutty. Add 1½ cups (350ml) of the cooking liquor from the celery followed by the warmed milk, a small ladleful at a time, until you have a smooth sauce. Stir in three-quarters of the Parmesan and turn the heat down so that the sauce simmers quietly for a good fifteen to twenty minutes. Chop the parsley not too finely, stir it into the sauce, then taste and correct the seasoning (I try to bear in mind that I will be adding more Parmesan shortly, which will be a little salty).

Pour the sauce over the celery. Mix the remaining grated Parmesan with the breadcrumbs, then sprinkle over the top. Bake for forty minutes or so, until the sauce is bubbling enticingly.

A soup of celery and blue cheese

Long associated with the finale of the Christmas meal, Stilton and celery is a fine combination and there is every reason to turn it into a soup. I'm not sure it matters which blue cheese you use but the saltier types tend to be more interesting here. A good Stilton will work well enough, but something with more punch—say Picos, Roquefort, Stichelton, or Cashel Blue—would get my vote, as would good old Danish Blue. Cream is usually a given with celery soup, but I am not sure you need it.

enough for 4
celery – a large head
an onion
celery root – half a head, about 9 ounces (250g)
butter – a thick slice
chicken stock – 4 cups (a liter)
a bay leaf
blue cheese – 4½ ounces (125g)

Give the celery stalks a really good wash, then chop them coarsely. Peel and coarsely chop the onion and celery root.

Melt the butter in a deep pan, add the chopped vegetables, and let them cook for about twenty minutes, until soft. Pour in the stock, add the bay leaf, and bring to a boil. Season with salt (remember that you will be adding a salty blue cheese later), then decrease the heat to a simmer, and leave for half an hour, stirring occasionally.

Purée the soup in a blender or food processor until really smooth. It may need a little longer than most other vegetables. Check the seasoning and ladle into warm soup bowls. Crumble the cheese into the soup at the table and stir until it is partially melted.

A simple sauté of chicken and celery

Some steamed or boiled potatoes, slightly fluffy at the edges, would be my choice of accompaniment here, with a plate of large, soft lettuce leaves for mopping up the juices.

enough for 2 or 3
chicken pieces (thighs, drumsticks, whatever) – 6
butter – 4 tablespoons (50g), and some more to finish the sauce
olive oil – 2 tablespoons
garlic – 3 cloves, peeled
half a head of celery

parsley – a small bunch
a glass of Noilly Prat or other white vermouth
lemon juice

Season the chicken all over with salt and black pepper. Melt the butter in a shallow pan and pour in the olive oil. Put the chicken in, skin side down, and allow to color lightly, then turn it over. Keeping the heat moderate, add the whole peeled garlic cloves and cover. Let cook for about forty-five minutes, checking regularly.

Break the celery into ribs and cut into short lengths. Once the chicken has been cooking for twenty minutes, add the celery. Continue cooking until everything is tender. Chop the parsley leaves; you will need a good handful.

Remove the chicken and celery to a warm place. Pour the vermouth into the pan and let it boil, scraping away at the sticky goodness at the bottom of the pan with a wooden spatula and stirring it into the bubbling vermouth. Let cook over high heat to bubble down a bit. It will never thicken, but will become slightly syrupy. Whisk in a thick slice of butter and the chopped parsley. Freshen with a squirt of lemon juice if it needs it. Return the chicken and celery to the pan, continue for a couple of minutes until all is hot, and serve.

A gentle vegetable dish of old-fashioned grace

Heads of celery, braised in good chicken stock, are a reminder of the elegant days of hotel dining rooms and railway dining cars. A flashback to times before chefs were ever talked about, let alone "celebrities," and the head waiter rather than the kitchen ruled the roost. Braised celery is what I want to eat with roast turkey and the trimmings.

enough for 4
celery – 2 heads
chicken stock – ¾ cup (200ml)
butter – 4 tablespoons (50g)
garlic – a fat clove, peeled and flattened
Madeira – 3 tablespoons

Preheat the oven to 350°F (180°C). Trim the bunches of celery, leaving the stalks attached at the root end and cutting each head down to about 8 inches (20cm) in length; keep the trimmings for stock. Cut each head in half lengthwise.

Heat the stock. Melt the butter in a heatproof dish and gently fry the heads of celery over low heat without letting them color. Add the garlic and Madeira, then pour over the hot stock. Cover with a piece of buttered wax paper or a pan lid, then bake for forty-five to fifty minutes, until the celery is tender.

Celery root

Knobbly, whiskery, and impenetrable, its roots curled round its feet like a viper's nest, celery root poses something of a problem for the newcomer. There are no crisp leaves to entice, no sweet juice to stir our passion, no perfume to inhale with closed eyes. In fact, no real clue at all to its reason for being. *Apium graveolens* seems an appropriately somber botanical name.

Brush off the encrusted soil, hack away at the thick, warty skin, and you have a clean, crisp bulb with the scent of freshly cut celery. Once you breathe in its cool notes of aniseed, hazelnuts, and clean, sweet earth, your gnarled root starts to develop distinct culinary possibilities. A soup yes, an ice-crisp salad with apples and jagged splinters of bacon maybe, a possible candidate for the roasting pan. Opportunities slowly start to present themselves.

This member of the celery family is often referred to as "turnip-rooted celery," as if that would do it any favors. The thin green stalks and their tuft of leaves that sprout from the bulbous root resemble the plumper, juicier ones of their better-known cousin, but they have all the bitterness of the wild variety. Put them on the compost. Most celery root from the produce market comes shorn of its stalks anyway.

The modern varieties are less rustic looking than the celery root of old. They have been bred to possess a smoother skin, without the tangle of roots at the base, and are of a decent enough size that you need only one to make a pile of buttery purée for four. Progress of a kind. That said, you still need to use a knife rather than a peeler to gain admission.

But why would you bother when celery is so readily available and user friendly? The answer is in the root's subtlety, its failure to dominate a stew or a soup in the way that one stalk too much of celery can, and its ease of growing. That you can mash and roast it should alone answer the question. I also value the craggy one for its keeping quality, and the chance of having a long-life vegetable other than butternut squash in the house.

In some parts of Britain celery root is known as "celery knave" or "celery knob," the latter sounding even more unfortunate than cauliflower ear.

Celery root in the garden

To the gardener, celery root has several advantages over its leggier cousin, the principal one being its robustness. A row of celery root will keep happily in the ground over winter, or will store patiently in a cool garage. There is none of the blanching or earthing-up process associated with celery, much less disease, and less demand for attention.

This is not a fussy vegetable (nor could it afford to be with those looks), and it will quietly do its thing in the most awkward corner of the vegetable patch. Full sun or partial shade, a soil of clay or sand, it will even withstand a bit of a drought later in its growth, but the fattest, whitest bulbs will come from well-manured, well-watered soil in good sun. If you can water it almost daily during its early stages, then all the better.

The seeds are tiny, and you should get them in early, by the end of March at least. Start them in small pots in a warm place, scattering the seeds over the surface of the compost, then covering with a very fine layer of vermiculite. They need to be kept at at least 60°F (15°C) to germinate—unusually warm for a vegetable seed. Transfer to larger pots when the seedlings are showing a good pair of leaves.

Don't shock the youngsters by putting them straight into cold soil, but get them used to the thought of a life outdoors by bringing them out during the day, then back in at night, for a week or two. Mid-May and June is probably early enough to plant out, each seedling about a foot (30cm) apart and with some slug protection such as a copper ring or a moat of coarse sand.

Water is essential until the plants have a chance to get settled; a wet summer has its uses, and it is a good idea to add a mulch around the plants to retain as much of it as possible. The idea is to get the plants well and truly established before the real heat of summer hits.

As they grow, the swollen stem bases will sit proud of the soil. If you have planted one of the older varieties, pull the lower leaves off over the summer to prevent your harvest getting too knobbly. As autumn approaches, cover the exposed crowns with soil to keep their flesh white. Many growers leave their celery root in the ground over winter, tucking it under a loose blanket of straw if there are long, icy periods.

Varieties

It is not so much the flavor that varies with the variety but other factors, such as appearance and ease of growing.

Monarch Probably the smoothest. A newish variety that discolors less than the older ones when cut.

Giant Prague* The one they grow at Heligan. Reliable and charmingly knobbly.

Brilliant* White flesh, quite craggy to look at, but good keeping qualities.

Prinz A knotty heirloom variety considered very fine by aficionados.

*Available from US seed sources. Note that seed sources usually call the vegetable celeriac, rather than celery root.

Celery root in the kitchen

The French probably got there first with celery root rémoulade—the classic salad made by dressing coarsely grated raw celery root with a mustardy mayonnaise. They spotted the nutty, mineral notes that set it apart from sweeter roots such as carrot and parsnip; even if you cook it there is much less sugar here. They realized that these mineral notes and its earthy quality are its trump cards (they appear almost nowhere else in the vegetable world) and that they are best captured with the bite of vinegar or lemon juice.

A sticky mayonnaise or robust vinaigrette, made on the rough side with a coarse hit of white or red wine vinegar, will show the raw bulb at its best. I'm not sure anything is to be gained by using a posh, timid version, though some berry vinegars have worked for me. To that you can add mustard, as much or as little as you like, and maybe some walnuts, whose nutty qualities bring out the same in the celery root, just as a spoonful of honey brings out the sweetness in a roasting parsnip.

This is one root that makes a sloppy mash and needs an equal amount of potato if it is to stand in a cloudlike mound. I'm not sure it matters, but others seem to think so. Mashed celery root with a plainly roasted pheasant is an autumn treat, especially with a curl or two of fat-marbled bacon. In a visual and textural sense it is difficult to serve with roast chicken if you are also having bread sauce. A dash of lemon in the cooking water will prevent a gray mash.

I have no doubt that the most delectable roast celery root is that which has been blanched in boiling water first (be generous with the salt). The inner core of each piece becomes meltingly tender and, though the outside never crisps quite as tantalizingly as a potato, it is still more than worth the trouble. Not giving them five minutes in boiling water first throws up the risk of them drying out as they roast.

As good as this branch of the celery family is when mashed or roasted, I have had the most heartening results when I have sliced it, then baked it in a slow oven with a moistening of stock and a tablespoon of butter. You can pair it with another vegetable—pumpkin is a good one—or leave it by itself. Either way, it emerges soft and earthy.

I try not to waste any vegetable. Even throwing them in the direction of the compost fills me, albeit briefly, with guilt. But sometimes we just have to go with it. Whereas celery has just a few stalks and leaves to trim, this needs a good strong chef's knife to cut away the rough skin and tuft of stem. You could put the trimmings in the stockpot, where they will be of genuine use, but I doubt anyone will grumble if you sneak them into the compost.

Seasoning your celery root

Lime juice An idea from Sarah Raven. The juice brings excitement to a salad of grated celery root and caraway seed.

Apples Use the two together in a soup or grated in a salad. I find the russets work best, but then I'm deeply biased in favor of our rough-skinned apples.

Mustard Yes, in a classic rémoulade, but also as a seasoning for soup or in a walnut oil and lemon dressing.

Celery seeds Not the overkill you might expect. The seed's musky flavors lend depth and mystery.

Honey A little in a salad dressing is good here, as is a spoonful tossed with hot roast roots in the roasting pan.

Thyme Not the easiest to match to a herb, celery root nevertheless enjoys the company of woody herbs such as thyme and rosemary and is, I think, lacking something when there's no parsley present.

Lemon Apart from making the flavor sing just that bit louder, a shot of citrus will halt the oxidation process, keeping your grated roots white.

Walnuts The raw bulb, grated and dressed with either mayonnaise or oil and vinegar, marries well with the flavor and texture of walnuts, even more so with cobnuts (a variety of hazelnuts) if you can catch their milky selves during their short season in early September.

Vinegar Rough vinegar lifts the bulb's white flesh to a more interesting level, especially the more astringent white wine varieties. Tarragon-infused vinegar works too (there's the aniseed connection), as does a slightly rasping red wine version. Celery root likes it rough, but don't rule out the fruit versions such as raspberry. A shake over celery root chips is a good thing in the way that fish-and-chip-shop vinegar does such wonders for chips.

And...

* As vegetables go, the length of time from sowing to harvest is among the longest: thirty weeks for celery root as opposed to twelve for carrots and fourteen for zucchini.
* The nutty notes signal the possibilities of this root working well with cheeses, and especially at the blue-veined level. Stir crumbled Stichelton, Stilton, Cashel blue, or Roquefort into a celery root soup; serve the wafer-thin slices of the root with a lump of blue cheese and a long, green, mild pickled chile; spread a creamy Gorgonzola on fingers of raw celery root.
* A soaking in lemon juice not only keeps the flesh white but also has the effect of tenderizing the starch.
* It is difficult to think of a meat with which celery root doesn't fit, but pork and beef are usually more appreciative than lamb.
* Mashed celery root is good with game birds, the denser and darker fleshed the better.

Celery root rémoulade—a contemporary version

Crème fraîche or strained yogurt offers many of the qualities of mayonnaise but with a cleaner, more piquant character. Beating in a small amount of olive or walnut oil will nudge it toward the perfect coating consistency of a classic mayonnaise-type rémoulade dressing. Using these tart alternatives lends a lightness, too.

enough for 4 as a side dish
the juice of half a lemon
celery root – about 1 pound (500g)
a raw medium beet
crème fraîche – 4 heaping tablespoons
whole-grain mustard – 2 teaspoons
a little olive or walnut oil
parsley – a small handful of leaves
walnut halves – a scattering

Squeeze the lemon into a bowl. Peel the celery root, then grate it coarsely. A food processor with the coarse grater attachment is easier than trying to do it by hand. Put into a bowl and toss gently with the lemon juice to keep it from discoloring. Grate the beet and add it to the celery root, but don't mix it up just yet.

Put the crème fraîche in a small bowl, and stir in the mustard and a little salt and black pepper. Gently mix in enough oil to make a coating consistency—probably about 2 or 3 tablespoons. Coarsely chop the parsley leaves and add to the dressing. Mix gently with a small whisk or fork, then fold into the shredded vegetables, mixing only lightly, so that the beet doesn't send everything pink. Toast the walnuts lightly in a small, nonstick frying pan, then scatter them over the salad.

A simple salad of celery root and sausage

Many of my most pleasing suppers have been one-off, chucked-together affairs made with whatever was to hand. A question of making do. I rarely write them down, assuming that no one else will be interested in something that simply filled a hole with whatever happened to be around at the time. This was one of those meals, taken as lunch in early March when the cupboard was pretty bare, but I thought I would pass it on for its frugal, done-in-a minute quality and as yet another opportunity to do something with the celery root that turns up in the organic veg box.

enough for 2
celeriac – about 1 pound (500g)
plump, garlicky sausages – 4
peanut oil – 3 tablespoons
walnut oil – a tablespoon
lemon juice – a tablespoon
smooth Dijon mustard – 2 teaspoons
flat-leaf parsley – a small bunch

Peel the celery root, dipping it into cold water containing a drop of lemon juice as you go. Cut into pieces a scant ⅛ inch (3mm) thick. Bring to a boil in a pan of deep water, add salt, then cook for seven to ten minutes, until tender when pierced with the tip of a knife.

Meanwhile, fry or grill the sausages as you think fit, then cut them into thinnish slices and drop them into a salad bowl. If they crumble, all to the good. Make the dressing with the peanut and walnut oils, lemon juice, and mustard, whisking the ingredients together with a grinding of salt and pepper. Chop the parsley and stir it into the dressing (the parsley is essential here, I think).

Drain the celery root. Now toss carefully with the sausage and the dressing.

A rémoulade of celery root and smoked bacon

As much as I appreciate the traditional rendition of the sort of celery root rémoulade you might get in a Parisian brasserie, I also like to shake it up a bit. Including the ham, or even bacon, in the salad rather than serving it alongside gives the meat a while to get to know the other ingredients, becoming more than just an accompaniment. An alternative to bacon would be shreds of smoked venison or prosciutto, or maybe smoked mackerel.

Radish sprouts are stunningly colored sprouted seeds with a spicy heat. Enterprising natural food shops and supermarkets have them, or you can sprout your own in a salad sprouter. If they evade you, you could use any sprouted seed here.

enough for 2 as a light main course

for the dressing
crème fraîche – 1 cup (250ml)
the juice of half a lemon
whole-grain mustard – 2 tablespoons

for the salad
parsley leaves – a large handful
celery root – about 1 pound (500g)
smoked bacon – 8 slices
radish sprouts or mung bean sprouts – 1¾ ounces (50g)

Mix the crème fraîche, lemon juice, and mustard together and stir in a little salt and black pepper.

Coarsely chop the parsley. Peel the celery root and shred it coarsely. I find this easiest with a food processor and a coarse grater attachment. Broil the bacon until it is starting to crisp and the fat has turned gold, then cut it into pieces the size of a postage stamp. Stir the celery root, radish sprouts, parsley, bacon, and dressing together. Serve while the bacon is still hot.

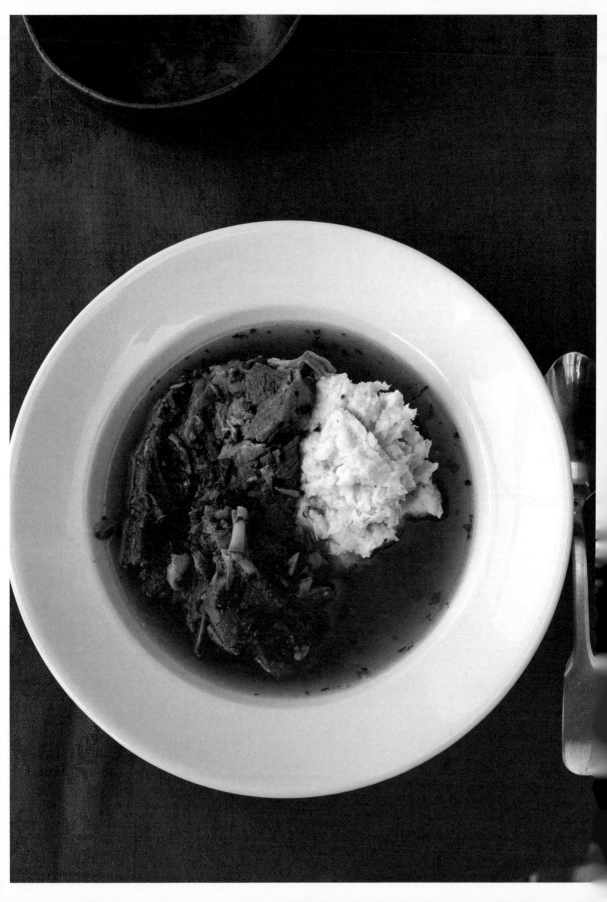

Steamed pork in an aromatic broth, celery root purée

Fresh pork hock is not an easy piece of meat to carve. I just do the best I can, cutting the soft meat away in pieces and laying them in a shallow bowl or deep plate. Then ladle the thin, aromatic broth around it.

enough for 4
fresh pork hock or sparerib chops on the bone – 4 pounds (2kg)
green onions – 10
a lump of ginger – 2½ ounces (75g)
garlic – 4 cloves
peanut oil – 2 tablespoons
sugar – 2 tablespoons
dark soy sauce – 2 tablespoons
rice wine – 3 tablespoons
salt – a level teaspoon
a whole star anise
five-spice powder – a teaspoon
crushed dried chiles – a teaspoon
a stick of cinnamon
stock – 4 cups (a liter)

for the celery root purée
a large head of celery root
butter – 4 tablespoons (50g)

Fill a large pan with water, add the piece of pork to it, and bring to a boil. Simmer for five minutes, then lift out the pork and set aside, pouring away the cooking water. While the meat is simmering, trim the green onions, discarding the darkest part of the green stalks, and chop them. Peel the ginger and cut the flesh into matchsticks. Peel and finely slice the garlic.

Put the pan back on the heat and add the oil. Warm it over medium heat, then add the green onions, ginger, and garlic and let soften, stirring so they do not color. Lower in the piece of pork.

Add the sugar, soy sauce, rice wine, salt, star anise, five-spice powder, crushed chiles, and cinnamon stick and then pour in the stock. Bring to a boil, decrease the heat so that the cooking continues at a comfortable simmer, then cover. Let cook gently for an hour, checking occasionally that there is plenty of liquid left in the pan. Turn the meat over, so that the other half is now under the broth, cover, and continue cooking for a further hour.

Peel the celery root, chop it up, and boil in deep, salted water until tender. It should be ready in about twenty to twenty-five minutes. Drain thoroughly and put into a food processor with the butter and some black pepper. Process to a smooth purée.

To serve, put a big spoonful of celery root purée in the middle of a large, shallow bowl. Carve the pork into coarse slices (it will fall apart as you do so) and lay it alongside the purée. Pour a ladleful or two of broth around the outside and serve. You'll need spoons for the broth.

A pot-roast pheasant with celery root mash

Pheasant and celery get on rather well. I sometimes put thick ribs in with the aromatics for a pot-roast bird, and have included shredded celery in a salad of cold pheasant with Little Gem lettuce and walnuts. Celery root seems to be one of the most successful mashes to serve with the mildly gamey flesh of this bird (parsnip is good, too).

enough for 4
olive oil – 2 tablespoons
pancetta cubes – 5 ounces (150g)
oven-ready pheasants – 2
garlic – 2 cloves
sage leaves – 4
dry Marsala – ¾ cup (200ml)

for the mash
potatoes – 4 medium to large
a whole head of celery root
butter – 4 tablespoons (50g)

Preheat the oven to 350°F (180°C). Warm the oil and the cubes of pancetta in a Dutch oven or other large, heavy pot set over medium heat. When the pancetta fat starts to color, add the pheasants and brown them lightly on all sides.

Peel the garlic cloves and slice each one in half lengthwise. Add them to the pot with the sage leaves, then pour in the Marsala. Let it come to a boil, cover the pot with a lid, and put in the oven for forty minutes. Turn the pheasants once during cooking.

To make the mash, peel the potatoes and celery root and, keeping them separate, cut them into large pieces, as you would for boiled potatoes. Put them in separate pans of cold water and bring to a boil, starting the potatoes ten minutes before the celery root. As soon as both are tender, drain them, mix the potatoes and celery root together, and mash with the butter. I do this with a potato masher, followed by a good whipping with a wooden spoon, but you could do it in a stand mixer if you don't mind the washing up.

To serve, divide the mash among four warm plates. Lift the pheasants from the pot and put them on a chopping board. Using a heavy chef's knife, cut each one in half lengthwise (this sounds scary if you have never done it before, but you will find one good push should do it). Place half a bird on each pile of mash, then spoon over the hot juices and pancetta from the pan.

A baked cake of celery root and parsnips

Once the snowdrops are out and the buds on the trees start breaking, I have usually had enough of mashed, roasted, and baked roots and am gasping for the fresh greens of spring. As the root season draws to a close, I find a dish of parsnips and celery root, thinly sliced and slowly baked, makes a pleasant enough change. Sweet and yielding, this is both an accompaniment and a vegetable dish in its own right. I have used the quantities below as a main dish for two before now.

enough for 4
onion – a large one
parsnip – 1 pound (500g)
celery root – 1 pound (500g)
butter – 5½ tablespoons (85g)
thyme leaves – a teaspoon
vegetable stock – 6½ tablespoons (100ml)

Peel the onion and slice it into thin rounds. Put them in a large bowl. Peel the parsnips and celery root and cut them into very fine slices. A sharp knife will work, but you could use a mandoline or the appropriate disk, on your food processor (it's the one at the very back of the drawer). However you go about it, your slices should be almost thin enough to see through. Toss them with the onion.

Preheat the oven to 375°F (190°C). Melt the butter in a shallow ovenproof pan, then add the vegetables, layering them neatly or just chucking them in as the mood takes you, seasoning with the thyme leaves, pepper, and salt as you go. Be quite generous with the salt. Now pour the stock over the top.

Cover with a round of wax paper or aluminum foil, pressing it down well on the top of the cake. Bake for about an hour and ten minutes, until tender when pierced with the tip of a knife. Remove the cover, increase the heat to 425°F (220°C) and bake for a further ten minutes, until the top has colored and crisped a little.

A crunchy celery root and blood orange salad for a frosty day

There is something uplifting about refreshing food eaten on a frosty day. What follows is a light, fresh-tasting salad that makes your eyes sparkle.

enough for 4
small kohlrabi – 2
a blood orange
the juice of half a lemon
capers – 12
olive oil – 3 tablespoons
raw beets – 2 small
celery root – a 7-ounce (200g) wedge
green onions – 3
flat-leaf parsley – a handful

for the dressing
thick yogurt (I use sheep's) – ¾ cup (200g)
olive oil – 3 to 4 tablespoons
garlic – a small clove, crushed

Slice the kohlrabi thinly and divide the slices among four flat plates. I don't think you have to peel them, but you can if you wish. The slices should be very thin, otherwise the whole thing loses its delicate quality.

Peel and thinly slice the blood orange and place on top of the kohlrabi. Add a pinch of sea salt to the lemon juice, stir in the capers and olive oil, then spoon it over the sliced kohlrabi. Set aside for a good half hour.

Peel and coarsely shred the beets and celery root. Finely shred the green onions and toss all together with the parsley leaves. Mix the yogurt and olive oil, stir in the crushed garlic clove, and add a pinch of salt and black pepper.

Pile the grated vegetables on the kohlrabi and add the dressing. Mix together as you eat, to retain the fresh crunch of the raw vegetables.

Chard

The garden sleeps. Here and there the white tear of a snowdrop, a late Crimson Bengal rose glazed with frost, a paw print deep in the snow. The few cabbages are battle scarred from the wind and freezing rain, their leaves like green-blue lace. If I had to live from this little garden I would starve.

Tucked behind the yew hedge that separates the vegetable patch from the rest of the garden, the dark green is suddenly shattered by a row of chard as bright as a jar of boiled sweets. Their maroon and bottle-green leaves, veins as thick as pencils, lie fallen from the cold, but their stalks—ruby, apricot, saffron, and ivory, and one the color of seaside rock—glow as if lit by candles.

Swiss, ruby, and rainbow chard are one of the few vegetables that remain in this plot in deepest winter, while I let the soil take a rest. The earthy, mineral notes of chard are detectable even in the youngest sprouting seed but get stronger as the leaves age. I have eaten the jewel-colored stems at every stage of their maturity, from when they are as young and fragile as mustard and cress right through to the point at which the stems are so old and thick that they need to be cooked separately from their leaves, lest the latter fall apart. Yet it is only relatively recently that I had even heard of this member of the beet family.

Cousin to spinach, along with purple orache, the wild "fat hen," and, oddly, samphire, this handsome vegetable gets its name from its thick, wide, heavily ridged stems, known as "chards." It owes its modern-day popularity to the organic-box schemes, which have keenly embraced its general good nature and cut-and-come-again qualities.

Commercially grown chard has changed since I first came across it in the mid-1990s, in that it is being picked younger, while the stems are more supple and less strident in flavor (there is sometimes a hint of bitterness in the older "chards"). Rarely now do I spot the wide, flat stalks of white Swiss chard that took forever to cook and had strings you had to peel away, like old-fashioned celery. Almost gone are the days when you had not one but two vegetables: the stalks to braise and the leaves to steam.

This is a vegetable taken further up the deliciousness ladder simply by picking it earlier. Immature leaves the size of your thumb are a true earthy delight in a salad. The honorable exception is Fordhook Giant, a magnificent sight on the allotment, its leaves like huge green waves. It is still grown by those who value its generous stalks.

Chard in the garden

It is a rare moment, perhaps when I have been overenthusiastic in clearing the vegetable beds on a winter's afternoon, when there is no chard in this garden. Once the seedlings have got away there is no stopping them, and I can pick the odd handful throughout the winter. Chard can be a good friend to the gardener-cook when there is no one else to play with.

I have had more success with sowing in seed trays and transplanting the finger-high shoots into the garden than I have had with direct *in situ* sowing. It seems a slug can spot the tiniest blood-red seedling from six feet (2 meters). Chard likes moist, quite rich soil. I dig in a shovel or two of compost every spring. If your chard lacks luster, add a little nitrogen.

I sow in April and May, a mixture of Jacob's Coat or Bright Lights and the single-color rhubarb chard, barely a half-inch (a centimeter) deep. You can sow in July and August for plants to carry you through the winter. Once established, chard plants seem to thrive on neglect. At least mine do. But they will bolt in very hot weather, though less dramatically than spinach. In theory, a good frost will kill them, but mine often shrug off a cold snap, even more so if I remember to put a wicker cloche over them.

There are two ways to pick chard: either as a salad leaf when the plants are still small (if you cut no less than a half-inch (centimeter) away from the soil, they will resprout) and after eight weeks or so, when the leaves are fully mature and the ribs firm and thick. Picking the outside leaves first gives the inner leaves a chance to fatten up. They will keep for several days, wrapped in newspaper in the vegetable crisper of the fridge.

A chard diary

Late May, early June I scatter the seed both into seed trays and over a square patch of ground that measures little more than a stride either way (I could have sown it as early as April or as late as August). Two weeks later, both the seeds in the tray and those in the ground continually sodden from endless rain have sprouted in clumps that look like cress, their red and yellow stems already plainly visible.

Just a few weeks or so after they first emerged, some of the larger leaves, now the size of a teaspoon, are ready to pick and add to a salad, but those in the seed trays are more prolific. The seeds grown in the open air have suffered at the hands of the snail population and the heavy rain.

So small, yet still with that distinctive earthiness that chard does so well, they end their short life with mild, crisp leaves of Little Gem lettuce, sliced, white-tipped radishes, and roughly broken shards of feta cheese—a simple salad of salty, earthy, hot, and mild notes that didn't require, or at least didn't get, any dressing whatsoever.

Early July I transplant the tray-grown seedlings into open ground.

Late July, early August Vast plumes of leaves with stems in shades of ivory, ruby, and a piercing yellow are coming nonstop. Like the sweet peas that stand beside them, the more you cut the more they come. The trick is to pull a few from each plant. The transplanted seedlings have generally fared better than those planted directly in the soil.

Mid-August The fox cubs visit one evening, curling up in the chard bed and crushing the crisp stems and leaves. The next day I cut off the leaves in the hope of a come-again crop.

Late September Up and running again.

November Some of the leaves have gone to seed, but I am still picking the larger ones for the kitchen. Rarely has a packet of seeds given me so much for so little.

Varieties

Swiss Chard* Classic variety with green leaves and very wide, flat stems. Sometimes known as silverbeet.

Wavy Leaf What it says on the packet.

Rhubarb Chard* Green-maroon leaves, vermillion veins and stems. Slightly less hardy than the others.

Bright Lights* Green leaves with veins and stems of raspberry pink, blood red, saffron, orange, and yellow. Similar to Jacob's Coat and Rainbow mixtures.

Oriole Deep gold veins, very dark leaves.

Fordhook Giant* Large, flat white stems, curling green leaves. This is one to cook leaves and stalks separately.

*Available from US seed sources.

Chard in the kitchen

When my first bunch of wide, white stalks, and their plumelike leaves turned up in the weekly organic box I had little idea of what it was. In true British style I boiled it, admiring the crunchy, deeply mineral flavor of its stalks but despairing at the overcooked and watery leaves.

Next time, I cooked the leaves and their stalks separately. Actually that is not entirely true. I twisted off the leaves and steamed them like spinach with melted butter and lemon juice, putting the stems back in the fridge for another day. A week later I guiltily turfed out the wilted, stringy things I had completely forgotten about. Then, just as I thought I had gotten away with it—the waste and the humiliating lack of inspiration—another bloody bunch arrived.

Treated with respect, both are good to eat: the stems keep their crunch even during slow cooking and the leaves can be almost as tender and silken as spinach. They are less sharp than spinach, tougher too, except when they are very young. Swiss chard has deepest emerald-green leaves and thick, cream-colored stalks. Ruby chard has translucent red stems and green leaves, while the almost maroon-brown leaves of rainbow chard are shot through with cream, yellow, orange, and red veins and stems, making this one of the most extraordinarily cheerful-looking vegetables you can have in the kitchen.

Anyone signed up for a weekly organic vegetable box will know that chard makes a regular appearance. Some might say too regular. The stems are interesting cooked in a way that celery—which they vaguely resemble— rarely is, and can, with olive oil, lemon juice, and garlic, be of real interest. In the kitchen, chard is also at home in a bean soup, heavy with thyme, garlic, and tomato.

Even under a blanket of richly savory cheese sauce (a little cayenne wouldn't go amiss here), the stalks keep their character and are better than you might expect alongside a piece of ham or even a pork chop.

The ivory stems seem to be crisper and cleaner tasting than the red, yellow, and orange. But I could be wrong.

Vegetables tend to prefer oil or butter as a cooking medium, but these stalks are happy with either. I generally use olive oil out of habit, but softened butter on the verge of liquidity, given an edge with a squirt of lemon, is very appropriate. Like leeks or celery, this is one for fairly gentle cooking. Nothing much will come from roasting the ribs, and they can become bitter when browned.

Seasoning your chard

Lemon juice and peppery olive oil ~~A ...~~

~~... and stalks.~~

Cream Especially as an ingredient in a gratin.

Mustard In conjunction with cream, or as a principal ingredient in a dressing for the stalks.

Nutmeg Perhaps as a seasoning in a gratin.

Anchovies Chopped and cooked to a pulp in olive oil, then used to dress leaves and stalks.

Parsley Seems to calm the excessive mineral notes of older stalks, especially when used with lemon juice and olive oil.

Cheese I go for the stronger varieties, but particularly the long-matured Cheddars.

And...

* I have boiled chard briefly in deep water, cooked it in shallow water under a lid in the way most people cook spinach, and steamed it over boiling water. To be honest, there's not a lot in it, but the colors tend to stay brighter in boiling water. A big plus when you are using rainbow varieties.
* If the stems are very wide or tough, they really do need to be cooked separately from the leaves. As a rule of thumb, I cook the two parts separately if the stalk is more than a good finger's width.
* When I do decide to cook the stems and leaves separately, I cut the stalk half an inch (a centimeter) or so below where the leaf starts. The stem is still very tender at this point but will help the leaf keep its shape better during cooking.
* In a gratin-type recipe, the chard leaves need a good squeeze to rid them of their water. If you don't do this, they will ooze liquid as they bake and water down the sauce.
* Yogurt, fromage frais, and mascarpone are all suitable as a dressing for freshly cooked chard. I add a drizzle of olive oil too, and maybe a scattering of paprika.
* Tatty outer leaves can be left in the ground over winter. They will protect the more fragile leaves coming up in the middle of the plant.
* Raw chard is really worth trying, but only when the leaves are small. They are exceptionally sweet until they get above the size of a teaspoon, when they start to develop their characteristic earthiness. You might like to add them to a watercress or other small-leaf salad and dress them with nothing but raindrop-sized splashes of olive oil and some crisp, salty croutons hot from the pan.
* I have never known chard stalks, no matter how thick, take longer to boil or steam than three or four minutes.

A chard gratin

The first time I cooked the stems separately from the leaves, I cut them into short lengths, boiled them until almost tender, then drained them and laid them in a buttered shallow dish. Covered with a classic cheese sauce, dusted with grated Parmesan, and baked till the top was golden, they made a perfectly fine gratin.

A better gratin, this time with whole-grain mustard

enough for 4
chard stems and leaves – 1 pound (450g)
whole-grain mustard – a tablespoon
heavy cream – 1¾ cups (400ml)
grated Parmesan – a good handful

Preheat the oven to 350°F (180°C). Cut the chard leaves from the stems. Chop the stems into short lengths, then cook briefly in boiling, lightly salted water until crisply tender. Dip the leaves in the water briefly, until they relax. Drain and put them in a buttered shallow ovenproof dish. Put the mustard in a bowl and stir in the cream and a grinding of salt and black pepper. Pour the seasoned cream over the stems and leaves, cover with grated Parmesan, and bake until the top has a light crust the color of honey.

A soup of lentils, bacon, and chard

On the right day, a deep bowl of lentil soup is all the food I need. The homey, almost spare quality satisfies me in a way fancier recipes cannot. The undertones of frugality, penury even, are avoided by rich seasonings of unsmoked bacon, herbs, and good stock. The blandness of earthiness is given a fresh top note with mint and lemon juice. You can keep your beef Wellington.

enough for 4
a large onion
olive oil
garlic – 3 or 4 cloves
unsmoked bacon or pancetta – a good handful, chopped
flat-leaf parsley – a small bunch
chard – a large bunch
Puy or Castelluccio lentils – 1¼ cups (250g)
stock or, at a push, water – 4 cups (a liter)
a bay leaf – optional
juice of a lemon
mint – a small bunch

Peel the onion and chop it finely, then let it soften in a deep pan over medium to low heat with a little olive oil. Peel the garlic, slice it thinly, then add to the onion with the chopped bacon or pancetta. Chop the parsley and stir it in.

Wash the chard thoroughly, set aside four beautiful stalks and their leaves, then separate the remaining stalks and leaves. Chop the stalks coarsely and set the leaves aside. Add the chopped chard stalks to the onion and bacon and continue cooking,

Wash the lentils thoroughly, then stir them into the onion and bacon. Pour over the stock or water and bring to a boil, skimming off any froth that comes to the surface. You can add a bay leaf or two if you like. Decrease the heat so that the lentils simmer merrily, then almost cover the pot and simmer until they are tender, but far from collapse—about thirty minutes, depending on your lentils.

Tear the reserved chard leaves up a bit. Stir them into the soup. Steam the reserved whole leaves and stalks until tender.

Season the soup with salt, black pepper, lemon juice, and the mint leaves, tasting as you go. Ladle the hot soup into warm bowls, add the steamed chard, and serve with more lemon and mint for those who want it.

Chard with olive oil and lemon

Perhaps because of the thickness of its stalks, or the unruly tangle of leaves on the plate, chard always manages to exude a rustic quality. It is not really a vegetable for "fine dining." Blanched and seasoned with young, mild garlic and a squeeze of lemon, the stems and leaves become a useful side dish for any big-flavored main course.

Allowed to cool, they also work with cold roast meats, thickly torn chunks of mozzarella, wedges of warm savory tarts, or coarse-textured "country" pâté. In other words, a distinctly useful thing to have in the fridge.

enough for 2 as a side dish
white-stemmed chard – 1 pound (450g)
young garlic cloves – 2 or 3 small ones
extra-virgin olive oil – 3 tablespoons
a lemon

Cut the white stalks from the leaves and keep both separate. Wash them thoroughly in cold water, rubbing any soil off the stalks with your thumb. Rinse both leaves and stems thoroughly.

Bring a large pan of water to a boil, salt it, and add the chard stalks. They will take three or four minutes to cook and should still retain some bite, rather than be softly tender (you could steam them if you prefer). Scoop out the stalks and drain them. Return the same water back to a boil and add the leaves. They will need barely two minutes. Take them out when they are tender but still bright green. Pour off the water, wipe the pan, and return it to the heat.

Peel the garlic and slice it finely, or chop it if you prefer. Pour the olive oil into the pan and let it warm over low heat. Toss in the garlic and stir it so that it softens without color. Add the drained chard leaves and stalks and gently fold them over in the warm oil and garlic. Grind over a little black pepper and sea salt, then cut the lemon in half and squeeze half over the greens.

Serve immediately, with the rest of the lemon on the side.

Potato cakes with chard and Taleggio

Bubble and squeak is an iconic British dish made by frying leftover boiled potatoes and cabbage to make a large, flat potato cake that is crisp outside and soft within. Bubble and squeak can be as simple as the traditional leftover cabbage and potato fry-up or somewhat more sophisticated, with the introduction of cheese, smoked pork, fish, or other vegetables. The bells-and-whistles versions can often successfully disguise the fact that your supper is made from stuff you found at the back of the fridge. Keeping the potato pieces quite coarse makes the texture more interesting.

makes 4, enough for 2
chard leaves and (only) the finer stalks – 7 ounces (200g)
basil – a large bunch
olive oil – ⅓ cup (75ml)
lemon juice – 2 teaspoons
Taleggio, Wigmore, Waterloo, or similar
    semisoft cheese – 5 ounces (150g)
cooked potatoes – 2½ cups (400g) coarsely mashed
all-purpose flour – a tablespoon
parsley – 4 tablespoons chopped
cornmeal (polenta) – 6 tablespoons
olive or peanut oil – a little for frying

Wash the chard thoroughly, then steam or boil until the stalks are tender. Drain well. Process the basil leaves and their stems and the olive oil in a food processor, then stir in a pinch of salt and the lemon juice. Set aside. Coarsely chop the chard, leaving four beautiful leaves on one side.

Cut the cheese into small pieces and mix with the coarsely mashed potatoes. Season generously with salt and black pepper, then stir in the flour, parsley, and chopped chard. Divide the mixture into fourths and shape each one into a rough patty about the diameter of a digestive biscuit. Tip the cornmeal onto a plate, then turn the patties in it to coat.

Warm a thin layer of oil in a nonstick frying pan. Set the patties into the pan and cook for about four minutes on each side, until golden. Let rest briefly on paper towels to drain while you dip the reserved chard leaves in the frying pan, just to warm them through. Serve the cakes topped with the chard leaves and a drizzle of basil oil.

A shallow tart of chard and cheese

Cheese is the savior of chard, as a crisp crust, a seasoning for soup,
a luscious sauce, bringing out its qualities while introducing a note of
luxury. Often, the bolder the cheese the more interesting the result, so
a well-matured British cheese is a wise choice for something like a shallow
chard tart. As a sort of double whammy, I add cheese to the pastry as well
as the filling.

enough for 6 or more

for the pastry
all-purpose flour – 2 cups (250g)
butter – 8 tablespoons (100g), cut into small dice
a sharp farmhouse Cheddar – 1¼ ounces (35g)
thyme leaves – a teaspoon
an egg, lightly beaten

for the filling
red or rainbow chard – 9½ ounces (270g)
green onions – 4 thin ones
eggs – 2
heavy cream – 1¼ cups (300ml)
Cheddar – 1¾ ounces (50g), grated
Pecorino, Spenwood, or Parmesan – 1½ ounces (40g)

Put the flour into a bowl and add the butter. Rub it into the flour until it
resembles coarse breadcrumbs (you can also do this in a food processor).
Grate the cheese and stir it in along with the thyme, a pinch of black pepper,
and the beaten egg. Bring together to form a soft ball, adding a little milk if
necessary.

Lightly flour a work surface. Roll the pastry out and use it to line a
12 x 9-inch (30 x 23cm) nonstick baking sheet (if your baking sheet isn't
nonstick, brush it with a little butter). Press the pastry carefully into the
corners and trim the edges, then chill for a good thirty minutes. Don't be
tempted to skip the chilling period, otherwise your pastry will shrink in
the oven.

Preheat the oven to 400°F (200°C). To make the filling, blanch the
chard in a little boiling water until soft and tender. Drain and squeeze as
much of the water out with your hands as you can, then coarsely chop the
chard. Finely slice the green onions and add to the chard with a seasoning of
salt and pepper.

Lay a piece of aluminum foil or wax paper in the pastry shell and weigh
it down with dried beans (I sometimes find a piece of aluminum foil is heavy

enough to do the job without the beans, though not so greaseproof). Bake for fifteen minutes or so, until the pastry is firm, then remove the paper and return the pastry to the oven for five minutes, until dry to the touch.

Put the chard into the pastry shell. Beat the eggs and cream until well mixed and season lightly. Scatter the grated cheeses over the chard and pour over the egg and cream mixture. Bake for twenty to twenty-five minutes, until the pastry is crisp and the filling has set.

Chard with black pepper and cream

The purity of a leaf and its edible stalk, lightly steamed and served "naked," is always somehow life enhancing. But occasionally I want a more sensuous treatment (a welcome lift in times of recession).

The spiced cream with juniper and peppercorns recipe that I occasionally use with green leaves makes them a particularly sound accompaniment for grilled or roast pork, or for poached ham or chicken, but I also find it perfectly acceptable with brown rice as a main dish in itself.

enough for 4 as a side dish
chard – 14 ounces (400g)
black peppercorns – 2 teaspoons
juniper berries – a teaspoon
butter – 2 tablespoons (25g)
heavy cream – ⅔ cup (150ml)

Shred the leaves into thick strips. Cut the stalks in half widthwise. Steam the leaves and stalks until tender, bright green, and perky, then drain.

Meanwhile, crush the peppercorns and juniper berries lightly with a pestle and mortar, or with a heavy object on a chopping board.

Melt the butter in a saucepan and toast the crushed spices in it for a minute or two, until fragrant. Pour in the cream and let bubble for a minute or so, until it starts to thicken slightly. Season with a very little salt and add the drained leaves and stalks. Toss them in the spiced cream until they are lightly coated. Serve straightaway, while the sauce is still piping hot and creamy.

The Chinese greens

There are moments when I long for a plate of steamed greens. This may be after the summer solstice, when I have had one too many salads, or in late autumn, when the kitchen has been inundated with sweet roots. Perhaps I have had too many rich meals in a row. But there are times when I want nothing more than emerald-green shoots, in quantity, brought still steaming and virtually unadorned to the table.

The greens I obsess over most, the leaves I will take an hour's bus journey simply to get my hands on, are usually the Chinese brassicas. The gai lan and bok choy, the choy sum, and mizuna leaves are ones I never seem to tire of, despite the singularly unadventurous way I tend to prepare them. Steamed, drained, tossed in hot oyster sauce, their bold green simplicity excites and pleases me.

No green shoots are more succulent or refreshing than those of gai lan or choy sum, and while I value them for their soft leaves and mild mustard flavors, I reserve most of my esteem for their fleshy stems. These are the greens you see being packed up into fat bunches in the back lanes of Chinatown, the ones that come to your table tossed in chopped garlic. Greens whose extreme juiciness tempers their traditional hot or salty seasonings.

I like to think of these faintly mustard-edged leaves as the future of our homegrown winter vegetables—they thrive in the cool and are a verdant shock in the dark days of March—but they are hungry feeders, who require not just good but excellent soil in which to grow, and are heavily reliant on our most precious resource, water. Succulence comes at a price.

I have given up trying to grow the plump, joyously crisp bok choy because of its ability to seduce a snail from twenty feet, but the long-stemmed gai lan and the yellow-flowered choy sum are worth dedicating our most humus-rich soil to.

Nothing good will come from getting too fancy with these greens. They bask in simple treatment and become shy when long lists of ingredients appear. The real moment of glory for the Chinese brassicas is when they team up with high-octane dressings such as salty oyster sauce, searing chiles, or chopped and sizzling garlic. The marriage of mild, juice-filled stems and hot, simple flavorings is reason enough for their place in the vegetable patch.

Chinese greens in the garden

Given the right conditions, these brassicas will grow very quickly but I have not found them to be the easiest of tenants. They are greedy, so you need to add manure to the beds the summer before you sow and then be prepared to add high-nitrogen fertilizer as they grow into mature plants. They are very thirsty too, so you can expect to get the watering can out regularly. The young plants have shallow root systems, so like a bit of mulching too, to keep the ground moist as the weather heats up.

I find they respond better to being grown in modules and transplanted when they are a few inches high than they do sown directly into the soil (I suspect my soil isn't fine or moist enough for them). Small coir pots are excellent to get your seedlings going.

The leaves of the young plants are delicate and dislike heavy rain, so growing under cloches is ideal. Sow again in autumn (I put them in after the peas come out), and with luck and a bit of protection they will stand throughout the winter. Although they are from the same family as sprouts and Savoy cabbage, they lack their coarseness, instead offering the sort of subtlety we expect from a spring shoot.

I have had little success with bok choy, whose juicy stems attract any number of marauding snails "popping out for Chinese." Gai lan has proved less demanding and can be made to last for several weeks if you pick the main shoot, allowing secondary shoots to appear from the stems.

Preparing the bed with organic matter the summer before you plant is essential unless your soil is naturally exceptionally fertile. Raised beds will help to keep snails at bay and a spraying of nematodes during warm weather will be worth the expense.

Choy sum

You see bundles of these greens and their tight yellow buds all over Chinatown. Their soft-textured, oval leaves are nice enough but it is the fleshy stems that are the real attraction. I steam the whole thing, buds and all, until they are bright and tender when pierced with the tip of a knife, then toss them with a little oyster sauce.

The flowers should be only just starting to open. Avoid any with yellowing leaves or fully blossoming flowers. You will need quite a bit of space to grow these yourself, but a row or two would be a beautiful addition to your patch.

Bok choy

These spoon-shaped annuals have not been easy for me to grow and I regard them as one of my failures. Mine come in a bag from Chinatown or from the farmers' market, where they tend to be stragglier than the usual squat form. Their unique selling point is their mild flavor and juicy stems, plus their ability to calm a pungent sauce. You eat every bit, the stems, leaves, and flowers.

Grown in China since the fifth century A.D., they come in several varieties, ranging from ones with green or white stems to others whose leaves are as long as rabbits' ears. I find the compact ones easiest to deal with and, for no reason other than their color, prefer the all-green ones. Their neatness appeals to my enhanced sense of order and, despite their ability to reach 12 inches (30cm) in length, I tend to ignore any that are longer than 6 inches (15cm).

The plump stems—they narrow toward the leaves—are decidedly crunchy and easy to overcook. They need barely five minutes in a steamer, maybe less. The faint hint of mustard rescues them from accusations of blandness. When the leaves are small, about the size of a teaspoon, they are refreshing in a salad, although they are generally eaten cooked. Sometimes the stems and leaves are cooked separately, the thick stems being added to the wok before the leaves.

Gai lan

Also called kai lan and Chinese broccoli, these long-stemmed, blue-green leaves are possibly the most delicious of all the cabbage family. Known as "mustard orchid" in China, they have an elegance on the plate and a gentility too rare in the vegetable world. It is surprising that they are not more popular here, being crisp, green, quick to cook, and mildly flavored. The purple variety (*zi cai tai*), like climbing beans of the same hue, tends to lose its color once it meets hot water.

I treasure them and their crisp stems lightly steamed and placed on an oval plate with a slick of oyster sauce, let down with a little stock and oil. Some shredded ginger warmed with the oil, oyster sauce, and a pinch of sugar would be heaven. Coarsely chopped, the stalks make a very good stir-fry with garlic, beef steak, oyster sauce, and green onion.

Sow seed in mid- to late summer for autumn and early-winter harvesting. You can plant seedlings out in the autumn that will last all winter. Once the plant is about 6 inches (15cm) tall, you can snip out and eat the main shoot, then break off and harvest the side shoots as they appear. It is slower growing than choy sum. The flowers, caught just as the yellow buds are opening, are charming in a salad of dark green leaves.

Mizuna

I have always thought of spiky, arugula-like mizuna as Japanese but it actually originates in China. The leaves are feathery and open and have an airiness to them that lightens a salad. I sometimes wonder if there could be a prettier edible leaf. They take a bit of chewing, but they are rarely anything but tender, even when they get to the size of a spoon. The oldest leaves might need cooking.

Mizuna is the current darling of the trendy salad bag, though its flavor is on the mild side. I use it principally in salads, to add body and a frilly texture to the mix, but it can be stir-fried very successfully too. Once it hits the heat, the characteristic spikiness is somewhat lost, and I can't help thinking of it as best in a salad. Like arugula, too much can tickle the throat and cause you to cough.

The plants, which form a bushy clump, can be vigorous and don't mind moderate shade. They rarely bolt, which is an unusual quality for a brassica. You can sow the seed in spring and be picking—albeit small leaves—three weeks later. They have shallow root systems so I use a seed tray lined with newspaper and some fine, organic seed compost. The little leaves love it. I have left sowing until late summer and been picking until the frosts. If I had more indoor space I would grow this leaf all year, but they are happy enough on a windowsill if it is just small, salad-ready leaves you are after.

Once the leaves are the size of a teaspoon, the plants can go out into the garden and be left to form unruly clumps.

Mibuna

I mention this only because it is growing in popularity and is one of the most versatile cut-and-come-again leaves. It is very easy to grow and can be cut four or five times—the new growth being more resistant to frost and cold than the fully matured leaves. Related to mizuna, it has long, softer-edged leaves, with none of mizuna's feathery quality. You should be able to pick a few of the larger leaves about six weeks after sowing. They can grow up to 6 inches (15cm) in length and have a pleasing, almost mustardy warmth to them, which gets stronger as the plants age. I prefer them lightly cooked rather than in a salad.

Sow from spring to late autumn. I have not had much luck transplanting young seedlings into the ground (though that may just be me) and I recommend you sow them directly where they are to grow.

Chinese mustard greens

This is a huge family of leaves of different shapes and textures, only a few of which are available in the UK and the US, even in seed form. They originate from the Himalayas, spreading first to China and then to India and beyond. Whatever their size or shape, they have in common their prominent mustard flavor. Although I can handle them in a salad when the leaves are small (I especially like the small mauve-blushed Osaka Purple leaf), they are generally best either steamed or added to a stir-fry.

The young growth of the mustard family has a sweetness to it that is missing in the older specimens, which get hotter as they get nearer to bolting. This is the leaf that takes you by surprise in harmless-looking mixed salad bags, the one that burns your tongue. But most of them provide a gentler heat, and especially so when they are torn up and used in a wok. They come in various guises, some with large, tight heads of wavy-edged leaves, others with long leaves, and still others like huge, unruly iceberg lettuces.

I grow these in shallow seed trays, planting both Osaka Purple and the jagged-edged Green in Snow (also known as *Shi-Li-Hon*). The first is very much a cut-and-come-again variety, for adding in small quantity to a salad. The latter germinates quickly and offers lots of small, hot leaves to tuck in a sandwich. The small leaves are peppery and fun when matched with something cool, like soft white bread, but can be eye-wateringly hot if left to reach their full, foot-long (30cm) potential.

Chinese greens in the kitchen

"Useful in a stir-fry" is one of those cop-out sentences that make this writer's blood boil. Except in this case it is true. No other member of the greens family takes so well to the intense heat and feisty seasonings associated with this way of cooking. The stems cook quickly, while the leaves soften and take up the garlic, ginger, chile, and liquid seasonings that are the heart and soul of the everyday Chinese or Vietnamese stir-fry.

I sometimes steam my Chinese brassicas lightly before they meet the stinging sides of the wok. It tends to produce a juicier result. The downside is that the extra water contained in a cooked stem of bok choy turns to steam in the pan and will lower the temperature of the wok, which is the last thing you want, so any precooked greens should be well drained.

You can eat the smaller leaves of all the Asian brassica family in salads, or wait a few weeks and then steam them. I find a large bamboo steamer placed over a wok of boiling water is the ideal way to cook them. Then I toss them in a mixture of oyster sauce and garlic, or chile sauce.

Outside the salad bowl, the steamer, and the stir-fry, there isn't much I would want to do with these vegetables. Using them in European recipes feels awkward. Rather like trying to make carbonara with Chinese noodles.

Seasoning your Chinese greens

All the flavors we associate with Asian cooking—chiles, ginger, garlic, fish sauce, soy, oyster, hoisin, and chile sauces—work perfectly with these greens. Any European ingredients, such as butter, are somehow just plain wrong.

And…

* Buy or pick only those with more bud than open flowers.
* The Chinese who sell these honorable vegetables have a habit of squashing them into a tight bundle, resulting in leaves that look squashed. This doesn't mean they are not fresh. The slender stems and their delicate leaves will be fine when they are cooked.
* The mustards tend to get hotter when they are deprived of water.
* Mizuna and mustard leaves aside, the Asian brassicas will keep in good condition for several days. Pop them into a plastic bag or newspaper and store them in the vegetable crisper of the fridge.

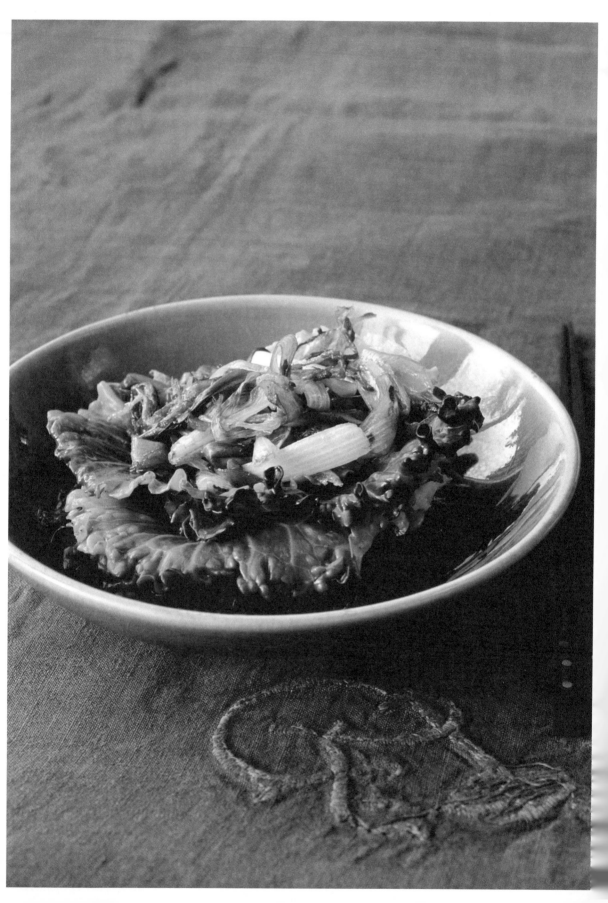

A Vietnamese stir-fry

Of all the flavors that seem to bring out the rest of the cabbage family's earthy greenness, few work as effectively as those of Southeast Asia. Ginger, green onion, and garlic have a natural affinity with chlorophyll-rich vegetables of any sort, but the saltiness of the fish sauces with which Thai and Vietnamese cooks season their food does much for cabbage leaves. I often serve this with roast duck, which appreciates such seasoning, or as a side order for a mushroom stir-fry hot with chiles and soy.

> *enough for 2 as a side dish*
> Chinese greens or small cabbage leaves – 12 stems or small leaves
> garlic – 2 large cloves
> ginger – a thumb-sized piece
> green onions – 6
> peanut oil – 2 tablespoons
> nam pla (Thai fish sauce) – a tablespoon

Bring a saucepan of deep water to a boil and salt it lightly. Wash the greens thoroughly. Peel the garlic and ginger, finely chop the garlic, and shred the ginger into matchsticklike strips. Trim the green onions and cut each into two or three.

Warm the oil in a shallow pan or wok. Toss the garlic, ginger, and green onions in the oil until deep gold, verging on being lightly browned and fragrant. Drop the greens, whole or shredded as you wish, into the boiling water. Leave for only a minute or so before draining. Pour the fish sauce in with the garlic and ginger—it will spit and sizzle—then toss with the greens and eat.

Chinese broccoli with garlic and oyster sauce

Any of the brassica family is good to go here. Most successful are gai lan (kai lan) and choy sum.

enough for 2 as a side dish
Chinese broccoli – 8 stalks
garlic – 3 cloves
shallots – 2
a little oil
oyster sauce – 3 heaping tablespoons
Shaoxing wine – 3 tablespoons

Steam the greens over hot water. Meanwhile, peel and finely chop the garlic and shallots. Fry them for a minute or two in a little oil. Stir in the oyster sauce and the wine and bring to a boil. Let the resulting sauce cook down for a minute, maybe two, then pour it over the steaming-hot greens.

Prawns, leaves, and limes

Bok choy or, better still, gai lan will be perfect here. Eat it hot and spluttering from the pan.

enough for 2
Chinese greens – 5 ounces (150g)
ginger – a thumb-sized piece
lemongrass – a large stalk
small, hot red chiles – 2
green onions – 2
peanut or vegetable oil – 2 tablespoons
large raw prawns – 1 pound (500g)
lime juice – 3½ tablespoons (50ml)
nam pla (Thai fish sauce) – 3½ tablespoons (50ml)
sugar – 2 teaspoons
cilantro leaves – a large handful
basil leaves – a large handful

Do the prep first, because everything happens quite quickly once you start cooking. Wash the leaves and remove any tough stems. Peel the ginger, then grate it or cut it into small, matchsticklike shreds. Remove the tough outer leaves of the lemongrass and very finely shred the tender heart. Finely chop the chiles, removing the seeds if you prefer cooler spicing. Finely shred the green onions.

Warm the oil in a wok or shallow pan. Add the ginger, lemongrass, chiles, and green onions and stir-fry for a couple of minutes, until the ginger starts to color. Drop in the prawns. As they turn opaque and color lightly, add the lime juice, nam pla, and sugar. When all is sizzling and fragrant, add the greens, turning them over in the pan as they start to wilt and darken. As soon as they are tender, add the cilantro and basil leaves and serve immediately.

Squid with greens and basil

I often come home from Chinatown with a squid and a bag of choy sum. The fishmonger will have done most of the dirty work for me, leaving me to give the body sac a final rinse before slicing. Squid is ideally suited to this quick, high-temperature cooking.

enough for 2
Chinese greens – 2 large handfuls
large red chiles – 2
ginger – a thumb-sized piece
prepared squid bodies and tentacles – 14 ounces (400g)
nam pla (Thai fish sauce) – 2 tablespoons
brown sugar – 2 teaspoons
lime juice – 2 tablespoons
vegetable oil – 2 tablespoons
basil leaves – a large handful

Blanch the greens in boiling water for a minute or two. Drain and set aside, chopping the stems coarsely.

Halve the chiles, remove the seeds, and slice the flesh thinly. Peel the ginger and grate or shred it finely. Wash the squid, dry it thoroughly with paper towels, then cut the bodies down one side and open them out. Wipe them clean (sometimes they have bits of yuck attached). Cut into large pieces and score each one carefully with the point of a sharp knife. Mix the fish sauce, sugar, and lime juice together.

Warm the oil in a wok or frying pan, then add the chiles and ginger. When it sizzles and the ginger starts to color, add the squid bodies and tentacles. Fry for two minutes, until the edges of the squid start to color, then pour in the fish sauce mixture. Take care, as it will spit and pop.

Continue frying briefly, then add the lightly chopped greens. Toss in the basil leaves, let them wilt, then eat immediately, from two warm bowls.

Eggplants

The eggplant seduces. No other vegetable can offer flesh so soft, silken, and tender. You don't so much chew an eggplant as let it dissolve on your tongue.

I fell in love at first taste: baked until its flesh had almost melted, heavy with olive oil, musky with cinnamon and allspice, cumin, and ginger, sweet with golden raisins. A dish in shades of chocolate, tobacco, and amber, heady with garlic and with a fragrance at once both ancient and mysterious.

The big purple shlong we know so well is just one of many varieties. Its beauty is nothing compared to the ivory varieties, their pale skins blushed with lilac or rose as if someone had taken an artist's brush to them. Finger eggplants, slender, cute in shades of lavender or black, are as elegant as any vegetable—or berry to the botanically pedantic. Some curl up at the end like Turkish slippers, others are ridged and bulbous, while some are as perfectly oval and unblemished as a duck's egg. I have always thought it a shame that commerce has chosen the glossy, long-keeping varieties over the softly hued ones with their sugared-almond colors.

The eggplant, *Solanum melongena*, is not of our world. A native of India and Sri Lanka, it thrives in long, hot summers, which we can only really replicate in a greenhouse. They have survived three summers out of four on my kitchen steps but truly thrived only once. China has long honored the eggplant in its cooking (stuffed with pork, battered and fried; steamed and tossed with chile sauce) and was the first to mention its existence, in *Qí Mín Yào Shù*, the ancient Chinese agricultural study.

More recipes for eggplants exist in Arabic cultures than in that of the Mediterranean, and most of what I do with them has a Middle Eastern or Indian feel. They are a member of the nightshade family, like tomatoes and potatoes, and initially aroused suspicion. They are still indigestible to a few and generally avoided, like peppers and tomatoes, by arthritis sufferers.

In the markets of Delhi and India I have seen this fruit the size and color of an ostrich egg, and in Bangkok as small and round as a malted milk ball. None relies on flavor to sell itself, but maybe we would use them more if we had a choice that included the exquisite Rosa Bianca or Turkish Orange.

The eggplant is at its most sensuous in a haze of olive oil and garlic, onions, golden raisins, pine nuts, yogurt, and fresh mint. The fragrance is beguiling, sumptuous, heady. The flesh of *Solanum melongena* loves the muskier spices such as cumin and saffron, the piercing sharpness of pomegranate seeds, the faintest breath of rose water. But nothing does quite so much for it as being grilled over charcoal. Smoke seeps into the spongy flesh, lending a note of intrigue and exposing an altogether darker undertone.

The thick stems, with their light, fine hairs, the mauve flowers drooping down as if in shame, the first hint of ivory or purple fruits, and the soft, jade-green leaves make this one of the most covetable plants to own. And if it gives us only two or three ripe fruits at the end of an infrequent hot summer, we should just be thankful. Rarely is the cook given anything quite so beautiful to work with.

An eggplant in the garden

With luck and a good summer, we can grow eggplants as successfully as anyone in the Med. I grow them in deep clay pots, against my warmest wall. The slimmer varieties do best in Britain, but given a long, hot ripening season, even the fat, mauve-blushed versions will come good.

We must replicate the conditions of their natural home, so growing them in a greenhouse is the most reliable way of ensuring your plants will fruit. They thrive in fine, well-drained soil and prefer masses of heat. I have no greenhouse, so they have to live in the biggest sun trap I can offer them— on the steps by the back door, their backs to a white wall. Neither are they fond of wind, so a sheltered place is essential.

The seeds need gentle heat to germinate, about 70°F (20°C). They will grow on a windowsill, but you need to start them early, sowing in late winter. The heat must be constant. Even given the right conditions, the seeds can refuse to germinate, so I plant two to a pot. Pot them on when they are about 1½ inches (4cm) high. Although you won't get much in the way of choice, you can also pick up small plants at farmers' markets, nurseries, and by mail order from specialty suppliers—the easy option for anyone without the space and heat to grow from seed.

It is a good idea to pinch out the tips of the growing plant when it reaches about 8 inches (20cm). You will get a less fragile, more bushy plant. As soon as the first flowers appear, mist them with a fine water sprayer to encourage the fruit to set, and feed the plants once every two weeks or so with tomato food. Keep an eye out for whitefly. They are rather partial to a young eggplant.

You will get about half a dozen fruits per plant, so we are not talking about vast crops here. But what a plant lacks in quantity it makes up for in the sheer pleasure of seeing the young fruits form on their furry stems. The mauve flowers are beautiful. Expect your first pick in early autumn, a little earlier if you are growing in a greenhouse.

Varieties

Violetta di Firenze* White fruit, flushed with violet.
Rosa Bianca* Creamy-white skin with a pink blush.
Applegreen* An heirloom variety, with pale green, egg-shaped fruits.
Thai Green* Small, ancient variety the size of a large pea. Often used in Southeast Asian soups.
Baby Rosanna Golf ball sized on dwarf plants (2 feet [60cm]).
Prosperosa* Large, somewhat flat-sided fruits that you could slice and fry as a steak.
Early Long Purple Lives up to its name, often with a slight bend at the end.
Black Beauty* Lustrous, handsome, extraordinary girth.

*Available from US seed sources.

An eggplant in the kitchen

The heart and soul of the eggplant is not its flavor but its unique texture. It has the ability to turn an outwardly spongy blandness into a mass of silky, melting flesh that is effortless to eat. But no amount of heat alone will work this magic. The eggplant relies on the cook's generosity with the olive oil bottle. It is the fruit's ability to soak it up that makes it interesting in the kitchen.

The skin is rarely eaten, but it can be. Much depends on the way it is prepared. Peel an eggplant to be sliced and stewed (say, with tomatoes, onions, cinnamon, and dried fruits) and it will collapse during cooking. Halved and baked, the skin can sometimes be tough and occasionally bitter. I usually serve it intact, then cut a piece off to try. If it is on the stringy side, I just scrape off all the flesh and leave the skin.

An eggplant has little going for it without other ingredients to add interest to its mild flesh (it is one of the few vegetables that is completely inedible raw). The simplest way to prepare it is probably to slice and grill it, but even that will need some form of dressing or sauce. No other vegetable needs quite so much help from its close friends as this one—by which I mean onions, tomatoes, garlic, and herbs.

You can fry an eggplant in shallow oil, most of which it will soak up, until its edges are crisp. You can bake it whole or cut in half, its skin scored to soak up more oil, or you can grill or stew it. Boiling and steaming do nothing for this one.

It is the blackening of its skin that gives many of the most famous eggplant dishes their character. *Moutabal*, or baba ghanoush, the soft purée of the roasted or grilled fruit beaten with olive oil and garlic, relies on the smoky notes of the charred skin for its essential flavor. Grilled eggplant with yogurt sauce again needs the smoky notes from having been cooked on the grill as much as it needs salt and pepper.

Classic eggplant recipes tend to involve spices rather than herbs. While fresh cilantro and basil appear at the end of many recipes, it is the spices—cinnamon, cumin, and coriander seed in particular—that are considered essential.

Salting—the process of leaving the sliced or cubed fruit in a colander, its cut surfaces encrusted with salt—is thought to remove the bitterness present in some varieties. Most of this attribute has been bred out, but I have experienced it occasionally in my homegrown fruits. Salting is still worthwhile, even for thirty minutes or so, simply to relax the cells of the flesh, preventing it from soaking up all your precious olive oil.

Seasoning your eggplant

Olive oil It is the fruit's ability to soak up copious quantities of liquid that makes our choice of oil all the more important. The eggplant's flesh is nothing without oil, and in particular a green and deeply fruity olive oil. Some of the light olive oils on the market are good for cooking, but ones such as peanut and vegetable add a fatty quality while offering nothing in terms of flavor. Walnut and other nut oils are too strong and burn too quickly for this use. Olive oil is what makes an eggplant worth eating.
Garlic You can throw any amount of garlic at an eggplant. They are in total harmony with each other.
Salt The addition of salt after chopping will draw out the eggplant's juices and relax the flesh. This means your eggplant will soak up less oil during cooking. If there is any bitterness present—the heirloom varieties occasionally carry a little—it should disperse that too. Use sparingly at the end of the dish.
Tomato A perfect pairing, especially when olive oil and garlic are involved.

Mint While basil and thyme also get on well with this particular ingredient, it is mint that is heavily involved in its history. Many Middle Eastern dishes include the clean taste of mint, which cuts the oiliness.
Onion Use as a base for any slow-cooked dish or include in a stuffing. Onions feature in the famous *imam bayildi*, the Turkish stuffed eggplant recipe.
Yogurt Spices, mint, and yogurt form a romantic seasoning for the eggplant. You can also stir it into a stew or curry, or drizzle it over grilled eggplant as a dressing.
Pine nuts Toast and scatter.
Walnuts Lightly crushed, sprinkled over grilled eggplant slices.
Spices Add depth and mystery. Cumin, cinnamon, paprika, and cardamom are the most comfortable here, but ground coriander and turmeric are very good in vegetable stews.
Parmesan Grated. Its fruity notes bring out the fruit's subtle flavor.
Pomegranate seeds Either fresh or dried. Scatter the little jewels over grilled eggplant, along with golden raisins and pine nuts. Add dried ones to stews.

And...

* Eggplant flowers droop, almost hiding themselves from the bees. Plant brightly colored flowers such as marigolds close by to attract the interest of passing insect life.
* Beware the pale green calyx at the stem end. It packs a number of small, sharp thorns.
* Certain varieties have seeds inside, and they can be quite pronounced in older specimens too. It is not necessary to remove them. They are perfectly edible when cooked.
* Indian cooks often refer to the eggplant as *brinjal*, a name that is sometimes used to label them in Indian markets. Generally, it refers to the slim, elegant fruits grown there rather than the fat, black whoppers we get in the UK.
* Eggplants dislike the fridge. Keep them at cool room temperature.

Baked finger eggplants, yogurt, and cucumber

The slim eggplant varieties, often with a lavender blush, that are to be found in Middle Eastern and Indian markets are especially suitable for grilling, since they cook quickly and evenly. I rarely salt these little chaps. Black onion seed (nigella sativa) is the seed of the nigella flower and is common to southwest Asia. It is best known as the black seeds used to decorate Indian naan bread and resembles black sesame seeds.

enough for 4
finger eggplants – about 8
olive oil

for the yogurt
half a cucumber
thick yogurt – ¾ cup (200g)
a clove of garlic
mint leaves – about 12
black onion seeds – a teaspoon (optional)
warm flat bread such as pita, to serve

Preheat the oven to 400°F (200°C). Wipe the eggplants and cut them in half lengthwise. Pour a thin layer of olive oil into a baking pan and place the eggplants, cut side down, in the oil. Bake until soft and squishy, about forty minutes.

To make the cucumber yogurt, wipe the cucumber half and grate coarsely. Sprinkle lightly with salt and set aside in a colander for half an hour. Squeeze the cucumber dry in the palm of your hand, then stir it into the yogurt. Peel and finely crush the garlic, chop the mint leaves, and stir both into the cucumber and yogurt. Toast the black onion seeds lightly in a nonstick pan. Transfer the yogurt to a serving bowl and sprinkle with the onion seeds.

Serve the eggplants on plates with the cucumber yogurt. Spread some of the baked eggplant onto a piece of the bread, spoon over a little of the yogurt, and eat.

Grilled eggplant, creamed feta

This is one of those recipes I find come in handy on several levels. I use it as both starter and main dish—often with parsley-flecked couscous on the side—but it is also a fine dish to bring out as one of the constituents of a laid-back summer meal in the garden. The sort where you just put a few simple dishes on the table and let everyone help themselves.

enough for 2
medium-sized eggplants – 2
feta cheese – 7 ounces (200g)
yogurt (preferably sheep's) – ¾ cup (200g)
chopped basil, parsley, and mint – a tablespoon of each
olive oil
warm flat bread, to serve

Slice each eggplant lengthwise into five or six long steaks. Sprinkle with sea salt and allow to stand for up to an hour or so while you make the creamed feta. This salting will ensure the eggplants soak up as little oil as possible.

Crumble the feta into a bowl and mash it with a fork. Stir in the yogurt, 3 tablespoons of water, and the chopped herbs. Season with black pepper, but not salt unless your feta was extraordinarily mild.

Rinse the eggplants gently and pat them dry. Brush with olive oil and place on a grill or a hot grill pan, the ridged sort that sits over the burner. When they are tender—a matter of five or six minutes on each side—and appetizingly charred in patches, lift them off the grill and place on a serving dish. Drizzle immediately with olive oil. How much they absorb will depend on the eggplants but make certain they are all thoroughly soaked. Leave them to cool a little, then serve with the creamed feta and flat bread.

Smoky eggplants and a punchy, bright-tasting dressing

I am always on the lookout for simple but interesting side dishes to eat with cold roast meats. A little pile of grilled eggplants, their smoked edges moist with a vibrant green dressing, wakes up yesterday's cold roast chicken or beef.

enough for 2
a large eggplant
olive oil
parsley leaves – a generous handful
mint – 6 bushy sprigs
basil leaves – a handful
garlic – 2 cloves, crushed
Dijon mustard – a tablespoon
capers – 2 tablespoons, rinsed
extra-virgin olive oil – 6 tablespoons
lemon juice – 2 tablespoons

Slice the eggplant lengthwise into five or six pieces. Brush lightly with oil and sprinkle with sea salt, then set aside for thirty minutes or so. Grill them over low to medium heat on both sides until they are soft and tender.

To make the sauce, chop the herbs quite finely, but not so small they look like tea leaves, then stir in the garlic, mustard, and capers. Slowly pour in the extra-virgin olive oil, beating with a fork. Stir in the lemon juice and season with sea salt and black pepper. Be generous with the seasoning, tasting as you go. The sauce should be lively and piquant.

Remove the eggplant from the grill, toss gently in the sauce, and serve.

A quick supper of eggplants and pesto

Cut the eggplants in half and score deeply almost down to the skin. Roast them in a hot oven with a good dousing of olive oil. When they are squishy and meltingly tender, spread them with pesto sauce and return to the oven for a few minutes. Serve hot.

Roast eggplants, chiles, and thyme

A sort of lazy guy's ratatouille this, but better, I think, for its freshness and clean taste. I keep the chiles large here, which is partly why I have suggested using the milder varieties but, as always, it's up to you.

This works hot as an accompaniment to so many main dishes—roast lamb comes to mind—but as a warm salad too, and indeed, piled on hot toasted ciabatta as a weekday supper.

enough for 4
medium-sized eggplants – 2
cherry tomatoes – 2 large handfuls
garlic – 3 cloves
bell peppers (red or orange) – 2
large, mild chiles – 2 or more
thyme – 6 to 8 sprigs
olive oil – ⅔ cup (150ml)
toasted ciabatta, to serve

Preheat the oven to 400°F (200°C). Wipe the eggplants and cut them into thick slices or segments (salting them if you wish). Put them into a roasting pan or baking dish with the tomatoes, halved if on the large size.

Peel and crush the garlic and add it to the eggplants. Cut the peppers in half, scrape out and discard the seeds and central core, then cut the flesh into thick pieces. Cut the chiles in half, remove the seeds, and slice the flesh thickly (cut it too thinly and it will burn). Add to the eggplants with the sprigs of thyme, olive oil, and a generous seasoning of salt and black pepper, then toss gently until everything is glistening with oil.

Bake for forty to fifty minutes, turning once or twice, until everything is sweet and tender. A little black here and there will only add to the deliciousness. Serve piled up on the toasted ciabatta, drizzling over any remaining sweet, garlicky roasting juices.

An eggplant bruschetta

I can live without nibbles with drinks (you might get an olive if you're lucky), but from time to time the genre gets an outing. They tend to be more substantial than most, as I have a fear of anything that might fit the name canapé. Little rounds of toast piled with grilled eggplant in a lemon and herb dressing is a tantalizing mixture of crisp and soft.

> *makes 4 to 6 small rounds of toast, maybe more*
> large eggplants – 2
> extra-virgin olive oil – 6 tablespoons
> the grated zest and juice of a lemon
> basil leaves – a small bunch
> mint – a small bunch
> country bread – 4 to 6 thick slices, toasted, then drizzled
>   with olive oil just before you add the eggplants

Cut the eggplants into ¼-inch-thick (6-mm-thick) slices about the thickness of two one-pound coins, put them in a colander, sprinkle with sea salt, and leave for half an hour. Get a grill or ridged grill pan hot. Rinse and dry the eggplants, then place them on the grill. While they are cooking, pour the oil into a bowl, then add the lemon zest and juice, and a mild grinding of salt and coarse black pepper. Tear the basil leaves into large pieces, then remove the mint leaves from their stems and toss them into the dressing with the basil leaves.

When the eggplants are tender and nicely charred on both sides, add them to the herbed oil. Toss gently and leave to marinate for a good fifteen minutes or so (longer will not hurt), then pile onto the hot toast. Drizzle over any remaining dressing.

Hot eggplant, melting cheese

It is essential to get an eggplant truly tender. The knife should barely have to cut it. This is easier to achieve when baking or frying than when an eggplant meets the grill. It is, I think, essential that the heat is lowered during cooking so that the inside of the slice has a chance to soften while the crust lightly browns.

> *enough for 2 as a light lunch*
> a large eggplant
> basil leaves – a small handful
> olive oil
> bocconcini (baby mozzarella) – 12

Cut the eggplant into long, thin slices. You should get about six from a large fruit. Salt them, leave for half an hour, then, when they have relaxed, wipe off the salt. Get a grill or ridged grill pan hot. Grill the eggplant slices until soft and lightly colored (four or five minutes on each side), then place on a baking sheet.

Tear the basil leaves, mix them with a couple of tablespoons of olive oil, then season with salt and pepper. Brush the slices of cooked eggplant with the seasoned oil. Slice each mozzarella in half and place the halves on the eggplant slices. Let the cheese melt under a hot broiler and serve immediately, before the cheese has a chance to color.

Moutabal—a heavenly purée

The smoky, parchment-hued cream *moutabal* is one of my desert-island dishes. Few recipes can produce anything as soft and sensuous as grilled eggplant, mashed to a pulp, and seasoned with lemon and sesame paste. The lemon is essential, working an ancient magic when involved with anything charred and smoky.

Many lightly bake their eggplant for this, but without a good charring they lack the mysterious, smoky back notes that I consider as much a part of the ingredients as the eggplant itself.

> *enough for 2*
> large eggplants – 2
> juice of a lemon
> garlic – 2 cloves, crushed
> tahini paste – 2 tablespoons
> olive oil – 3 tablespoons

Preheat the oven to 400°F (200°C). Slit the eggplants here and there with a sharp knife and bake them until their skin is black and charred and they are melting and tender inside—about forty minutes. When they are cool enough to handle, scrape out the flesh with a teaspoon. This is a messy business, but try not to get any of the skin in with the flesh. Mash the flesh with a fork, beating in the lemon juice, crushed garlic, tahini paste, olive oil, and a good seasoning of salt. It may look a little curdled but it will taste wonderful.

A classic caponata

Sicily's cooks make much of the eggplant. They fry it in crisp disks, with mint and vinegar; bake it with tomato sauce and salty caciocavallo cheese; stuff it with anchovies, parsley, and capers; or grill it over charcoal before seasoning with garlic and oregano. Occasionally, they will roll up a thick jam of eggplant in soft disks of dough like a savory strudel, called *scaccie*, while all the time matching it to the Arab-influenced exotica of their cupboards: anchovies, olives, fennel, mint, pomegranates, currants, and pine nuts. The thin, Turkish eggplant with the bulbous end is the one they prefer, though you could use any shape for their famous caponata, the rich sweet-sour stew braised with celery, golden raisins, vinegar, and bell peppers. I can eat this fragrant, amber slop at any time of year, but somehow I always end up making it when the sun is shining, eating it outside with flat, chewy bread and maybe some grilled sardines flecked with torn mint leaves and lemon. If you make it the day before, its character—salty, sweet, and sour—will have time to settle itself.

enough for 4
very large eggplants – 2
a large onion
olive oil
garlic – 2 cloves, sliced
celery – 2 large stalks, thinly sliced
a large red bell pepper, cored and sliced
tomato paste – a scant tablespoon
tomato purée – scant 1 cup (200ml)
golden raisins or raisins – 2 tablespoons
red wine vinegar – 4 tablespoons
sugar – a tablespoon
capers – a tablespoon
green olives – a handful

Peel the eggplants and remove their stems. Cut them into large chunks, place in a colander, and sprinkle with salt. Set aside for an hour.

Peel the onion, slice it thinly, and add it to a large, shallow pan coated with a shallow layer of oil. Let the onion soften—but not color—over medium heat. Add the garlic toward the end of cooking. Remove the onion and garlic from the pan, and put in a bowl. Fry the celery and pepper in the pan until soft. Remove and add to the onion.

Rinse the salt from the eggplants, pat dry with paper towels, then soften in the same pan. As they approach tenderness, return the onion, garlic, celery, and pepper to the pan, stir, and continue cooking over gentle heat until the eggplants are truly tender.

Stir in the tomato paste, tomato purée, golden raisins, vinegar, sugar, capers, and ⅔ cup (150ml) water. Season and simmer gently for about twenty-five minutes, keeping a careful eye on it to ensure you end up with a soft tangle of sweet-sour vegetables. Chill overnight, then serve with bread.

Eggplants baked with tomato and Parmesan

Eggplant and tomato are excellent bedfellows; the sweet sharpness of the tomato adding much in the way of succulence to the bland flesh of the eggplant. Garlic and olive oil are almost certain to come along for the ride. What follows is a recipe I use over and again as a relatively quick supper, occasionally introducing mozzarella instead of Parmesan, and sometimes adding basil with the tomatoes.

enough for 4
eggplants – 2
olive oil
tomatoes of assorted color – 12 ounces (350g)
a red chile
a clove of garlic
grated Parmesan – 6 tablespoons

Preheat the oven to 425°F (220°C). Slice the eggplants into thick rounds, place them on a baking sheet, brush generously with olive oil, and season with salt and black pepper. Bake for twenty to twenty-five minutes, until soft and tender.

Chop the tomatoes, chile, and garlic and cook them in a shallow pan with a little olive oil and plenty of salt and black pepper for twenty minutes or so, until cooked down to a mush.

Pile the tomatoes in the middle of each slice of eggplant, scatter over the grated cheese, and bake for fifteen to twenty minutes, until sizzling. If there is any tomato mixture left over, serve it on the side.

Baked vegetables with an eggplant sauce

enough for 4
tomatoes – 4 large or several smaller ones
zucchini – 3, cut into quarters lengthwise
bell peppers – 2, cored and thickly sliced
an onion, peeled and cut into wedges
olive oil
ground cumin – a teaspoon
harissa paste (or other hot sauce) – 2 teaspoons
pine nuts – a handful
raisins – a handful

for the eggplant cream
large eggplants – 2
olive oil
creamy yogurt – scant ½ cup (100g)
mint leaves – a handful, chopped

Preheat the oven to 400°F (200°C). Make the eggplant cream: cut the eggplants in half lengthwise, score the flesh with several deep etches, then sprinkle generously with salt and set aside for half an hour. Wipe off the salt, place in a baking dish, pour over a few glugs of oil, then bake until thoroughly soft. You should be able to crush the flesh with a fork. Leave the oven set to 400°F (200°C).

Scrape the eggplant flesh from the skin and mash with the yogurt and enough olive oil to make a paste that is thick enough to drizzle. Season with salt, black pepper, and the chopped mint.

Meanwhile, put the tomatoes, zucchini, bell peppers, and onion in a roasting pan or baking dish, toss with olive oil and a little salt, and roast for a good forty-five minutes to an hour to become tender. Toward the end of cooking, gently stir in the cumin, harissa paste, pine nuts, and raisins. Remove from the oven and serve with a drizzle of the eggplant sauce.

Baked eggplant, miso dressing

You could probably use any finely ground dried chile for this, but I like the mixed ground seasoning known as nanami togarashi. Togarashi is simply the Japanese term for red chile, but this one is blended with orange peel, sesame seeds, and ginger. It has a slight grittiness that works well with the silky softness of the eggplant. You can find it in any Japanese market. Get the yellow miso, by the way, not the darker and substantially saltier one. Small eggplants are best for this, available from Chinese and Asian markets.

serves 4 as a side dish

for the eggplants
small, long eggplants, about the size of a zucchini – 6
mirin – 2 tablespoons
peanut oil – 2 tablespoons

for the miso dressing
mirin – ½ cup (120ml)
yellow miso paste – 2 level tablespoons
sugar – 1 tablespoon
togarashi – a half to a teaspoon

Preheat the oven to 350°F (180°C). Cut the eggplants in half lengthwise, or, if they are on the large side, into thick slices.

Score each one across the cut side, cutting almost down to the skin. Lay them in a baking dish.

Mix a couple of tablespoons of mirin with the oil and brush it over the eggplants. Cover the top with aluminum foil and bake for forty minutes to an hour, until they are truly soft and melting. You can brush them with a little more of the mixture if you think they need it.

To make the miso dressing, pour the ½ cup (120ml) of mirin into a saucepan and warm gently. Stir in the miso paste and the sugar. When they have dissolved, remove from the heat and stir in the togarashi.

Remove the eggplants from the oven, toss them in the dressing, and return them to the dish. Bake for five minutes or so, until the dressing starts to lightly caramelize.

Eggplants with mint and feta

Slice a large eggplant thickly, salt it if you wish, then brush it with a little oil and grill on both sides until completely tender. Make a dressing with four parts olive oil, one of red wine vinegar, a little salt, and plenty of chopped fresh mint.

While the eggplant slices are hot from the grill, toss them gently with the mint dressing, then serve with thick slices of feta cheese and warm flat bread such as pita.

Spiced eggplant stew

A lovely, deeply flavored vegetable stew. This is one of those dishes that is all the better for a day in the fridge, during which time the flavors seem to mellow. I have kept it quite spicy but the final seasoning will depend on how hot your chiles are, and you will need to adjust it accordingly. Something to take your time over. I eat it with steamed basmati rice.

enough for 6
eggplants – 2 pounds (1kg; 2 very large ones)
medium onions – 3
peanut oil – 2 tablespoons
green cardamom pods – 8
coriander seeds – 2 tablespoons
black peppercorns – 2 level teaspoons
garlic – 4 plump cloves
fresh ginger – a thumb-sized piece
ground turmeric – 2 rounded teaspoons
medium tomatoes – 10
vegetable stock – 2 cups (500ml)
coconut milk – 3½ cups (800ml)
small, hot red chiles – 4, finely chopped
mint – a small bunch
cilantro – 2 small bunches

Wipe the eggplants, cut the stems from them, and cut them into fat chunks. The dish will be more interesting to eat if you don't cut them too small. Put them into a colander, set in the sink, and sprinkle sea salt over them. Leave them for a good half hour, longer if you can.

Peel and coarsely chop the onions, then cook them with the oil in a large pan over medium heat until they are soft, translucent, and sweet.

While the onions are cooking, crush the cardamom pods with the flat blade of a knife or a rolling pin and shake out the little black seeds into a mortar or spice grinder (or a clean coffee grinder). Add the coriander seeds and the peppercorns and grind them to a coarse powder. The smell as you grind will convince you that there is much to be missed in buying ready-ground spices.

Thinly slice the garlic. Peel the ginger and cut it into thin, matchstick-like shards. Stir the garlic and ginger into the onions along with the turmeric and ground spices. Peel and seed the tomatoes and add them to the pan.

Rinse the eggplants of their salt and pat dry. Without oiling them, grill them on a ridged cast-iron grill pan until they are starting to soften and have dark grill lines across them. Turn them as you go, so that they are cooked on both sides, removing them as they are ready and replacing them with another batch. Add them to the onions, then pour in the stock and bring to a boil. Add the coconut milk, chiles, and a little salt and continue cooking at a simmer for about forty-five minutes. The eggplants should be very soft and silky but not actually falling apart.

Lift out the eggplants, tomatoes, and some of the onion with a slotted spoon. Reduce the rest of the sauce by boiling hard for five minutes or so. Now ladle most, but not all, of the sauce into a blender and blitz until smooth and thick (take care to cover the top before you turn it on, the sauce is very hot). Return the vegetables and the sauce to the pot, then chop the mint and cilantro leaves and stir them in, together with a final seasoning of salt and black pepper. Serve with rice.

Grilled lamb with eggplants and za'atar

Za'atar is a mild spice mixture available in Middle Eastern markets and some supermarkets. Fragrant and green, it is usually prepared using dried thyme, oregano, marjoram, toasted sesame seeds, and salt. Some varieties may add savory, cumin, coriander, or fennel seeds.

enough for 2
eggplant – 12 ounces (350g)
olive oil – scant ½ cup (100ml)
za'atar – 2 teaspoons
a lemon

for the lamb
lamb rib chops – 6 nice little ones
olive oil
homemade or good-quality purchased hummus – ⅔ cup (150g)

Preheat the oven to 400°F (200°C). Cut the eggplant into quarters lengthwise, then into fat chunks. Put them into a bowl and pour over half the olive oil, then season with sea salt and black pepper. Put the eggplant on a baking sheet and bake for twenty minutes, until the flesh is truly tender.

Rub the lamb chops with olive oil, salt, and black pepper and grill them until they are sizzling outside and still pleasingly pink in the middle. While they are cooking, turn the hummus into a bowl and drizzle it with a little olive oil.

Warm the remaining 3½ tablespoons (50ml) olive oil in a shallow, nonstick pan over medium heat, then add the za'atar. Transfer the eggplant to the pan and let it cook, turning the pieces occasionally, for three or four minutes. Squeeze over the lemon juice and serve with the lamb cutlets and hummus.

A hot stew with tomatoes and cilantro

Hot, clean, and vibrant, a mouth-popping stew for scooping up with soft, warm naan or, if you prefer, rice. Should you want something richer and less spicy, then stir in a carton of yogurt, about 1 cup (250g), at the end and simmer for a further seven or eight minutes.

> *enough for 4*
> medium-large eggplants – 2
> ginger – a thumb-sized piece
> garlic – 4 cloves
> the juice of a large lemon
> medium tomatoes – 4
> small, hot red chiles – 2
> cilantro – a large bunch (about 1½ ounces [40g])
> peanut oil – 4 tablespoons

Cut the stems from the eggplants and discard. Slice each fruit in half lengthwise, then again, then cut the long strips into short, fat chunks. Put these in a colander and sprinkle generously with sea salt. Let them sit for a good thirty minutes.

Peel the ginger and chop it finely, then do the same with the garlic. Put them into a blender (or a food processor) along with the lemon juice. Whiz till you have a smoothish purée. This may take a bit of doing.

Coarsely chop the tomatoes. Slice the chiles thinly, without removing the seeds; you want the dish to be really quite spicy. Coarsely chop the cilantro.

Once the eggplants have relaxed, rinse them of their salt and pat them dry. Heat the oil in a large pan, then, when it starts to sizzle, add the eggplants, letting them color on their cut edges, turning them so that they are golden all over.

Add the garlic and ginger paste and stir to coat. Mix in the tomatoes and chiles, shortly followed by the cilantro and 4 tablespoons of water. Season with salt and let simmer gently for four or five minutes, until the eggplants have softened further. Taste for seasoning, check the eggplants for tenderness—they should be soft to the point of collapse—and serve with warm naan to mop it up.

A fragrant supper for one

I make the most of cooking just for myself, with a supper of intense frugality that might not appeal to others. A favorite is a bowl of white rice seasoned with Vietnamese fish sauce and masses of mint and cilantro, eaten from my most fragile and precious bowl. A humble meal of consummate purity.

A baked eggplant may not sound like an indulgence, but its luxury and richness lie in its texture rather than its price. A simple supper that feels more expensive than it actually is. Some soft Middle Eastern bread would be good here.

> *enough for 1*
> a large, firm eggplant
> olive oil, a good everyday one
> garlic – 2 cloves
> yogurt, sheep's if you can – 3 or 4 tablespoons
> paprika – a pinch or two
> mint leaves – a small palmful

Preheat the oven to 400°F (200°C). Wipe the eggplant, removing its leaves, and slice it lengthwise down the middle. Score across the cut sides, going deep down into the flesh, in a lattice pattern. This will help the heat and olive oil penetrate the eggplant.

Place the halves, cut side up, in a small baking dish or roasting pan, then drizzle generously with olive oil. Grind over a little salt, then flip the eggplant halves over, so that their cut sides sit flat on the dish. Put the garlic cloves, whole and unpeeled, into the dish too. Bake until the eggplant is tender and melting, the flesh translucent with oil. This will take a good forty-five minutes, but much will depend on the size of your eggplant, so keep an eye out.

When the eggplant is totally soft and juicy, lift it onto a plate, squeeze the soft garlic flesh from its skin, and smooth it into the eggplant. No need to make a big deal of this, just wipe it over the flesh. Spoon over the yogurt, dust very lightly with paprika, and scatter the mint leaves on top. Scoop the flesh from the skin as you eat it, mashing it with the yogurt and mint.

Baked eggplants with thyme and cream

This is a gorgeous dish, sumptuous and rich, a perfect accompaniment to grilled lamb or to steak. I have served it as a vegetable main dish with brown basmati rice too. By rights, cream and eggplant should never meet, but here they seem to work splendidly.

enough for 2 as a main dish with rice, 4 as a side dish
eggplants – 1 very large or 2 smaller
a medium onion
olive oil
garlic – 2 juicy cloves
thyme – a few bushy sprigs
whipping or heavy cream – 1¾ cups (400ml)
Parmesan for grating

Wipe the eggplants and cut them into long slices, about ¼ inch (6mm) thick. Put the slices in a colander and sprinkle with salt. Leave for a good half hour, until they have relaxed (each piece will go a bit floppy), then rinse and dry. Preheat the oven to 350°F (180°C).

Peel and thinly slice the onion. Cook it in a little olive oil until it has softened, but stop before it colors. Peel and slice the garlic and add it to the onion as it cooks. Lift out the onion and garlic and place in a shallow baking dish. Put more olive oil into the pan and add the rinsed and dried eggplant. As each slice starts to color, turn it over, then, when all are golden—though far from brown—drain them thoroughly on paper towels. This is essential if there is not to be too much oil in the finished dish.

Lay the eggplant slices in the baking dish on top of the onion, scattering with salt, pepper, and thyme leaves as you go. Pour the cream over the eggplant and onion, scatter over a couple of spoonfuls of grated Parmesan, and bake for thirty-five to forty-five minutes, until bubbling and lightly browned here and there.

Oh, and can I remind you of the Green Curry of Shrimp and Thai Eggplant in *The Kitchen Diaries*?

Fava beans

I only truly appreciated fava beans once I had seen them growing. The flowers, pure white, black and white, or the deep crimson-pink of an archbishop's robe, have a scent that wafts lightly on the air. The smell takes you by surprise on a cold spring day, like a sudden blast of winter jasmine, hitting you when you least expect it. As a child, I wouldn't eat the bean, and yet for all its faults—mealy texture, musty smell, papery skins—I knew that the fava bean was essentially a beneficial thing. I wanted to like it. It wasn't until my teens, finding my stepmother's tiny homegrown offerings under a white sauce speckled with parsley (and alongside a slice of steaming, fat-framed pink ham), that I found them acceptable. The sight of them in our new country garden, festooned with smart black-and-white flowers and held up by sticks and brown string, amused a displaced and lonely city boy. Their ability to stay green even in the coldest weather, their gentle scent, and the fact that the seed germinated so reliably made me think differently about the bean I had previously refused to eat.

The first pink-flowered variety I saw was at the Chelsea Physic Garden in a bed behind the pelargonium house, three feet high, its deep magenta blossoms singing out against soil the color of wet tobacco. I guess that is when I truly fell in love with them. I could have been persuaded to relish them sooner had they been served without their gray, parchmentlike skins. But it was the sight of their flowers, like butterflies clinging to a stick, that finally seduced me.

Now I respect them and their fur-lined pods in much the same way that others revere asparagus or artichokes. In a salad with crumbly white cheese, baked with cream and parsley, tossed with chopped dill and fat bacon, they take on a must-have quality. I grow them in my own garden now, the ancient Aquadulce, Grando Violetto, and the crimson-flowered variety, too.

A fava bean in the garden

We have cultivated this flat, wide bean since the Bronze Age. I have grown it for the last seven years. The only truly frost-hardy bean, it will usually survive throughout the coldest winter. Autumn planting is popular, to get a head start, picking them in early summer before many other crops have crossed the starting line. But you can, and I often do, sow as late as April.

I have found this bean to be the least fussy vegetable of all. Wherever I plant it, in my clay soil or cosseted in warm pots of compost, the seeds germinate without fail. If only everything was as good-natured and tolerant. Generally it is accepted that fava beans do well in deep, heavy soil. They have long roots and do like the ground to have had a digging over before they go in.

There are two distinct cultivars: those with a long pod such as the Aquadulce I grow each year, and the shorter "Windsor" pods with three or four plump beans, such as Jubilee Hysor or Crimson Flowered. I get on well with the long-podded types, apart from the odd bit of blackfly here and there.

Sheltered gardens allow seeds to be sown directly in October, but most survive more reliably if sown indoors, then planted out in early spring. As a rule, spring sowing can be done under cover in February or March (plant out in late April or early May and water in well) or in April where they are to crop. They need 8 inches (20cm) between each plant and 18 inches (45cm) between the rows, although I have often allowed less.

I keep blackfly to a minimum by picking out the top shoots two weeks or so before the pods are ready to pick. You can stir-fry the young leafy tops with garlic.

A fava bean diary

The catalogues are offering Aquadulce Claudia for autumn sowing (and for which I am too late), Giant Exhibition, which sounds like a tough old man fit only for winning awards at country shows, and The Sutton Dwarf, a bush variety and apparently prolific. One or two mention the magenta-flowered bean that stole my heart.

I order Aquadulce, a nineteenth-century Spanish variety. The Catalans have wonderful bean recipes, including one where the beans are cooked in earthenware with pork fat, onion, parsley, oregano, rosemary, and olive oil and served with blood sausage. You don't need a recipe—just pile the ingredients in, cover with a little stock and a lid, and let cook in a slow oven for a couple of hours.

March 11 I plant the seeds, pale gray-brown and the size of my thumbnail, in peat-free potting compost in tall, root-trainer pots, two to a pot. Not too deep, barely an inch (2.5cm) below the surface. I put wet newspaper in first, which they seem to like, then compost. The surface smoothed off, the pots go into the cold frame. Others are dibbled straight into the soil, each one marked by a copper ring to ward off slugs and to remind me of life below the surface. More organized gardeners will have planted theirs in January to grow more slowly and to give a late-May or early-June harvest.

Unable to resist, I also plant the ancient Grando Violetto and once again the red-Xowered beans I picked up from the Chelsea Physic Garden whose seeds are the most beautiful of all, a sultry jade-green color and slightly smaller than Aquadulce.

March 24 A pool of water has frozen solid on the buckled top of the garden table. Before the cold, gray light fades, I spot the first beans poking through the compost, a single stem, pointed like a bird's beak, poised, ready to unfurl.

May 4 The Grando Violetto, red flowered, and Aquadulce Claudia have germinated with just a single failure. Those sown outside are shorter by half, but seem stronger and stiffer than those wallowing in the luxury of the cold frame, whose swollen stems are already in need of a stick. Once they are 4 inches (10cm) high, I plant the indoor-grown ones out on the cool, moist side of the garden, about 8 to 10 inches (20 to 25cm) apart and with sticks for each to climb.

May 24 The stems are full of carmine and white flowers and the first plump bean pods are the length of my little finger. I tie the stems to stiff canes.

June 6 A few straggling flowers still grace the plants but it is the beans that are the stars now, their pods quickly thickening up with the heavy rain. I pick almost constantly for a full month.

July 20 I rip up the bare stems that are now crisping in the sun to make way for cabbage plants. Any legume leaves behind a quantity of nitrogen in the soil that is heartily welcomed by members of the brassica family.

Varieties

Aquadulce Claudia A long bean of good flavor and disease resistance. Comes up trumps for me every time.

The Sutton Dwarf A short bushy bean, barely 14 inches (35cm) in height, so useful for small gardens like mine or on windy sites where a taller bean would come to grief. The beans are small, the flowers black and white.

Green Windsor One of the deepest-flavored varieties, but inclined to be tender, so best for spring sowing. A short bean, it has been with us since the 1750s. The original "unimproved" variety, with short, plump pods and beans of incomparable flavor, can be found in specialty seeds catalogues like those of Thomas Etty or the Organic Gardening Catalogue.

Crimson Flowered* An enchanting sight in the spring garden, alongside pale green pea shoots and young mint. The jury is out on the flavor, but I find it delicate and appealing; others feel it is more of an ornamental addition to the allotment.

Bunyard's Exhibition A long pod and a prolific cropper. Yet another long-lived vegetable from Bunyard, the eighteenth-century nursery. Good flavor. Will need some support in the form of sticks and string.

Grando Violetto Old variety with purple beans in green pods.

D'Aguadulce a Tres Longue Cosse* Lovely black-and-white blossoms and plump pods; disease resistant.

Cascine* Italian variety with small, slender pods and tender beans.

*Available from US seed sources.

A fava bean in the kitchen

Vicia faba, incidentally the only bean native to Europe, has three stages when it is of interest to the cook. The first is when the pods are the size of an index finger, the immature beans barely the length of a large vitamin pill. It is at this point that I have cooked them whole, pod and all, with cubes of bacon, olive oil, mint, and a little water. Stewed for twenty minutes, the pods become tender enough to eat as they are, with hunks of bread to dip in the oily juices.

The second stage is when the pods are plump, the shadowy undulations of the beans visible through them, the skins bright and shiny. They are at their most useful point and work as well in a salad as they do in a risotto.

At the end of their lives, the beans start to get mealy, losing their nutty sweetness. Even now there is no reason to despise them. I often make a purée of these older specimens, thinning it to the consistency of hummus with olive oil and chopped dill or mint—a treat with roast lamb.

Had my first experience been of a sweet, young specimen, or of a larger one that had been skinned, then I might have taken to them earlier. Gray food tends not to win a child over.

I don't bother to skin young beans. Their skins are thin, pale green, and dissolve sweetly in the mouth. Anything larger than a thumbnail and I skin them. Popping them out of their parchmentlike skins after cooking takes but a minute, and is actually a rather agreeable kitchen task.

Seasoning your beans

Pork Of any persuasion, but especially in the form of blood sausage, prosciutto, and bacon.
Onions Particularly green onions and even onion tops.
Mint Perhaps in a sauté of beans, green onions, and olive oil.
Dill In a salad or for a purée of the beans with oil and hot sesame bread.
Salty cheeses Such as ricotta, goat, or sheep's cheese, especially feta, where it works well in a salad with cilantro and radishes. Blue cheeses, used in a salad or risotto, can intensify the sweetness of young, mild beans.

And...

* Although I have included a recipe for beans with cream, mint, and parsley, I also make a side dish for fish by stirring boiled and skinned fava beans into a classic parsley sauce. Sublime with any white fish or, indeed, a lump of gelatinous boiled ham.
* Planting summer savory between the rows will deter aphids. Blackflies hate the smell (or so they tell me). The savory can always be chucked on your pizza.
* I scatter a layer of grit around the stems of my newly transplanted young plants to stop the slugs getting too close.
* The beans keep better in the pod than out of it. I store mine in a thick brown paper bag in the fridge. Their sugar turns to starch quickly, so the less time they spend in storage the better. They freeze exceptionally well, possibly better than any other vegetable, but should be removed from their pods first.
* Cooked beans don't store very well. If I have cooked a glut and find them having to "overnight" in the fridge (say, for a salad with bacon and mint tomorrow), I pour in a glug of olive oil, toss well, and cover the dish with plastic wrap to prevent them from drying out.
* Fava beans like a bit of acidity. I find them at their best with goat cheese, tossed with a little thick yogurt and olive oil, served with a shaving of lemon zest, or dressed with a vinegar-heavy vinaigrette. The sharpness is an effective contrast to their slightly mealy quality.

"Mangetout beans" for eating with ham or roast lamb

I was wary of the idea of eating the pods until I grew my own beans; young vegetables tempt in a way that full-sized specimens often don't. The recipe is only worth doing when you can get your hands on unblemished beans without the cotton-wool lining to their pods and no longer than a middle finger. If you can catch them at this point in their lives, then you can eat them whole, like mangetout (snow peas). Serve warm, with thick pieces of bread or as a side dish for roast lamb or cold ham.

enough for 4
olive oil – ⅔ cup (150ml)
a medium onion
smoked bacon – 3½ ounces (100g)
very young fava beans in their pods – 1 pound (500g)
water – 1¾ cups (400ml)
a bunch of fresh mint
a lemon

Warm the olive oil in a large pan. Peel and finely chop the onion and add it to the oil. Cut the bacon into bite-sized chunks and stir it into the softening onion. The bacon fat should turn pale gold; the onion should soften without color.

Put the fava bean pods into the pan and pour in the water. Bring to a boil, then decrease to a light simmer, and simmer for fifteen to twenty minutes, until the pods have lost their bright color and are meltingly tender.

Coarsely chop the fresh mint and stir it into the beans. Serve with a thick wedge of lemon to squeeze over, and torn hunks of crusty bread to mop up some of the golden olive oil dressing.

A risotto of young beans and blue cheese

Green stuff—asparagus, nettles, peas, spinach, and fava beans—adds life and vigor to the seemingly endless calm of a shallow plate of risotto. My first attempt found me convinced that I didn't need to skin the beans. In theory it works, but the skins interfere with the harmony of stock, rice, and cheese and add an unwelcome chewiness. I am not sure you should ever need to chew a risotto.

enough for 4
shelled fava beans – 2 cups (300g)
butter – 4 tablespoons (50g)
a small onion
arborio rice – 1⅔ cups (300g)
a glass of white wine
hot stock – 6½ cups (1.5 liters)
soft blue cheese, such as Gorgonzola or Cashel – 7 ounces (200g)

Cook the fava beans in deep, lightly salted boiling water for four or five minutes, then drain and set aside. Unless the beans are very small, you may want to pop them from their skins. The choice is yours. Melt the butter in a heavy-bottomed pan. Peel and finely chop the onion, then leave it to cook in the butter until it is soft but shows no sign of browning. Add the rice, stir briefly to coat in the butter, then pour in the wine.

Little by little add the hot stock, stirring pretty much continuously, adding more only when each ladleful of stock has been absorbed by the rice. Check the rice for tenderness as you go; it should be ready about twenty minutes after adding it to the onion, and should still have a bit of bite. Stir in the cooked beans and the cheese in pieces, check the seasoning, and serve.

Green beans, cool white cheese, and hot radishes

The tiniest of fava beans have an affinity with young, snow-white goat cheeses. I like to use them in an early summer salad with Ticklemore, the cheese that Robin Congdon makes at his farm in Devon with milk from Sharpham Farm, the Buddhist retreat. Otherwise, I'll use whatever is suitably crumbly, milky, and mild. It is a salad that seems to gain much from being eaten outside, under the shade of an umbrella, when there is much new, pale green growth in the garden.

For two of us I use a little over 4 ounces (125g) of podded beans, an equal weight of cheese, ten radishes, and three or four sprigs of parsley. I use the parsley leaves whole, adding them to the boiled and skinned beans, the cut radishes, and the thinly sliced cheese with just a splash of olive oil, the mildest I have. The coolness of the cheese, the heat of the radishes, and the buttery taste of the beans make a fresh, clean-tasting salad of utmost purity.

The Italians, and especially the Florentines, who were known as "the bean eaters," have some noteworthy recipes for this mild bean. In the late 1980s I ate them lightly cooked and skinned in an arugula salad, then on the same trip, in a risotto with Gorgonzola. At home, I have also used the beans in risotto with goat cheeses the texture of fudge and with the saltier blues such as Beenleigh and the majestic Stichelton.

Fava beans and the pig

Fava beans have a kinship with ham in all its forms. At its most basic, raw fava beans can be slit down the middle with a thumbnail and eaten in the same bite as a piece of thinly cut ham. The most interesting version of this I have eaten involved newly picked beans from a friend's garden, each the size of a jelly bean, tucked inside slivers of dark, moist Joselito Gran Reserva ham from acorn-fed pigs. At a less rarefied level, bacon and boiled fava beans tossed in the bacon fat is a supper to which I return time and again.

A lump of smoked ham, served hot with some of its thin cooking juices and a thick mash of the beans, is warming on a chilly summer evening. (It works even better in winter if you remembered to freeze a few beans in the summer.) Ends of fatty bacon, which you can often buy for a song from a deli, make a quick weekday meal when chopped and sautéed with lightly boiled fava beans and lots of flat parsley, its leaves thrown almost whole into the pan. The merest splash of dry sherry will turn it into something altogether more soulful.

Fava beans, herbs, bacon, and its fat

enough for 2
shelled fava beans – 1⅔ cups (250g)
green onions – 6
a small bunch of dill
a small bunch of mint
white wine vinegar – 2 tablespoons
olive oil
smoked back bacon – 4 slices

Cook the fava beans in a deep pan of lightly salted boiling water. They should be tender in four or five minutes. Cool them under running water, popping the bright green beans from their pale skins with your finger and thumb and dropping them into a bowl as you go. If the beans are really small and young, I sometimes leave the skins on.

Finely slice the green onions and drop them into a bowl. Chop enough dill to give you a couple of heaping tablespoons. Pull a loose handful of mint leaves from their stems and add them to the onions with the dill and white wine vinegar. Crumble in a little salt and some coarse black pepper, then stir in enough olive oil to make a slushy dressing. I find 5 to 6 tablespoons (80 to 90ml) are enough.

Lay the bacon in a nonstick frying pan with the merest drop of olive oil and let it fry until the fat is golden and verging on the crisp. Fold the skinned beans into the herb dressing and divide between two plates. Put a couple of slices of bacon on each, tipping any hot fat in the pan over the beans.

The simplicity of fava beans and Spanish ham

There is a Spanish stall at the market. Each Saturday in midsummer I wait patiently at the counter while the *jamon* is carved. I am unsure which is more beautiful: the long, elegant leg on its steel stand or the fluid, methodical way in which the carver slices the gossamer-thin morsels of meat from the bone. I never take much, its price is breathtaking, but once home I savor every mouthful, as much out of respect for my wallet as for the pig. If I find young fava beans, or the ones in the garden are ready to pick, I marry the two—a simple plate of densely flavored, fat-besplodged ham the color of dried blood and fresh, bright-green beans. There is usually soup on the table too, watercress or spinach or fresh pea, and some scraps of dry, mild-tasting Manchego.

enough for 4 as a starter or as part of a light lunch
fava beans in their pods – 2 pounds (1kg)
air-dried ham – 3½ ounces (100g), very thinly sliced

for the dressing
sherry vinegar – a tablespoon
smooth Dijon mustard – half a teaspoon
olive oil (a fairly light one is best here) – 3 tablespoons
a handful of parsley leaves

Bring a pan of water to a boil. Shell the beans. Very lightly salt the water and add the beans. Return the water to a boil, then decrease the heat so that they boil merrily for three or four minutes or until they are tender. The exact cooking time will depend on the size and age of your beans but generally they take less time than you might expect. Drain them and cool under running water.

Pop the beans from their skins, unless they are very young and the size of a fingernail. This is a very pleasant way to spend ten minutes on a lazy afternoon. Place the pieces of ham, which should be in snippets about twice the size of a large postage stamp, on a serving plate.

Make the dressing by adding a small pinch of salt to the sherry vinegar and letting it dissolve. Add half a teaspoon of mustard—no more—then whisk in the olive oil with a fork. Chop the parsley leaves quite finely and add them to the dressing. Lastly, a few grinds of pepper. Toss the beans gently in the dressing and set aside for twenty minutes or so (they are fine for several hours if it makes life easier).

Scatter the beans over the ham and eat.

Creamed beans with mint

Fava beans are gentle, soothing, calm (particularly so when they have been skinned), a vegetable without the vibrancy of spinach or even peas. Surely we don't always want vegetables to be full of fireworks? Rather than fight this mild character with an addition of spice or bright tastes, I go along with it, and often serve the beans as a side dish with cream and perhaps a stirring of parsley. A dish as soporific as it is beautiful. Some poached ham would be nice here, as might a piece of lightly cooked white fish. Though I would be more than satisfied with some triangles of hot brown toast.

Should you happen to have any summer savory in the herb bed, this is your chance to use it.

enough for 4
shelled fava beans – 2⅔ cups (400g)
heavy cream – 1 cup (250ml)
a knifepoint of ground nutmeg
a handful of parsley leaves, chopped
mint – the leaves from 3 or 4 sprigs, chopped

Boil the beans in deep, very lightly salted water. When they are tender, drain them and put them back into the pan. Pop them out of their skins, if you like. Pour in the cream, add a little salt, some black pepper, and the nutmeg, perhaps, then fold in the chopped parsley and mint. I tend to keep it quite fine for this dish. If you are using savory, introduce it now. Bring the mixture to a quiet simmer, then spoon it alongside your ham, halibut, or whatever.

A green hummus

Elderly fava beans are possibly not on everyone's shopping list, but in late July, when their sugar has turned to starch and their skins are as thick as writing paper, I have still made a good meal of them. They make a fresh-tasting hummus that always surprises people with its green notes. A silk purse out of a sow's ear if ever there was one. There is another recipe for this in *The Kitchen Diaries*, but with dill. Good with bread, roast lamb, even alongside a piece of grilled fish. Like the popular chickpea recipe, somewhat addictive.

enough for 4
fava beans in their pods – 3 pounds (1.5kg)
olive oil – about 4 tablespoons
the juice of a small lemon
mint – the leaves from about 8 stems

Shell the fava beans and check for blemishes. Boil them in lightly salted water for six to nine minutes, depending on their size. The longer cooking time is because of the beans' age. Big brutes may take up to ten minutes. Drain and purée in a food processor with the olive oil, lemon juice, and mint leaves. I continue to purée, adding more oil if necessary, until I have a smooth pulp the consistency of cake batter.

A fava bean frittata

This little pancake has a springlike freshness with its filling of young, peeled fava beans and freckling of feathery dill. Curiously, it is not at all "eggy." In fact, a devout noneater of eggs, I have been known to finish a whole one by myself. A drizzle of yogurt over its crust or a few slices of smoked salmon at its side are possibilities too.

I really think this is only worth making with the smallest of fava beans, and they really must be peeled.

enough for 2 as a light main course
shelled young fava beans – 1⅓ cups (200g)
Parmesan – 1¾ ounces (50g)
eggs – 3
dill – about 2 tablespoons chopped
butter – a rounded tablespoon

Bring a deep pan of water to a boil, drop in the fava beans, and boil until tender. They should be ready after four or five minutes, depending on their size. Drain, cool slightly under running water, then pop the beans out of their little skins. Chop them roughly and set aside.

Finely grate the Parmesan. Break the eggs into a small bowl and mix them lightly with a fork. Stir in the Parmesan and the chopped dill. Preheat the broiler.

Melt the butter in a shallow pan, about 8 inches (20cm) in diameter. When it starts to froth, pour in the egg-and-cheese mixture. Add the peeled fava beans and let the frittata cook over a relatively low heat until the bottom has formed a golden crust. Lift the pan from the heat and slip it under the broiler until the eggs have set and the top is lightly colored.

Cut into wedges, like a cake.

Jerusalem artichokes

I almost missed the dusty brown wicker basket with its cargo of palest-ivory artichokes. Rolling them over in my hand and brushing the loose soil from them with my thumb, I wasn't even sure if they were artichokes at all. Slender and smooth, with the smell of fresh earth, they lacked the warts, knobs, and tight crevices that I associate with the root vegetable known for its capacity to produce velvety soups and triumphant wind. They had long tails and whiskers, too. When I got them home in their brown paper bag it was like washing baby mice under the cold tap.

I steamed the artichokes unpeeled, then browned them in a shallow pan of butter and oil, parsley, and a last-minute shot of lemon juice.

I had expected the usual earthiness, and the introduction of lemon juice only went on to highlight that, but what surprised was the warm nuttiness of the little tubers and the pleasing roughness of their skins. The outside was all texture, like eating walnuts, the inside a mouthful of ivory-hued, fudgy delight, with a whiff of the artichoke hearts with which they are often confused.

Beside them in a small pile were several slices of cold roast pork as thin as paper and three long shards of crisp crackling, its skin blistered with golden bubbles. No condiments save the buttery, walnut-colored juices and a scattering of burnt bits from the pan. Rarely has a meal of cold meat and vegetables been so satisfying, its sepia tones perfectly suited to the gray of a cold November day.

Despite its dullness of hue, the artichoke is a member of the sunflower family, and may take its name from the Italian *girasole*—because of the flowers' habit of moving with the sun. There is another line of thought, which I prefer, that the name is from Terneuzen, the third largest Dutch port and home to the Flying Dutchman, from where they were first imported to Britain. While either explanation makes sense, this artichoke's homeland is neither Holland nor Jerusalem but North America.

Jerusalem artichokes make you fart. This has probably cost them more than a few friends, but they have so much going for them, both as a vegetable for the allotment—their height makes an efficient windbreak for more tender vegetables such as spinach or peas—and in those legendary smooth cream soups, that I do everything I can to encourage people to try them. I have been known to add them quietly to a mixed-vegetable soup and not tell anyone. Perhaps quietly is not the right word.

And while the odd bay leaf in the cooking water or a thorough peeling may (or may not) calm their side effects, it really is just a case of learning to love them.

A Jerusalem artichoke in the garden

Once the stems are fully grown and the flower buds open, the artichoke's connection to the sunflower is unmistakable. The flowers are delicate, others might say pathetic, so I dig in a few Velvet Queen sunflowers among them to add a touch of opulence to their section of the garden. Their thick stalks and spreading roots take up quite a bit of space, which is why it is best to grow them near the back of the vegetable border. In a windy autumn, their stems may need tying back.

Prolific is a word I heard more than once before I planted my own artichokes. You get a lot going on underground from planting time in January and February (you can put them in as late as May) through to what can be a copious harvest in late autumn and winter. Many gardeners trim the flowers and the tallest of the shoots in midsummer to encourage the plant to plow all its strength into the slowly fattening tubers. I find this neither necessary nor aesthetically pleasing.

The tubers overwinter well enough in deep ground (pile soil on top if you think they might be too near the surface) and keep better there than in the house. If your ground freezes and you do need to bring them in, they will keep well if the air is a little damp. The vegetable crisper of the fridge is ideal.

I am looking out at mine as I write, their swaying stems and rich, tobacco brown winter foliage stands striking against the row of golden hornbeam that does its best to shield the garden from the worst of the west wind. The tallest and most elegant of vegetable plants, even in repose.

Topinambours, as the French know them, thrive on rich soil and sunshine and the slugs are partial to their tender new shoots, but they have few other demands. They will grow on a shady site, and even suffer neglect from the watering can. A patch will last for years if you wish it to, though replanting regularly will, say the experts, give you smoother tubers. And while everyone seems determined they will become a weed if you fail to clear the ground properly, I can think of worse weeds to deal with than one that will bring me soup of such solace.

An artichoke diary

February 23 A paper bag of beige tubers dusted with fine, black soil arrives on a winter morning, when the earth is white with frost. Artichokes will survive shade, and I decide to grow them close to the thick yew hedge that acts as an impenetrable boundary for the vegetable garden; a patch where little has previously even survived, let alone flourished. I fork the area lightly. The soil is rich but light, and surprisingly less sticky than it has been in past years. The recent frosts have broken down the soggy clods into something altogether more friable.

The tubers are Fuseau, unusually smooth, each with a pink nose at the pointed end. Ten small holes, 6 inches (15cm) deep and a good 8 inches (20cm) apart, are to be their home. I put them in nose up, then cover them with soil and a forest of hazel twigs to give any inquisitive foxes a poke in the eye.

April 16 First signs of life, here and there a furry shoot pokes through the soil like the ears of a startled hare. I run out with the coffee grounds and organic slug pellets.

May 4 Tufts of matte green leaves sprout from stems white with hairs, their edges cut as if with pinking shears.

May 15 Eighteen inches (45cm) high, the hairy stems and their long ears are leaning away from the hedge and toward the light, as befits their other name, the sunchoke. I tie them up with strong brown string.

November 9 The stems are taller than a man, and sway back and forth in the wind. The leaves have almost blackened with the first frosts, and are leaning across the path. They rustle as you push past them on the way to the compost. An eerie sound on a dark evening. If they were in a more exposed site, such as an open allotment, I would cut the stalks down and lay them over the soil to keep the tubers cozy through the winter.

November 17 The garden fork goes in and I lift out a huge root dripping with twenty or more long, smooth tubers. It is one of many, but I take only half of them, leaving enough behind to sprout next year.

Varieties

Not many, but I recommend Fuseau for a smooth, delicately flavored tuber; Stampede for a knobbly variety with the look of a Henry Moore sculpture, and Dwarf Sunray for those who prefer not to peel their 'chokes. Both Fuseau and Stampede are available from US seed sources.

A Jerusalem artichoke in the kitchen

The smoother varieties and those with fine, pale skins often need nothing more than a good wash under running water. The knobbly ones are likely to hold onto their mud like a rabbit holds onto its coat. I take a scrub brush to them; it's often the only way to get the soil out from the deeper notches and dimples. Once you break the skin you are in trouble, and will need the action of lemon juice to stop the white flesh browning. A bowl of acidulated water will do. Resist the temptation to peel them and instead celebrate the vegetable's wholehearted earthiness.

You can eat them raw, thinly sliced and tossed with parsley, nut oil, and the juice of an orange or lemon, or perhaps with shredded salami and again, more parsley. Artichokes like to be steamed or cooked in butter. Simmered only with stock or water, a soup of Jerusalem artichokes can give the impression of having been laced with cream, even when the only dairy product it contains is a tablespoon of butter.

Peeled, they are likely to turn to wet mush in the pan, so I scrub them instead. You can boil them with a little lemon in the water, but better, I think, to steam them in a colander set over merrily simmering water, in which case their flesh is less likely to collapse. Marry them to parsley, to lemon (to emphasize their earthy qualities), or to seafood and anoint them with butter. But the real trick is to bring them to tenderness in stock instead of water. Chicken or vegetable broth, and a careful eye for any signs of approaching tenderness, will reward you with a soup that has both sweetness and body. The tubers love a good chicken stock above all, and simmered together they will produce a soup far superior in terms of flavor and texture than mere water alone will ever produce. Boiled in water, they sometimes take on a disinfectant note.

If you are cooking them in oil or butter, they will benefit from five or six minutes in the steamer first. This will tenderize the innards, leaving less risk of them toughening in the frying pan.

When I first came across a recipe that married the root with scallops, I assumed it was an affectation—a plea from a chef desperate for attention. Who else could have contrived a terrine of thinly sliced scallops and artichokes framed with sprigs of chervil? Then, a while later, I came across a mention of artichokes with shrimp; then a soup, a salad, a posh restaurant dish that again brought together the earthiest of tubers and the most delicate of seafood. Warily, I tried them. Wonderful. The most successful partnership seems to be with scallops, particularly if you include the crescent-shaped corals.

Seasonings for the artichoke

Parsley The most fitting of all herbs, earthy but fresh, a perfect match. Fold a handful, coarsely chopped, into an artichoke salad, or more finely chopped into a soup. To my taste, the two are inseparable.

Lemon The best way to keep the vegetable from turning gray, but also as a welcome shock of freshness and light to balance the mineral tones.

Orange Finely grated and added to a dressing in an artichoke salad. Use with care.

Butter Even a thin slice added to oil for frying or roasting is rewarding.

Hazelnuts and almonds Toast and scatter over the surface of a soup; include in a warm salad of artichokes and young spinach leaves.

Walnuts and their oil Add toasted walnuts to artichoke soup; toss them into a salad of artichokes and lemon; use the oil to dress the warm tubers straight from the pan.

Bay leaves A must in artichoke soup.

Cream It is not always a necessary addition to soup, but even a mere swirl of heavy cream will introduce a little gentility into the proceedings. Until later, of course.

Scallops, shrimp Steam your artichokes and toss them with freshly cooked shrimp or queen scallops, a mass of chopped cilantro, and a dressing of olive oil and lemon juice.

And...

* The tubers first appear in the shops in late autumn, continuing throughout the winter, and should snap crisply. I avoid any that bend.
* I find artichokes keep best with a little of their soil attached—or at any rate unscrubbed—wrapped in newspaper, in the vegetable crisper of the fridge. A cold garage or shed will work just as well. Home growers, such as myself, will find they keep freshest when left in the soil.
* Peeling isn't always necessary. A good scrub is often enough. I chuck any trimmings in the stockpot.
* Once the artichokes have been trimmed, the discoloration of their white flesh can be halted not only by the usual lemon juice but also with a dash of wine vinegar in the soaking water. You won't taste it in the cooking.
* The extraordinary affinity that the artichoke has for shrimp and scallops is at its most simple and charming in a soup of puréed artichoke with a scattering of lightly fried scallop on top.
* Puréed or mashed artichokes work beautifully with almost any white fish, but sautéed hake, parsley sauce, and mashed artichokes is especially pleasing.
* Nutty, firm-textured cheeses—think of the Cheddars and Dales varieties, along with the Beaufort, Gruyère, and farmhouse Gouda-style cheeses— partner this root more successfully than the strongly flavored, softer varieties, which tend to bring out its bitterness.
* Though they are good enough with pork, the sweet, mild flavors of the roasted roots make a particularly fine contrast to the exceedingly savory pan stickings of a beef roast.
* Wind is almost inevitable. Just go with it.

A salad of raw artichokes

The juicy crunch of a raw artichoke bears many of the qualities of a water chestnut. Few ingredients pack such snowy crispness. I use them in a parsley-flecked salad to add a snap to baked pork chops, but have also offered them at a Saturday bread'n'cheese lunch of Cornish Yarg and Appleby's Cheshire. Lemon is essential if the peeled tubers are not to discolor.

> *enough for 2*
> a medium lemon
> olive oil
> walnut oil
> Jerusalem artichokes – 14 ounces (400g)
> parsley

Make the dressing first. Dissolve a good pinch of salt in the juice of the lemon, twist in a few turns of the peppermill, then whisk in enough olive and walnut oil to make a thickish dressing. I usually find two tablespoons of each is about enough. You want the lemon to really sing rather than sit quietly in the back row. Peel the artichokes, then slice them thinly, using a vegetable peeler. They will be almost transparent. I usually let the shavings of artichoke fall into the dressing so that they don't discolor.

Chop the parsley, but not too finely, then toss gently with the salad. Add any of the ingredients below or not, as the mood takes you.

Good things to add to your artichoke salad

* Hazelnuts, skinned and toasted.
* Toasted walnuts.
* Thin slices of grilled scallop.
* Peeled shrimp.

A warm salad of artichokes and bacon

"Monday cold cuts" is a key dish in our house: it shows our intent to use every scrap, to make the most of what we have, but it also gives me a break. It is one meal I don't have to think about other than sharpening the carving knife. The appearance of thin slices of cold meat on the first day of the week also gives me a chance to consider a side dish more interesting than a baked potato. Sometimes I bring out a bubble and squeak, fried in my old cast-iron pan, or some leftover mashed root vegetables warmed in a bowl over hot water with a tablespoon of butter; other times it's red cabbage, shredded with pickled walnuts as black as coal. Another favorite is a warm salad of some sort of root vegetable, fried or steamed, then turned in a mustardy dressing.

enough for 2
Jerusalem artichokes – 1 pound (500g)
smoked bacon – 7 ounces (200g)
olive oil – 3 tablespoons
walnut oil – a tablespoon
lemon juice – a tablespoon
whole-grain mustard – 2 teaspoons
flat-leaf parsley – a small bunch

Peel the artichokes, dipping each one into cold water containing a squeeze of lemon juice as you go. This will stop them browning. Pile into a steamer basket or colander and steam over boiling water until tender when pierced with the tip of a knife.

Meanwhile, cook the bacon in a nonstick pan until lightly crisp—you probably won't need any fat—then cut into finger-thick strips and drop into a salad bowl. Make a dressing with the olive oil, walnut oil, lemon juice, and mustard, whisking the ingredients together with a seasoning of salt and pepper. Chop the parsley and stir it into the dressing (the parsley is essential here, I think).

Slice the artichokes thickly, I like them quite chunky for this recipe. Over medium heat, warm the pan in which you cooked the bacon, then add the sliced artichokes, letting them cook until nicely colored on both sides. Now toss them carefully with the bacon and the dressing.

Serve with cold roast beef or chicken.

Roast artichokes

Preheat the oven to 400°F (200°C). Scrub the artichokes, say four or five per person, then slit them in half down their length. Warm a thick slice of butter and a glug of peanut or sunflower oil in a roasting pan. Put the artichokes in, cut side down. Crack open a whole head of garlic, squash 2 or 3 cloves per person with the flat of a knife—just enough to break the skin—then chuck them in the pan.

Roast for twenty-five to thirty minutes in the oven until the underside of the artichokes is crusty. Squeeze over the juice of half a lemon, maybe more, and a handful of coarsely torn parsley.

Jerusalem artichokes with walnut oil and lemon

Having discovered the delights of raw artichoke with lemon and walnut oil, it was only a matter of time before the ingredients took the leap into the pan. A main course of artichokes is probably more than most gentle people could take, so I use this as something to cuddle up to a main course. It is very good with smoked mackerel.

enough for 4 as a side dish
Jerusalem artichokes – 1½ pounds (750g)
butter – 5 tablespoons (75g)
walnut oil – a tablespoon
an open-textured loaf such as ciabatta – 4 slices
lemon juice
parsley leaves – a handful, coarsely torn

Wipe, scrub, or peel the artichokes as you think fit. Steam in a colander balanced over a pan of boiling water, or simply cook in boiling water, until just yielding to the point of a knife. Drain.

Melt the butter in a shallow, heavy-bottomed pan and add the walnut oil. When the fat is sizzling, add the artichokes and a generous grinding of salt. Leave them to color, then shake the pan or stir them to color the other sides. Tear the bread into wide hunks and tuck them among the vegetables. Leave to color here and there and soak up the pan flavors. Squeeze over a little lemon juice to lift the general earthiness, then toss with the parsley and eat.

A panfry with duck fat and bay

Jerusalem artichokes share with the potato an ability to drink up both dressings and the fat in which they cook. Roll a still-warm steamed artichoke or potato in a sharp oil and vinegar dressing and it will soak up the liquid like a sponge. It is this quality that makes them a candidate for cooking in luxurious mediums such as bacon fat or, better still, duck fat.

This contemporary twist on the sautéed potato is, as you might expect, something with which to garnish a steak. An ice-crisp salad of winter leaves (Belgian endive, radicchio, frisée, maybe) would slice the edge off its richness.

enough for 4 as a side dish
Jersusalem artichokes – 3 pounds (1.5kg)
a lemon
duck fat – 3 generous tablespoons
thyme – a couple of sprigs
bay leaves – a couple

Bring a deep pan of water to a boil. Scrub the artichokes, removing the most awkward of the lumps and bumps and dropping them into a bowl of water into which you have squeezed a little lemon juice. Steam the artichokes for seven minutes until almost tender. If they break a little, then it is all to the good.

Melt the duck fat in a shallow, heavy-bottomed pan and, once it starts to sizzle, add the thyme leaves and bay leaves. These are not an affectation—their effect is subtle but essential. Put the artichokes in the pan in one layer and season with salt. Let cook until the roots are crisp, golden, and tender, shaking the pan from time to time. They should be ready in thirty to thirty-five minutes.

A Middle Eastern seasoning for an earthy roast

December 2007 and a net of ivory and pink artichokes has turned up in the organic box, as knobbly as a bag of vertebrae. We have had them twice out of the garden already this week and I am not sure whether to laugh or cry. Sound and clean, they have a pink blush to them that makes them appear more delicate than they probably are. They tempt, though, and I decide to roast them to serve with the sliced cold ham and jar of fruit jelly in the fridge.

The tubers get a brief once-over under cold water, which makes their soft colors shine like young flesh, then I put them on the chopping board and whack each with a can of chickpeas. I could have used a rolling pin to break the rough-sided tubers but I like the squat heaviness of the can in the hand—it feels like the right tool for the job. The idea is, I suppose, to crack each one open so that the roughly broken insides as well as the skin might caramelize in the oven's heat.

For no particular reason, I decide to follow the earlier roast artichoke recipe but to season the sweet, earthy roots with the piquancy of a couple of chopped pickled lemons, a teaspoon of crushed coriander seeds, and the throat tickle of large, coarse parsley leaves. The contrast with the pan-cooked ones with fresh lemon I mentioned previously is striking.

A new artichoke soup

I have long made a simple artichoke soup by adding the scrubbed tubers to softened onions, pouring over stock, and then simmering until the artichokes fall apart. I often add a little lemon juice, bay leaves, and sometimes a thumb of ginger. I blitz it in the blender, then stir in lots of chopped parsley. Some might introduce cream at this point but I honestly don't think it's necessary. The soup is velvety enough. It has become a staple in this kitchen over the last few winters; its warm nuttiness is always welcome on a steely-skied January day.

Late in the winter of 2008, possibly having had one day too many of what Beth Chatto calls "dustbin-lid skies," I changed the soup's tone by adding a stirring of bright green spinach. As often happens, it came about by accident—a bowl of creamed spinach left over from a boiled ham lunch—added to the soup just to use it up. The magic in this soup is in the marriage of earthy cold-weather food and a shot of mood-lifting chlorophyll. Spring is obviously stirring.

enough for 4 to 6
large leeks – 2
butter – 3 tablespoons (40g)
Jerusalem artichokes – 1 pound (450g)
bay leaves – 2
light stock or water – 4 cups (a liter)

for the spinach
butter – a thick slice
large spinach leaves – 1 pound (500g)
crème fraîche – 2 heaping tablespoons
ground nutmeg

Finely slice the white and palest green part of the leeks, wash thoroughly in plenty of running water, then drain. Melt the butter in a heavy-bottomed saucepan, add the sliced leeks, then let soften over low to medium heat for fifteen to twenty minutes. They need to remain green and white and shouldn't brown at all. I find the easiest way to achieve this is to place a round of wax paper on top of the leeks, followed by the pan lid. A regular stir will help.

Rinse and coarsely chop the artichokes and add them to the leeks. Continue cooking for a few minutes, then add the bay leaves and stock or water, and bring to the boil. Decrease the heat so that the soup bubbles gently, partially covered. It will take about twenty-five minutes before the artichokes are tender. Blitz the soup in a blender until smooth. I should probably remind you not to overfill the blender container. Pour into a bowl.

Make the spinach cream: Melt the butter in the artichoke pan and add the spinach. Turn it from time to time until it softens. Press the spinach against the side of the pan and drain off the liquid. Do this thoroughly. Transfer to a blender and add the crème fraîche, a tiny pinch of ground nutmeg, and a little salt and blitz.

Warm the artichoke soup (it may be hot enough already if you have worked quickly), spoon into soup bowls, then add a couple of spoonfuls of the spinach to each bowl and mix the two lightly together as you eat.

A casserole of artichokes and pork for deepest winter

A damp January morning (2006) and a walk round the vegetable patch reveals only two herbs in reasonable condition: rosemary, which loses some of its potency in winter, and parsley, most of which has collapsed in a dead faint to the ground. I value both enormously, feeling even now that they have an edge on the imported basil and spindly thyme in the markets. Both respond well to earthy winter cooking.

Chilled to the bone (I find it's the damp that gets to me more than the temperature), I come in and use the parsley where it really matters: in a pan of braised artichokes and pork sausage, whose brown depths I freshen up with Italian lemons and, at its side, some crisp and chewy greens.

enough for 4
pork sausages – 8 really good ones
olive oil
onions – 4 medium
garlic – 2 cloves
small mushrooms – 9 ounces (250g)
Jerusalem artichokes – 1 pound (500g)
a large lemon
fennel seeds – a teaspoon
light stock or water to cover – about 2 cups (500ml)
flat-leaf parsley – a small bunch, coarsely chopped
steamed cavolo nero, spring cabbage, or purple sprouting, to serve

Brown the sausages all over in a little oil in a Dutch oven or other heavy pot. Set aside. Peel the onions and cut them into thick sections, then add to the pot in which you browned the sausages, pouring in a little more oil if you need to. Let the onions soften over medium heat until they are tender enough to crush with a wooden spoon. Don't hurry this; it should take fifteen to twenty minutes. Peel and finely slice the garlic and add it to the onions. Halve the mushrooms and add them too.

Peel or simply scrub the artichokes, then cut them in half. Add them to the pot, pushing the onions aside, and let them color slightly. Now return the sausages back to the pot. Cut the lemon into fat chunks and tuck them in along with the fennel seeds and a good seasoning of salt and black pepper.

Pour over enough stock or water to cover and bring to a boil. Decrease the heat and simmer for about thirty minutes, until the vegetables are truly tender. If there is too much liquid, increase the heat and let it reduce a little. Stir in the parsley, check the seasoning, and eat with the greens.

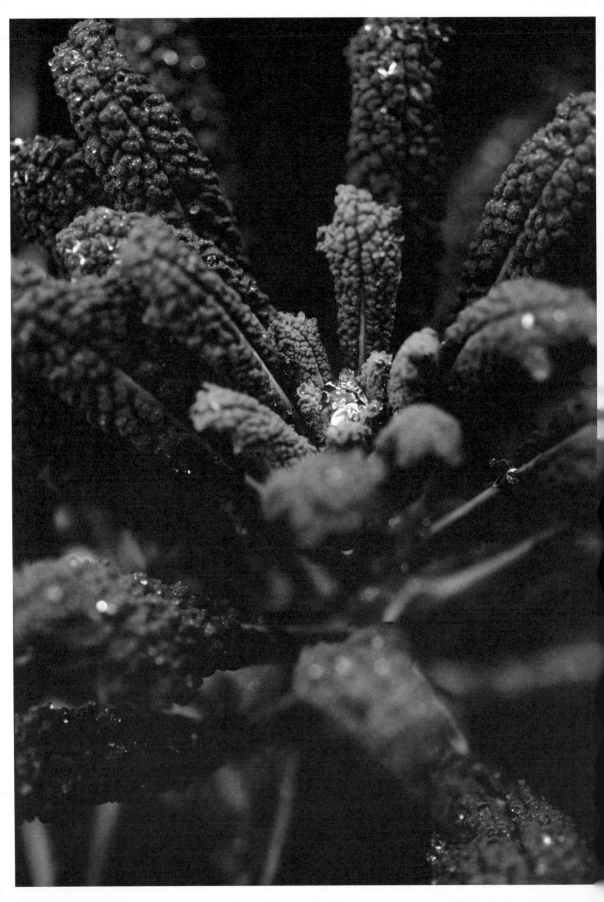

Kale and cavolo nero

From a distance, huge undulating pillows of green and dusky blue. Close up, coarse, frilly leaves with a tough central rib. In the mouth, richly textured, a little chewy, sweet, and slightly bitter. Kale is both pleasingly humble yet vibrant and big flavored, a forerunner of the full-headed cabbages we know today.

The leaves are long, plumelike, and run from the mildly serrated through to the heavily fringed and indented. They are so beautiful they could be grown as an ornamental, while their texture can be softer than spring greens or so tough you feel like a donkey chomping at thistles. Much depends on the variety.

Since earliest times the kales have kept us going during the hungry gap from January to March. So important was the crop that the Romans referred to the month of February as Kalemonath. It was often the only leaf crop standing in late winter—good enough reason for them to be thought of as a survival vegetable, something to chew our way through when the land is bare, but our attitude is changing. Kale has gone from a food of poverty to one of supreme trendiness. Much of its current popularity has to do with the leaves' high vitamin content and the fashion for growing your own—kale is an easy and reliable crop. The plants are relatively pest free too, which is partly why they are the winter darlings of our organic farmers (though they are apparently the very devil to pick in quantity).

There are four kales of real interest: red Russian, which is a soft silver-green edged with pink; black, which is better known as cavolo nero; curly kale, whose leaves are almost as tightly clenched as old-fashioned parsley; and the late, flat-leaved form often called Hungry Gap.

Where we might harvest a cabbage for its entire head, kale leaves tend to be picked individually in a cut-and-come-again fashion. At least they are on my patch. Sometimes, especially from organic-box growers, they arrive in a whole, gracefully arching bunch. While fans like me get overexcited at the sight of a crate of curly kale leaves at the market in January, I should probably mention that others find this member of the brassica family rather coarse and difficult to deal with.

I am heartily grateful that what was once consigned to cattle (and still is at the end of the season, when the herds are allowed into fields of unsold crops) is now the most fashionable of all the green vegetables. Some of its new popularity is due to the publicity the leaves have received for their apparent cancer-fighting abilities, more to the new varieties whose bitter notes have been somewhat bred out, but I suspect the true breakthrough is due to Ruthie Rogers and Rose Gray at the River Café in London. Their full-bodied bean soups, richly laced with garlic and Parmesan, often feature the black-green kale we know as Nero di Toscana, cavolo nero, or black palm cabbage. I like to think it is because of them that you can now pick up a bag of black cabbage, albeit mild and ready-trimmed, in the more enterprising supermarkets.

Cavolo nero was the first of the cabbage family to be planted in my garden, and I welcome its presence in the bone-chilling patch after New Year, when it stands, embarrassingly ragged but curiously elegant, against the frost-white soil. Those frosts, incidentally, sweeten its character. Its long, blue-black leaves are pretty much all that is left on my vegetable patch in February. Well, that and Jerusalem artichokes. A combination best avoided by the easily embarrassed.

Kale in the garden

The fancier-leaved forms of kale are the most hardy and the most pest resistant. The softer, wavy-leaved plants are slightly less hardy and will attract the attention of the cabbage white butterfly. I throw a net over mine in summer, removing it only when the weather is too cold to entice a butterfly out to play.

You can grow plants from seed either in situ or in seed trays, moving them on to small pots and then, when they are feeling strong enough, to the garden. Sow from April to June in order to harvest in late winter. Sown under glass or on a windowsill, your seedlings should be through in ten days or so.

At six to eight weeks old, the seedlings should be sturdy enough to transplant. I use a dibble to make a deep hole, then lower the young plant in. A thumb will do. About 16 inches (40cm) is usually enough between the plants, certainly in my garden. Rather than pushing the soil back into place with my hands, I puddle water in from a watering can and leave them to sort themselves out. I put a stick in, to which I should tie them, but I find the heavier, more indented leaves generally hold on without any help from garden string. They hook themselves round the stick. The plants need regular watering but are less capricious than other cabbages, even tolerating a little shade, and will withstand any amount of frost. Some varieties, such as Russian kale, don't show their true colors till the air is cold enough. Few sights, vegetable or otherwise, are more breathtaking than a patch of Russian kale in the snow, its leaves the hauntingly beautiful dusty greens and faded pinks of an old tapestry.

Varieties

Dwarf Green/Blue Curled* Exceptionally hardy, positively thrives in the cold.
Frosty A very curly form, growing taller than most.
Winterbor* The young leaves are tightly curled and frilled, opening to a somewhat flatter leaf as they mature. The pale blue-gray of Paris at dusk. I have much success growing this variety.
Hungry Gap Robust, reliable, heavily curled leaves.
Winter Red* Flat type with gently frilled edges. Colors well once the frost is here.
Redbor* Deeply frilled, dark pink form. Pleasing color in the winter vegetable patch.
Red Russian* Pink-purple veins and rose edges to sweet and tender leaves. Only colors up in exceptionally cold weather.
Nero di Toscana* What the Italians mean when they say cabbage. Long, almost black, blistered leaves with wide stems. Strongly flavored, will withstand virtually any amount of cold. A very popular variety with my snails.

*Available from US seed sources.

Kale in the kitchen

I particularly look forward to the arrival of the greens we pick by the leaf rather than by the whole head. Flat leaved from the garden; deeply curled from the box scheme in Buckfastleigh; purple stemmed from the market in the East End. It enriches my life even before I put it in the pot. Just heaped into the sink, the leaves are handsome against the stainless steel. Once the icy water collects in droplets, glistening like diamonds in their frills and waves, I feel uplifted, invigorated.

I have shocked people by adding curly kale, tugged from its stalk in stamp-sized nuggets, to a salad. It works if the produce is young and there is grilled bacon involved, or slivers of speck or salami or chorizo, and if the dressing has a dab of mustard in it. Lemon, too, will make your lunch sing, but not in the same salad as bacon. You can dip the leaves into deep boiling water and come up with an accompaniment of vivid purity—wonderful on a bowl of white rice with a drizzle of toasted ginger and soy—or you can steam and toss it in almost-melted butter and lemon juice.

Kale lends itself to many of the same treatments as cabbage and several of the Asian greens. It is worth checking out those sections in this book and using the softer-leaved kales in their place. The tough kales—robust, literally bouncing with health—need careful handling. With their tough stalks, they are apt to get stuck in your teeth. At least, they do in mine. In my kitchen, the leaves are shredded, stalks and all, and plunged into boiling, unsalted water before being chucked into a smoking pan of oil, garlic, sliced red chiles, and shredded ginger. Tossed briefly, then quickly out on to warm plates. The chiles get stuck in the leaf folds and offer occasional and unexpected fireworks in the mouth. Either that, or I tear the leaves from their thick stems, trudging the latter to the compost heap the next day.

Seasoning your kale

Cream, mustard, juniper, caraway, bacon, and the other flavors so happy
to coexist with the headed or sprouting brassicas are appropriate here, but
there are a few others that seem to work especially well with the strong-
leaved kales.

Eggs A softly poached egg dropped onto a plate of steamed kale makes
a quick and cheap supper dish.
Anchovies Chopped finely and "melted" into warm butter, then tossed
with the greens.
Ham Stridently flavored leaves work well stirred into soups made with
ham stock.
Vinegar Use to temper kale's more ribald notes. Use it generously in
a dressing for steamed or raw (young) kale.
Potatoes Work well in a soup with the tougher leaves. Add chunks
of garlicky sausage too.
Lemon A pacifier.

And...

* Bacon is not the only cured pork to get on with the kale family. Cured
  sausages, chorizo, speck, and coppa all marry well, as do pancetta and lardo,
  the preserved pork fat from Italy. Apart from making good additions in
  their own right, they will all soften over heat to form an excellent cooking
  medium in which to toss the leaves.
* The kales become bitter as they age. Stick to the smaller fronds if this
  worries you.
* I have met people who put raw kale in their smoothies (gawd luv us).
  They did look exceptionally healthy.
* We are now starting to see kale all year round in supermarkets. Rather than
  bemoan the merging of the seasons as I usually would, I feel pleased that the
  lowly ancestor of the cabbage is getting more popular. Though I still think
  it looks out of place in July.
* Steamed kale, energized with a squirt of lemon, is an acceptable side dish
  for most of the fishes, especially the gelatinous skate and the cheap and
  rather more sustainable mackerel.

A soup-stew of beans and cavolo nero

The soup-stew, a bowl of spoon-tender meat, beans, and aromatics that partly collapse into the surrounding stock, is one of the suppers I hold dearest. More often taken as lunch, this is food that feeds the soul as much as the belly, enriching, calming, quietly energizing. This is the cooking on which to lavish the cheapest cuts going, the fatty, bony lumps that butchers sell at reduced prices: mostly cuts from the neck and lower legs. Ingredients whose sole purpose is to give body to the liquid in which they cook.

A knuckle end of prosciutto would be a sound addition here, if your local deli will sell you one. Most will charge very little. Butchers are an excellent source of ham bones with much meat attached. Failing that, I use a lump of ham, complete with its thick layer of fat.

enough for 4 to 6
dried beans, such as cannellini, butterbeans, or borlotti – 8 ounces (250g)
bay leaves – 2
olive oil
pancetta in the piece – 5 ounces (150g)
large onions – 2
carrots – 2
garlic – 2 large cloves, chopped
tomatoes – 14 ounces (400g), chopped
water or vegetable stock – 4 cups (a liter)
a small butternut squash or pumpkin
a meaty ham bone or knuckle of prosciutto
a short length of rind from a lump of Parmesan
flat-leaf parsley – a handful, coarsely chopped
cavolo nero – 2 large handfuls, or half a small cabbage, cut into wedges

Soak the beans overnight in deep, cold water. Drain, put them in a large, deep saucepan, and cover them with fresh water. Bring to a boil, then remove the froth from the surface with a slotted spoon. Drop in the bay leaves and a tablespoon or so of olive oil and let boil merrily for forty-five minutes to an hour, until tender (older beans tend to take a little longer). Add salt to the water about twenty minutes before the end of cooking. Drain and set aside. (I sometimes put a shot of olive oil over them at this point to prevent them sticking together.)

Cut the pancetta into short lengths or fat cubes, put them in a deep pan with a couple of spoonfuls of oil, and set over medium heat. Peel the onions, halve them, and slice them thinly. Once the pancetta has begun to sizzle, add the onions and stir them from time to time until they soften.

Scrub the carrots, cut them into large dice, and add to the onions with the garlic. Let everything soften without coloring, lowering the heat as and when you need to. Add the tomatoes and let them soften and melt a little into the other vegetables before pouring in the water or stock. Peel and coarsely chop the squash or pumpkin and stir it in.

Now is the time to add the ham bone and Parmesan rind. Either one will make a huge difference to the finished flavor. Bring the soup almost to a boil, then decrease the heat so that it simmers gently. Cover with a lid but set it askew, so that some of the steam escapes. Let simmer, with only the occasional stir, for an hour and a half, by which time the soup should be thick, rich, and heavy.

Add the beans to the pot along with the parsley and cabbage leaves. Continue cooking for ten to fifteen minutes. Serve with grated Parmesan.

Black cabbage and bacon—a fry-up

A fantastic little recipe, cheap, simple, and fast. I usually have some bread with this, if only to rub round the plate afterwards. This is best on very hot plates.

> garlic – 2 cloves
> butter – a thick slice
> mildly smoked bacon or pancetta – 5 ounces (150g)
> cavolo nero – 4 handfuls

Peel the garlic and chop it finely. Let it soften fragrantly with the butter in a shallow pan over a sprightly heat.

Cut the bacon into chunks or thick strips, whatever tickles your fancy, then let it fry with the garlic until its fat is pale gold. If the cavolo nero leaves are large, tear them up a bit, then add to the sizzling bacon and toss in the garlicky fat. As soon as the leaves relax, put them and the fat onto hot plates.

Young kale with lemon and garlic

I often take bright young leaves and their sprouting shoots, cook them briefly in boiling water, then toss them into sizzling butter seasoned with garlic and lemon as an accompaniment for grilled pork belly, a roast fillet of lamb, or a nice piece of fish. That said, it still takes up more room on the plate than the meat.

Red Russian kale, which I often cook in this way, is finer boned than the curly plumes we know so well. The heavily laced leaves have a fragility to them, and wilt quickly after picking. For all their gentility and mauve-pink blush, they still carry something of the coarseness of the stronger stuff.

enough for 2 as a side dish
kale or any tender young greens – 2 large handfuls
butter – 2 tablespoons (30g)
olive oil – a little
garlic – 2 cloves
lemon zest – a little
the juice of half a lemon

Wash the greens and set them aside. Bring a pan of water to a boil, salt it lightly, and cook the greens for no longer than a minute or two. They must retain their crispness and vigor. Drain and set aside.

Meanwhile, warm the butter and oil in a shallow pan, peel and crush the garlic, and soften it in the butter and oil. Add a little grated lemon zest (a couple of teaspoons should suffice), then, as the butter starts to froth, squeeze in the lemon juice. Lower in the greens and toss them gently in the hot, lemony garlic butter. Correct the seasoning and serve immediately.

Kale with golden raisins and onions

Even though much of the bitterness of this cultivar has been bred out, some extra sweetness is often welcome. Casting around for something sweet to scatter over a plate of steamed kale, I suddenly remembered the Sicilian habit of adding golden raisins to soft, sweet onions. The contrast between the leaves and their seasoning is strangely comforting. Quite when you might eat this is debatable. We first ate it with treacly rye bread and Gruyère cheese, next to fillets of smoked mackerel. It is tricky to know where it would sit most comfortably.

enough for 2
kale or cavolo nero – 2 large handfuls
a medium onion
olive oil
golden raisins – 3 tablespoons

for the dressing
a blood orange
white wine vinegar – 2 tablespoons
extra-virgin olive oil
capers – 2 tablespoons

Wash and trim the leaves. Peel the onion and slice it thinly into rings. Pour a thin layer of oil, say a couple of tablespoons, into a shallow pan and let the onion cook for fifteen minutes or so, until soft and sweet. It will need the occasional stir to stop it browning beyond a pale honey color.

While the onion cooks, squeeze the orange juice into a small bowl, add the wine vinegar, then beat in up to five tablespoons of olive oil, to give a sweet-sharp dressing. Stir in the capers and a grinding of black pepper. Steam the greens briefly.

Pour the blood orange dressing into the pan with the onion, shake in the golden raisins, and spoon over the leaves.

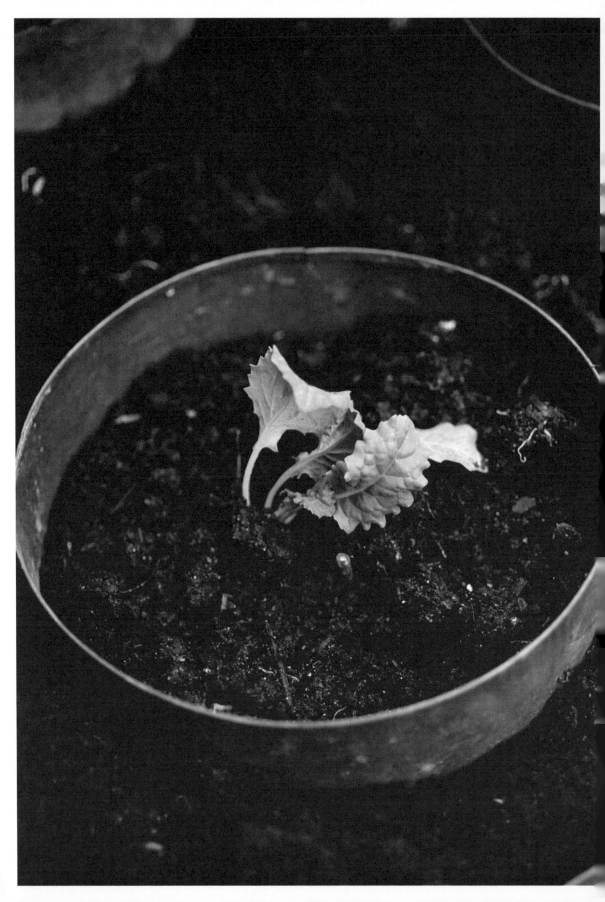

Chicken broth with pork and kale

Kale is just one possibility for bulking out this supper of pork balls and broth. I use it because I like the fullness of its leaves with the smooth pork balls. You could use any member of the greens family, and particularly Savoy cabbage. The important bit is not to overcook the greens.

enough for 3 to 4

for the pork balls
ground pork – 14 ounces (400g)
small, hot chiles – 2
green onions – 4
garlic – 2 cloves
parsley – 6 bushy sprigs
mint – 6 bushy sprigs
a little oil

for the soup
chicken stock – 4 cups (a liter)
kale leaves – 4½ ounces (125g)

Put the pork into a mixing bowl. Finely chop the chiles and add them with their seeds to the pork. Chop the green onions, discarding the roots and the very darkest tips of the leaves, peel and crush the garlic, and add with the green onions to the pork. Pull the parsley and mint leaves from their stems and chop coarsely, then add to the pork mixture with a generous seasoning of salt. Mix thoroughly, then roll into about sixteen balls.

Warm a shallow film of oil in a nonstick pan and add the pork balls, and cook until they are nicely toasted all over.

Pour the stock into a saucepan and bring to a boil, season carefully with salt and black pepper, then lower in the pork balls. Decrease the heat and simmer for five to seven minutes, until they are cooked through.

While the balls are cooking, pull the kale leaves from their tough stalks and cook them briefly—about one or two minutes only—in boiling salted water, then drain (don't be tempted to cook them in the stock). Lower the kale into the soup and serve immediately.

Leeks

The leek is the vegetable of clear, white winter skies and kitchen windows fogged up with condensation. It is garden soil glistening blue with frost; grainy potato soups the color of antique linen; itchy socks that have slid down the back of your Wellingtons, toes numb with cold. I like the gardener's expression, "a good stand" of leeks, and that the upper green part is called a flag. For that is what they do, stand and wave, when all else in the garden or allotment has collapsed in a tangle of crisp, brown stems.

The leek is the onion's refined sister, brought here by the Romans, for the times you want the latter's silken texture but less of its bold sweetness. The white stalk is especially delicate, tender, succulent, subtle. But unlike more extravagant cooks, I make use of the coarser green leaves too (in soup, mostly, and in chicken stock). Musselburgh is the one I grow. Renowned for its long, green leaves, it's an essential ingredient in cockie-leekie (potato and leek soup).

Although of the same family, the leek has none of the sugary stickiness you get in a slowly baked onion. Less rugged and hearty, the slender green one turns up not as the backbone of a rustic dish but in an altogether subtler role. It is linked with gentle, even genteel, cooking, such as chilled vichysoisse in a fine china bowl, leeks vinaigrette, leeks mimosa (steamed, chilled leeks with finely grated hard-boiled egg yolks the color of primroses), and Scotch broth to heal the sick.

As a farm crop, leeks are backbreaking work. They cannot be machine harvested and rely on handpicking in freezing weather. A sobering thought as we tuck into our steaming bowl of potato and leek soup.

A leek in the garden

You can sow leek seeds under cover in early spring, planting them out in early summer. Having limited indoor space, I buy mine as immature plants in May and June for harvesting from late autumn through to next spring. I rarely pick before November. These "plugs" require a nice, deep hole—use a pencil if you have no dibble—and should be lowered in without crushing the fragile roots. The plants need around 6 inches (15cm) between them. Rather than filling the hole around their stems with soil, pour water in from the watering can and let them sort themselves out.

Young leeks need plenty of water but, once established, they are good-natured and undemanding. More than enjoying a drop now and again, they like a thorough soaking every fortnight or so. During the growing season, pile earth up around the shaft of the leek; this will encourage extra-long growth of the white part that is so useful in the kitchen.

Unlike onions, which have to be lifted and dried, leeks will stand in the patch all winter. Pick as you need them.

A leek diary

Leeks wallow in moist, dense soil. They don't like their long, white roots to be waterlogged in cold weather, but will take a bit of shade if they must. A good frost usually sees off the rust to which they are prone.

July 22 The "leeklets" that arrived a month ago, wisplike in their plastic tray, are now almost pencil thick, and I plant them, the splayed width of my hand apart, in a partly shaded, damp bed near the medlar tree. As usual I'm growing the old Scottish variety, Musselburgh, a blue-green-leaved leek of mild flavor and medium size that should plump up by late autumn and still be standing in the new year.

I make deep holes, a good 6 inches (15cm) deep, with an oak dibble, then drop the young leeks into the hollows, taking care not to bash their roots. Instead of pushing the soil in around them, I "puddle" them in as is traditional, filling the hole around each leek with water from the watering can instead.

August 1 A sultry morning, still and strangely ominous. The foxes have dug up the leeks, leaving them and their fragile roots scattered over the garden like bits of green and white string. I replant them all, cursing.

Throughout the autumn, the shafts continue to thicken, the leaves change from green to blue. They get the odd watering and an occasional stroke.

January 31 A stand of leeks means a great deal to me at this point in the growing year. Little else is around, and I love the way they stand proudly through heavy frosts and even deep snow. A midnight walk up through the vegetable patch reveals leeks sparkling in the frosty night air, as if sprinkled with sugar. I normally start digging them up, one or two at a time, around now. I have only a few, and to be honest they are not very straight, but they will last me through until the finger-thick ones arrive once more at the market.

Varieties

Leeks for winter and spring eating
Sow in spring, plant out in June and July.

Musselburgh* A late Scottish variety from before 1834, known for its mild flavor and long, thick stalks.
Blue Solaise* A French variety known for its hardiness and its ability to stand in the garden in good condition for longer than most. Wonderful blue-green flags.
King Richard* A slender, long-shafted early variety. Plant in April for August pulling. Will keep well until after Christmas.
St. Victor Established French variety with distinctive blue leaves. Very hardy and very late; plant out in July for pulling the following late winter/spring.
Siegfried Late-maturing, tough old thing, especially suited to chilly areas of the country. Invaluable for those with long, cold winters.

Leeks for summer and autumn eating
Sow indoors in winter, plant out in April.

Toledo A popular, late leek with a long shaft.
Pandora* An early, well-flavored variety for autumn eating. Will stand a bit of frost, but not a hardy leek.
Varna* A tall, slim leek suitable for summer eating. Mild enough to eat in salads like a spring onion if picked small enough.

*Available from US seed sources.

A leek in the kitchen

Leeks are a little more demanding of the cook. Whereas an onion caught around the edges by a bit of overcooking will take on a welcome rustic note, a leek scorched is a leek ruined. You cannot rescue a pan of browned leeks. Their flesh should remain pearlescent, which is why I cook them with a gentler hand than I would an onion: in a taller pan, over a lower heat, covered not only by a lid but with a round of wax paper, albeit carelessly torn, that ensures the vegetables steam rather than fry.

When they have been steamed or softened in butter, leeks are very pleasing with eggs, especially in a soufflé, stirred into scrambled eggs, or caught within the tender folds of an omelette.

A leek is what you reach for when a fish dish requires a touch of onion. Fish pie, made with haddock and mussels, climbs to a different level when you add the fish to a tangle of lightly stewed leeks. Creamed leeks with grilled scallops is a very fine dish. Leeks are more appropriate—less overbearing, subtler, more integrated—than onions in a fish soup.

The leek collects grit between its layers as it grows. No other vegetable needs such careful attention in the sink. No cursory rinse here, but a thorough cleansing in ice-cold water to extract every last speck of trapped grit. I peel back and discard the outer layer, which is often tough, then slit the leek down its length, stopping shortly before the root. First I hold it under the cold tap, opening the layers out like a fan, then swish it around in a bowl of cold water. If I am washing shredded leeks, then I let them sit in water for a few minutes, to give the fallen grit time to settle at the bottom of the bowl.

It is butter rather than oil that brings out the best in this member of the allium family, which is another reason to keep the heat low. Their pale green leaves love cream too, and I often stir a spoonful or two into a pan of shredded and softened leeks to go with a grilled ham steak or to slide into the crack of a baked potato. Wonderful, too, with mackerel, especially when its skin is charred black from the grill. Oil, with the exception of that in a French dressing, does very little to enhance the flavor or texture of this vegetable.

Seasoning your leeks

Butter The preferred cooking medium for all leeks, thin or fat.
Cheese Most cheeses have an affinity for any member of the onion family. Use saltier sheep's cheeses for the crust of a leek gratin or to amplify the flavor of a sauce.
Blue cheese In a soup, gratin, or sauce. The more strident cheeses work better than the timid.

Anise Tarragon, chervil, and fennel all flatter the flavor of a leek stew or soup.

Bacon Add diced bacon to a leek soup; wrap slices around blanched leeks before sliding them into a gratin; add snippets of broiled bacon to a leek tart.

Chicken Of all the meats you can partner with this allium, chicken seems the most comfortable. Particularly in broths and stews or baked together in a pie.

Potatoes Perhaps most famously married in a soup, the two can also be baked slowly with a little stock, or the leeks used as a stuffing for a baked potato.

Mint The most useful herb next to parsley when cooking with this elegant vegetable.

And...

* The deeper the trench you dig, the longer your leek will be. Exhibitionist growers have been known to employ old drainpipes to get the length they need.

* Short, fat leeks are hardier than more elegant strains, which is why our own tend to that shape rather than to the slim ones from warmer European climates.

* Washing a leek can be a peaceful, if finger-chilling task. Split the leek right down the shaft, splay out the layers, and rinse long and carefully under running water. Leaving a split leek in cold water will make it curl.

* The top part of the green flag is usually too coarse to interest anyone but a keen composter, but farther down, where the color starts to soften, it is worth using if you cook it slowly enough with plenty of butter or stock. Tough leaves really should be added to the stockpot.

* It is worth trying a leek instead of an onion in many classic onion dishes. The result is often more delicate.

* If I'm honest, I use leeks so much because onions make me cry and I don't have to peel them.

* A lovely way to present this vegetable is to cut the stalk and pale green bit into short lengths, then simmer it, covered by a lid, with a generous slice of butter, a glass of white wine, and a spoonful or two of water. Simmer until it is soft and tender when pierced with the tip of a knife. Leeks, butter, and wine are a threesome that deserves to be better known.

* You can grill leeks of small to medium girth with great success. I prefer to blanch them for a couple of minutes in boiling water first, then place them on the grill or a grill pan until their sides start to color. Dress with olive oil and squeeze lemon over while they are still warm.

Potato soup with leeks, blood sausage, and parsley

The potato and the leek are happy bedfellows, as anyone who has eaten a good vichyssoise will know. Softer than potato and onion, more graceful than a chowder, warm potato and leek soup has a peaceful, almost soporific quality. A silky, cool-weather soup that somehow manages to taste creamy and rich with only the smallest amount of butter and no cream in it.

> *enough for 4 to 6*
> large leeks – 2
> butter – 3 tablespoons (40g)
> medium celery ribs – 4
> floury potatoes – 14 ounces (400g)
> light stock or water – 6½ cups (1.5 liters)
> parsley – a small bunch, chopped
> blood sausage, boudin noir, or morcilla – 9 ounces (250g)

Discard the toughest of the leaves from the leeks, then cut the tender white and palest green flesh into thin rounds. Rinse thoroughly under running water to remove any trapped grit, then add them to a heavy saucepan with the butter. Let them cook over low to medium heat for a good fifteen to twenty minutes, without letting them color, until they are soft enough to crush between your fingers.

Once they have started to soften, you can finely slice the celery and add it to the pan, then peel and chop the potatoes and stir them in too. Cover the pot with a lid and let the vegetables sweat and soften without coloring, then pour in the stock or water and bring to a boil. Decrease the heat so that the soup bubbles gently and partially cover it with a lid. It will take about twenty-five minutes for the potatoes to become truly tender. Blitz the soup in a blender or put it through a food mill, stir in the chopped parsley, and check the seasoning.

Cut the blood sausage into slices and grill until crisp. Ladle the soup into bowls and float the sausage slices on top.

A chowder of mussels and leeks

Onions have always had a slightly awkward relationship with fish. They seem particularly ungainly and rough edged alongside the white varieties or shellfish. Shallots work better, with their milder notes and less significant dose of sugar, but of all the alliums it is the leek that marries most successfully. The white of the leek has an elegance and subtlety that is unlikely to overpower any fish you put it with. In a soup or pie, it dances with the piscine ingredients where an onion would tread on their toes.

Chowder is traditionally a hearty bowl of food. The one I make with mussels and bacon is a short step away from the big clam and potato numbers I have eaten in Boston, in that it is somewhat lighter and less creamy, but it is still essentially a big soup for a cool day.

enough for 4
leeks – 3
smoked bacon – 5 ounces (150g)
butter – 3 tablespoons (40g)
mussels – 2 pounds (1kg)
white vermouth – 2 glasses
potatoes – 1 pound (450g)
heavy cream – ¾ cup (200ml)
bay leaves – a couple
thyme – 4 sprigs
parsley – a few sprigs, chopped

Thinly slice the leeks and rinse them very thoroughly. No vegetable holds its grit like a leek. Cut the bacon into short, thin strips and put them into a deep, thick-bottomed pan with the butter. Let the bacon color lightly over medium heat. Decrease the heat, add the leeks, and cover with a lid. Let them cook for twenty minutes or so, with an occasional stir, until they are soft and sweet—they should not color. Remove from the heat.

Check the mussels and pull away any beards. Discard any mussels that are broken, open, or exceptionally heavy. Put them in a large pot, pour in the vermouth, and cover tightly with a lid. Place over high heat until the mussels have opened (a matter of minutes), then remove each mussel from its shell.

Peel the potatoes and cut them into large dice. Put them in a saucepan with 1¾ cups (400ml) of the mussel cooking liquor, drained through a sieve. Add the cream, bay, thyme, and a little black pepper (no salt). Bring to a boil, then decrease the heat so that the potatoes simmer gently for about ten minutes.

Add three-quarters of the cooked potatoes to the leeks and bacon. Put the remainder in a blender with the cream (pick out the herbs first) and blitz briefly until smooth (too long and it will turn gummy). Pour into the pan and add the mussels and parsley. Bring all to a boil and serve.

Braised lamb shanks with leeks and haricot beans

Users of *The Kitchen Diaries* may feel they recognize this recipe. Previously I have always made it with cubed lamb, but I recently tried it with lamb shanks and left it overnight before reheating it. The presence of the bone and fat and the good night's sleep have made such a difference that I thought it worth repeating here. You could make it a day or two in advance to good end.

enough for 4
dried haricot beans – 1½ cups (300g)
bay leaves – 3
olive oil
small lamb shanks – 4
large leeks – 4, trimmed
butter – a thick slice, about 4 tablespoons (60g)
garlic – 2 cloves
thyme leaves – a tablespoon, chopped
all-purpose flour – a tablespoon
light stock or water – 2¾ cups (650ml)
the juice and zest of a lemon
a handful of parsley, chopped
a handful of mint leaves

Soak the beans overnight in cold water. The next day, drain them, put them into a deep saucepan, and cover with fresh water. Bring to a boil, skim off the froth, add a bay leaf, and a drop or two of olive oil and simmer for about forty minutes. Turn off the heat and leave them in the water.

Warm a glug of olive oil in a Dutch oven or other heavy pot. Season the lamb shanks all over with salt and black pepper, then lower them into the pot. They should sizzle when they hit the oil. Turn the meat from time to time until it has colored nicely on all sides (we are talking pale honey color rather than deep brown). Remove the meat from the pot and set aside on a plate to catch any escaping juices.

Preheat the oven to 325°F (160°C). Cut the leeks into chunks roughly the length of a wine cork, wash them thoroughly, making sure no grit or sand is trapped in their many layers, then put them in the casserole together with the butter, keeping the heat low. Cover with a piece of wax paper or parchment paper, then cover with a lid (the paper will encourage them to cook in their own steam rather than brown). Cook them on the stove until they have started to soften, a good twenty minutes or so. You will need to give them an occasional stir.

Remove and discard the paper. Peel and thinly slice the garlic and add it to the pot with the thyme and the remaining bay leaves. Sprinkle the flour over the top and continue cooking for three or four minutes, stirring occasionally. Pour in the stock or water, then drain the beans and add them too. Season with salt and pepper.

Return the shanks and any collected juices to the pan and bring to a boil. Cover the pot with a lid and place in the oven for an hour and a half, or until the lamb is completely tender. Sometimes it takes two hours. You should be able to remove it from the bone with little effort (then again, it shouldn't actually be falling apart). Remove from the oven, stir in most of the lemon juice and zest, parsley, and mint, then scatter the rest.

Leek and cheese mash

A good side dish for Monday's leftover cold roast meat. The quantities are deliberately vague because of the nature of leftovers. A recipe for which we must use our instinct.

a large leek
butter
leftover mashed potatoes
cheese – anything you have around that needs using

Wash and chop the leek, then let it cook in a generous amount of butter, covered with a lid and a piece of wax paper if you wish, until soft. Season with salt and then scoop into a shallow ovenproof dish.

Tip the mashed potatoes on top of the leeks. Level them a little without packing them down too tightly. Dot small knobs of butter over the surface, cover with grated or crumbled cheese, then bake in a hot oven until the cheese has melted and the potatoes are heated through.

A soup of roots, leeks, and walnuts

Good cooking often comes from simply going with what is around at the time. Ingredients that are in season at the same time tend to go together—in this case, the last of a hat trick of leek soups made with all that is left in the depleted winter vegetable patch.

enough for 4 to 6
large leeks, with plenty of green – 2
butter – 3 tablespoons (40g)
medium celery ribs – 4
Jerusalem artichokes – 14 ounces (400g)
light stock or water – 4 cups (a liter)
parsley – a small bunch, chopped

for the spice mix
coriander seeds – a teaspoon
shelled walnuts – about ¼ cup (30g)
ginger – a 1-ounce (30g) lump
peanut oil – 4 teaspoons

Discard the toughest of the leaves from the leeks, then cut the tender white and palest green flesh into thin rounds. Rinse thoroughly under running water to remove any trapped grit, then add them to a heavy saucepan with the butter. Let them cook in the butter over low to medium heat for a good fifteen to twenty minutes, without letting them color, until they are soft enough to crush between your fingers.

Once they have started to soften, you can finely slice the celery and add it to the pan, then peel and chop the artichokes and stir them in too. Cover the pot with a lid and let the vegetables sweat and soften without coloring, then pour in the stock or water and bring to a boil. Decrease the heat so that the soup bubbles gently and partially cover it with a lid. Cook for about twenty-five minutes, until the artichokes are very tender.

Grind the coriander seeds to a fine powder with a pestle and mortar, then add the walnuts, mashing them briefly to a pulp. Peel the ginger and slice it thinly, then cut it into thin matchsticks. Warm the oil in a shallow pan, add the ginger, and fry for about thirty seconds, until it is golden and crisp. Toss in the crushed walnuts and coriander, let them sizzle briefly, then turn out onto paper towels.

Blitz the soup in a blender or put it through a food mill, stir in the chopped parsley, and check the seasoning. The soup should be mild and almost nutty tasting. Ladle into bowls and top with the spice mix.

A tart of leeks and cheese

There is a point in the year, usually after the Christmas decorations have been put away, when the house gets too cold to sit still in without a wrap around you. I have always kept a cold house; hot rooms make me feel unhealthy. But sometimes the only way of getting warm here is to eat. Carbohydrate-rich meals, such as the tart of leek and cheese and pastry I made on the coldest day of the year, warm you in a way few others are capable of.

enough for 4
waxy potatoes – about 1¼ pounds (650g)
medium leeks – 3 (about 1½ pounds [750g])
butter – 4 tablespoons (50g)
crème fraîche – ¾ cup (200ml)
Cheddar – 6½ ounces (180g), grated
a little freshly grated nutmeg
puff pastry – 1 pound (500g)
beaten egg for glazing

Preheat the oven to 400°F (200°C). Bring a large pan of water to a boil. Peel the potatoes and cut them into slices about ⅛ inch (3mm) thick. Salt the boiling water, add the potatoes, and let them simmer enthusiastically until tender—they can be almost falling apart. Drain and put into a large bowl.

Meanwhile, remove the greenest part of the leeks and discard it. Slice the white and pale green part into rings, then rinse thoroughly under running water. Melt the butter in a saucepan and add the leeks. Cover with a lid and cook over low to medium heat until thoroughly tender; this will take a good twenty minutes. Put the leeks in with the drained potatoes, then add the crème fraîche and grated Cheddar. Season with salt, black pepper, and nutmeg.

Roll the pastry into two rectangles approximately 9½ x 12½ inches (24 x 32cm). Lay one on a nonstick baking sheet. Pile the filling into the center, then brush the edges with beaten egg. Lay the second piece of pastry over the top and press the edges down. Trim around the edges, then pinch firmly to seal. Brush the top with beaten egg and cut equally spaced slits across the width of the top piece of pastry. Bake until the pastry is crisp and golden, about forty to forty-five minutes.

Spring leeks, fava beans, and bacon

In spring, the young leek is a welcome sight with its stick-thin body and compact green flags, particularly after the thick winter ones with their frozen cores. They are worth steaming and dressing with a mustardy vinaigrette or, as here, using as a base for a fava bean and bacon lunch. We sometimes have this in the garden, with inelegant hunks of bread and sweet Welsh butter.

enough for 2 as a light lunch
young, slim leeks – 3 or 4
unsmoked bacon or pancetta slices – 6
butter – a thick slice
a clove of garlic, peeled and squashed
fava beans – 2 pounds (1kg; weighed in the pods)
tarragon leaves – 2 loosely packed tablespoons, chopped
flat-leaf parsley – a handful, chopped

Bring a deep pan of water to a boil. Wash and thickly slice the leeks. Remove the rind from the bacon slices and cut each slice into finger-thick strips. Warm the butter in a shallow pan and add the strips of bacon. Let the bacon color lightly in the hot butter until its fat is starting to turn pale gold, then add the sliced leeks and the garlic clove. Partially cover with a lid and let the leeks soften but not color.

While the bacon and leeks are cooking, shell the beans and add them to the boiling water. Salt the water and let the beans cook for four or five minutes, until tender. Drain and rinse in cold water until cool enough to skin. Leave the tiniest of beans unskinned, but it is probably better to skin anything larger than a thumbnail—just squeeze each bean between thumb and finger and pop it out of its skin.

When the leeks and bacon are soft and fragrant, stir in the tarragon, parsley, and the drained and skinned beans, then season. Stir gently, allow to heat through for a minute or two, then serve on warm plates.

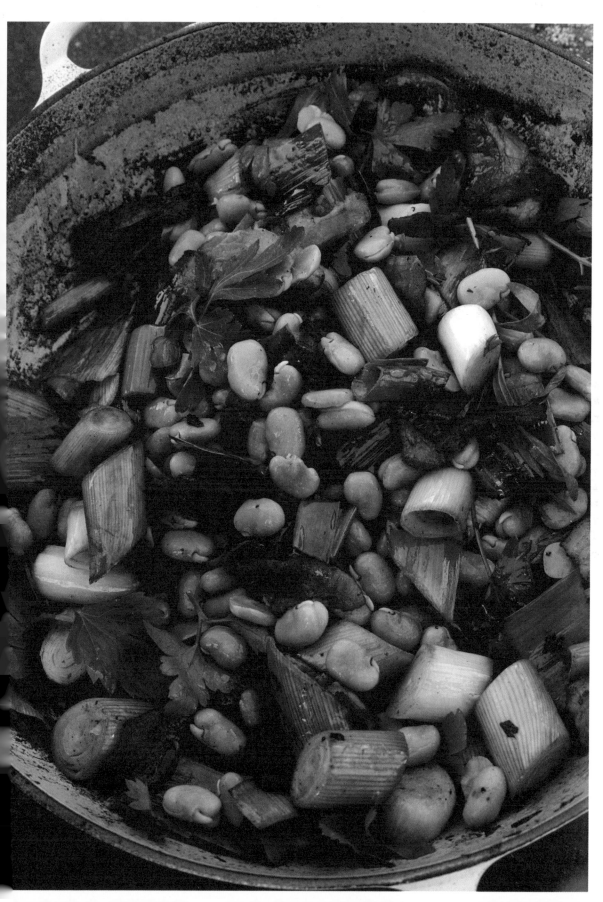

Pork, leeks, and green peppercorns

To our list of ingredients that balance the leek's (and onion's) tendency toward sweetness, we can add green peppercorns. Outside the anise-scented emporiums of Chinatown they are difficult to track down in their fresh state, but bottled ones in brine are perhaps even better here. Deep-winter stuff, this. Some fresh, crisp greens might be appropriate with it, some winter salad leaves or maybe a plate of lightly cooked spinach. Whatever, I do recommend some plain, steamed potatoes to balance the general richness.

Green peppercorns in brine are available in cans or bottles from well-stocked specialty markets and delicatessens.

enough for 4
leeks – about 1¼ pounds (650g)
butter – 3 tablespoons (40g), plus a little more
cubed pork – 1 pound (500g)
mushrooms – 1 pound (500g)
all-purpose flour – a heaping tablespoon
stock – 2 to 2½ cups (500 to 600ml), hot
bay leaves – 2
parsley – a small bunch
green peppercorns in brine – 4 teaspoons
heavy cream – a scant ⅔ cup (140ml)

Trim the leeks, discarding the dark, outer leaves. Slice the leeks about ¾ inch (2cm) wide and wash thoroughly. Warm the butter in a large, heavy-bottomed pot, add the leeks, then cover with a lid and let cook slowly for ten to fifteen minutes. You want them to end up bright and almost tender but without color. Lift them out and set aside.

Return the pan to the heat, let it get a little hot, then add the pork. Let it color lightly on all sides, then remove and add it to the leeks.

Preheat the oven to 300°F (150°C). Cut the mushrooms into halves or quarters, then fry them in the pot until they are golden and slightly sticky. Add a little extra butter if they need it. Return the leeks and pork to the pot, scatter over the flour, and let cook for a minute or so. Slowly pour in the hot stock. Stir in the bay leaves and a grinding of salt and black pepper. Bring slowly to a boil, then cover with a lid, and transfer to the oven. Leave for fifty to sixty minutes to cook its way quietly to tenderness.

Chop the parsley and stir it into the pot with the peppercorns and cream, then either return it to the oven for five minutes or heat through on the stove. Check the seasoning and serve with steamed, unbuttered potatoes (see facing page).

The potatoes

Either steam or boil large, floury potatoes, then drain them. Put them back on the stove over low heat for a few minutes, so that they are completely dry, then gently shake the saucepan back and forth so the edges of the potatoes "bruise" and crumble slightly. Eat them with the casserole, mashing the floury, crumbly spuds into the sauce from the casserole with your fork.

Chicken with leeks and lemon

To balance the sweetness of leeks, we can use a little white wine vinegar, especially tarragon, or lemon juice. The addition of either removes any risk of the dish cloying. The recipe that follows is one of my all-time favorites for a good, easy midweek supper. What especially appeals is that although the sauce tastes rich and almost creamy, it has no butter or cream in it at all.

> *enough for 4*
> olive oil – 2 tablespoons
> chicken thighs – 8
> medium leeks – 4
> dry vermouth such as Noilly Prat – a glass
> the juice and zest of a lemon
> chicken stock – 2 cups (500ml)
> parsley – a small bunch

In a large casserole, warm the olive oil over medium heat. Add the chicken pieces, skin side down, and cook until pale gold in color. Wash the leeks thoroughly, shake them dry, then cut them into pieces the length of a wine cork. Lift the chicken out of the pan and add the leeks. Cover and let them cook gently until they are soft but relatively uncolored. Whatever happens, they should not brown. Once they start to soften, add the vermouth, the zest and juice of the lemon, and the chicken stock. Bring to a boil, return the chicken and its juices to the pan, season with salt and pepper, then cover and simmer for about twenty minutes.

Chop the parsley, taste the sauce for seasoning, and stir the parsley in.

A risotto of leeks and pancetta

Like asparagus, leeks produce a particularly subtle risotto. The crucial point is not to let them color. Cook them over low heat, with a lid on if you wish, or maybe with a piece of wax paper on top. Either way they must not brown.

enough for 2
medium leeks – 2
butter – about 4 tablespoons (50g), plus a walnut-sized lump to finish
arborio or other risotto rice – 1⅔ cups (300g)
dry vermouth such as Noilly Prat – a glass
chicken stock – 4 cups (a liter), hot
thin slices of pancetta – 6
grated Parmesan – 3 tablespoons, plus more to finish

Wash the leeks thoroughly, splitting them down their length and rinsing under a running cold tap, then slice them finely. Melt the butter in a wide, high-sided pan over low heat and add the leeks. Let them soften without coloring, stirring from time to time.

Stir in the rice, then pour in the Noilly Prat. Let the mixture boil until the alcohol has evaporated, then add in the first ladleful of hot stock. Continue stirring, adding the stock when the rice has absorbed almost all of the previous ladleful, until the rice is plump, tender, and yet has a little bite left in it—a process that will take about twenty minutes. Meanwhile, broil the pancetta, or cook it in a nonstick frying pan (no oil necessary), until truly crisp. Cut into pieces about the size of a large postage stamp, leaving a couple of slices whole. Fold the cut pieces into the risotto.

Stir in the walnut-sized lump of butter, adding the 3 tablespoons of Parmesan as you go. Divide between warm dishes and finish with a piece of pancetta and more grated Parmesan.

Little cakes of leeks and potatoes

This sounds too spartan a recipe to be true but, when cooked slowly in butter, the leeks take on a deep sweetness that makes these cakes so much more than the sum of their simple parts. They are great with broiled bacon or cold roast beef.

makes about 12 cakes, enough for 4
medium potatoes – 5
large leeks – 2
butter – 4 tablespoons (50g)
milk – scant ½ cup (100ml)
vegetable or peanut oil for shallow-frying

Peel the potatoes, then boil them in deep, salted water. Trim and rinse the leeks, discarding the dark outer leaves, and slice them thinly. Melt the butter in a shallow pan and cook the leeks in it over low heat, stirring from time to time, until they are soft and melting; they should be ready in twenty minutes or so. If they color they will turn bitter, so cover them with a lid or a piece of wax paper.

Bring the milk to a boil in a small saucepan, then switch off the heat. When the potatoes are tender, drain them, put them back on the heat for a minute, covered with a lid or a kitchen towel, to dry out, then mash them with a potato masher, pouring in the warm milk as you go. You are after a thick mash, not a sloppy one, so stop adding milk when the consistency is thick enough to make into patties. Stir in the leeks and season generously.

When the mixture is cool enough to roll, shape it into rough patties. Don't be tempted to make them perfectly smooth; they will be all the more interesting if they are a little rough.

Heat some oil in a shallow pan. When it is hot, slide in the patties, not too close together, and let them color lightly on both sides. They will cook quite quickly, about three or four minutes on each side. Lift the patties out with a spatula and drain briefly on paper towels.

Onions

I regard a baked onion as a fine but humble supper. It will probably have been steamed first to keep its flesh juicy, then left in a low oven to bake with a little butter and salt until its translucent, golden layers are at the point of collapse. Its edges may have caught and even blackened here and there, and the few juices may come embellished with a little cream and grated pecorino or perhaps our own Spenwood. There will be hand-torn bread, and maybe some lightly cooked spinach at its side. Oh and a glass or two of wine, something quite velvety, would do nicely.

Onions are often described as the backbone of a stew, a sauce, a casserole. I think of them more as the heart of a dish, their vital activity rarely considered, quietly beating away in the background. They provide sweetness, mellowness, depth, warmth, tenderness, suavity, and body, and seem to have a steadying influence on all the other ingredients. This is why the way in which we treat them in the pot is crucial. Why we must never hurry the onion's slow progress toward sweetness or burn its delicate edges or, worst of all, fail to cook them enough. Get the onion part of a dish right and you are halfway towards a good supper. Get them wrong and no amount of cooking and clever stunts can quite put matters to rights.

Anyone who has cooked a stew without a member of the allium family knows how they settle a dish and, in the case of a casserole, give it a sense of being. We have always cooked with them—they appear in our oldest recorded recipes and may well have come to us with the Romans. Certainly they were widely used in the Middle Ages. In Britain, we briefly supplied most of our needs ourselves, with Bedfordshire the center of production. Now, with most of the supplies coming from Egypt or China, the only way to get our hands on a locally grown onion is to bring them back from the farmers' market or grow them ourselves. A row or two in the garden gives us the chance of cooking with a traditional old school Ailsa Craig, named after the craggy island off the Scottish coast, or a Red Baron.

From a purely aesthetic angle, a soldierly row of neatly tied onions sitting proudly on dry autumn soil is a sign of a well-ordered allotment. Onions will not do well grown higgledy-piggledy in a badly tended site, and tend to struggle among weeds. Hating the hoe—their roots lie too close to the surface to rely on this easy way to weed—they require more hands-on care than you might expect.

The onion is probably the one vegetable that even the most thoughtful food shopper tends to take for granted. We are not helped by the fact that onions are almost never labeled with their variety. Growing our own introduces more possibilities for getting to know this aromatic bulb in all its forms than picking one up from the corner store or supermarket. There are soft-fleshed Spanish onions, sweet enough for eating raw in a Cheddar sandwich but whose keeping qualities are low; hard, crisp-skinned golden onions for general cooking and long winter storage; red onions, for where a mixture of strong flavors and intense sweetness is required; shallots for when mildness is key—in a sauce, for instance; and long, thin green onions for crunching raw in a salad. One might say an onion for almost every culinary occasion.

An onion in the garden

Decent onions, firm, sweet, and unblemished, are available in almost any shop that sells food. They are a mainstay of the organic box, a stalwart of the farm shop and delicatessen, and part of the wallpaper in every produce market in the land. The question is, why would anyone want to grow their own?

Those of us lacking much in the way of outside space have to be ruthless about the plants we grow, and onions are often the first we cross off the list. I grew them initially as a way to deter slugs—they hate all members of the allium family—but soon found that the space they took up was too valuable. Onions are generally grown from "sets"—immature onions—though they are more cheaply grown from seed. The sets for an early-autumn crop are sent out in early spring. They need to be planted right up to their necks, about 6 inches (15cm) apart. Small varieties can be closer, with 2 to 4 inches (5 to 10 cm) between them, but in either case just the tip should be visible. Any more and they will be pulled out by the pigeons.

Onions like a cool start to the year, in rich but not freshly manured soil (do it the autumn before), and plenty of sun later on. Their pet hates are being waterlogged or choked by weeds that nick their nutrients. It is essential that the bulbs have a good amount of space between them for airflow. Cramped, wet conditions will encourage rot and bolting. Avoid watering much once they are established.

In the cool part of the season, the bulbs will send up green shoots, then, as the weather warms, the bulbs themselves slowly fill out. The onions are ready to pick once the leaves start to yellow in late July or August. They store well, but they need to dry out before we put them away for winter. Pull them out of the ground with the help of a garden fork so that the roots come too, and leave them in a dry place for a day or two before storing. Make sure that the air can get round each bulb and they are not touching one another. If the weather is good, it will help to do this out in the sun. Bring them into store only when they feel dry in the hand and the skin is crisp.

Golden onions will keep for months in a cool, very dry place, red ones slightly less. They will go moldy in humidity. Tying the dried leaves together in the style of a French onion seller is a good way of storing them, as is keeping them (don't laugh) in a pair of panty hose hanging from the ceiling. Sprouting in spring is natural, but a sign that the bulbs are past their best.

Varieties

Suppliers often give two choices for the home grower: packets of seed or "sets," the immature onions that are grown from seed planted the previous summer. More varieties are available as seed than as sets, but many find sets more reliable. I grow from immature plants.

Red onions
The red onion has gained in popularity over the last decade, offering a mild character, rather sweeter than the yellow. It cooks to a slightly disappointing murky purple and lacks the savor of the traditional golden onion. It generally keeps less well. Simmered slowly with oil and thyme, red onions break down to a sweet "marmalade" that is good with cheese.

Red Baron* Everyone seems to swear by this sweet, reliable red onion.
Rossa Lunga di Firenze Mild, slightly elongated onion that can be eaten raw.

Golden onions

Senshyu Yellow* Slightly flattened, yellow-skinned mild onion for August planting. Overwinters well, ready in June. I have had much luck with this one.
Santé A popular choice for spring planting.
Ailsa Craig* Mild, large variety, an excellent all-rounder. Originating in Scotland, it is also a popular "showing onion" for those who think growing is something to do with getting a rosette.
Sturon Mild, reliable, round onion.
Candy* Flattened globe prized for its sweetness; not a long keeper.

*Available from US seed sources.

An onion in the kitchen

The golden skin of an onion will lend a warm, amber glow to a stock, keep a baked onion moist, and prevent a boiled one falling apart in the water, but most of the time a recipe will tell us to peel it.

I was taught to peel an onion whole, in the old-school manner, by slicing off both root and tip and peeling away the skin with an oversized chef's knife. Now I do it my own way, by cutting the onion in half from root to tip while still in its skin. It is then easy to pry off even the most tenacious skin. I use a very small, sharp knife too. Cooking isn't about rules, it is about whatever makes the cook feel comfortable.

Unless we are baking our largest alliums whole or boiling them for stuffing (with anchovy, parsley, lemon, and ricotta, maybe), we need to decide whether to slice or chop them. Much will depend on how you want them to look in the finished dish. A tangle of hairlike slices and melted cheese is essential to a classic onion soup. Thickly cut, meltingly soft slices are what you want in a baked onion salad; *imam bayildi*, the famous stuffed eggplant of the Middle East, needs onions chopped in such a way that they will easily melt into a silken pulp. Whether I am chopping coarsely for a beef stew or finely for a rosemary and breadcrumb stuffing, I keep the root intact for as long as I can. It holds the layers in place and stops them slithering around.

It is worth mastering the chopping of an onion. Apart from the physical pleasure of holding a knife, its thick handle cushioning the cold sharpness of the steel, an onion swiftly chopped with a knife of almost surgical sharpness is less likely to end in tears. Heavy work with a blunt blade will bruise the vegetable's cells and send a fine spray of juice into your eyes.

The villain of the piece is lachrymator, the chemical that sets our tear glands off. Not everyone is affected to the same extent. It sometimes seems as if every cook save me has a tried-and-true method to sabotage the work of the evil lachrymator. I find peeling onions such torture that I often choose a recipe that uses leeks instead. Some of the ways other sufferers might like to try include:

Peeling them under the hood of an exhaust fan.
Chilling the offending onions in the fridge to slow down the release of their oils.
Slicing from root end along.
Removing the skin under running water.
Holding a piece of bread in your mouth to absorb the lachrymator.
Wearing swim goggles.

In my experience, none of these seems to make any difference at all. Much depends on the season and how old an onion is. Fewer tears are shed in summer.

During cooking, an onion will behave differently according to the variety and the time of year. In summer, onions contain more water and tend to steam in the pan, taking longer to caramelize. If you absentmindedly cook them with the lid on, you will end up with a pan full of juice. They may brown less successfully, too, because their sugars are less concentrated, and should you lack the time to let the juices evaporate, you will end up with a watery mess.

A soup, a sauce, or a risotto generally starts with the chopping of an onion and its slow journey toward tenderness in hot butter. Including bacon fat or olive oil will add flavor while lessening the risk of the onion burning. Only when the onion is glossy and the color of honey can we add garlic, celery, or tomato and any spices or herbs. To add the garlic at the same time as the onion would risk it browning too much (fine in Chinese cooking but not what you want for a risotto).

Older onions, those that feel heavy for their size or seem particularly reluctant to shed their skins, are often piercingly strong. Offensively pungent onions can sometimes be tamed with cold water or vinegar. A short soak in ice water will often quell a sliced onion's anger so successfully that it can be eaten raw. Cut no thicker than garden twine, raw onion can be rustically satisfying in a doorstop sandwich with sharp Cheddar and soft white bread. Finely diced bullies destined for a salad dressing can be calmed by five minutes in a puddle of red wine vinegar.

Cooked long and slow in earthenware, steel, or cast-iron pans, onions are often enriched with olive oil and butter, thyme, garlic, parsley, and not mere bacon but expensive, faintly herbal pancetta. This scented base will act as a backbone around which we can build a dish with meat or beans or both, to which we can add diced root vegetables, mushrooms, or spices and moisten with stock, wine, or water. The onion is the aromatic foundation stone on which the cook can build. A level floor capable of taking any amount of our creativity and imaginative cooking.

Seasoning your onions

The twiggy herbs, such as rosemary, thyme, and bay, have an elemental
pull toward the onion, as do beef stock, white wine, and butter. Onions
and cheese have a longstanding affair with one another, especially the more
piercingly flavored farmhouse varieties. Onions flatter all meat and poultry
and have a deepening effect on the flavor of most vegetables. So useful and
versatile is the onion that it would probably be easier to say what doesn't go
particularly well with it. I say probably, because it is surprisingly difficult to
think of anything, at least in a savory sense.

A few special partnerships

Cream Add heavy cream and a spoonful of Dijon mustard to a pan
of caramelized onions to make a luxurious sauce for steak.
Woody herbs Add thyme and rosemary to softened onions, then scatter
them over a focaccia dough with olive oil and flakes of sea salt. A slow stew
of butter, onions, and woody herbs is a sound base for all manner of recipes.
Anchovy Chopped finely and stirred with onion until it melts, this salty
little fish balances the bulb's inescapable sweetness. Add to potato gratins
and bean dishes.
Butter Onions cooked slowly in butter take on a mellow sweetness.
Oil, duck or goose fat, and beef dripping are often used too, but butter
is the only one that seems to have a sweetening effect.
Parmesan It is difficult to think of two ingredients more flattering
to each other.

And...

* Twigs laid over newly planted onion sets will deter birds from pulling them out or squirrels looking for something to play ball with.
* I buy onions by feel. They should be hard, the skins crisp, and showing no signs of sponginess round the shoulders. Any with mildew or a moldy smell should be dismissed. I don't buy if they are sprouting or damp to the touch. Produce vendors are prone to throw them around, upending the traditional orange net bag into the onion bin, but that doesn't mean they won't bruise. The care with which the French have long wrapped theirs in trailing strings, using the dried leaves like twine, is more like the consideration we should show them. A bruised onion will rot.
* Dark-skinned varieties store better than pale ones.
* The green shoot that appears inside an aging onion is simply the leaf forming for the next planting. Many people find it indigestible and bitter.
* The darker your storage, the longer your onions will keep from deteriorating.
* Avoid putting a cut onion in the fridge. It will taint everything that is in there, especially the milk.
* The marriage of sweet onions and salty ingredients is particularly pleasing. Try the obvious anchovy or Parmesan mentioned above, but feta and olives are also worth bearing in mind.
* Shallots are an invaluable addition to a salad. I chop them into fine rings, letting them sit in the vinegar for a while before I add the oil and pepper.

A few words about shallots

Refined in flavor and possessing an extraordinary elegance, the shallot has a milder taste than the onion. Its golden skin and the flesh beneath tend to have a pink blush, and it is usually easier to peel. Shallots are often flat sided from where they have grown together in a huddle.

High-level restaurant cooking is this allium's natural home, as a base for classical French sauces, but they are worth giving a more down-to-earth treatment too. I cook them slowly in a shallow pan with butter and thyme, letting them soften and take on a coat as sticky as molasses. A little sugar, a drizzle of balsamic or sherry vinegar, and just a little salt is all that is needed in the way of seasoning. Grilled fish welcomes this accompaniment, as do cold roast meats, especially slices cut from a joint of pork.

The larger form, often sold to the shopper as "banana shallots," is good roasted, when the flesh softens meltingly inside the crackling skin.

Fried onions to accompany liver or steak

Onions were never a big deal at home when I was a kid. One or two turned up in the occasional stew, floating in the languid stock along with thickly sliced carrots, parsnips, and a bay leaf, but they were not stalwarts of our kitchen.

In my teenage years I was finally introduced to the liver and onions so hated by most of my school friends, the onions cooked lovingly in our battered aluminium frying pan, blackened from years of Sunday fry-ups, until they took on the color of varnish and their flesh turned from acrid to a deep, honeyed sweetness. I took to this marriage of the intensely savory meat and sugary-sweet onions straightaway, though more for the glistening alliums than the panfried organ.

My first attempts at cooking onions to match those luscious little nuggets I had been enjoying at home failed for lack of a heavy-bottomed pan and a little patience. The gorgeous, caramel-edged stickiness of a fried onion needs time in which to develop. A quick ten minutes in the thin frying pan that accompanied my crummy bedsit was never going to work.

To make perfect fried onions, you need a shallow, heavy-bottomed pan. The temperature should be low to medium and the onions should be allowed to soften slowly. Winter onions, which contain less water, will produce a sweeter and deeper gold result. Summer onions, full of water, will produce rather a lot of liquid, which will have to be evaporated away by turning up the heat.

The essence of frying onions is to let them soften in an unhurried manner with only the occasional stir to stop them sticking. You want their sugars to caramelize on the bottom of the pan; it is what gives fried onions their characteristic gloss and sweetness.

enough for 2 or 3
large, golden onions – 3
butter – a thick slice
oil – a small glug

Peel the onions. Cut them in half from root to tip, then slice each half into thick segments. Melt the butter in a shallow pan, add the oil, and then the onions. Cook over low heat until the onions are sweet and soft enough to squish between thumb and forefinger. Salt only at the end of cooking, otherwise they will fail to soften.

There is no hurrying this. Turning the heat up will result in the onions browning, and what you are after is onions that are deep honey gold rather than the color of creosote. Stir them as they soften so they do not stick, but not so often that they fail to leave a glossy, sticky residue in the pan. There will be much flavor there.

The fusion of onions, beef, and beer

Cooking onions slowly and without color produces an aromatic backbone to a dish that is less sweet than one where the sugars in the onion have been allowed to caramelize. To do this successfully, I keep the heat low and stir the pot regularly. This is not something for the impatient cook. They need a watchful eye if they are not to color, and can take up to twenty minutes or so to become a pale, translucent gold. They are ready when each piece is easily squashable between finger and thumb.

My early casseroles were complex, made up of layers of onion, celery, carrot, bay, thyme, red wine, and meat juices, simply because that was the way I was taught to make them. It is what comes from learning to cook in cooking schools and restaurants rather than at your mother's knee. It has taken a while for me to appreciate the simpler style of slow-cooked stew such as the Lancashire hotpot and the French pot-au-feu.

Beer and onions is a merry little friendship. It works in hot dogs, the ploughman's lunch, and Flemish beef casseroles. The Belgians often use beer instead of wine, stock, or water. As it cooks, it loses its alcohol content but adds a characteristic sweet-sharp note that is difficult to introduce in any other way.

A simple stew of onions, beer, and beef

This extraordinarily deep-flavored stew is one for a day when there is
frost on the ground. The inclusion of applesauce isn't quite as daft as it
sounds, and there is much magic to be found at the point where the sharp
applesauce oozes into the onion gravy. Boiled potatoes as big as your fist,
their edges bruised and floury, are the ideal accompaniment.

enough for 4
butter – a thick slice
stewing beef in one piece – 1½ pounds (750g)
large onions – 2
thyme – a few sprigs
all-purpose flour – 2 heaping tablespoons
Trappist beer – 2 small bottles
bay leaves – 2 or 3
red currant or apple jelly – a tablespoon

for the apple sauce
apples – 5 or 6, the sharper the better
butter – a walnut-sized knob
sugar – a little to taste
ground cinnamon – a pinch

Preheat the oven to 350°F (180°C). Melt the butter in a large Dutch oven
to which you have a lid. The heat should be quite sprightly. Cut the beef
into four pieces, each nicely seasoned with salt and black pepper, then lower
into the lightly sizzling butter. Let the meat color on one side, then turn it
over. Peel, halve, and thinly slice the onions while the meat browns. Once
colored, remove the meat to a plate and decrease the heat.

Add the onions to the pan, with the leaves from the thyme sprigs, and
cook over low to medium heat until the onions are soft and pale gold.

Stir in the flour and cook until it is the palest gold color, then pour in
the beer and add the bay leaves. Once the sizzling has subsided and it is
approaching the boiling point, return the beef and its juices to the pan and
decrease the heat. Season with salt and black pepper, cover with a lid, and
place in the oven. Bake for a good hour to an hour and a half.

Peel the apples for the sauce, core them, and cut into coarse chunks.
Put them into a pan with a little water and the butter and bring to a boil.
Decrease the heat, cover with a lid, and let cook to a sloppy mass. Sweeten
with a little sugar and the ground cinnamon, then beat with a fork or
wooden spoon until smooth.

Lift the lid from the pot and stir in the jelly. Check the seasoning,
adding salt, pepper, and jelly as you go. Serve with the applesauce.

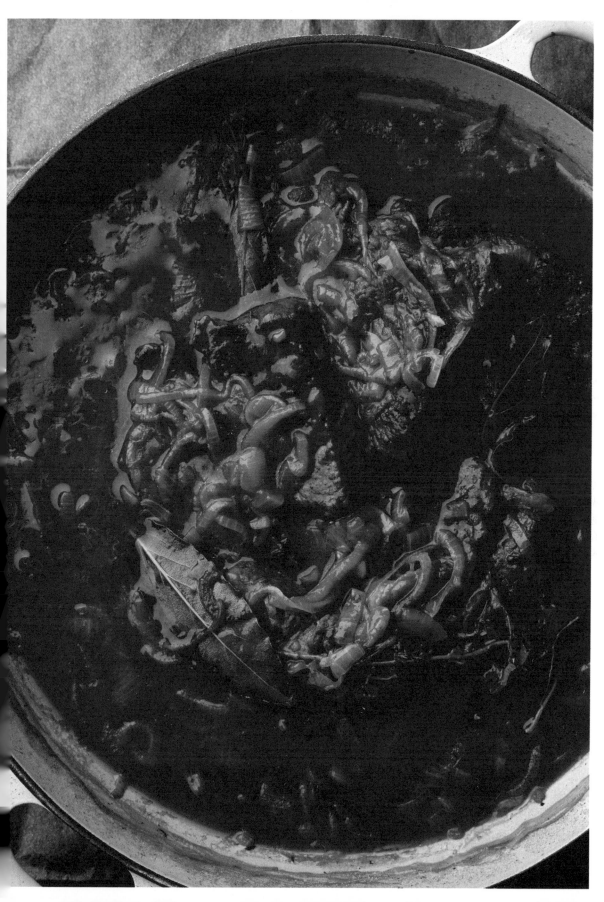

A classic meat and onion pie

Onions make an important contribution to the filling of pies, providing a sweet balance for the savoriness of the meat and a necessary change of texture, too. A meat pie with no onions would be hard going.

I rarely make a meat pie. It is one of those recipes I reserve for a cold autumn day, when it's too wet to go out.

enough for 4
rump steak, cut into large bite-sized pieces – 1½ pounds (750g)
thyme – 4 sprigs
rosemary – 2 bushy sprigs
bay leaves – 2
red wine – 2 glasses
ox kidney – 1 pound (450g)
all-purpose flour – 2 tablespoons
butter – a thick slice
medium onions – 2, chopped
chestnut mushrooms – 8 ounces (250g)
beef stock – 2 cups (450ml)
puff pastry – 12 ounces (350g)
a little beaten egg

Put the steak into a china or stainless-steel bowl, add the thyme, rosemary, and bay, and pour in the red wine. Cover with plastic wrap and refrigerate overnight.

Preheat the oven to 400°F (200°C). Cut the kidney into large, bite-sized pieces removing any fat or sinew. Toss it in the flour with the drained steak (reserve the marinade). Melt the butter in a deep pan and add the floured meat. Let it sizzle for a minute or two. As soon as it is lightly browned on all sides, add the onions, letting them soften for a few minutes, then the mushrooms, cutting them into quarters as you go. Pour in the reserved marinade and the stock, season with salt and pepper, cover with a lid, and let simmer for a good hour and a half, until the sauce is like a thick gravy. Let cool.

Put the filling into a pie dish, or divide among four small dishes. Roll out the pastry, then cut off strips to cover the rim of the dish. For the large pie, you may need to put a pastry funnel, eggcup, or tumbler in the dish to hold up the pastry. Brush the rim of the dish with beaten egg and press the pastry strips into place. Now brush that with beaten egg, then lower the pastry lid or lids into place. Cut a slit in the top for the steam to escape and bake for forty to fifty minutes, until golden.

An onion rabbit

Of all the hot snacks I put together, it is this unctuous topping of onions, thick toast, and highly seasoned melted cheese that pleases most. The onions need to cook, with the occasional stir as you pass, for a good fifteen minutes or so. They are ready only when they are truly soft and golden—there is no shortcut. The leftover cold beer solves the problem of what to drink with your meal.

makes 2 rounds
small to medium onions – 2
butter – 3 tablespoons (35g)
Cheddar – 5 ounces (150g)
all-purpose flour – 1 heaping tablespoon
dark beer – ½ cup (125ml)
milk – ⅓ cup (75ml)
English mustard – 1 to 2 teaspoons
thick slices of brown bread – 2

Peel the onions and cut them into rings or thin segments. Cook them slowly in the butter over low to medium heat for fifteen minutes or so, until they are softly sweet and pale gold. While the onions are softening, grate the cheese.

Stir the flour into the onions with a wooden spoon, letting the mixture cook gently for a few moments, then slowly stir in the beer, followed by the milk. You should have a thick sauce. Stir in the mustard and a grinding of black pepper, then introduce the grated cheese.

Preheat the broiler. Toast the bread lightly on both sides on a baking sheet. Spoon over the rabbit mixture and leave under the broiler for a few minutes, until the crust is scorched here and there.

A stew of oxtail and onions for a cold night

The animal's tail has a gentle life, the occasional swish in a buttercup-strewn meadow, and I like to think that is reflected in how we choose to cook it. Oxtail is a meal of almost soporific qualities. It will not be hurried toward tenderness any more than the animal will be hurried along a country lane. After a long, slow baking with a lot of finely sliced onions and a little aromatic liquid, the velvety fibers will fall away from the bone in brown and pink flakes. Some spinach, very lightly cooked and served without butter, will flatter the meat and melt into the creamy sauce.

enough for 4
olive oil
oxtail – 4 pounds (1.75kg)
large onions – 2
3 bay leaves
a glass of white wine
heavy cream – 1¼ cups (300ml)
smooth Dijon mustard – a tablespoon
whole-grain mustard – a tablespoon

Warm a little olive oil in a Dutch oven or other heavy pot. Season the oxtail all over with salt and black pepper. Lower into the oil and let color on all sides. Meanwhile halve, peel, and thinly slice the onions, while occasionally turning the meat so that it browns lightly and evenly. Remove the oxtail from the pot and add the onions, letting them soften a little but not color.

Preheat the oven to 325°F (160°C). Hide the meat among the onions, tuck in the bay leaves, and pour over the white wine. Lay a piece of buttered or oiled wax paper over the top, then cover with a lid. Bake for two and a half hours, checking now and again that it is not dry. If it is, add a little more liquid. Remove from the oven.

Lift the lid and remove the meat to a warm dish. Pour off any obvious fat from the pan, then stir in the cream and the mustards, and check the seasoning. Bring to a boil on the stove and bubble hard for five to ten minutes to reduce the quantity, stirring in any pan stickings as you go.

Spoon the mustard sauce over the oxtail and eat immediately.

Roast lamb, couscous, red onion

Onions are used in most stuffings, both lightening the rice, couscous, or breadcrumbs and introducing sweetness. As they melt down, they keep the filling moist.

Ask the butcher to prepare your shoulder of lamb for stuffing. When the bone is removed, it provides a neat pocket that will hold just the right amount.

enough for 6
a large red onion
olive oil
fine couscous – scant ⅔ cup (90g)
boiling water – scant 1 cup (200ml)
golden raisins – a handful
ground cumin – half a teaspoon
ground cinnamon – 2 large pinches
a shoulder of lamb – about 3 pounds (1.3kg), prepared for stuffing

Peel and thinly slice the onion, then let it soften in a little olive oil over medium heat, stirring from time to time. It is ready when soft and golden. Put the couscous in a bowl, pour over the water, and leave for ten minutes. Preheat the oven to 425°F (220°C).

Fluff the couscous with a fork to separate the grains. Stir in the softened onion, the raisins, and the spices. Season generously, then stuff the mixture into the pocket inside the lamb. Pull the meat over the stuffing and seal with a skewer or tie with string.

Place the meat in a roasting pan, scattering any spare stuffing around the outside, and rub a little olive oil over the fat. Pour a glass of water into the roasting pan and place in the oven. Roast the lamb for twenty minutes, then decrease the heat to 400°F (200°C) and continue roasting for forty minutes, until the fat is crisp and golden and the juices run clear when the meat is pierced with a skewer. Remove from the oven and let rest for ten minutes before carving.

Grilled ham, baked onions

This is a lovely dish, old-fashioned and what I call "great-grandmotherly." I sometimes find white sauces a bit heavy, so I have lightened this one by using half vegetable stock to milk.

The sauce is worth seasoning generously, with salt, pepper, grainy mustard, bay leaves, and a (mild) grating of nutmeg. I leave the bay in even when the sauce is finished and poured over the onions. It adds much in the way of subtle flavor.

Should you not fancy grilled ham, then I would still urge you to make the onions—they would be good even on their own, perhaps with a mound of buttery mashed potato or, better still, golden rutabaga with lots of butter and pepper.

serves 2, with second helpings of onions
medium onions – 6
butter – a thick slice
all-purpose flour – a heaping tablespoon
vegetable stock (see above) – 1 cup (250ml), hot
milk – 1 cup (250ml), hot
bay leaves – 3
nutmeg
whole-grain mustard – 2 teaspoons
parsley leaves – a small handful
a little oil
ham steaks – 2, about 5 to 6 ounces (150 to 175g) each
dried oregano

Preheat the oven to 350°F (180°C). Bring a deep pan of water to a boil. Peel the onions, add them to the pan, then decrease the heat and let them simmer until they are tender when pierced with the tip of a knife. This will only be a matter of twenty to twenty-five minutes or so. Drain them and discard the water (don't try using it in the sauce, the flavor can be too strong).

Put the pan back on the stove, melt the butter in it, and stir in the flour, keeping the heat low to medium. Let the flour and butter cook for a couple of minutes, stirring often so the mixture doesn't burn, then increase the heat, pour in the stock and milk, and whisk together for a minute until there are no lumps.

Season the sauce with salt and black pepper, the bay leaves, a gentle grating of nutmeg, and the mustard. I cannot emphasize enough the importance of these seasonings: they add depth and savor to the sauce and make the whole dish "work." Let the sauce simmer gently for a good ten minutes or more, stirring regularly so that it does not catch on the bottom.

Cut the onions in half from stem to tip—take care, they are slippery—and place them, flat side down, in a shallow baking dish. I use an oval enameled gratin dish. Chop the parsley, but not too finely, and stir it into the sauce, then scoop the lot over the onions. Their caps will probably be poking out, but no matter, just bake for forty to forty-five minutes until the sauce is bubbling.

Turn off the heat, but leave the onions in the oven while you cook the ham. If your broiler is, like mine, in the oven, then move the onions to the bottom and put the broiler pan two-thirds of the way up, so that it blocks the onions from the broiler (if you prefer, you can cook the ham on a stove-top grill).

Oil the steaks lightly and season them with pepper, a very little salt, and a light sprinkling of oregano. Now broil them for three or four minutes on each side, until golden. Serve the broiled ham with the baked onions and their sauce.

Shallots with raisins and cider vinegar

I have eaten these onions, at once caramel sweet and pickle sour, with bread and cheese, and that is really what I meant them for. But they also make a sticky accompaniment for a roast—maybe a fillet of lamb or pork—and are good on the side with cold roast beef, kept pink and sweet. I serve them warm rather than hot or chilled.

enough for 4 as a side dish
shallots – 30
olive oil – 2 tablespoons
butter – a thick slice
a clove of garlic
thyme – 4 bushy sprigs
cider vinegar – 3 tablespoons
raisins or golden raisins – 2 tablespoons
light muscovado sugar – 2 tablespoons

Preheat the oven to 375°F (190°C). Peel the shallots. Warm the olive oil and butter in a small roasting pan or ovenproof baking dish. Peel the garlic and slice it thinly, add to the butter, then put in the shallots and the thyme leaves, stripped from their stems. Add the cider vinegar, an equal amount of water, the raisins or golden raisins, and the muscovado sugar. Season with salt and black pepper and bake for forty to fifty minutes, stirring once or twice, until the shallots are sticky and sweet-sour. They should be soft enough to crush between your fingers and thumb. If they are browning too quickly, then cover with aluminum foil.

Lentil soup with lemon, pancetta, and mint

One of those soups that doubles as a main course, earthy, filling, and beefy. The soup relies on the onion to add depth and body.

enough for 4
onions – 2 small or 1 large
olive oil
garlic – 3 or 4 cloves, sliced
unsmoked bacon or pancetta – a good handful, diced
flat-leaf parsley – a small bunch
French or Castelluccio lentils – 1¼ cups (250g)
stock or, at a push, water – 4 cups (a liter)
spinach – 2 large handfuls
a lemon
mint – a small bunch, leaves torn

Peel the onions and chop them finely, cook them over medium to low heat with a little olive oil, the sliced garlic, and the diced bacon. It should all be golden and fragrant. Chop the parsley and stir it in.

Wash the lentils thoroughly, then stir them into the onions and bacon. Pour over the stock or water and bring to a boil, skimming off any froth that comes to the surface. You can add a bay leaf or two if you like. Decrease the heat so that the lentils simmer merrily, then almost cover the pot with a lid and leave until they are tender but far from collapse—about thirty minutes, depending on your lentils.

Wash the spinach thoroughly and tear it up a bit. While it is still wet and dripping, put it into a shallow pan over high heat and shut the lid tightly—you need to cook it in its own steam. After a minute or two it will be limp and bright emerald green. Lift it out, squeeze it dry, then divide it among four warm bowls.

Season the soup with salt, black pepper, lemon juice, and the torn mint leaves, tasting as you go. Ladle the hot soup on top of the spinach and serve with more lemon and mint for those who want it.

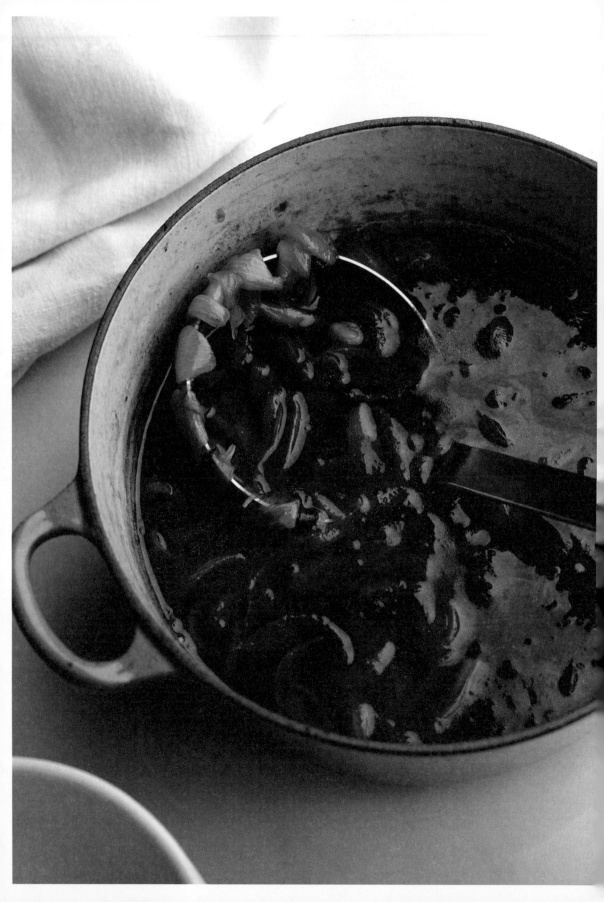

Onion soup, Madeira, and Gruyère toasts

I relish the frugality and bonhomie of a bowl of onion soup. This is slightly richer and thicker than the one in *The Kitchen Diaries*, possibly for colder weather. I don't often use flour to thicken a soup but in this case it produces a particularly velvety texture.

enough for 4
butter – a good thick slice
large onions – 3, sliced
bay leaves – 2
all-purpose flour – 2 tablespoons
white wine – 1 cup (250ml)
chicken stock – 4 cups (a liter)
Madeira – 3 to 4 tablespoons
sourdough bread – 8 small slices
Gruyère – 2½ ounces (75g), thinly sliced

Melt the butter in a heavy-based saucepan, add the sliced onions and the bay leaves, and let them cook, without coloring, over medium heat. You want them to be soft and slightly sticky, which will take a good twenty-five minutes. When they are ready, stir in the flour, cook for a minute or so, then pour in the white wine, followed by the stock. Bring to a boil, season with salt and black pepper, then decrease the heat so that the soup simmers and simmer, with just an occasional stir, for thirty minutes. Add the Madeira and continue simmering for five to ten minutes.

Preheat the broiler. Toast the bread on one side, then cover the other side with the sliced Gruyère. Check the soup for seasoning, then spoon into heatproof bowls. Float the slices of bread on top and place under the broiler for a couple of minutes, until the cheese has melted.

Baked onions

Banana shallots (sometimes known as torpedo), the most generously proportioned and mild tasting of the shallot family, roast superbly, their translucent flesh almost melting inside their skins. I have eaten them this way with creamy goat cheese mashed with herbs (thyme, tarragon, chives) and with a lump of good, mouth-puckering Cheddar too. Yet they will also stand as a vegetable. I think it worth including them here for that alone.

banana shallots – 4 per person
olive oil
thyme sprigs
a little cheese, such as Caerphilly or Cheddar

Preheat the oven to 375°F (190°C). Bake the shallots in their skins, with a light drizzle of oil and a few sprigs of thyme, for about thirty minutes, until soft to the touch. Test one; it should be meltingly soft inside.

Put the shallots on serving plates, cut into each shallot, then pour in a drop or two of olive oil and add a few thyme leaves and a few thin scraps of cheese. Press together until the cheese softens. Push the shallot from its skin and eat while hot.

Baked onions, porcini, and cream

These are *the* onions to have alongside a few slices of rare roast beef. The marriage of flavors is superb. If they are to be truly tender and silky soft, it is crucial to take them as far as you dare in the pre-cooking stage, before you scoop out the center and stuff them. They need to be boiled for a good half an hour, depending, of course, on their size. Any layers that are not supple and easy to squash between your finger and thumb should be discarded.

There is no reason why these onions with their mushroomy, creamy filling couldn't be served as a main dish. You would need two each, I think, and maybe some noodles, wide ones such as pappardelle, on the side, tossed in a little melted butter and black pepper.

enough for 4 as a side dish
dried porcini mushrooms – ½ ounce (15g)
medium to large onions – 4
butter – a thick slice
garlic – 2 small cloves, crushed
thyme – 5 sprigs (you can use dried thyme at a push)
heavy cream – ¾ cup (200ml)
grated Parmesan – 5 tablespoons (40g)

Put the porcini in a small bowl and cover with warm water. Peel the onions, then boil them in deep, salted water for about thirty minutes, until they are tender and the layers will come apart when pulled. They mustn't be hard in the middle. Drain them, slice the top off each one to give a flat edge, then put them in a small ovenproof baking dish, one in which they will fit snugly. Using a teaspoon, scoop out most of the inside of each onion without splitting the sides and base.

Preheat the oven to 400°F (200°C). Chop half of the scooped-out insides (you can discard the other half, you won't need it) and warm it with the butter and crushed garlic in a small, shallow pan. Drain and chop the porcini, pull the thyme leaves off their twigs, and chop them finely, then add both porcini and leaves to the onions and continue cooking, stirring from time to time. As the onions continue to soften and color and the mixture starts to smell interesting, pour in the cream, season with salt and black pepper, and remove from the heat.

Stir in most of the grated cheese, then spoon the stuffing into the hollows of the onions. Add the remaining cheese on top and bake for twenty minutes, until bubbling.

Couscous, red onions, parsley, pine nuts

I have eaten this for supper with a spot of harissa sauce stirred in (let down with a little water) but that is not really the idea. It is meant as an accompaniment to grilled lamb or fish, or perhaps some spicy meatballs. Instantly comforting, and as soothing as a pashmina.

enough for 4 as an accompaniment
couscous – ⅔ cup (100g)
large red onions – 2
olive oil
bay leaves – 3
pine nuts – 4 tablespoons (35g)
flat-leaf parsley – a small bunch

Put the couscous in a bowl, sprinkle with a cupful of water, and let sit for ten minutes.

Peel the onions and cut them into thin slices. They should be no thicker than your little finger. Warm a little olive oil in a heavy frying pan—just enough to cover the bottom—then add the onion rings and bay leaves and cook until golden brown. Do this over low heat, and expect it to take a good fifteen minutes, maybe longer. That way they will soften without burning and caramelize to a sweet, deep golden color. Cook them too quickly and they will take on a bitter note.

Put the couscous into a steamer basket lined with damp cheesecloth or into the top of a couscousier, suspended over a pan of boiling water. Steam for ten minutes, then remove and sprinkle with a little more water and a shake or two of olive oil. Let it swell for five minutes, then return it to the steamer for ten minutes.

Stir the pine nuts into the onions and let them color lightly. Chop the parsley leaves and stir them in too, with a seasoning of salt and black pepper. As soon as it is tender and fluffy, add the couscous to the onions and stir.

Parsnips

The soil-encrusted root, gnarled like the bark of an old tree, hides a creamy flesh that is both earthy and sweet. Snapped in half, it smells of freshly dug ground. Roasted in butter, it smells of warm heather honey. I value the parsnip for its gentle sweetness, its happy marriage with the crusted edges of a piece of roast beef, and the velvety soup you can make even from its woody core. Steamed, mashed, and softened to a purée with warm cream, the frugal root becomes a deceptively luxurious accompaniment to roast lamb. Baked in a slow oven with cream and the milder spices—cumin, nutmeg, a few specks of mace—the parsnip makes a sensual supper on a day when you are expecting someone to arrive home cold and sodden.

Medieval cooks, to whom sugar and honey were expensive, were glad of its sweetness. The plump varieties we enjoy now did not appear until the 1850s, a deliberate attempt to improve upon the wild one with its thin, strong-tasting tail. I buy my first bag in autumn to eat with a curl of Cumberland sausage and a bottle of cider, the last some time around April, when I have had my fill of sugary roots.

I haven't always loved the parsnip. It is extraordinary that a child so fond of sugar managed to find no comfort in the sweetest of all the root vegetables. But then I mostly knew the parsnip as the yellow chunk among the orange, brown, and white ones in a Wednesday neck of lamb stew. The whispering cloud of sweet mash, the fluffy chip, and the slice of sugary root bathed in spices and cream were all parsnip recipes I would meet up with only later in life.

Almost more than any other vegetable, the parsnip is linked to cold climates (you will see beets for sale in warm countries but rarely parsnips). As a kid, I would dawdle in the woods on my way home, particularly on Sunday afternoons in winter, when the hazels were bare and the twigs underfoot were as brittle as icicles. I would sometimes pretend to be lost, though in truth I never really went so deep into the trees as to lose sight of the glow from the cottages that lined the main road. Somehow, an imaginary adventure made arriving home to the smell of roast beef and baked apples all the sweeter. My dad insisted that the odd parsnip should be tucked in among the potatoes that sat, gently crisping, round the Sunday roast. The woods around Knightwick are still there, though now they have more elder and are no longer threatening or even exciting. To this day, I find parsnips are at their most welcome after a cold walk, and I too hide the odd parsnip among the Arran Victory and Maris Pipers in the roasting pan, a sugary surprise for those who fail to check what is on their fork.

It is worth making sure that everyone is happy with this arrangement. While the parsnips take on the juices of the roast and turn a pleasingly chewy gold, they don't meet with everyone's approval. Especially when they are disguised as a potato.

It was "Gaudy Bohemian" Molly Parkin and the food doyenne Jane Grigson who saved the parsnip from a life of endless stews. The writer, celebrity, and fashion editor Molly Parkin ("two ex-husbands, nine ex-fiancés, and a galaxy of glorious lovers") invented a recipe from which the sleepy root has never looked back. Parsnips Molly Parkin is initially an unconvincing-sounding dish made up of layers of tomatoes, parsnips, brown sugar, and cream. It tastes less sugary than it sounds. We first bumped into each other (the recipe that is, not Ms. Parkin and I) when I was given the task of producing a daily vegetarian option in a busy metropolitan café. Original, profitable, and really rather delicious, the recipe gathered fans to the point where we barely dared take it off the menu. For all its richness, the idea is still valid, though I think it is probably better as a side dish. The cream and the acidity of the tomatoes make this a sound enough accompaniment to anything you might serve with a classic potato dauphinoise. It's a good dish with a roast shoulder of lamb and one of the few times tomatoes can be said to go successfully with root vegetables.

A less jazzy treatment involved the late Jane Grigson's 1960s idea of stirring a cautious amount of curry powder into a parsnip soup. Warmly sweet and with a curious depth, the soup has become a modern classic and is one I make, with endless variations, to bolster us on a winter's day. These two treatments took the humble root to another level of sophistication altogether.

Parsnips did rather well out of the period that saw a panoply of peasant foods adopted by chefs looking for "beyond the pale" ingredients with which to surprise and amuse their customers. While the Jerusalem artichoke fared best of all, the parsnip was not overlooked. I once ate a roast fillet of lamb sliced and arranged in a spiral (you know the sort of thing) encircled by a purée of parsnip scattered with pine nuts. Back at home, where the cooking tended to be somewhat less precious, I served a mound of the mashed roots gussied up with a little cream, grated nutmeg, and toasted pine nuts alongside a roast leg of lamb. It has remained a favorite to this day and deliciously gets rid of the wizened roots from the larder.

Today the parsnip is the darling of the organic movement, which values its solid reliability and the ease with which it wards off predators. The brown roots are a stalwart of my organic box from November to April. Most of us have usually had enough of them long before Easter. The mash turns up both in gastropubs alongside lamb shanks and in avant-garde splatters across Michelin-starred plates. In my kitchen they are often seen in the company of thyme, mustard, cream, and curry spices.

A parsnip in the garden

You probably only need to know that the parsnip's umbrella-like flowers are a pale mustard yellow if you have planted them next to the carrots—whose flowers are white—and forgotten to label them. They must look charming against their native chalk and limestone soil. Yes, they are a weed. As a plant, *Pastinaca sativa* lacks the carrot's delicacy of form (its leaves are coarse, like lovage or celery root), but in the kitchen it has a charm and shyness that can make the bright orange carrot look a bit crass.

I have never grown them, enjoying reliable supplies from the organic-box delivery or from the farmers' market (those from the Fern Verrow stall at Borough Market are hauntingly beautiful). Arriving dirty, with their long rattails intact, they are tougher skinned than the polished ivory roots from the produce market or the supermarket, which, like sheep, have had their tails docked (in truth, the thin roots are useless and tend only to dry up in the oven). Two- and three-pronged parsnips, while amusing the shopper, are given withering looks by show gardeners, who blame a split root on heavy or badly prepared soil. Me, I rather like their random shapes and forked tongues. There is little enough to make a cook smile in February.

Those who grow their own seem to favor the long-rooted varieties such as Excalibur, Gladiator, and Javelin (one is led to assume the varieties were all named by men), appreciating their generous yield and resistance to canker. Home gardeners and allotment holders need some patience here.

The seeds take forever to germinate, and are usually sown in late winter and early spring in rows about 12 inches (30cm) apart. They like their feet in deep, sandy soil (you can get away with shallow soil if you plant a stubby variety such as Evesham). My rich clay would smother them. Lumpy soil will make the roots turn a corner. A vigilant gardener will thin the seedlings to a good hand's width apart, then water them when and if they remember. The parsnip is quite tolerant of drought, so useful for the forgetful gardener.

The old wives' tale about this vegetable tasting better after a good frost or two has sound foundations. In practice, the frost turns the starch into sugar, giving a more rounded flavor. Older gardeners have told me they really need four or five hard frosts to make a difference. I am tempted to suggest we leave them in the ground until the roast beef is in the oven, but they can be frustratingly difficult to extract if the ground is frozen.

Varieties

I have never seen parsnips sold under their varietal names. "It's just a parsnip, guv." If we want to know which is which, we apparently must grow our own. As a cook, I remain unconvinced that there is a huge difference between one and the other, but allotment holders and farmers may know better. Besides Excalibur, Gladiator,* and Javelin,* other varieties you might like to grow are:

Hollow Crown* Named for the way in which its stem seems to be sunk deep into the top of the root, this is one of the oldest varieties in cultivation, if not the oldest. Paler flesh than some, and mellow rather than "in your face" sweet.
The Student* Grown initially from wild seed, this thick variety was the work of one James Buckman, professor of geology, natural history, and botany at the Royal Agricultural College, who donated his prize seed to Suttons in 1860. Painfully slow to germinate.
Harris Model* Smooth, long roots with no side roots and an especially sweet flavor.

*Available from US seed sources.

A parsnip in the kitchen

The hidden treasure here is sugar. To get the best out of this vegetable, you need to caramelize the sugars present in the flesh and introduce an element of richness with butter, cream, or spices. There is little excitement in a plainly boiled root.

Simmering in water until they yield slightly to the touch will soften the starch. It's generally a good idea to do this before roasting or baking, otherwise they tend to become a boring chew. Shocking them in sizzling butter or a mixture of butter and oil helps to get a good crust going. Slow roasting, with the occasional turn, should achieve a tender, nuttily flavored vegetable that is pleasurable in small quantities. Two or three cork-sized lumps per person are usually enough.

Where the 'snip reaches glorious heights is when you tuck a handful around the Sunday roast, when the roasting juices get a chance to caramelize with the roots' own sugars, or if you bake them in layers with cream to which you have added a few spices. Thickly sliced, they have the ability to soak up the cream and develop a soft, undulating crust similar to potatoes cooked à la dauphinoise. The combination of sweetness, spice, and cream is extraordinary.

There are still many who fail to get the point of this overblown wild root. Others have questioned why I give it such high billing in my kitchen. In its defense, the parsnip possesses a rare quality that will introduce body to soups, stocks, and stews. Lamb stew without a touch of parsnip always seems to have something indefinable missing. The vegetable has a grounding, steadying effect and seems to bring the other aromatics together.

As a mash to accompany a chicken casserole, a pork roast, or a pile of sausages, parsnip makes a fine alternative to the usual potato. The inherent sweetness is a good contrast to the umami notes of the meat and its glossy, sticky skin. That mash, if made dry enough, can be used as a base for parsnip patties flecked with parsley and bacon or as a thick crust for a shepherd's pie. For which you might like to see my recipe in *Real Cooking*.

Roasted, the root will provide the necessary sweet note to balance a meal that might otherwise be monotonously savory. The occasional mouthful of sugary root, its edges browned and tacky with caramelized sugar, is entirely at home with roast beef and pork.

A soup of parsnips—bland, sweet, calming—is pleasing on a gray day. A version with apple is surprisingly "unsweet," especially if you add a crisped slice or two of bacon.

A fried parsnip can also be a good thing. The trick is to blanch chunks of the vegetable first in boiling water, then fry them in deep peanut oil. The resulting sweet, hot chips are tempting when dipped into hollandaise sauce, especially if it contains more than the classic proportion of lemon juice.

One of the curious facts about the parsnip is how it shines all the more brightly with the addition of a bit more sugar. In theory this should be too much of a good thing. In practice it is what the root needs if we are to see it at its best (which is, after all, why we are here). A scattering of Demerara sugar before baking, a spoonful of runny honey or maple syrup before the chopped roots meet the roasting pan, is all it takes.

When parsnips are sold away from the scrubbed and sanitized supermarket shelves, some shoppers find the sight of this long root and its casing of soil less than inviting. I disagree, but then I like to buy my veg dirty. Once home, it will keep best in its protective layer of earth. If it has been scrubbed, keep it in a cool, dry place; the vegetable crisper of the fridge will do. In the kitchen the parsnip needs peeling—the skin tends to toughen on cooking and will refuse to mash, or will turn to leather when roasted— and when you do you are left with a sweet, ivory-cream root with which to play. Curious, though, how a peeled and rinsed parsnip becomes as slippery as a bar of soap.

Seasoning your parsnips

With the exception of thyme and rosemary, herbs are of little interest here. Spices, on the other hand, work like a dream. As a cooking medium, butter, dripping, and duck fat are more appropriate than olive oil—often the case with things grown underground.

Beef and its dripping A scattering of parsnips around the roast is invariably a good thing.

Gravy A pitcher of hot gravy poured over a mound of mashed roots is even better if the gravy was made yesterday and has had time to "ripen" in the fridge. Both gravy and mash should be piping hot.

Spices Cinnamon, cumin, and nutmeg added to the onions at the outset flatter a smooth parsnip soup, as will a spoonful of the mild garam masala stirred in toward the end.

Mace If there is a single spice that seems made for the parsnip it is powdered mace. In a parsnip cake, or as a pinch of seasoning in a creamy dauphinoise, mace's subtle, musky sweetness is extraordinary.

Butter Use to enrich a mash or for frying thickly sliced steamed roots. A fat knob added after draining will brighten even the lowliest offering of boiled roots (surprisingly luxurious when eaten with boiled ham).

Cream It may seem altogether too bland to match such a sweet vegetable but cream will seduce when used to bake a dish of sliced parsnips. The addition of some softened onions or a little pancetta is also worthwhile.

Mustard Mild whole-grain mustard balances the inherent sweetness in gratins and soups.

And...

* Due to their excellent storage qualities, parsnips are in markets all year. At their best after a good frost, their sweetness is welcome in any month from October to March. They feel awkward in summer.
* I have been known to stick a box of them outside when there is frost around. They seem all the sweeter for it.
* The small, round parsnips that appear in late summer are exceptionally mild (one could say tasteless) but are good for introducing the root to skeptical newcomers.
* I have very little spare room in my vegetable patch, so I plant no parsnips. They hog a lot of space throughout summer.
* The sweetness of this root is particularly appropriate with beef and all the game birds and ravishing with innards. Mashed, it forms a sincere partnership with liver, bacon, lamb shanks, and oxtail. This is not the vegetable to force into a marriage with fish. It is just plain wrong.
* The sweet mash likes some gravy to play with. I include it on the side of unctuous, sloppily sauced suppers like braised oxtail, ham and parsley sauce, lamb stew and liver, and sausage hotpot.
* Parsnip fries rarely crisp as successfully as potato ones. But blanching or steaming the vegetable first, then frying it once in hot oil, then again in very, very hot oil will bring us as near as we can get.
* If you grow parsnips, they will keep splendidly in the ground until you need them. If you buy them, then try to find dirty ones. The presence of soil seems to have a preserving effect. I keep mine in a cool scullery (the coldest room in the house) in a brown paper bag. They remain in fine condition for a week or more. The fridge is fine too, even more so if you wrap them in newspaper.

The perfect roast parsnip

Among the potatoes there were clearly parsnips, their cut sides straighter, their color darker and showing the odd flash of glowing, deepest yellow. There was beef, a small rib, its three wide bones sticky, its fat incandescent in the metal roasting pan blackened and buckled from a decade of Sunday lunches.

The beef was lifted out to a warm place to rest under a dome of crumpled aluminum foil and its juices left to settle. The potatoes and parsnips were emptied into a dish and briefly returned to the oven. There was a last-minute stirring of gravy on the stove, the mixing of grated horseradish root and cream in a cup, wedges of cabbage were drained and buttered. Plates clattered.

You could argue that the perfect roast parsnip had a lot of help—the gravy, the odd savory crumb of fat from the beef, the faintest dab of heat from the creamed horseradish to kick its sweetness into touch—but it was as fine as a swollen, starchy root could ever be, both savory and stickily sweet on the outside and softly yielding within. It had picked up the soul of the roasting juices and toasted onion in the pan.

Roasted alone with just dripping, oil, or butter, plus salt and thyme leaves pulled from the branch, a parsnip can be treat enough, yet allowed to catch here and there with the other elements from the pan, the parsnip can excel. A nugget of sweet gold among a plate of serious savor and celebration.

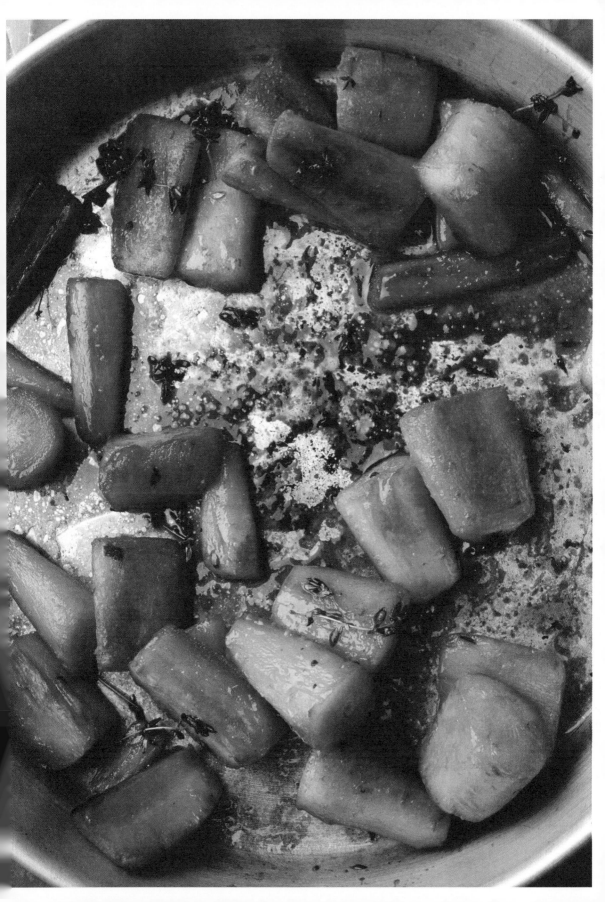

Roast parsnips

I cook them in dripping or butter for preference. Peanut oil if there is nothing else. They take forty minutes to color interestingly but an hour will turn them into vegetable toffee. The initial steaming is worth the ten minutes' wait and the pan to rinse and dry, helping as it does to keep them moist during the roasting and preventing them from toughening up in the heat.

enough for 4
parsnips – 1 pound (450g)
dripping, duck fat, or butter – a couple of spoonfuls

Preheat the oven to 350°F (180°C). Peel your parsnips, cut them into fat lumps, and steam them for ten minutes in a colander over a pan of boiling water. Warm a couple of heaping spoonfuls of fat in a roasting pan in the oven, then add the steamed parsnips. Roast for forty-five minutes or so, until their insides are soft and creamy, their exterior gold, brown, and, here and there, almost black. An occasional turn in the pan is a good thing, but too much meddling will prevent them achieving the ultimate sticky crust (the same goes for sausages, which I mention only because the two make a lovely pair). Inevitably the parsnips will have one side—that which lies underneath—darker and chewier than the others. It is part of the pleasure.

... and with thyme and maple syrup

The thyme is essential here, adding an important herbal note to the general sugar-fest. You need something savory alongside, and nothing works quite so well as gloriously rare roast beef. Sausages come a close second.

enough for 6
parsnips – 6 large
butter – a thick slice
a little beef dripping (or extra butter)
thyme – about 8 small sprigs
maple syrup – 4 teaspoons

Preheat the oven to 400°F (200°C). Peel the parsnips and remove the tops. Slice each in half unless they are truly enormous, in which case quarters might be better. Put them into a roasting pan with the thick slice of butter and a spoonful of beef dripping (or more butter). Season with salt and black pepper, then roast for thirty-five to forty minutes, until the parsnips are soft and golden. Remove the leaves from the thyme sprigs and add them to the vegetables with the maple syrup, turning the parsnips over as you go. Continue to roast for twenty minutes or so, until the surface of the vegetables is sticky and golden, the flesh soft and sweetly tender.

... and with sesame and honey

Whatever magic it may contain (and I certainly believe it does), honey is still sugar, and it seems extraordinary to add it to an already sweet root. But for some reason it works, bringing out the vegetable's flavor and lending it a distinct depth. I can't think of any better accompaniment to roast pork.

enough for 4
parsnips – 2 pounds (1kg)
a little peanut oil
a little rosemary
sesame seeds – 2 tablespoons

for the dressing
honey – 4 level tablespoons
sherry vinegar – 3 tablespoons
peanut oil – 3 tablespoons
sesame oil – a good splash

Preheat the oven to 350°F (180°C). Bring a pan of water to a boil. Peel the parsnips, cut them in half lengthwise, and then into fat chunks. When the water boils, lower them in and simmer for ten minutes, until they show early signs of tenderness. Remove from the heat and drain.

Pour a glug of oil into a roasting pan, add the drained parsnips, and toss them with sea salt, pepper, and some chopped needles of rosemary. A tablespoon or so will do. Roast for about forty minutes, turning them in the pan occasionally, so that they end up with a pale, golden crust on all sides. In a dry, shallow pan, lightly brown the sesame seeds. They will take barely a minute or so to color.

Put the honey into a small bowl and whisk in the vinegar, peanut oil, and sesame oil with a small grinding of salt and black pepper. Remove the parsnips from the oven and immediately toss them in the honey dressing, scattering over the toasted sesame seeds as you go.

How to make the silkiest purée

Parsnips make a better purée than a mash. Their fibers, coarser than potatoes or carrots, demand that extra bit of trouble from the cook, but they are easy enough to reduce to a fluffy cream in a food processor or stand mixer (use the beater attachment). Butter, hot milk, or a dollop of crème fraîche helps smooth the resulting starchy pulp to a soft and extremely silky purée. Beat it in with a whisk or wooden spoon to introduce air. The trick to a mash that is smooth but not wet is to steam the roots rather than boil them and a generous hand with the dairy.

The moment of bliss is when the parchment-colored purée slides into hot roasting juices or gravy on the plate.

A contemporary parsnip purée

Peel and boil, rather than steam, your parsnips here. The extra water will help with the texture. When they are tender to the point of a knife, blitz them in a food processor until smooth. Put into a bowl and beat in enough butter and crème fraîche to turn it into a shapeless purée. Season with a little smooth mustard and black pepper. Serve with grilled lamb chops.

A rich root and cheese soup for a winter's day

The tools for my winter gardening sessions tend to lie on the kitchen floor from one week to the next: the pruning knife, my leather-handled pruning shears, the largest of the two spades, the rake. They serve as a reminder that even though the garden may look crisp and neat from the window, there is still work to be done. It is during these cold, gray-sky days that I sometimes feel as if I live on soup. Roots—fat carrots, artichokes, and woody parsnips— are part of the lineup, along with onions and the occasional potato. I take much pleasure in the way something can be both earthy and velvety at the same time. Rather like my gardening gloves.

enough for 4
a medium onion
large parsnips – 2
butter – 4 tablespoons (50g)
garlic – 2 plump cloves
a little flour
dried chile flakes – a teaspoon
turmeric – half a teaspoon
vegetable stock – 4 cups (a liter)
light cream – scant ½ cup (100ml)
mild, grainy mustard – 2 tablespoons
Cornish Yarg, or perhaps Gruyère – 3½ ounces (100g), diced

Peel and coarsely chop the onion and parsnips. Melt the butter in a large, heavy pot, add the onion and, once it has started to relax, add the parsnips.

Peel the garlic, squash it flat, then add to the pan. Cook over medium heat, lid on, until the onion has colored lightly and the edges of the parsnips are mostly golden. Resist disturbing the vegetables too much as they cook: a slight browning of the parsnips here and there is essential to the flavor of the soup.

Sprinkle a dusting of flour into the pot, stir in the chile flakes and turmeric, then cook for a minute or two to remove the raw taste of the flour. Add the stock, stir, and bring to a boil. Decrease the heat to let the soup to sit at a light boil and continue until the vegetables are soft, about twenty minutes.

Pour into a blender or food processor and whiz to a creamy purée. Add the cream and mustard and salt and freshly ground pepper to taste. Drop the cubes of cheese into four warm soup bowls, then ladle the soup over. Serve immediately.

Ham with apple juice and parsnip purée

A poaching broth for fish, a chicken, or a lumbering piece of ham is all the more interesting for the inclusion of a leek or two. They soften the stock, bringing the flavors of onion, carrot, and herbs together.

The ham recipe here is my standard "food for a crowd." Poached ham slices neatly, even when it falls off the knife in chunks, and can be kept waiting patiently in its own stock without coming to any harm. I often serve it with creamed spinach. I include it here partly to show ham's affinity with parsnips and also because it's a useful recipe and I wanted to get it in somewhere. This seemed as good a place as anywhere.

I usually buy a ready-tied piece of boneless ham from the butcher for this. It needs no soaking, but will benefit from being brought to a boil in water, drained, and then rinsed before being cooked in the apple juice.

enough for 6
boneless ham, tied – 4 pounds (2kg)
leeks – 2
large celery ribs – 2
a carrot
unfiltered apple juice – 8 cups (2 liters)
juniper berries – 15
a cinnamon stick
black peppercorns – 9
parsley stems – 6 or so
bay leaves – 2

to serve
parsnip purée (page 342)

Put the ham in a large saucepan; it should fit snugly. Cover with water, bring to the boil, then pour the water away. Rinse the ham and return to the pot.

Split the leeks in half, discarding most of the tough, dark green tops. Rinse them thoroughly under cold running water to remove any trapped grit that may be lurking between the layers. Cut the celery into short pieces and tuck them into the pot with the leeks and the whole carrot. Pour in the apple juice, adding a top-up of water if it doesn't quite cover the ham.

Lightly crush the juniper berries with the flat side of a large knife, then add them to the pan with the cinnamon stick, peppercorns, parsley stems, and bay leaves. Bring to a boil, decrease the heat to a jolly simmer, then scoop off the froth that floats on top. Cover partially with a lid and leave it to get on with things for a couple of hours, checking from time to time that it isn't bubbling too fiercely or hasn't stopped altogether.

After two hours, check the ham for tenderness. Leave in the cooking liquor, the heat switched off, for anything up to twenty minutes before carving. Serve in thickish slices, drizzled with a spoonful of the hot, appley cooking liquor, with the vegetables if you wish, and the puréed parsnips.

A dish of cream and parsnips to accompany a roast

Eventually, possibly toward the end of your meal, you reach the point where the salty, herbal juices from the meat mingle with the sweet creaminess of those from the parsnips, a moment of intense pleasure.

While winter was in its death throes, and the first white narcissi were starting to peak through the damp earth, I produced this for Sunday lunch with a leg of lamb spiked with tough old rosemary twigs. We passed round a bowl of winter chicory and watercress for everyone to take handfuls with which to clean the mixture of juices from their plates.

Parsnips

347

enough for 4 to 6
parsnips – 1 pound (450g)
a tablespoon of butter
heavy cream – 1¼ cups (300ml)
whole milk – scant ½ cup (100ml)
thyme
a lump of Parmesan
breadcrumbs

Preheat the oven to 325°F (160°C). Peel the parsnips and slice them thinly from stalk to tip. The slices should be only slightly thicker than ⅛ inch (3mm). Bring to a boil in deep, unsalted water, simmer for five to seven minutes, then drain carefully so that they don't break up.

Butter a large ovenproof baking dish or roasting pan. Lay the sliced parsnips in the dish, neatly or hugger-mugger as the mood takes you. Mix the cream and milk in a pitcher and season with salt and pepper. Pull a tablespoon of thyme leaves from their stems and stir into the cream, then pour over the parsnips. Grate over enough Parmesan and breadcrumbs to cover the surface lightly. Bake for forty to fifty minutes, by which time it should be bubbling and golden.

A soup of toasted roots with porcini toasts

Dried porcini are expensive, but even a small handful added to a soup will bring with it a wave of smoky, almost beefy notes. A general instruction with parsnip soup is to prevent the vegetables coloring, presumably to keep the soup pale, but I suggest the opposite. You want the parsnips to cook to a gentle golden color before you add the stock; that way the soup will have a deeper flavor and a color reminiscent of heather honey.

enough for 6
dried porcini mushrooms – a handful
onions – 2 medium
olive oil – 3 tablespoons
a large tablespoon of butter
parsnips – 1¼ pounds (600g; 2 large ones)
light stock – 5 cups (1.2 liters)
a rib of celery, chopped
garlic – a plump clove, peeled and squashed

for the porcini toasts
dried porcini mushrooms – a handful
the leaves from a small bunch of parsley
a small clove of garlic
walnuts – a handful, chopped
butter – 4 tablespoons (50g)
interesting bread – 6 pieces, toasted

Soak the porcini in about 1¼ cups (300ml) warm water for thirty minutes.

Peel the onions, chop them coarsely, and put in a heavy-bottomed pan with the oil and butter. Cook until soft and translucent, stirring regularly. Peel the parsnips and cut them into large chunks. Add them to the pan and let them color lightly on all sides. They need to be evenly but gently toasted—a pale honey gold rather than mahogany brown. This will take seven to ten minutes with the occasional bit of stirring.

Pour in the stock, then add the celery, garlic, the porcini, and their soaking water. Season and bring to a boil. Decrease the heat so that the soup simmers merrily for about forty minutes.

This is one of those soups that are best eaten smoothly puréed, so push it all through the blender until smooth. Check the seasoning; it may need more salt and pepper. Serve with the toasts below, if you wish.

To make the toasts, soak the porcini in warm water for half an hour. Squeeze dry, then chop together with the parsley and garlic. Stir in the walnuts. Melt the butter in a small pan, add the mixture, and stir until warm and fragrant. Spoon onto the pieces of toast and float them on your soup.

A root vegetable korma

The kormas of India, serene, rich, silken, have much in them that works with the sweetness of the parsnip—cream, yogurt, nuts, sweet spices. The Mughal emperors who originally feasted on such mildy spiced and lavishly finished recipes may not have approved of my introduction of common roots but the idea works well enough. Despite instructions the length of a short story, I can have this recipe on the table within an hour. For those who like their Indian food on the temperate side.

enough for 4 with rice or Indian breads
onions – 2 medium
ginger – a fat, thumb-sized piece
garlic – 3 cloves
a mixture of parsnip, rutabaga, carrots, Jerusalem artichokes –
    2½ pounds (1.5kg) in total
cashews – ⅔ cup (100g)
green cardamom pods – 6
cumin seeds – 2 teaspoons
coriander seeds – a tablespoon
vegetable or sunflower oil, or butter – 2 tablespoons
ground turmeric – 2 teaspoons
chile powder – half a teaspoon
a cinnamon stick
green chiles – 2 smallish ones, depending on their heat, thinly sliced
light or heavy cream – ⅔ cup (150ml)
thick plain yogurt – ⅔ cup (150g)
cilantro, chopped

Peel the onions, cut them into large pieces, then blitz in a food processor until coarsely minced—you don't want a sloppy purée. Peel and coarsely grate the ginger on the coarse side of a grater. Peel and finely slice the garlic cloves. Peel and coarsely chop the vegetables. Coarsely chop half of the cashews.

Now deal with the spices: open the cardamom pods with your nails and scrape out the seeds, then crush them to a gritty powder. Grind the cumin and coriander seeds to a fine powder.

Put the oil or butter into a deep, heavy-bottomed pan and stir in the onions, letting them soften but not color. Stir in the grated ginger and sliced garlic, continue cooking over gentle heat for a couple of minutes, then introduce the spices—cardamom, cumin, coriander, turmeric, chile powder, and the cinnamon stick. Continue cooking, stirring for a couple of minutes, until the fragrance of the spices begins to rise, then add the chopped root vegetables and the chopped nuts. Season with the thinly sliced chiles, salt, and black pepper.

Stir in 3 cups (750ml) water, partially cover with a lid, and let simmer gently for forty-five to fifty minutes, until the roots are tender when pierced with the tip of a knife. Toast the reserved whole cashews.

Carefully introduce the cream and yogurt to the pan, letting them heat through but not boil. Should the mixture boil, it will curdle, and though the flavor will be fine, the grainy texture will be offputting. Check the seasoning, adding more salt or pepper if necessary. Scatter over the toasted cashews and some chopped cilantro.

Another supper of young parsnips and sausage

At the top of the garden, past the sunny stone terrace, the little beds of vegetables and the unruly shrubs, is a thicket, less than ten feet (three meters) deep but just enough to give the whole garden an unkempt, relaxed feel. Here lie the compost bins with their lids of rotting carpet, green plastic bags of decaying leaf mold, and four small trees of damson, hazel, mirabelle, and a King James mulberry—the latter being a "guardian" tree planted in the northernmost corner to protect the garden from the north wind. In between grow drifts of snowdrops, wild garlic sent by a friend from Cornwall, and *fraises de bois*, with which this garden is littered, and whose flowers twinkle like tiny stars in spring.

The work in this part of the garden is mostly done in winter, if only because the leaflessness of the trees makes it possible to see what you are doing. It is always dark and cold here, and damp, too. I come in from turning the compost or cutting hazel twigs with my feet like ice, my fingers numb. Invariably it's a Saturday, when I have been early to The Ginger Pig for my sausages. I leave them to bake with parsnips and stock. A slow bowl of food, which often sits patiently until I come in, too chilled to the bone to do anything but eat.

enough for 4
onions – 4 medium
peanut oil – 3 tablespoons
parsnips – 1 pound (500g)
butcher's sausages – 6 thick, juicy ones
thyme – a few sprigs
chicken stock – 2 cups (500ml)

Preheat the oven to 375°F (190°C). Peel the onions and slice them in half from root to tip, then cut each half into six or eight pieces. Soften them slowly in the oil in a flameproof baking dish or roasting pan over medium heat.

While they are softening, peel the parsnips and cut them into short, thick chunks, about the length of a wine cork. Add them to the onions and let color, increasing the heat a little if need be. Remove the onions and parsnips from the pan.

Cut each sausage into thirds, put them in the pan, adding a little more oil if it appears dry, and let them color. Return the onions and parsnips to the pan. It is important everything is a good color before you proceed. Strip the leaves from the thyme and stir them in, together with the chicken stock. Bring to a boil briefly, then put in the oven to bake for thirty-five to forty minutes, until the sausages are cooked right through, the parsnips are truly tender, and the stock has reduced a little.

Parsnips baked with cheese

It is often worth introducing some sort of richness to vegetables with a heart of starch. Ideal suitors include butter, cream, bacon fat, and honey. Jane Grigson suggests cheese, often in the form of Gruyère or Parmesan, as do others, who have been known to roll a stiff parsnip mash in grated Parmesan and deep-fry it as a croquette. To this list I add my own, a shallow cake along the lines of a pan haggerty (potatoes and onions topped with cheese), made with thin slices of the root layered with grated cheese and herbs. Parsnip haggerty, anyone?

> *enough for 2 as a main dish, with winter salad at its side*
> a large onion
> butter – 5 tablespoons (75g)
> parsnips – 2 large
> thyme – the leaves from 3 or 4 sprigs
> cheese – 3½ ounces (100g), I use Cornish Yarg or sometimes Gruyère
> vegetable stock – a scant ½ cup (100ml)

Preheat the oven to 400°F (200°C). Peel the onion and cut it into paper-thin rings. Melt half the butter in a shallow ovenproof pan and gently fry the onion until soft and translucent. Stop before it colors.

Peel the parsnips and slice in fine disks. I like to make them so thin you can almost read through them. Remove the onion from the pan, place a layer or two of parsnips in it, then brush with more melted butter and scatter over salt, pepper, some of the thyme, and a little of the cheese. Do this twice more, ending with cheese. Pour over the stock.

Cover with lightly buttered wax paper or aluminum foil, then place on a high rack in the oven and bake for twenty-five to thirty minutes. Remove the paper and test the parsnips with a sharp knife; it should glide in effortlessly. Return to the oven, uncovered, for about ten minutes to brown. Serve straight from the pan.

Peas

Walking around your garden or allotment at midnight is a gentle but sensuous pleasure, and never more so than in midsummer when the pea flowers, and those of the fava beans, shine as white as bone in the moonlight. Sometimes, just before I go to bed, I like to walk along the paths, the gravel crunching under my feet, taking in the eerie shadows cast by the crooked cane wigwams of climbing Viola Cornetti beans, their tendrils reaching out from the shadows. On a still night the scent of the roses is joined by that of the sweet peas—Cupani, Black Knight, the snow-white Dorothy Eckford—fava beans, and jasmine. To burst a pod of peas and eat them in the dark is a sweet joy.

I am not sure how much space you need to be self-sufficient in peas, but more than any allotment or average garden can offer. No matter. The pleasure from a row or two held up with hazel canes and string, their young growing shoots whispering in the night, is enough to make the planting and potting and watering and podding worth every second of our time. And how could anyone fail to find romance in a pea called Serpette Guilloteau (named after a sickle-shaped pruning blade) or any one of the endless stories of "mummy peas" that are rumored to have originated—or not—in several of the Egyptian tombs? As if to fire our imaginations even further, there is an old variety named Tutankhamun.

You could, of course, open a bag. Frozen peas are a dependable delight. Though the pea has been dried, soaked, and used as basic sustenance since earliest times—the poor ate them as a porridge, like a bland dhal—they have only been eaten fresh since the thirteenth century, when the Italians made them fashionable. The plants were, by all accounts, gangly specimens that required ladders for picking. Duke of Albany and the rarer Magnum Bonum are tall varieties still hanging on, being grown like runner beans, though they have generally been superceded by shorter varieties such as Hurst Greenshaft.

More peas are eaten raw than cooked in my house. They end up in salads of crab and cilantro, or tucking themselves into the crevices of pale green Buttercrunch lettuce. Many are eaten straight from the pod. They don't age well, so I cook them the day they are picked, and certainly so if I have bought them from the produce market. In truth, store-bought peas can disappoint, but then maybe I'm unlucky, even though I always seek out plump pods that are bright green and unblemished.

The pea has a simple nature. In the garden, the plants like much moisture and a cool spot in which to grow; in the kitchen they can be boiled, preferably in deep, lightly salted water at a merry boil, and will cook in four or five minutes. Often less. Nothing good will come from getting convoluted with them. It is for their sweet simplicity that we value them.

The perfect pea

1970 and the lane down to Collins Green Farm is steep, on one side a meadow dotted with plantain and long-stemmed buttercups, the other a kitchen garden with fava beans, swaying hollyhocks, and here and there discarded bikes with stabilizers and children's anoraks. Near the walls of the house itself is a stand of long canes, secured halfway with string, tightly bound against the wind. It is what I would expect runner beans to grow up.

The canes are full of peas, taller than usual, growing higher than even the tallest runner beans. No one knows the variety—it could well be Alderman, one of the few survivors of the many varieties of tall peas we once had, or Telegraph, Telephone, or Duke of Albany, which can grow taller than a man. Being tall, they need more water than the dwarf varieties, but are less backbreaking to pick.

My trips down the lane were for bales of hay for my rabbit or for runner beans for tea, but sometimes I would come back with a basket of peas as a gift for my parents. Still wet with dew, they should have been the sweetest peas ever, but rarely matched those from the bag in the freezer.

Frozen peas never vary in sweetness or flavor. No vegetable is as successful at being bred for a consistent taste. They are never tough or sour or pallid, or just "not the same." The frozen pea is a testament to uniformity and reliability. Pity it so lacks romance.

A pea in the garden

Most crop twelve weeks after planting (plant in March or April, harvest in June and July), though this will vary according to variety and the conditions. You can plant outdoors in March and April if the ground is not too cold, in trenches 2 inches (5cm) deep and 4 inches (10cm) wide. Most experienced growers claim that peas do better when planted from early autumn onward, giving an earlier and more reliable crop. They are not frostproof in the way of a fava bean, so unless you have somewhere cool and frost free to keep them until the ground has warmed up, spring planting may be a safer option.

A pea diary

April 6 I have a fancy to plant a row or two of peas, not purely for their pods but for their delicate, curling shoots and tendrils, which I find an extraordinary and enchanting addition to a salad. There is something fairylike about their presence in a bowl of early summer leaves, romantic wisps of palest green perched on top of all the other fronds and fragile greenery. The dressing must be so light as to seem almost nonexistent. I wake to find a layer of thick snow has fallen during the night, turning my grubby, rundown corner of London into a scene of peace and piercing-white light. I long for these rare moments. Each shivering stamen on the white pear blossom outside the kitchen window is sparkling with flakes of freezing snow. A single set of prints tells that a brave bird came looking for crumbs early this morning.

By midafternoon the sun is on my back, shining so brightly I almost wish I were wearing a T-shirt, as I dib dried peas into pots of deep, wet compost. It's a risk—peas hate going into cold soil—but I am testing Douce Provence, an ancient French pea that is said to withstand frost and whose robust qualities belie the tenderness of its pods. Douce Provence is a forgotten pea, from a time when legumes were grown more for drying than for eating fresh. The habit of boiling fresh peas may well have been introduced by Catherine de Medici, whose gardeners are said to have brought them from Italy. Loving them the way we do (for some, peas are the only truly acceptable vegetable), it is a habit for which we should be more than grateful.

May 4 The plants, fragile, dull green leaves from cotton-thread stems, are already a good ¾ inch (2cm) high. The ground they are to go in, on the cool side of the garden, has been dug, lightly manured, and rested for six weeks. Now I cover it with a roll of garden fleece to keep it warm. Peas tend not to germinate in cold ground, but when the weather heats up they will value the moisture-retaining quality of cool, rich soil.

May 5 I plant Hurst Greenshaft, a more popular variety. A week later to the day, they are up too, their plump green tips unfurling. Many allotment holders will regard this as exceptionally late, peas hating the strong heat of summer, but I find they soon catch up with those you plant earlier.

May 28 Roots are showing through the bottoms of the pea pots. I move them to the bed, making two long, shallow trenches with a trowel (for want of a hoe), 8 inches (20cm) apart, then gently pushing each seedling into the soil, ¾ inch (2cm) apart. Each plantlet gets its own stick, and here and there a brittle hazel twig, stripped of its leaves, to give it something interesting to climb. Chicken wire would work too, as would a cat's cradle of string. I water them in well.

May 31 Most peas of both varieties have survived, save a couple that lie in a dead faint. Several are bursting into flower. Pale, ivory-white blooms against fine, twining stems.

June 25 We pick the first peas and their tendrils, splitting the pods with a childish pop, then worrying the contents out with our thumbs. They never make it as far as the kitchen.

Varieties

Hatif d'Annonay Small bushes that need little support. Dark green pods with smooth seeds. Sow and pick early.

Amelioree d'Auvergne Early or main-crop pea with short, plump pods held on plants just over 3 feet (a meter) high.

Pilot A tall, fast-growing pea for planting in autumn or early April.

Alderman* One of the few tall varieties left, growing to 6 feet (2 meters) or more. Good flavor but won't hold up in a drought.

Early Onward Early, bushy variety with excellent flavor.

Feltham First Short-growing, very early pea, but needs picking while young.

Kelvedon Wonder Good flavor, a much loved favorite of many allotment holders.

Little Marvel* A reliable, early-maturing dwarf pea, good for those with limited space.

Hurst Greenshaft Along with Kelvedon, one of the most popular and flavorsome varieties. Long pods and good cropping from plants about 2 feet (60cm) high.

Lincoln* High yielding, easy to shell, and heat tolerant bush type.

Maestro* Shelling pea on vines about 2 feet (60cm) long; best in full sun but tolerates cool days.

Mr. Big* The name says it: large peas in stocky pods; for cooks who like extra-sweet peas.

Other reliable varieties are the heavy-cropping Lincoln and Onward, a delectably sweet pea that is probably the widest grown. The snow pea is not for me. I find it tastes more of sugar than of pea, but those who like its flat, pale crunch could do worse than grow Carouby de Maussane, sweet pea pods with brilliant purple flowers, or Dwarf Sweet Green—a variety that lives up to its name.

*Available from US seed sources.

A pea in the kitchen

Tiny peas straight from their pods need three minutes in frantically boiling water. That's all. I never salt them. Ready-shelled fresh peas from the supermarket provide the most instant gratification in the vegetable world, but in our house rarely make it to the pot, being eaten straight from the bag like vegetable Smarties.

Peas destined for a risotto can be added at two specific points. First, just before the rice, giving them time to truly flavor the dish, and second, about five minutes before the risotto is due to finish cooking, offering a sparkle of fresh pea flavor. That way, you get both depth of flavor and freshness, but you also get two distinctly different shades of pea.

For emerald soups (of lettuce and bacon or spinach), the peas need little more than seven to ten minutes if they are added with the onion base, before the stock. They work well enough when chucked raw into the filling for a chicken or fish pie but should be cooked in boiling water before being tossed into a dish of freshly drained pasta. I don't add them to a stir-fry. They like a bit more moisture to cook in than such a recipe has to offer. Peas and chopsticks are an accident waiting to happen.

To purée them, I use a food processor or a blender, adding olive oil or melted butter to speed the process. To crush them for a coarser texture, I find a potato masher or fork helpful.

Seasoning your peas

The pea shares its Christmas card list with the fava bean, numbering
bacon and smoked pork products as its best mates. It has many close friends;
indeed, it is difficult to think of anything it doesn't get on with.

Pancetta Warm cubes of pancetta or smoked bacon in a shallow pan until
the fat is gold, then stir in freshly cooked peas. Serve with cauliflower cheese
or a similar comfort supper.

Cheese A controversial marriage this, but I stand by it. Feta, in jagged
pieces, chalky goat cheeses, and thick, quivering slices of buffalo mozzarella
all work well with the pea's sugary notes. Others claim that peas in a
Cheddar cheese sauce as a side dish for bacon or ham makes the heart sing,
but I have yet to try it.

Lemon A revelation. Shake cooked peas in a pan with a liquid seasoning
of lemon juice, finely grated zest, and olive oil. A lively addition to a plate
of steamed halibut, grilled plaice, or breaded fish strips.

Lettuce The classic recipe of *petits pois à la française* involves simmering
soft-leaved lettuce with fresh peas until the peas are dull green and soft.
The two make a curiously moreish marriage, rich and yet homey.

Mint Yes, I know it's unfashionable. Do I care? No. This is the number-one
herb for the pea, although basil comes in a surprising second. Mint goes in
the water as they cook; basil is best shredded and mixed with the melted
butter you will toss them in.

And...

* While it is difficult to find anything that a spoonful of peas would not grace, it is worth making sure that we experience them with some of the ingredients whose sweetness they flatter most. Young lamb, battered cod, grilled plaice, poached ham, salmon in any guise, goat cheese, are all enhanced by our little green ones.
* I often don't put the peas into the boiling water until the meat is resting on the (warm) plates. I have known the tiny petits pois variety to be done in the time it takes me to carry the plates to the table.
* Peas do like a tablespoon of butter when they are cooked, but increasingly I find they also lap up melted bacon fat. It's a pukka marriage and you can add them, straight from the boil, to a pan in which you have fried a slice or two of bacon.
* Peas and new potatoes don't appear on the same plate just because they share a season but because the sweet greens and nutty potatoes form a thoroughly pleasing partnership in the mouth. Some might say inseparable.
* Don't put peas in a quiche. They may go nicely with a ham or crab filling but they make the custard fall apart. Not to mention the fact that a spotty quiche looks a bit silly.
* Peas are not always the easiest things to get from plate to mouth. At home I was taught to mush them on to the back of my fork with my knife. Now no one is looking, I use my fork as a shovel. I lose fewer that way. Others, perhaps a little greedily, use a spoon. Ideally, serve them with something they will stick to, like steamed fish and parsley sauce, roast beef and horseradish, even a dab of mashed potato.

A salad of beans, peas, and pecorino

Among the charcoal and garlic of midsummer's more robust cooking,
a quiet salad of palest green can come as a breath of calm. Last June, as
thousands joined hands around Stonehenge in celebration of the summer
solstice, I put together a salad of cool notes: mint, fava beans, and young
peas—a bowl of appropriate gentility and quiet harmony.

enough for 4
shelled fava beans – 1⅔ cups (250g)
shelled peas – 3 cups (400g)
ciabatta – 4 small slices
a little olive oil
salad leaves – 4 generous handfuls
mint leaves – a good handful
pecorino sardo cheese – 3 ounces (80g), in thin shavings

for the dressing
a lemon
olive oil (fruity and peppery) – 4 tablespoons
balsamic vinegar – a teaspoon

Bring a pan of water to a boil, then salt it lightly. Cook the beans in this,
drain them, then rinse in cold water. Put more water on and cook the peas.
Drain them and mix with the beans. Both peas and beans will need barely
more than a couple of minutes if they are small and sweet.

Make the dressing by dissolving a good pinch of salt in the juice of the
lemon, then using a fork to beat in the olive oil, balsamic vinegar, and a
grinding of black pepper (alternatively put all the ingredients in a screw-top
jar and shake).

Toast the slices of bread on both sides and tear them into short pieces.
Drizzle a little olive oil onto each one, then shake over a light dusting of
sea salt.

Toss the salad leaves and mint in the dressing, then add the peas, beans,
and pecorino shavings. Tuck in the toasted ciabatta and serve.

A green soup for a summer's day

Midsummer is a time of extraordinary activity in my garden. Every day brings with it a new shoot, a newly opened rose, a froth of lettuce seedlings. At this point I make a soup of the older lettuces and peas, and yet there is no reason why I shouldn't make it throughout the year with frozen peas and produce-market lettuce.

> *enough for 6*
> a large, round lettuce – about 14 ounces (400g)
> a thick slice of butter
> a couple of shallots
> shelled peas – 1 pound (500g)
> chicken or vegetable stock or water – 4 cups (a liter)
> mint – 3 bushy sprigs

Separate the lettuce leaves and stalks and wash thoroughly. Even the smallest amount of grit will ruin the soup. Melt the butter in a deep saucepan over low to medium heat. Peel the shallots and slice them thinly, then let them soften in the butter. When they are tender but have yet to color, chop the lettuce up a bit and stir it into the butter. As soon as it has wilted, add the peas, stock, and mint leaves and bring to a boil. Decrease the heat, season with salt and black pepper, and simmer for no longer than ten minutes.

Remove the pan from the heat and purée the soup in a blender until smooth. Check the seasoning, then serve hot.

Minted pea purée

> shelled peas – 3 cups (400g)
> mint – 4 sprigs
> olive oil – 3 tablespoons

Boil the peas and mint sprigs in lightly salted water until tender, then drain. Whiz the peas and mint in a food processor with the oil until smooth.

A lamb steak with peas and mint

It's mid-June and I have returned home with four lamb steaks. It's the sort
of thing I buy when my mind is elsewhere. I think I was after a "nothing-
special" lunch of ease and straightforwardness, yet once the steaks and their
fine frame of white fat had been brushed with olive oil and the leaves and
flowers of thyme, and were sizzling on the blackened garden grill, I realized
I had an extraordinary treat on my hands. Instead of a mound of petits
pois at the lamb's side, I blitzed the peas to a smooth purée with mint and
melted butter.

enough for 4
thyme – 6 bushy sprigs
a little olive oil
lamb steaks – 4, or 12 small rib chops

for the pea purée
shelled peas – 3 cups (400g)
mint – 4 sprigs
melted butter – 4 tablespoons

optional
pea shoots – 4 small handfuls
extra-virgin olive oil

Chop the thyme, then mash it in a pestle and mortar with a large pinch of
salt. Stir in the olive oil and a grinding of pepper. Brush over the lamb and
set aside for thirty minutes.

Boil the peas in lightly salted water until tender. Meanwhile, put the
mint leaves, butter, and a pinch of salt into a blender or food processor
and whiz until smooth. Drain the peas and whiz them in the blender or
processor with the mint butter until you have a thick, green cream. If you
need to keep it warm, put it in a bowl covered with aluminum foil in a pan
of hot water.

Grill the lamb on both sides until the outside has crisped and the inside
is still rose pink and juicy. Depending on the thickness of your lamb and the
heat of your grill, this will take about four minutes on each side.

Divide the pea cream among four warm plates. Place the cooked lamb
on top, then a handful of pea shoots on the lamb. Shake a little olive oil over
the lamb and pea shoots and serve.

A salad of hot bacon, lettuce, and peas

Anyone who has shelled a bag of peas will know how good they are raw.
Far too little is made of their scrunchy sweetness, and I put forward the
pod-fresh raw pea as an idea to throw into salads of pale yellow butterhead
lettuce, cracked wheat, or dishes of cooked fava beans. They work in their
uncooked state only when very young and small. Old peas are mealy and
sour. One rainy lunchtime in June, I put them into a simple salad of Peter
Rabbit lettuce, crisply cooked smoked bacon, and hand-torn ciabatta. The
result—restrained, refreshing, and somehow quintessentially English.

enough for 4
smoked bacon – 8 slices
a little oil
white bread – 5 ounces (150g)
a large, soft-leaved lettuce
a small bulb of fennel
shelled peas – 1 cup (150g)

for the dressing
Dijon mustard – a teaspoon
red wine vinegar – a tablespoon
olive oil – 4 tablespoons

Trim the bacon and discard its rind. Cut it into short lengths and cook in
a nonstick pan, with a little oil if necessary, until crisp. Remove the bacon
from the pan and drain on paper towels.

Tear the bread into small, jagged-edged pieces, discarding the crusts as
you go. Fry in the pan in which you cooked the bacon, adding more oil as
necessary. As soon as the pieces are nicely golden and blessed with the flavor
of the smoked bacon, remove to paper towels to drain and salt them lightly.

While the bread and bacon are cooking, wash the lettuce, separate the
leaves, tear them into manageable pieces, and put them in a serving bowl.
Finely shred the fennel and toss it into the lettuce leaves with the peas. Make
the dressing by mixing the mustard, vinegar, a grinding of salt and pepper,
and the oil in a small bowl or shaking them together in a small jar.

Put the hot bacon and bread in the salad, gently toss with the dressing,
then serve immediately.

Peppers

Without heat—from a grill, an oven, a cast-iron pan blackened with age—there is little point to the pepper. Raw, green, and unripe, its waxy, plastic skin and lack of obvious juice offer little but crisp nothingness. Refreshing, yes, but somehow an imposter in a green salad; an annoying intruder in a Bloody Mary; an unimaginative addition to a rice dish. Wherever it appears, the raw green pepper seems uncomfortable.

Left to ripen to a sunset orange or scarlet (a few varieties remain green even when ripe), then blistered over a hot flame or baked in a scorching oven, the pepper will show us its true heart and soul. By roasting or grilling, we do more than soften it, we create sweet juice with notes of caramel, tomato, honey, and smoke. The crisp shell relaxes to the texture of soft, moist flesh. Our "crisp nothingness" becomes the most tender and sensuous of vegetables.

The variety we know intimately, the bell pepper or capsicum, was originally Mexican, though the recipes we use tend to originate in the Middle East, the Mediterranean, or Eastern Europe. It is a fruit really, though we eat it as a vegetable, and a member of the nightshade family, along with the potato, eggplant, and the smaller, hot chiles. In mid-August we get the homegrown ones, twisted like a sultan's slipper; difficult to stuff neatly but more interesting than the bell pepper of dumpy uniformity. Horn-shaped varieties offer more of a clue to the fact that they are sisters to the chile, but there is no heat here, just slinky, silky flesh and a shape that begs more than anything else in the vegetable rack to be used to carry a cargo of spicily seasoned grain.

Stuffing aside, the pepper's proudest moment must be when it has been grilled or baked, stripped of its blackened skin, then laid in long, blood-red strips on an earthenware dish. Moistened with a bright, fruity olive oil and seasoned with the occasional slice of new, mild garlic and some torn basil, the pepper carries with it an almost erotic pleasure.

A pepper in the garden

The pepper only just survives the British climate. Night temperatures need to be above 70°F (20°C) for the seedlings to endure. In this country they will need a greenhouse to protect them, but as the bushes get stronger you can plant them outside. Mature plants do well in large pots, polytunnels, grow bags, and especially with their backs against a heat-retaining wall. If you can grow tomatoes, you can grow peppers.

Experts recommend planting seed in late winter, at a minimum soil temperature of 70°F (20°C). Use a thermometer rather than making an attempt to guess. Having no indoor growing space, I have yet to grow any from seed. My plants tend to arrive as "plugs" in late spring, and remain in 3½-inch (9cm) pots in the cold frame until early summer. I don't pinch out the tips as others do, but give them a high-nitrogen feed at this point. I transfer them to deep, 12-inch (30cm) pots once their roots have filled the small pots. They spend their days and nights on the stone steps near the house, their heavy harvest and thin stems supported on sticks, soaking up the residual heat. Once the flowers appear, the plants like good ventilation and an occasional feed with liquid fertilizer (I use bog-standard tomato food). They need plenty of late summer sun, more so than tomatoes, if they are to ripen, and—if you can find such a thing nowadays—the odd sprinkle of Epsom salts to quench their thirst for magnesium.

Varieties

I buy my plug plants ready for potting on, from a catalogue that includes the following:

Ace* An unusually good-tempered variety that ripens even in the coolest of summers.

Gourmet* Snooty name, but hides a glowing, orange pepper with a good, long season.

Gypsy* Narrow, bell-shaped, orange-red pepper.

Giant Szegedi* Popular Hungarian variety with high yields that will probably need support. Its thick flesh makes it sound for stuffing.

Red Knight* Early ripening and forgiving of the British summer.

Bounty Long, slender, deep-red pepper that lives up to its name.

*Available from US seed sources.

A pepper in the kitchen

A latecomer to the British kitchen, *Capsicum annum* is still rarely used as the principal ingredient in a meal. The 1960s and 1970s were a time of culinary adventure, a discovering and celebration of the heady flavors of the Mediterranean and, with it, the red pepper. Elizabeth David's books, written a decade earlier, became the blueprint for restaurants such as the Elizabeth in Oxford and the Hole in the Wall in Bath, whose menus consecrated the warm flavors of olive oil, eggplants, basil, and ripe peppers that are now firmly a part of Britain's diet.

From Mrs. David's books and these pioneering kitchens came *piperade*, a dish of eggs and sautéed peppers, which I never made, and gazpacho, a chilled vermillion soup of finely cut cucumber, garlic, tomatoes, and red peppers, which I did. With its raw garlic and pimiento, I remember it as a fiery, heart-pounding soup, an open window to the passionate flavors of its homeland.

In the 1980s Britain's chefs discovered the "coulis," a thin, brightly colored liquid somewhere between juice and purée, which modern-thinking French chefs were using to accompany a piece of meat or fish. The coulis— of anything from tomato to raspberry—was drizzled like an edible moat around (rather than over) noisettes of lamb, fillets of salmon, and fanned-out duck breasts. In some establishments the moat itself would be dotted with artfully turned vegetables and even flowers. A passing culinary fad, whose positive legacy has been to encourage a lighter style of cooking. The red pepper, perhaps because of its vibrant color, became the most ubiquitous coulis of all. In theory, the idea of using a thin sauce of red pepper to flatter a pastry parcel of ratatouille seems sound enough. The flavors should sit together happily but the effect was contrived. A proud fruit humiliated.

Of all the luscious, sun-soaked recipes we have borrowed from the Med, peppers Piedmontese, with its flashes of orange, pillar-box red, and deep olive green, is the one in which the pepper shows us what it is truly made of. No treatment quite gets this fruit to shine like roasting it with olive oil and a hint of anchovy. I don't always include the little fish. I add basil leaves to the open halves of pepper too, so that the copious olive oil, nuggets of garlic, and tomatoes tucked inside feel at home. It is a fragrant kitchen the day we have *peperoni alla piemontese* for lunch.

Elizabeth David wrote of this vivacious dish a few years before I was born. Delia Smith made it a star of the 1990s dinner party. But in our house it is one of those dishes that appears, oblivious to fashion, in late summer and early autumn—made with the fat, barrel-shaped ripe peppers that turn up in the organic box—sometimes in the classical form, other times with a basil dressing poured in at the very end of cooking. Sometimes it shows up with a slice or two of mozzarella and on other occasions with the anchovy reinstated. It's a humble dish, yet pulsating with the flavors of another place, another climate—an edible postcard from headier, sun-soaked kitchens.

In the autumn of 1988 I went from being someone who could take or leave these red and green fruits to someone who craved them as others might a steak, and a bloody one at that. I was casting around for vegetables to roast. The peppers' startling colors caught my eye. I tucked them whole, stalks intact, in among the eggplants and tomatoes. They went into the oven and then by chance I forgot them (a clear case of "out of sight, out of mind"). The dish that emerged looked at first like burnt offerings but was to change everything, opening up a whole new chapter of deliciousness.

Externally, the capsicums had blackened, one step away from charcoal. Inside, however, was a different story. Their flesh was slithery and a deep, angry red, at once smoky and sweet, and beguilingly delicious. I have "overcooked" my peppers ever since.

Seasoning your peppers

Tomato Offers the piquancy missing in the pepper's sweet flesh.
Use as a stuffing instead of ground meat.
Basil The pepper's best friend. The combination, especially when olive
oil and garlic are invited along, is the essence of the Mediterranean.
Warm, sweet spices Cinnamon, cumin, cardamom, and allspice work
nicely in starchy stuffings, making the pepper feel very much at home.
Anchovies The salty, oily quality of this little fish has a natural affinity
for the pepper.
Garlic Roasted, the caramel notes of garlic blend almost perfectly with
that of the roasted pepper. Raw, they can both be indigestible.
Goat cheese The sharp tingle of acidity in a slice of chèvre is a welcome
contrast to the sweetness of a cooked pepper.
Vinegar Use a little more than usual in a dressing destined for grilled
pepper. It will make the fruit's natural sugar sing.

And...

* Pepper plants are tricky to raise at home. I sometimes buy a couple
  of relatively mature plants from the farmers' market in early summer.
  They stand a better chance of survival.
* If summer is especially wet or miserable, peppers simply won't ripen.
  They need our sunniest corner.
* Keep the plants well ventilated and avoid putting them in a humid
  atmosphere. They will rot if kept too damp.
* Roast peppers in their skins, letting them go almost black. Put the roasted
  peppers in a bowl, cover tightly with plastic wrap or a plastic bag, and let sit
  for fifteen minutes before peeling off the skin with your fingers. You will be
  left with pieces of soft, skinless pepper for dressing with olive oil and basil.
* Red, yellow, and orange peppers are considerably sweeter than green ones.
  Those who usually find peppers indigestible may have no problem with the
  ripe, red roasted fruit.

Baked peppers for a summer lunch

My version of classic Italian baked peppers, but without the anchovies and with a last-minute stirring in of basil. There are some gorgeous flavors here, especially when the tomato juices mingle with the basil oil.

enough for 4
large peppers – 4
small or cherry tomatoes – 12 to 16
olive oil
basil leaves – a couple of handfuls

Preheat the oven to 400°F (200°C). Cut the peppers in half lengthwise and discard the seeds and white core. Put the halved peppers, cut side up, in a roasting pan or baking dish. Cut the tomatoes into halves or quarters, depending on their size, and season with salt and black pepper. Divide between the peppers. Pour a little olive oil into each pepper and bake until the tomatoes and peppers are lusciously soft, about forty-five minutes to an hour.

Blitz the basil leaves and about ⅓ cup (70ml) olive oil in a blender (sometimes I use a pestle and mortar), then pour into the peppers. The basil dressing will mingle with the warm tomato juices.

Stuffed peppers for an autumn day

Rice has for centuries been the obvious contender for stuffing a pepper—and indeed eggplant or a beefsteak tomato—flavored with caramelized onions, golden raisins, and musky raisins, and seasoned with capers, anchovies, cinnamon, or cumin. Small grains—cracked wheat, brown rice, the underused quinoa—are eminently suitable fillings, as is any type of small bean, lentil, or the plump, pearl-shaped couscous known as *mograbiah*. Vegetable stuffings can set the pepper alight. Piercing, cherry-sized tomatoes, such as Sungold or Gardener's Delight, or chunks of sweet steamed pumpkin offer more than just jewel colors to lift the spirits. They have a brightness of flavor very different from the humble, homely grains. They offer a change of step. A few hand-torn chunks of mozzarella and some olive oil will produce a seductive filling. Ground beef, the knee-jerk filling, somehow makes my heart sink.

Mograbiah, sometimes known as pearl couscous, takes the idea on a bit, having the comforting, frugal qualities of rice but possessing an extraordinary texture, poised between pasta and couscous. Made of wheat and similar to Sardinian *fregola*, it is available at Middle Eastern markets.

enough for 4
medium to large ripe peppers – 4

for the stuffing
mograbiah (pearl couscous) – about 1 cup (200g)
olive oil
green onions – 6
garlic – 2 cloves, sliced
ground paprika – half a teaspoon
the grated zest and juice of half a lemon
mint leaves – a large handful, chopped
cilantro leaves – a large handful, chopped
pine nuts – ½ cup (75g), toasted

for the yogurt sauce
thick yogurt – ¾ cup (200g)
cilantro and mint – a handful each, chopped
a pinch of paprika

To make the stuffing, cook the couscous in plenty of well-salted boiling water (use the same amount of salt you would to cook pasta) for about fifteen minutes, until tender. Drain and toss lightly with a little olive oil to stop the "pearls" sticking together.

Meanwhile, finely chop the green onions, discarding only the very darkest of the green shoots, and let them soften over medium heat in a glug or two of olive oil. Just before they start to color, add the garlic, then the paprika and the grated lemon zest. Stir in the chopped herbs and the toasted pine nuts. When all is fragrant and starting to darken a little in color, stir in the drained mograbiah and the lemon juice. Season carefully.

Preheat the oven to 350°F (180°C). Cut the peppers in half, tug out the seeds and cores, and lay the halves, cut side up, in an ovenproof baking pan. Pile the filling into the peppers, drizzle over a little more olive oil, and cover loosely with aluminum foil. Bake for about forty-five minutes, until sizzling.

To make the sauce, mix the yogurt with the herbs, paprika, and a grinding of black pepper. Spoon it over the peppers at the table.

Peppers with pork and rosemary

The deep sweetness of a roasted pepper makes it a suitable candidate for an exceptionally savory filling. I have tried several over the years: beef with cinnamon and tomato; minced chicken, lemon, and chiles; and more recently mozzarella and cherry tomatoes. Each had its merits, especially the latter with its tart juices. The latest manifestation of the stuffed pepper in my kitchen is one of highly seasoned ground pork with rosemary, Parmesan, and garlic. I think of it as the best yet.

enough for 4
a large onion
olive oil – 2 tablespoons, and a little more
garlic – 2 cloves
rosemary – 3 bushy sprigs
large tomatoes – 2
ground pork – 12 ounces (350g)
breadcrumbs – 1 cup (50g)
small red peppers – 6
grated Parmesan

Preheat the oven to 400°F (200°C). Peel and finely chop the onion, then put it into a large, shallow pan with the oil over medium heat. Let the onion soften without coloring. Peel and slice the garlic, chop the leaves from the sprigs of rosemary, and add to the onion. When all is soft and fragrant, chop the tomatoes and stir them in. Continue cooking until the tomatoes have collapsed into the sauce. Season with salt and black pepper, then stir in the ground pork and the breadcrumbs. Remove from the heat.

Cut the peppers in half lengthwise, remove the seeds, then lower them into a pan of boiling water and cook for six to eight minutes, until they are slightly limp. Remove them with a slotted spoon and put them, skin side down, in an ovenproof baking dish.

Divide the pork mixture among the peppers, then moisten with a little olive oil. Scatter grated Parmesan over the top and bake for thirty-five minutes, until sizzling.

A handful of stuffings for baked peppers

* Onions softened until sweet and golden, then stirred into cooked brown rice, golden raisins, and toasted almonds. Season with allspice, dill, black pepper, and cinnamon.
* Simmered green lentils seasoned with mashed roasted garlic, green onions, and mushrooms that you have sautéed until sticky. Season with sherry vinegar, lemon juice, cinnamon, and parsley.
* Onions softened in butter, then stirred through with cooked pearl barley, sautéed mushrooms, chopped preserved lemon, thyme, a little garlic, and parsley. Dot with butter before baking.
* Steamed couscous seasoned with fried onion, raisins, toasted pine nuts, cinnamon, ground cardamom, and toasted garlic. At the table, drizzle with yogurt into which you have stirred cilantro, olive oil, and fresh mint.
* Mozzarella, torn into chunks, pushed into the open pepper halves with cherry tomatoes, fresh basil, olive oil, black olives, and chopped anchovy, then baked until fragrant.

A Hungary-inspired stew for the depths of winter

Peppers, the red, collapsed horns in particular, are heavily linked with Hungary and its rust-colored stews. The Hungarians make ground paprika from them too, which has become their most famous culinary export. Despite their South American origins, Hungary is where I have found the most dazzling displays of peppers in the markets.

Two minutes, even less, from the river and the Szabadsag Bridge, Budapest's market stalls glow deep rust and gold with tins of paprika and strings of dried mahogany chiles. I love the crumbling wooden stalls of scarlet-capped mushrooms with their stray pieces of iridescent moss, wicker baskets of black sloes, and small sacks of red berries, and the apparently precarious piles of peppers, Christmas red, clean white, and burnt orange turning scarlet.

The long peppers that curl back on themselves have the intrigue of Aladdin's lamp but are awkward in the kitchen, tending to tip their stuffing out into the baking pan. You can roast them, though, with olive oil and lots of salt, and eat them with sesame bread torn into chunks.

The most useful, called Gypsy and the size of a fat rodent, are perfect for stuffing: with spinach and cream; translucent onions, capers, parsley, and garlic; cracked wheat, green olives, and toasted pine nuts; ground lamb and cumin. But mostly they are baked with a shake of the olive oil bottle and a grinding of salt until they collapse, wrinkle, and melt into silken strips. You'll need bread then, in fat, rough chunks, and maybe a glass of bright beer.

From August to the close of the year is when the market has the most from which to choose. After that the peppers come dried, in long strings of tobacco, madder, and soot. They shouldn't be despised. By then the stalls are mostly piled with roots and cabbages, endless sausages, and wholesomely fatty pork. The paprika stalls, stacked with red and gold tins, are kitsch in a Hansel and Gretel way, their shelves covered in fastidiously ironed lace, like the old women who run them.

Gulyas, or goulash, means "cowboy" and was traditionally cooked over an open fire. My paprika-scented pork stew—you could use beef—departs not too radically from the classical dish. I include dried mushrooms and cook it in a low oven, giving it a particularly deep, smoky flavor.

enough for 4
medium onions – 3
olive oil or dripping – 2 tablespoons
a medium-sized hot chile
sweet paprika – a heaping tablespoon
cubed pork (shoulder or leg) – 1⅔ pounds (800g)
all-purpose flour – a tablespoon
dried porcini or other dried mushrooms –
⠀⠀⠀⠀a handful, soaked in 1¾ cups (400ml) warm water for an hour
large, mild red peppers – 2
plum tomatoes – 14-ounce (400g) can
stock, white wine, or, if nothing else, water – ¾ cup (200ml)
caraway seeds – a level teaspoon
sour cream – scant ½ cup (100ml)
wide noodles or boiled potatoes, to serve

Preheat the oven to 275°F (140°C). Peel and thickly slice the onions and soften them slowly in the melted fat in a deep, heavy-bottomed pan—they should be soft and crushable, and a pale, appetizing gold. Chop and seed the chile, stir it into the onions with the ground paprika, and cook for a minute or two. Remove from the pan and set aside, leaving behind any fat you can. Increase the heat a little, add the cubed meat to the pan, and let it color on all sides, adding more fat if you need to.

Return the onions to the pan, sprinkle over the flour, cook briefly, then stir in the mushrooms and their soaking liquid. Halve and seed the peppers, cut each half into thirds, and stir them in together with the tomatoes, liquid, and caraway seeds. Bring everything to an enthusiastic simmer, season generously with salt, then cover with a lid and transfer to the oven. Bake, unpestered, for a good hour and a half. Remove from the oven, check the meat for tenderness, and remove some of the fat from the surface. Pour the sour cream over the top and stir once so that the surface is merely rippled with the cream. Serve with noodles or potatoes.

Pole beans

It's the second week of August, the air heavy with the smell of overripe figs from the tree on the terrace. Golden mirabelles hang like glass beads at the far, dark end of the garden. Only the distant laughter of a child breaks the oppressive silence.

The dark bronze stems of the beans I planted in late spring are curling their way up their frame, looping around the dead sweet pea husks that a neater gardener would have taken out. The buds of Cosse Violette—the beans I grow every summer—are shining an intense violet among the green leaves. The beans, some of which ripen while others are still in bud, are a dusky purple-black. I will admit to finding the marriage of violet, deep green, and inky black one of the most beautiful and tranquil a garden has to offer.

The term "pole" beans covers both the "green" bean in all its colors, and the longer, wider runner bean. "Green" beans, introduced to Britain by the Huguenots, are the more refined cousins of our much-loved cottage-garden runner bean. They have names like Rocquencourt, Fin de Bagnol, and Chevrier Vert, are a little less resilient, and need more careful nurturing early in life. Instead of the stinging scarlet of the runner, their flowers are ivory, cream, and soft lavender. Not that any of this makes them better of course, only different.

Pleasing as they are to eat, if I am honest, I grow green beans as much for their beauty as for their usefulness in the kitchen. I am unsure exactly why we have taken to the green bean rather than the yellow. There is much gentle beauty in a dish of butter-yellow pods glistening with almost-melted butter and a few grains of black pepper. Oval Yellow China, St. Esprit Jaune, and Mont d'Or are varieties worth seeking out. Eyes closed, they taste very little different from a green one, but their beauty is threefold.

The runner bean (*Phaseolus coccineus*) is flat and slightly coarse to the touch. I regard hearing its loud snap as one of the highlights of the British summer, just as others do the crack of a cricket ball on willow. The green beans (*Phaseolus vulgaris*) are mostly round and shorter than the runner, and come in all sizes, from the pencil-thin Blue Lake to the plump and knobbly borlotti. Their skins can be green, yellow, purple, or mottled like a bird's egg. Some, such as borlotti and Cream Splash, can grow to over 8 inches (20cm), the seeds clearly visible through the bean's skin.

I particularly mention the borlotti as it is the bean I am asked about more than any other. Its cream and bright-pink speckled pods make it one of the most beautiful of all the beans. Inside, the jade and pink seeds have a singular fresh greenness to them. They are increasingly being seen as something to eat fresh rather than dried, which is how many of us know them best. I grow them, sharing a frame with purple beans or maybe a climbing miniature pumpkin such as Munchkin. I should mention that this bean is one variety that needs a good hard boil for ten minutes. When borlotti are undercooked, some people find them indigestible.

Pole beans in the garden

No peony, full-blown rose, or wandering clematis could ever bring me as much delight as the sight of a cane wigwam of beans. There is much childish delight in making one too, tying the thin ends of the long, sturdy canes with tarred string; getting the thick ends equidistant in the ground; the constant shaking to test how secure they are; and that proud moment when all is complete. Passersby might see you as a dedicated gardener, but only you know you are secretly seven years old again and making a den.

While I am not sure a vegetable patch is worthy of the name without its pointed frame of scarlet-flowered runners, it is a fact that this bean was first grown for its flowers rather than for the table, and Native Americans still eat their roots as well as the long, flat bean itself.

I have been besotted with the sight of beans growing up rickety canes since I was a kid. The bean fields of the farmer next door were my hiding place as an eleven-year-old, sitting cross-legged among the heart-shaped greenery and its vivid blossoms for hours on end. We knew them as "scarlet" runners, but their flowers can be anything from red and white (Painted Lady) to pure ivory (Desirée).

I built my first wigwam for beans one day after school, on the precipitous slope of the family vegetable patch, with odd canes of assorted lengths. An unimaginably difficult task handed out by my father. Now I build them on the flat, each cane about 2½ inches (6cm) or so apart, one in the middle of each of my vegetable beds (and last year another, less secure than usual but just as useful, in a giant terra-cotta pot). Such tall, thin frames make sense for the gardener with limited space. The plants, which hate wind, protect one another as they huddle together, and take up less space than those grown in a long row.

One June, as I traveled from the station in a country taxi, the driver asked me, "Have you got your beans in yet?" It seemed an odd question to ask a perfect stranger. He then proceeded to tell me how he dug a square hole, two spades deep, in early spring, filled it with shredded newspaper, which he watered and covered with a layer of "well-rotted 'orseshit," then piled rich garden soil on top of that. He felt that the newspaper held water and that the beans then thrived without much need for the hose. He was right, and I have done it ever since. Though I fancy my "two spades deep" is more like his "one."

Pole beans of all sorts need warmth. They will germinate in soil above 54°F (12°C). I sow mine in pots of seed compost in May and start them in the cold frame. Prior to that, I just used my kitchen windowsill until all danger of frost had passed. They grow quickly enough for you to consider a late planting, say at the end of July. Green beans are happy to ramble over a wicker cloche (I once saw them growing through a large rose). I pick the round pole beans while they are still no longer than a finger, and up to pencil thickness.

Runners, named for their ability to climb, are much longer and heavier and need a strong frame. They were introduced to England by Tradescant, King Charles I's gardener, who also brought us my beloved cottage-garden phlox. The dark red roses growing in pots outside my back door are named for him.

My beans, the prolific Scarlet Emperor, Viola Cornetti or Cosse Violette, and Blue Lake, are a follow-on from the sweet peas that start to go downhill around the summer solstice. Last year, when my borlotti beans failed to germinate, a neighboring Connecticut squash gratefully squatted in their place and utilized the frame until the first frosts turned its stems to slush.

In all the years I have grown beans this way, it was Christopher Stocks, in his book *Forgotten Fruits* (Random House, 2008), who first brought to my attention the fact that runner beans climb clockwise, while all other beans clamber up in the opposite direction.

A bean diary

May 5 I plant four varieties of pole bean in seed compost in deep pots: the French; sulfur yellow Merveille de Venise; the sultry, purple Cosse Violette; the mysterious Black Knight that arrived by mistake; and the Scarlet Emperor runner bean that grows in virtually every cottage garden in Europe (in the United States their flowers are said to attract the hummingbird). Well watered, the seeds sit in the open cold frame for ten days or so before I notice their tips peeping through the black soil. Few seeds germinate at so satisfying a pace.

May 20 I put sticks up the stems as soon as they are tall enough to bend. I don't tie them; they generally hold on of their own accord.

June 1 About 16 inches (40cm) tall, their stems entwined like necking swans, the beans go into the prepared ground, four plants around each side of the climbing frames. The French Merveille de Venise, with long leaves like iron-age arrows, is planted in a deep terra-cotta pot around a tepee of long, bamboo canes, just as I have seen them growing on a barge in Venice. The others go into the garden, the Cosse Violette shares a bed with jewel-stemmed chard, globe artichokes whose leaves look as if they are glistening with frost, and Dahlia Black Monarch, whose flowers are of a deep, arterial red. Each bean has its long white root tucked deep into the soil and well watered, then surrounded by spent coffee grounds to ward off the garden snails. As usual, some seeds are tucked in among the growing plants to extend the season well into the autumn.

August 8 Much is starting to ripen. We continue to pick through to October.

Varieties

Green beans
Expect to start picking eighty days after planting.

Cosse Violette A good tall bean, with a long cropping period. I pick until the first frosts. Similar to Purple Tepee.
Blue Lake* An easy-to-grow variety, stringless and, despite its name, green. I like seedsman Thomas Etty's catalogue note that Blue Lake originated with the Native Americans on the banks of the Missouri.
Merveille de Venise A flat yellow pod, rather like a yellow runner bean. I sometimes entwine its yellow stems among those of the Cosse Violette.
Neckargold* A straight, round yellow bean.
Anellino Giallo* Elegantly curls back on herself, like a giant comma.
Aiguillon Like Blue Lake, this is a true haricot vert, waxy green, long, and pencil thin.
Rose d'Eyragues A parchment-hued bean with splashes of rose. A rare form from Avignon I am desperate to grow.

Also worth trying are Coco Noir, a beautiful, earthy black bean (just saying the name is enough for me); the Prince,* which is both stringless and flat podded; and Blauhilde,* a long, purple-black bean that can also be left and eaten as "flageolet."

Runner beans
Usually ready about ninety days after planting.

Painted Lady* An ancient variety introduced in the seventeenth century and occasionally known as York and Lancaster.
Red Rum Reliable and early to mature.
Scarlet Emperor* Copious orange-red flowers from black and purple speckled seeds. My favorite runner.
White Emergo* Slimmer pods than most and quite prolific.
Czar White-flowered runner from the nineteenth century.

Also worth looking out for are the almost-stringless Butler, Polestar (keep well watered), and Pickwick, a somewhat dwarf variety good for small gardens.

*Available from US seed sources.

Pole beans in the kitchen

What we are eating here is an immature bean, which we can enjoy pod, barely visible beans, and all. Runner beans are harvested slightly nearer maturity, so the pink bean inside the pod is quite visible. At the market, it is worth trying one before you buy. They toughen if left on the vine too long. Some require their edges peeling—a task known as "stringing" the beans. Runners need "topping and tailing," which simply means they need their ends cutting off before cooking, as do green beans. However, though I totally see why no one wants to eat the knobbly stalk end, I tend to leave the elegant tail ends intact. They are tender and sweet and I see no real reason to remove them.

Beans are a pleasure to grow, to witness in flower, and to pick. There is much happiness to be had in rummaging through the leaves in search of the elegant, dangling pods. I often eat a plateful with a roast tomato sauce. All red, green, and yellow, like a kid's painting.

Too much is made of undercooking. The flavor, what there is, develops only once the bean is tender, so a crisp green bean cooked for seconds rather than minutes is all very well, but it will never have the flavor of one that is cooked until it bends. A perfect bean should have some bite to it, but be incapable of standing to attention. I take a sample out of the pan every now and again. They will probably take only three or four minutes if the beans are young and the water boiling merrily. They are done when dark emerald green and visibly starting to relax.

There are few ingredients that can do anything for a green bean, and even fewer for a runner, but a little chopped shallot, melted butter, or a crushed clove of young garlic are all worth a try. Olive oil does it no favor other than in a salad, with sun-scorched tomatoes, torn mozzarella, and basil leaves. Nasturtium flowers look gorgeous, the orange and red petals falling like paint splatters over a dish of freshly cooked green beans, but add little in terms of flavor. But who cares when you have painted such a picture?

Purple beans such as Blauhilde and Viola Cornetti lose much of their color once they hit boiling water. Sometimes they turn completely green. But that is all they lose, though there is little to say about the flavor of green beans—purple, yellow, or green. What matters is youth and texture.

If enough ripen at once or I have picked some up from the farmers' market, I throw them into boiling water to which I have added a little salt, then drain and toss them in soft butter and very, very finely squashed garlic or chopped shallot. I have been known to use green onion. Anything else would interfere with their subtle "green" flavor. They rely on a cook with nothing more than a stopwatch. Imagination is unwanted here.

And...

* Some runner beans have a thin string down each long edge that needs removing before you slice them. If you insert a knife at the stalk end and pull along, the string will sometimes pull off easily. Other times, you need to slice it off. Much depends on your beans.
* Strings running down the edge of a runner bean are not necessarily a sign that the bean is old (though it often can be the case). It may just be the variety. Generally though, the younger a runner bean is picked, the less stringy it will be.
* About 6 to 7 inches (15 to 18 cm) is the right length to start picking your runner beans. Green beans should be picked well before they get to that length.
* If a runner bean doesn't snap when you bend it, then it is probably past its best.
* There is nothing you can do to stop purple beans turning green in the cooking water.
* Green beans can sometimes squeak as you eat them, especially if you undercook them. I rather like this attribute, but those who find it disturbing might like to toss them in butter. It quietens them down.
* If you can see the seeds clearly bulging through the pod, then it is probably on the tough side.
* Any green bean thinner than a pencil will need only two to three minutes in boiling water or a steamer. Runners need three to four.
* The flavor of round pole beans becomes deeper the longer you cook them, but at the cost of loss of color and texture.
* There is a point in the pole green bean's life when it is past being tender enough to eat as a whole bean, "pod'n'all," but not yet plump enough to be shelled and dried. This is the "flageolet" stage. The beans can be popped straight from their shells and boiled. Wonderful tossed with olive oil and lemon juice and eaten warm.

Warm chicken with green beans and chard

As much as I like big flavors, I sometimes want something more gentle,
a little genteel even. French beans lend themselves to such cooking.

enough for 2
chicken – 2 plump breasts
a little oil
rosemary – a bushy stalk
green beans – 7 ounces (200g)
chard – 12 thin stems and their leaves
tomatoes – 6 small ones, cut in halves or quarters
      depending on their size
a few nasturtiums, if you wish

for the dressing
a small shallot
lemon juice – 3 tablespoons
olive oil – 6 tablespoons
mint – a small bunch

For the dressing, peel and chop the shallot very finely. Put it into a screw-top
jar with a good pinch of salt, the lemon juice, olive oil, and the leaves from the
mint, lightly chopped (discard the stems). Screw on the lid and shake the jar
to mix the dressing.

Brush the chicken with oil, season with salt and black pepper, and scatter
with the finely chopped rosemary needles. Grill or roast until cooked right
through and the skin is golden. Set aside for ten minutes, perhaps with a bowl
over the top to keep it warm, saving any cooking juices that come from it.

Trim the beans, cut the chard stalks into similar lengths, and remove and
reserve their leaves. Boil the beans and the chard stalks in boiling water until
tender—a matter of two or three minutes in each case (I prefer to do this in
two pans, as the red from the chard water darkens the beans, but it is up to
you). Dip the leaves into the water for thirty seconds. Remove and drain.
Pour the dressing into a bowl, then add the drained green beans, chard leaves
and stalks, the tomatoes, and the nasturtium flowers if you are using them.
Divide the salad between two plates or lovely white bowls. Cut the chicken
breasts into thick slices—about four each—and place on top of the salad.

Beans in the steamer

I have said elsewhere that I often prefer green vegetables boiled rather than steamed, but I find the opposite with beans. There is something about the bean family's flesh that works exceptionally well in the steamer. I trim my beans, then cook them in a covered steamer basket over boiling water. I find this way they keep their color and the flavor is often better. Steamed runners work especially well.

French beans with shallot butter

Boil your beans, nicely trimmed as you think fit, in lightly salted water, or steam them if you prefer. They need about four minutes or so; they should be dark green and bend a little. Meanwhile, melt a little butter in a shallow pan, stir in some finely chopped shallot, and let it soften without coloring. Drizzle in a little white wine vinegar, then drain the beans and toss them with the shallot butter.

Beans and cheese

Parmesan and beans sounds an unlikely coupling but I recommend it. Pecorino, a young one, is a possibility here too, or one of the hard sheep's cheeses British cheese makers are getting so good at.

    green, purple, or yellow green beans or runners
    butter
    Parmesan

Trim the beans (I suggest a good handful per person), then boil them in deep, salted water or steam over boiling water.
    Have ready some almost-melted butter and some grated cheese. As you lift the beans from the water, toss them in the butter and cheese.

Another way with beans and cheese

For each fat handful of green beans, I allow about 2½ ounces (75g) of cheese, such as Wigmore, Waterloo, or any of the other white-bloomed, melting-textured cheeses. If I can get nothing "local," then I use Taleggio or Camembert. Cut the cheese into small pieces. As soon as the beans are cooked and drained, toss them with the little cubes of cheese. The heat from the beans will melt the cheese so that it forms a thick, savory dressing.

A chicken lunch for a searingly hot summer's day

Roast a chicken, perhaps with olive oil and lemon, and set it aside to cool. I don't think it should be cold, just vaguely warm. Make an aioli or mayonnaise. Cook freshly picked green beans in lightly salted water. Use a spoonful of the cooking water to thin the mayonnaise to the consistency of thick cream. Drain the beans and toss them in the thinned mayonnaise. Eat them with the cold roast chicken. The moist, just-warm chicken, lightly cooked beans, and garlicky mayonnaise come together perfectly.

A crisp salad of pole beans, fennel, and Parmesan

enough for 2
green beans – 7 ounces (200g)
a medium fennel bulb
small, hot salad leaves, such as arugula and watercress –
    4 double handfuls
white bread – 2 thick slices
oil for frying the bread

for the dressing
tarragon vinegar – a tablespoon
Dijon mustard – a teaspoon
an egg yolk
olive oil – a scant ½ cup (100ml)
grated Parmesan – 3 tablespoons, plus a block of Parmesan for shaving
lemon juice – 2 teaspoons

Trim the beans and boil them in lightly salted water or steam them, until tender. Drain them under cold running water. Cut the fennel bulb in half and shred finely. Make the dressing by whisking the vinegar, mustard, and egg yolk together with a little salt and black pepper, then beating in the oil followed by the grated cheese. It should be thick and creamy. Squeeze in the lemon juice, stir, then set aside for a few minutes.

    Put the salad leaves in a large bowl with the cooked beans and the fennel. Cut the bread into small squares and fry in shallow oil until golden on all sides. Drain the croutons on paper towels. Toss the leaves and beans lightly with the dressing. Pile the salad on to two plates and shave pieces of Parmesan over with a vegetable peeler. I usually do at least eight per salad, depending on my dexterity with the peeler. Tip the hot croutons over the salad and eat straightaway, while all is fresh and crunchy.

Green beans, red sauce

The smell you get from slicing freshly picked runner beans and the warm, herbal notes attached to the stalk of a tomato are, to my mind, the very essence of summer. Put those scents together and you have a recipe that is pure pleasure to make. A dish that could only mean midsummer—something to eat with cold salmon, a slice of crab tart, or a plate of grilled sardines.

enough for 2
tomatoes – 1 pound (500g)
olive oil
bay leaves – 2
a little red wine vinegar
runner beans – 1 pound (450g)
grated lemon zest

Preheat the oven to 400°F (200°C). Put the tomatoes into a roasting pan or ovenproof baking dish; they should fit snugly in a single layer. Pour over enough olive oil to wet the fruit and to form a thin layer at the bottom of the dish. Season generously with salt and black pepper, tuck in the bay leaves and sprinkle a little red wine vinegar over (a teaspoon will do). Now leave in the hot oven for about thirty minutes, until the skins have started to blacken here and there and there is much juice in the dish.

Crush the tomatoes with a fork, check the seasoning, and correct it with a little salt and pepper if necessary.

Trim the beans and slice them thinly. Steam for three or four minutes, until tender but still crisp and bright, then toss them with the tomato sauce. Grate some lemon zest over the hot beans and their sauce.

Potatoes

The flowers of the potato, delicate petals whose stamens bunch together to form a point, are among the most charming in the vegetable garden. Marie Antoinette wore them in her hair. The flowers of the Salad Blue are perhaps the most beautiful of all, an ethereal lavender and white, with deep orange-gold stamens often heavy with pollen. Charlotte, a soft candy pink; Kestrel, a piercing lilac and white. Summer rain and even clouds make their flowers close and droop like a swan in repose. As dusk falls, they gently close.

Once you have seen the delicacy of the potato's blossom you feel differently about what lies beneath the soil. In late summer, when you unearth the early, pale yellow Duke of York, the ivory-skinned Pentland Javelin, or the creamy Snowdrop, you do so with a certain tenderness, brushing the soil from their thin skins as gently as you might wipe the tears from a child's cheek. The idea of throwing them around the way Alf the greengrocer does suddenly seems as wrong as putting a box of eggs at the bottom of your shopping bag.

One of the more extraordinary details of my garden is its potato bed. A little over six feet (two meters) square, surrounded by a tightly clipped box hedge, it is on the cool side of the garden and is damp enough never to need watering. Against all sensible advice, it is heavily sheltered by a six-year-old medlar tree. What is more, the soil can be heavy, a tad clingy even. And yet, potatoes work well for me here. Having such success with them has been one of the greatest joys of "growing your own." I would probably plant them even if I didn't eat them, if only to give them away.

So firmly do potatoes feel part of our culinary heritage that it is odd to think that we had none until they came over in the cargo holds of Spanish ships in the late 1500s. Medieval Britain had no potatoes at all (nor carrots, parsnips, or many other roots) and it is hard to think of our diet without these beloved lumps of starch. *Solanum tuberosum* was first cultivated in the Andes, and was treated with suspicion when it arrived in Europe because of the flowers' similarity to those of the deadly nightshade plant. They are indeed from the same family.

That we love the potato so much is partly down to its versatility and, it must be said, its ability to fill us up cheaply. Potatoes calm and comfort, satisfy and satiate us, but in truth they have little nutritional merit. Yes, the public relations people can scrape around for the presence of vitamin C and a few minerals but the real reason we eat so many is simply because of their power to soothe and fill.

Apart from a freshly dug tuber, steamed and eaten for its earthy taste, we tend to take our tatties with fat. Boiled and buttered, mashed with milk, baked in cream, smothered in cheese, fried in oil, tossed in mayonnaise—be it a single potato chip or a spoonful of *pommes à la dauphinoise*, fat and the potato go hand in hand. Even the celebrated Jersey gets its time-honored brushing of melted butter or—heaven forbid—marge. Fat, in one form or another, makes the potato tempting.

The humble spud really got into its stride during the eighteenth century, and it is that period that gave us many of the dishes we still enjoy today. The French, who initially banned them, developed most of the lexicon of classic potato recipes (the Italians were slightly less gung ho, perhaps because they had their own favored carbs). While French cooks baked them in stock, fried them to a crisp, and let them tenderize in a slow oven with thick cream and garlic, the British simply boiled them. Whether they were large, small, new, or main crop, we took our starchy tubers cooked in boiling, salted water.

This is one vegetable that is losing its popularity. Yes, we are eating food from other cuisines, and growing and eating many new vegetables and fruits, but the real reason is our gradual slide toward eating less starch. The nutritionists' disdain of "empty calories" has done the spud no favors at all. They are one of the first foods to be removed from most weight-loss diets. French fries and potato chips are blamed for childhood obesity rather than the more obvious lack of exercise.

I see only good coming from this movement away from having a pile of potatoes on our plate. From it will come a new appreciation of an ingredient whose qualities have long been measured only in quantity. We shall learn that this vegetable is so much more interesting than simply a "filler," that it is something whose character can vary dramatically according to season and variety. A vegetable to be explored with a new vigor. It may yet be seasoned as much with restraint as with fat. That said, I will happily eat a plate of *pommes à la dauphinoise* with simply a green salad at its side. I just wouldn't do it every day.

Varieties

Potatoes are divided into two main groups, earlies and main crop. The first can be referred to as either first earlies or second earlies, according to when they are ready. You can pick them as soon as the flowers appear. Main-crop potatoes, which I tend to start eating in late summer, can be dug up once their stems have collapsed and started to die down.

The variety of potato will, to a certain degree, decide what we use them for. Those with a dry texture will make a light mash or roast crisply but will fall apart in salads. Waxy-fleshed varieties will make a gluey mash but hold together in the rough and tumble of a salad. In no other vegetable are the varieties so distinct from one another. Like grapes, a tuber's flavor will be affected not only by the variety but also by the soil and the climate in which it was grown. In general, cold climates tend to produce a more interesting-tasting spud, which may well be why so many of our best-loved names hail from Scotland.

The early potatoes have a thin-skinned delicacy to them and a nutty sweetness. They are what we call "new" potatoes, and rarely need peeling (though are very elegant when you scrape them to shed their flaky skins). Rarely larger than a hen's egg, some of them have a waxy quality that makes them appealing in a salad. They take on a pleasing fudgy texture when sautéed in butter and can even be roasted, the sticky gloss that accumulates on their young skins only adding to their pleasure.

Varieties to look for in late spring and early summer

Duke of York A Scottish variety bred by William Simi in 1891, with floury flesh and exceptionally fine flavor. A very good roaster.
Epicure Introduced in 1901 by Charles Sharp, this almost pear-shaped "early" has smooth skin with a waxy texture and good flavor. It remains a classic in Scottish gardens.
International Kidney (called "Jerseys" when grown there) Despite the drone of those who insist they "don't taste like they used to," the Jersey, when properly grown and dug young, is a good, waxy little spud. Left in the ground, it becomes floury with age.
Edzell Blue Bright, violet-blue skin, white flowers, and floury flesh.
Kestrel A creamy yellow, oval potato with purple-blue eyes, which roasts, fries, and chips well. A joy to grow.
British Queen Another Scottish variety with a good dry texture and excellent earthy flavor. Archibald Findlay's Victorian masterpiece makes some of the best mash.
Charlotte* A waxy variety with excellent flavor.
Belle de Fontenay* An old French variety, kidney shaped and slightly curved, with waxy flesh. Very nice cold, when its deep flavor really shines.

Adirondack Red* Oblong, purplish-red skin, and pink flesh with excellent flavor; good for boiling, frying, in salads.
Russet Norkotah* Netted russet skin and white flesh; high yielding.

And in late summer and autumn

Snowdrop Sometimes called Witch Hill, a white potato with slightly waxy flesh and a fine, earthy flavor. A medium-sized potato, good for boiling or roasting.
Kerr's Pink* An heirloom variety with pale pink skin and floury flesh. An exceptionally fine potato for roasting and mashing.
Arran Victory An old, purple-skinned potato from the Isle of Arran, this late main crop, bred by Donald Mackelvie, is legendary. With its violet skin and snowy white flesh, it is the oldest Arran potato still available. Its floury flesh makes an exceptional mash, cumulus like but with plenty of body and a depth of flavor that may (or may not) come from the local habit of putting kelp on the fields.
Golden Wonder One of my favorites for frying and roasting. A russet-skinned, white-fleshed Scottish variety of great beauty. Easy to grow.
German Butterball* Pale russet skin and yellow flesh with medium-dry texture and buttery flavor; stores well.
Russian Banana* Small fingerling with pale yellow skin and flesh and waxy texture; easy to grow.

Of great visual charm are the "blues," those extraordinary varieties that have not only blue skin, like the Edzell Blue, but also violet-blue flesh. They are tricky to find in markets, but farmers' markets provide a good hunting ground. Blue seed potatoes for growing at home are available from seed suppliers such as Alan Romans and Carroll's. I keep a look out for Shetland Blue, Salad Blue, and the rare, gray-skinned Vitelotte Noire. (All Blue and Adirondack Blue are two good choices for US gardeners.) If their exquisite violets and indigos were matched by their flavor they would probably be better known, but they are worth having now and again just for their beauty.

*Available from US seed sources.

A potato in the garden

I grow my own, but have only taken it up recently—twenty years later than I first grew tomatoes, ten years later than I planted my first beans. They are now one of my most successful crops, both in terms of quality and yield.

When I sowed that first grubby handful of Charlotte seed potatoes, it was as an experiment. I had no intention of making a potato bed a permanent fixture in my garden. There is too little room, and I somehow felt they were so cheap and plentiful that there was little reason to chit, plant, and dig my own. There was also the idea that they are difficult to grow organically.

Once Charlotte's pink flowers had passed and the stems had grown leggy, I dug them up, half expecting to find a few moth-eaten tatties. What sat on my garden fork was a veritable nest of small, perfect potatoes, oval, golden, and smelling of sweet earth. I think I was even a bit proud of myself. The following year I planted five varieties, only one of which (Pink Fir Apple) didn't do particularly well. The others were pretty much picture perfect and cooked beautifully.

Potatoes like deep, well-drained soil that gets some sun for at least part of the day. I grow mine in the shadiest beds of all, which enjoy direct sunshine only for a couple of hours around midday. It's not perfect, but they cope. The crop will benefit from a good manuring the autumn before you sow. I dig in a couple of bags after harvesting and let it enrich the soil over winter. I alternate my planting between two beds, both on the shadier side of the garden, to stop the buildup of soil-borne viruses. A gap of three years between planting on the same site would be even safer. You can also grow a small crop in deep terra-cotta or plastic containers. This works especially well for early, waxy potatoes. The confined space is not a problem, as they need room to spread down rather than across.

Seed potatoes can be planted directly in the soil but most people find it better to "chit" them first. This is simply another word for letting them sprout for about a month, until they have a few short, strong shoots. I find egg boxes ideal for this, the hollows holding the potatoes securely while they sprout. They need some light, otherwise the shoots will grow long and weak, as they do when you forget them in the vegetable rack.

Once the shoots are about ¾ inch (a couple of centimeters) long, and the risk of frost is over, the whole potato can be planted outside. I make individual holes 6 to 8 inches (15 to 20cm) deep (you can dig a trench, if you prefer), then gently plant each potato with the healthiest-looking shoots uppermost. They need 12 to 16 inches (30 to 40cm) between the rows. Label the varieties clearly and write them down too (the foxes ran off with some of my wooden labels one year, so I could have been confused had I not kept a separate note).

The time it takes for your potatoes to mature depends on the variety, the weather, and your location. A hundred days is about the minimum between planting and digging up. It's a good idea to plant an early variety, then a couple of others for later in the year. Generally, early potatoes are ready once the flowers appear; main crops are ready once the flowers have faded and the tops have started to collapse.

And...

* If you want an early crop, lay garden fleece or black plastic over the soil to warm it up for a week or two before planting.
* Plant with the sprouting end up.
* You can start with "earlies" in March, covering them with deep "earthed-up" soil or a cloche to keep the frost out.
* Potatoes like to grow in soft soil. You can use up old compost and anything from plant pots in the trench. I use the contents of last year's tomato pots.
* As soon as the shoots show above ground, pull the soil up around them to protect against late frosts. It is worth remembering that some parts of the country can experience frosts as late as May.
* A layer of horticultural fleece to cover the shoots at night is a good investment.
* You can store main-crop potatoes in paper bags in the dark for weeks, even months. Whatever you do, keep them away from the light.
* And yes, it is true that they keep better with their soil on.

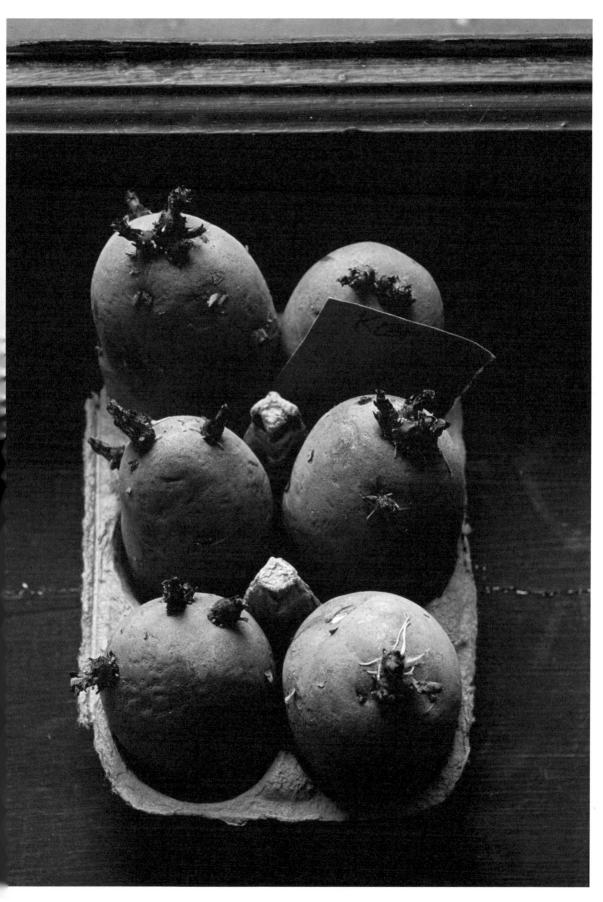

A potato diary

February 24 Five varieties of seed potato arrive from Scotland: Arran Victory, Kestrel, Golden Wonder, and Pink Fir Apple. There's a rare and capricious blue one too, which I intend to grow more for its flowers than any hope of a crop.

I put the tubers to "chit" in egg cartons—that is, to develop strong green shoots. I use the coldest room in the house for this, warm temperatures giving rise to thin, weak shoots. The tubers stay in their egg cartons until Good Friday.

April 9 I plant them out. No matter whether Easter is early or late, I do this on Good Friday. It is an ancient tradition among allotment holders and I have stuck to it. But then, I always trim my hedges around Derby Day too.

May 4 Almost a month to the day, the first shoots push through, teased through the wet soil by a succession of drenching showers and piercing sunshine. First up is Kestrel, with its tight tufts of hairy, bottle-green leaves. A day later I spot the first signs of the Salad Blue, dense clusters of violet-black leaves edged with a single line of green, barely visible against soil the color of molasses. The dark leaves intrigue, exuding an air of mystery and poison. You are reminded that the potato is but a short hop from deadly nightshade, with its jet-black berries and threat of death.

I protect them from the snails and slugs with spent coffee grounds and copper rings.

May 15 Every potato is up 15 inches (38cm), standing proud against the damp soil, which is now scattered with a confetti of white medlar petals.

Late June The potatoes are in flower. Since I have previously grown only varieties with pink flowers, the violets, mauves, and deep indigo shades come as an unexpected and graceful joy.

July 28 Most potatoes are ready to dig when the flowers are open. They generally keep well in the ground, so I tend to leave them there till they are needed. We start digging on July 28 (wonderful, purple-skinned Salad Blue) and continue till late October, when the last of the Golden Wonder are dug.

A potato in the kitchen

Nowhere else in the vegetable kingdom does "the right one for the right job" matter quite so much. The texture of a potato after cooking depends on its flesh structure and water content. Some varieties have a low water content, resulting in a "fluffy" texture when cooked and making them good for mashing, roasting, and baking. They are often referred to as "floury." Others have a high water content, giving them a waxy feel and letting them keep their shape when cooked. They are especially good for gratins and salads. These are the ones to use when a recipe suggests a "waxy" variety. Their flesh is often more yellow in color than the "floury" varieties. There are also many that sit on the fence and can be used for different kinds of recipes.

Seasoning your potatoes

Fat Butter, olive oil, bacon fat, duck and goose fat, beef dripping—all have much to offer the plain and floury potato. The best cooking medium seems to me to be duck or goose fat, or beef dripping.

Cheese Sharp, piquant cream cheeses, robust, mouth-puckering British farmhouse Cheddars, melting cow's milk cheeses with rind the color of snow—all marry beautifully with potatoes. I sometimes break little nuggets of soft cheese over a boiled and softly floury King Edward or Maris Piper, then squash the melting cheese into the spud with my fork.

Spices Cumin, turmeric, chile, ground coriander, and the spice mix garam masala do much for a floury variety. Anise-flavored spices (fennel seed, aniseed, star anise) less so.

Herbs Rosemary, thyme, bay, parsley, cilantro, tarragon, and mint are the most obvious, and it is indeed difficult to find any herb that does not contribute something to potatoes. Despite my comment about anise, chervil is delightful with the new and very waxy. Unusually, sage gets a look in too. Normally too pungent for use with vegetables other than onions, this musky-tasting leaf finds a friend in a slow-cooked potato. Chives are especially good when the potato is eaten cold, in a salad or perhaps a chilled soup.

Cream The flesh of both floury and waxy varieties will, to differing extents, soak up cream or milk. Be it mash (floury) or slow baked (waxy, in a gratin), the effect of this vegetable combined with cream is thoroughly calming.

All meat, game, and most fish are happy to share a plate with potatoes in pretty much any form, though I can't say I have ever managed to marry them with crab particularly successfully. Smoked and pickled fish are at their most comfortable with a potato salad at their side. Ask any Scandinavian.

Mashed potatoes

The perfect mashed potato is one that manages to be both fluffy and buttery at the same time. Too much butter will make it heavy; too little and it will fail to satisfy. The mixture of starchy carbs, butter, and, sometimes, warm milk produces what is possibly the most soporific vegetable dish of all.

Mashed potato is often at its most blissful when we use it to soak up gravy or sauce. For many, it is the ultimate side dish for ham and parsley sauce, or rich stews whose gravy can seep into the mound of starch. Generally, the richer the sauce with which it is served, the less butter I put in. It is also used as a crust for fish pies or ground lamb or beef, and as the backbone of a fish cake.

Traditionally, a floury potato is used. The high percentage of dry matter in large, white potatoes produces a fluffy, light result. Beaten hard with an electric mixer or a wooden spoon, a floury potato will hold air and produce a mash of extraordinary volume.

In recent years, a new style of mash has become popular using waxy-fleshed varieties, which produce a creamy, almost puréelike finish. Mixing is kept to a minimum, as the starch grains would turn gluey if beaten as much as when using a floury potato. Introduced by restaurant chefs to anchor their griddled scallops to the plate, this mash is too rich and buttery to have in great steaming clouds with your sausages but is very soothing under a hunk of roast cod. Butter is used in this, but sometimes olive oil is beaten in too. You can often tell by the slightly green color.

The drier the potato is before mashing, the better. Much is made of the idea that the best results come from potatoes steamed in their jackets—it prevents them getting waterlogged—before being peeled and mashed. I have done this, but I find the difference not dramatic enough to go through the trauma of peeling steaming-hot potatoes while trying to get dinner on the table.

You can make excellent mash from a potato that has been peeled before boiling or steaming, providing you dry it out beforehand by letting the steam leave the potato after draining. The most successful way to do this is to drain the potatoes, leave them in the pan, then cover with a clean kitchen towel for three or four minutes. The towel will absorb the steam while keeping the spuds warm. You can then mash them and beat in the butter.

The mashing varieties

Some floury, some a little waxy, but they all make a good mash. Arran Victory gets my vote as the best choice for producing a fluffy, well-flavored cloud. Others will have their favorites but the varieties that follow are among the most suitable:

Fluffy mash Arran Victory, Avalanche, Dunbar Rover, Kerr's Pink, King Edward, Epicure, Kestrel, Maris Piper, Record, Santé, Snowdrop, Estima, British Queen, Wilja, Norgold Russet, Goldrush, Russet Burbank.
Silky mash Accent, Desiree, Edzell Blue, Majestic, Nadine, Picasso, Romano, Maris Peer, Yukon Gold, Kennebec, Katahdin.

* Cut the potatoes into large pieces before cooking. Small cubes of potato are likely to produce a sloppy mash.
* There is a long-established rule that "old" potatoes are put into cold water and brought up to the boil, while "new" potatoes are best dropped directly into boiling water. The theory behind this is that the slow heat involved in bringing the water to a boil allows the inside of the potato to cook at the same time as the outside. I have found this to be true, even though the science of it sounds a bit dodgy. Much depends on the variety of potato and the size to which it is cut.
* Check for doneness with a skewer. As soon as the point will slide in without much pressure, they are ready.
* Once the potatoes are drained, leave them in the hot pan covered with a kitchen towel to steam for three or four minutes. They will lose moisture this way and produce a fluffier mash.
* Add the butter, and the milk if you are using it, before you start mashing. The extra heat will help the butter melt properly.

A classic fluffy mash for sausages

enough for 4
floury potatoes – 2 pounds (900g)
butter – ½ cup (100g)
hot milk – scant ½ cup (100ml)

Peel the potatoes and boil them in deep, salted water until tender when pierced with the tip of a knife. Drain them, then return to the pot, cover with a kitchen towel, and let steam for a few minutes. Mash them with the butter, using a potato masher or an electric mixer fitted with the paddle attachment.

Now beat in the milk, either with the paddle or a wooden spoon. Check the seasoning.

A lovely soft mash with milk and bay

I love buttery, cloudlike mash but sometimes I want something softer. I use a floury-textured winter potato beaten with butter and hot milk to produce a snow-white mash suited to mopping up the juices of winter recipes. The quantity of milk will depend on the level of starch present in the potatoes, so I simply stop adding the warm milk when I have the texture I like.

enough for 4
medium to large floury potatoes – 6
bay leaves – 5
milk – ¾ cup (200ml)
butter – 5 tablespoons (75g)

Peel the potatoes and boil them in deep salted water until tender. Put the bay leaves into the milk in a separate pan and bring to a boil. Turn off the heat and set aside. The bay leaves will gently flavor the milk.

Drain the potatoes, then return them to the pan, cover with a kitchen towel, and let sit for a few minutes. Put the potatoes into a stand mixer fitted with the paddle attachment and beat with the butter and a little black pepper. With the mixer on slow, pour in the milk, leaving the bay leaves behind, and continue beating until almost sloppy. Season and serve immediately.

* You can make a deeper-flavored, more "earthy" version, by melting the butter and milk together, then whizzing them in a blender with a handful of chopped parsley. The mash will be pale green in color.

Mustard and parsley mash

Add a small handful of chopped parsley and 2 tablespoons of whole-grain mustard to 1 pound (500g) buttery mashed potato.

Wasabi mash

Stir 2 teaspoons of ready-made wasabi paste into 1 pound (500g) mashed potato.

A mash with olive oil (and the merest whiff of garlic)

enough for 4
mashing potatoes – 1 pound (450g)
olive oil – 4 tablespoons (60ml)
garlic cloves – 2, squashed flat but not peeled
thyme – a bushy sprig
a thick slice of butter

Peel and cook the potatoes in the usual manner. Warm the olive oil, garlic cloves, and thyme sprig in a small pan, then turn off the heat and leave the aromatics to do their work while the potatoes cook.

Mash the potatoes as usual, introducing the butter and oil and holding back the garlic and herbs as you go. Grind in a little pepper and serve.

A Parmesan and olive oil mash

enough for 4
mashing potatoes – 1 pound (450g)
olive oil
finely grated Parmesan – a large handful

Peel the potatoes and steam or boil them. When they are tender, drain them, then leave for three or four minutes in the empty pan covered with a kitchen towel. Mash them, either by hand or using an electric mixer, beating in a couple of tablespoons of olive oil and then the grated Parmesan. The mash should be smooth and slightly glossy.

A soft mash with cream and parsley

The affinity between potatoes and parsley is usually demonstrated by tossing new potatoes in butter and the chopped herb. I like to take it one step further and put the parsley in a soft, almost sloppy purée of potatoes. It excels as a side dish for white fish.

enough for 4
large floury potatoes – 4
parsley – a large bunch
light cream – ⅔ cup (150ml)
butter – 4 tablespoons (50g)

Peel the potatoes and steam or boil them until tender. As the potatoes approach tenderness, finely chop the parsley and warm the cream in a small pan.

Drain the potatoes, then return them to the pan, cover with a kitchen towel, and let sit for a few minutes. Mash the potatoes with the butter, then, when all is light and fluffy, stir in the cream and chopped parsley. Put the potatoes into a stand mixer fitted with the paddle attachment and beat with a little black pepper.

Check the seasoning and serve immediately.

The mashed potato cake

Mash, if not made too soft with butter or milk, can be shaped into a patty and fried until crisp. White, floury potatoes give a suitably firm yet tender texture. A mash of waxy potatoes can almost liquefy if you try to fry it. Thyme can be stirred in as you shape your potato cakes, or cooked and chopped greens—cabbage, broccoli, sprouts—or snippets of bacon, a crumbling of blood sausage, or simply a dusting of ground nutmeg. In so doing, a dollop of mash becomes an entire main course.

I disagree with those who claim you need eggs to hold everything together. A little flour will do the job if you really think your cake will collapse in the pan. Test the mixture by squeezing it in the palm of your hand. If it sticks together, then it won't need the adhesive addition of flour. Leaving it to fry unheeded will also help it keep its shape. When fish cakes and the like have fallen apart, it is generally because the cook couldn't resist the opportunity to play.

Famous potato cakes such as bubble and squeak, made with leftover cabbage and mashed potato, were traditionally meant as an accompaniment to Monday's cold cuts from Sunday's roast. The sizzling crust of the reworked mash is a pleasing contrast to the softly pink cold meat.

It is hard to think of anything I haven't tried in a potato cake, from the shredded corned beef of my first student digs to flaked kippers and even smoked salmon. When I was in my twenties, a popular supper involved potato molded into patties with canned salmon and fried, then later, much later, Arbroath smokies (smoked haddock) and a sauce of cream and curly parsley. The most successful, to my mind, was some duck confit, pulled off its creaking bones with a fork, then folded into smooth mash, floured lightly, and fried in duck fat. Another good one involved a cold sausage, sliced into thick coins.

Much effort is made getting the potato as smooth as silk, but I also like the effect when it is mashed coarsely, leaving much of it in uneven lumps. When this is pushed together, thoughtfully seasoned and fried in butter or oil, the texture is more interesting than that of a cake made from a smooth mash, in much the way a crumpet ripped in half by hand toasts more interestingly than one sliced flat with a knife. If that sounds like Zen and the art of the potato cake, then so be it.

A cake of potato and goat cheese

Goat cheese—sharp, chalky, a little salty—makes a sound addition to
the blandness of a potato cake. The fun is coming across a lump of melting,
edgy cheese in among the quietness of the potato. This is what I eat while
picking eagle style at the carcass of a roast chicken or wallowing in the
luxury of some slices of smoked salmon. It also goes very well with a humble
smoked mackerel.

enough for 2
cooked potato – 14 ounces (400g)
goat cheese – 5 ounces (150g)
herbs (thyme, tarragon, parsley) – 4 tablespoons, chopped
all-purpose flour – a tablespoon
cornmeal (polenta) – 6 tablespoons
olive or peanut oil

Mash the potatoes with a masher or a fork until they are a mixture of sizes
from gravel to pebbles. Cut the goat cheese up into small pieces and fold
it into the mash with the chopped herbs. Season generously with salt and
black pepper, then stir in the flour.

Divide the mixture into fourths and pat each one into a rugged patty
roughly 2½ inches (6cm) in diameter. Empty the cornmeal onto a plate,
then turn the patties in it.

Get a thin layer of oil hot in a shallow, nonstick pan. Lower the patties
into the oil and, without moving them, cook for about four minutes,
until golden and lightly crisp underneath. Turn them quickly and carefully
with a spatula and cook the other side. Drain briefly on paper towels
before serving.

Roast potatoes

Roast potatoes are as much a part of the Sunday roast as the roasting juices or gravy, providing crispness to contrast with the soft tenderness of the meat. Although you could bake them alone, the best flavored are those cooked around the meat. As they cook, they soak up some of the meat juices, whose natural sugars caramelize around the potato, resulting in a crisp and deeply savory crust.

You can get a good result by using vegetable oil, butter, or lard instead of the roasting juices, but these fats tend to produce a slightly second-rate result, losing out on the heart and soul of the meat. Butter alone, without any meat juices, will produce a burned taste; olive oil should always be a light version. Heavy oils will prevent your tatties from crisping. Dripping or goose or duck fat, on the other hand, can be almost as good as cooking them round the roast itself.

The crispest results will come from potatoes that have been boiled or steamed before you add them to the roasting pan. Roasted raw, the potato's surface can often harden instead of crisping deliciously.

The single thing that will improve the crust of a "roastie" is to bruise the edges of the lightly cooked potato before roasting. The bashed edges become frilly and crunchy in the sizzling meat juices.

The roasting varieties

A floury variety produces a roast potato that, cooked correctly, will be crisp on the outside and fluffy within. The actual variety is less critical than the way it is cooked, but the following is a list of suitable candidates:

Accent, Arran Pilot, Arran Victory, Cara, Desiree, Dunbar Standard, Duke of York, Epicure, Golden Wonder, Kestrel, King Edward, Maris Piper, Navan, Osprey, Picasso, Romano, Sharpe's Express, Russet Burbank, Norgold Russet, Long White.

* The crispest results of all come from using duck fat.
* Summer potatoes usually contain more water than those in winter, which have been stored.
* There is no ideal way to keep roast potatoes warm without them going soft, but the best way is to leave them uncovered in a cooling oven. Failing that, a very loose dome of aluminum foil will help, though inevitably at the expense of some of the crispness.
* You can cook new potatoes this way too. Their flesh becomes sweet and fudgy inside but their skin rarely forms a crust.

Classic roast potatoes

Peel the potatoes, cut them into pieces large enough for you to take two bites at each, then bring to a boil in deep, generously salted water. Boil for five minutes or so, then drain and return to the pan. Take the pan in both hands and give it a couple of good shakes. The idea is to fluff the edges of the potatoes so that they become crisp and frilly as they roast.

Arrange them around the roasting meat, then turn each one over so that it is coated in the roasting juices. If you are cooking them separately, use a shallow pan containing a little dripping, lard, or duck fat (or olive or peanut oil, if you must), then roast them at 400°F (200°C). They will need a good forty-five minutes, maybe a bit longer. Move them once or twice during cooking, so they crisp nicely all round.

If you are cooking the potatoes around the Sunday roast, remove the meat to rest before carving but return the potatoes to the oven. If they look less than crisp and golden, whack the heat up a few notches until they are perfect.

Sea bass with lemon potatoes

Baking a big piece of meat or a large fish on top of a layer of potatoes is a reliable way of ensuring they stay moist. The juices from the roast are soaked up by the potatoes, making sure that not a drop of flavor is wasted. Large fish such as sea bass and sea bream can be cooked in this way, as can Cornish mullet. Line-caught, ocean-friendly sea bass is not too difficult to find. I reckon on a 2-pound (1kg) fish being enough for two.

enough for 2

for the fish
sea bass – a whole fish, cleaned but left on the bone
olive oil
a little dried or fresh oregano

for the potatoes
waxy-fleshed potatoes such as Charlotte or Red Bliss – 1 pound (500g)
olive oil – 4 tablespoons
a large lemon
anchovy fillets – 12
vegetable stock – 1 cup (250ml)

Preheat the oven to 400°F (200°C). Slice each potato three or four times. If you do this lengthwise you will end up with long, elegant pieces. Warm a couple of tablespoons of olive oil in a roasting pan over medium-high heat, then put the potatoes in and let them color on both sides. They cook best if you leave them alone for several minutes in between stirring. You want them to be pale gold on both sides. Cut the lemon in half, then into thick segments. Add to the potatoes with the anchovy, and a grinding of black pepper and then pour over the stock.

Lay the fish on top of the potatoes, brush with a little olive oil, then add the herbs and a mild seasoning of salt and black pepper. Bake in the preheated oven until the flesh will slide easily away from the bone in big juicy pieces. This will take a matter of twenty-five to thirty minutes. Serve the fish with the potatoes and spoon over the stock.

Roast new potatoes and salami

Young potatoes of any sort roast sweetly, especially if scrubbed hard so
their skin almost disappears and they are allowed to develop a sticky, golden
coating in the oven. They need a few minutes in boiling water before they
hit the oven if they are not to toughen as they roast.

I match them with robust ingredients—slices of fat-flecked salami or
perhaps a spoonful of softly fibrous pork rillettes—as a Saturday lunch.

enough for 4
new potatoes – 16 to 24, depending on their size
extra-virgin olive oil
a bushy sprig of rosemary
salami – 24 slices
black olives – 16

Preheat the oven to 400°F (200°C). Rub the loose skin from the potatoes,
then boil them in salted water until tender. Drain and put them into a
baking dish or roasting pan. Using the back of a spoon, press down on each
potato, crushing it slightly—you just need to break the skin and flesh a little
in order to allow the oil to penetrate and the potato to crisp.

Pour a good glug of olive oil onto each smashed potato, then chop the
rosemary spikes finely and crumble them over the potatoes. Season and
roast for thirty-five to forty minutes, until the potatoes are golden and crisp
around the edges.

Divide the salami among four plates, then add the olives, the roast
potatoes, and a drizzle of olive oil.

Roast potatoes with duck fat and garlic

This is the classic accompaniment to duck confit, though I make it all the time—as a side dish for baked mushrooms or a steak, or sometimes as a main dish in its own right, in which case I make a salad too, perhaps with frisée or green beans.

enough for 4, as an accompaniment
medium potatoes – 4
duck fat – 3 tablespoons
the leaves from a couple of sprigs of thyme
garlic – a single clove, chopped

Preheat the oven to 400°F (200°C). Peel the potatoes and slice them as thinly as you can. They should be no thicker than ⅛ inch (3mm). Melt the duck fat in a shallow, heavy pan—I use a cast-iron skillet—turn off the heat, and add the potato slices, neatly or hugger-mugger, seasoning them with salt, black pepper, thyme leaves, and a little chopped garlic as you go. Bake for thirty-five to forty minutes, until golden brown.

Fried potatoes

There are two types of fried potato: French fries, which are deep-fried, and those that are sautéed in shallow oil or fat. I can think of few things I would rather eat than a French fry, hot and salty, dipped into a dish of béarnaise or hollandaise sauce. Yet I rarely make them at home, partly because we don't eat that much fried food and partly, if I am honest, because I dislike the terror of cooking with deep pans of boiling oil. Whenever I do dig out my deepest pan, half fill it with oil, and make a batch of fries, I always fry them twice: first, at a moderate temperature to cook them right through to the middle and then at a higher one to crisp them.

I tend to make sauté potatoes as a way of using up leftover boiled spuds. I often find they fry all the better for having spent the night in the fridge. They dry out overnight and seem to crisp up more reliably.

The frying varieties

I regard pretty much any fried potato as delicious, no matter whether it is waxy or floury, old or new, large or small. Bad fries are better than no fries at all. But just as there are good mashers, there are some potatoes that will fry better than others. I find Golden Wonder the ultimate frying potato for crispness and flavor, and grow it specifically for that. Of the more accessible varieties, it is worth looking at Accent, Cara, Desiree, Kerr's Pink, Kestrel, King Edward, Majestic, Maris Peer, Pentland Javelin, Premier, and Winston. Many people, and many fish-and-chip shops, swear by Maris Piper.

Chips

enough for 2 to 4
large floury potatoes – 4
dripping, lard, or sunflower oil for frying – 8 cups (2 liters)

Peel the potatoes and cut them into long, thick sticks, putting them into cold water as you go. The water has the effect of preventing them browning while also washing away some of the starch. Drain and pat dry with a cloth or paper towel. Heat the oil to 300°F (150°C) in a large, deep pan. Lower the potato sticks into the hot oil—it will bubble up alarmingly—and fry for six or seven minutes, until they are pale and soft. Lift them out and let drain while you bring the temperature of the oil to about 350°F (185°C). Lower the sticks into the hot oil again and fry for three or four minutes, maybe less, until they are crisp and golden.

Drain on paper towels and dust enthusiastically with salt.

A crisp cake of shredded potato

I had heard about Golden Wonder, the rock-hard potato with a deep honey-brown skin that roasts like a dream, but only came across my first a year or so back, at the farmers' market. Hard as ice and crisp white inside, the golden one turns out to hate water and will turn to soup if you attempt to boil it. Give it olive oil, butter, or goose or duck fat instead. This is the potato for frying in little cubes with rosemary and salt, and for French fries.

If you plant Golden Wonder in April, and are lavish with the water, it will reward you with charming, snow-white flowers flushed with palest lilac and, come September, perhaps the best frying potatoes of all, to be finely shredded and cooked in a flat cake with goose fat and garlic.

> *enough for 4*
> Golden Wonder potatoes – 1 pound (500g)
> goose fat – about 3 tablespoons
> garlic cloves – 4

Peel the potatoes (the skins are tough) and grate them finely. I have done this by hand but it takes just seconds using a food processor fitted with a medium-fine grating blade. You want the strands of potato to be roughly the same thickness as the wool for knitting a sweater.

Melt the goose fat—I sometimes use butter—in a wide, shallow pan and add the grated potato. Grind over a little sea salt, then squash the garlic cloves flat and tuck them in among the strings of potato. Cook over low to medium heat for fifteen to twenty minutes, until the underside is crisp and golden. Loosen the edges with a spatula as they cook, pushing it farther under the cake until it is free enough to slide about.

Lay a heatproof plate on top of the pan, then, holding it firmly in place, turn the whole thing upside down (I find doing this with one positive movement and no dithering tends not to end in tears). Now slide the potato cake back into the pan and cook the other side.

When it is truly golden, crumble over a pinch of sea salt flakes and serve, hot and crisp, from the pan.

Potato cake with thyme

Good with lamb.

enough for 6
medium potatoes (floury are best) – 5
butter – 7 tablespoons (90g)
thyme – the leaves from 4 sprigs

Preheat the oven to 400°F (200°C). Peel the potatoes and slice them thinly. They should be so thin that you are almost able to see through them. If you tend to work slowly, put the sliced potatoes into a bowl of cold water to prevent them browning.

Melt the butter, then brush some of it on to the bottom and sides of a loaf pan (or use a round cake pan, if that is what you have). Cover with a piece of wax paper, leaving a little extra overlapping the sides to get hold of when you come to turn out the cake. Cover the bottom of the pan with slices of potato, brush with more butter, and season with salt, pepper, and a light sprinkling of thyme leaves. Continue layering the potatoes, adding the butter and seasonings every two or three layers, until you have used them all up. Pour any remaining butter over the top. Bake for forty to fifty minutes, until the top is golden and a skewer can be inserted effortlessly into the layers of tender potato. To serve, lift the potato cake out by holding both long sides of the wax paper and pulling upward. Cut into six pieces. If it falls apart, and well it might, just push the slices back together.

Potatoes with goose fat and thyme

For each person, cut a medium to large potato into large dice. Squash a clove of garlic flat and warm it in a shallow pan with a couple of good tablespoons of goose fat (or oil) and a couple of hearty sprigs of thyme. Introduce the potatoes and let them cook for fifteen to twenty minutes, until they are tender. Increase the heat so they crisp, dust with salt, then eat as soon as they are cool enough to do so. I sometimes make this just for myself, occasionally scattering the crisp potatoes onto arugula leaves to make me feel virtuous.

Steamed and boiled potatoes

Steaming or boiling a potato is often the most successful way to showcase its flavor. The nutty, lemony, or earthy notes are at their most obvious when a vegetable has met nothing but steam or water before we eat it. This alone makes it worth hunting out a really good spud. Local markets are excellent places to track down something more interesting than the average supermarket variety, but nothing beats steaming potatoes we have grown ourselves.

The most important characteristic after flavor is that of holding together during cooking: a potato that doesn't collapse in the steam or break up in the water. Our choice will depend very much on the time of year but also on whether we want a neat, fudgy little potato to serve whole, perhaps rolled in melted butter and parsley, or a big, fat lump of tatty potato, all floury edges and fluffiness. The sort of spud to mash into your gravy with your fork.

I use as little water as possible and salt it generously, but I prefer to steam them where I can. When they are cooked without water, their flavor seems truer and their flesh stays firmer.

Best for boiling and steaming

For small potatoes, to be served whole Anya, Edzell Blue, Pink Fir Apple, small Maxine and any of the very early varieties such as International Kidney (called Jerseys when grown there), Foremost, Duke of York, Accent, Epicure, French Fingerling, Russian Banana, Red Gold.
For big, fluffy results to accompany a stew or sloppy braise Arran Victory, Cosmos, Maris Peer, Maris Piper, Estima, King Edward, Nadine, Saxon, Kestrel, Wilja, Norgold Russet, Kerr's Pink, Adirondack Red.

Potatoes, crème fraîche, and dill

It's the last week of June and the pink-mauve flowers of the Charlotte potatoes have started to fade. The stems are thick like old rhubarb, yet almost transparent in the evening sun. Once the flowers have gone, it's okay to lift them.

The tallest stalk doesn't disappoint. A good dozen potatoes are attached to its fine, creamy-white roots—pale, golden eggs against crumbly black soil. Not just hen's either, there are diminutive spuds the size of quail's eggs and others more like duck's. It is said that they are best left to "set" for a day before cooking. We don't, and they are rubbed clean with a thumb under running water, then boiled in heavily salted water for fifteen minutes, eighteen for the duck's eggs.

Gently rub the potatoes clean, washing them well under running water. Leave the skin be if it is young and thin. Peel it if not. Put the potatoes into cold water and bring to a boil. Salt generously, then simmer until tender when pierced with the tip of a knife—a matter of anything from ten to twenty-five minutes, depending on the variety of your potatoes. Drain and return them to the stove, this time over gentle heat.

Put a large dollop of crème fraîche into the pan and a handful of chopped dill fronds. Cover with a lid until the cream has melted. Fold the potatoes gently over in the melted cream and herbs until they are lightly coated, then eat with ham or oily fish.

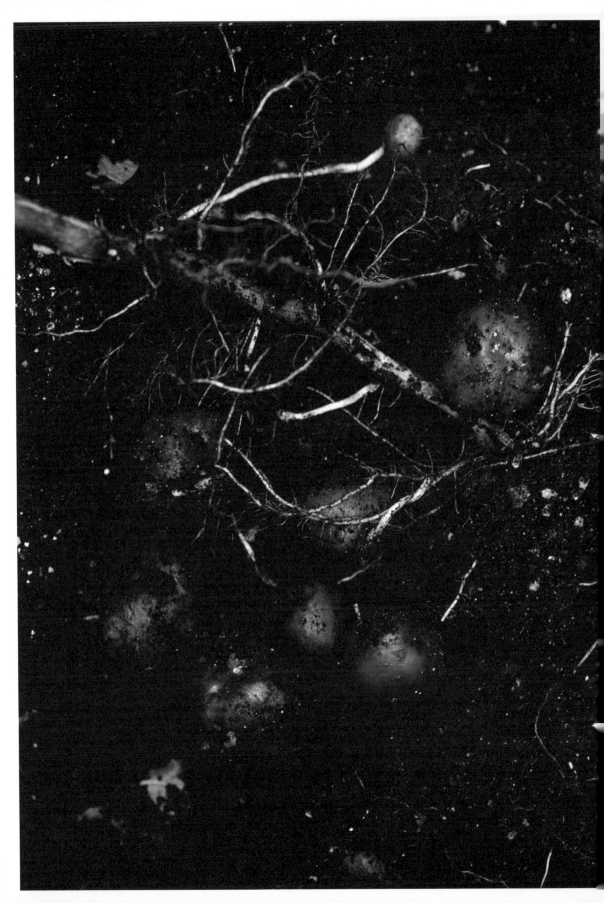

Crushed potatoes with cream and garlic

If you crush a cooked potato with the back of a spoon or fork, its broken edges are receptive to any dressing you wish to drizzle over it. Cream and garlic is a rather sumptuous treatment for a virginal new potato, but it works very well.

enough for 4 as a side dish
new potatoes – 1 pound (500g)
new garlic – 3 juicy cloves
heavy cream – 1 cup (250ml)
thyme – about 8 sprigs

Scrub the potatoes but do not peel them. Boil them in a pan of deep, lightly salted water for fifteen to twenty minutes or so, until tender.

While the potatoes are boiling, peel and lightly crush the garlic cloves. Pour the cream into a small saucepan, and add the leaves from the sprigs of thyme, the garlic, a little salt, and some black pepper. Let the mixture simmer over medium heat until it has reduced by about a third.

Once the potatoes are drained, put them in a shallow dish and crush each one lightly with a fork—you want to break the skin and flatten the potato just enough for its flesh to soak up some of the hot cream. Pour the cream and thyme over the crushed potatoes and eat while hot.

Sorrel with new potatoes

Occasionally in spring I find myself with a bunch or two of sorrel (it is often sold at the farmers' market by the handful). The lemony notes work well with tiny boiled potatoes. Sorrel collapses when it gets hot, loses its color, and almost disappears. But it leaves behind a soft green purée that is very good for tossing freshly boiled Jerseys in.

Cook new potatoes in deep, salted water until tender (you will need about 1 pound [500g] for four). Meanwhile, make a dressing with a little oil and vinegar, then add salt, pepper, and the shredded sorrel. As soon as the potatoes are drained, while they are still piping hot, toss them with the sorrel dressing, letting them rest for ten minutes before serving.

New season's potatoes with pancetta, walnut oil, and sherry vinegar

Steam 14 ounces (400g) of new season's waxy or floury potatoes until tender when pierced with the tip of a knife. Leave the skins on. They will be used uncut, so you need them to be as small as possible.

Put a tablespoon of Dijon mustard in a small bowl with a pinch of sugar and three pinches of sea salt. Whisk in a tablespoon of sherry vinegar, then four of walnut oil. Stir in a tablespoon of cold water and a little pepper.

Broil eight thin slices of pancetta until crisp. Snap them into short pieces. Coarsely chop a little parsley.

Spoon the warm potatoes into a serving dish, toss gently with the dressing, then fold in the parsley and pancetta.

The perfect baked potato

A baked potato can be a perfect thing, brought rough skinned from the oven between warm oven mitts, its crust sparkling with salt like a pearlescent frost, its interior the texture of deep snow. I have made many a meal of a single baked potato, huge like a boulder, with ice-cold butter tucked into a craggy slit in its skin. I usually have a beer too and a bowl of salad, whose peppery leaves I stuff into the empty, salt-encrusted skin. It is something to eat alone, a big fat spud all to yourself, a meal of utter simplicity and quiet solace.

When I was a kid, baked potatoes appeared on the table having had their filling removed and whipped up with mashed corned beef or grated cheese, piled back in, and baked briefly until the surface was crisp with golden furrows. I rarely go in for that and tend to present them on the table with a packet of butter, a tub of crème fraîche, and a bowl of crisp salad, Belgian endive, and watercress in a mustardy dressing being a favorite. Supper becomes a delicious assembly job.

In theory, you can rinse your potato, prick it with a fork, and stick it in the oven and you will get a perfectly fine result. However, even a baked potato has levels of perfection, and there is little point in not at least trying to make each one the best baked potato we have ever eaten.

* While the skin is still damp from washing, a little sea salt can be dusted over the surface. This will help it to crisp.
* A metal skewer pierced right through the potato and left in position while it is in the oven will help your supper cook more quickly.
* The cooking time will depend on the size of your potato, but even the smallest will take a good fifty minutes at 350°F (180°C). For a guaranteed crisp skin, bake them at 400°F (200°C).
* To achieve a fluffy interior, the steam must leave the flesh quickly. A good karate chop will suffice, though wrapping a kitchen towel around the hand first is worth thinking about. Your blow should be hard enough to break the skin but not so hard as to send potato shrapnel all over the kitchen. In time, you can perfect it.

The baking varieties

A variety with a dry, powdery flesh will produce a light, open-textured baked potato—one that is capable of soaking up butter, crème fraîche, salad dressing, or whatever lubricant we throw at it without becoming heavy. As a general rule of thumb, any that mash or roast well will usually produce a good, light result when baked.

No single potato will be everyone's preferred "baker," and some favor a more waxy texture. Many regard Red Duke of York as one of the finest in terms of texture and flavor, but King Edward and Arran Victory have more than a few fans. I find homegrown Kestrel, with its flashes of violet, one of the most enjoyable. Marfona tends to be the one the supermarkets push as the potato for baking but I find it too waxy. Below is a list of suitable candidates:

Arran Pilot, Arran Victory, British Queen, Desiree, Duke of York, Edzell Blue, Epicure, Estima, Foremost, Kestrel, King Edward, Maris Peer, Maris Piper, Nadine, Pentland Javelin, Pentland Squire, Picasso, Romano, Saxon, Swift, Vanessa, Wilja, Winston, Burbank Russet, Atlantic, Viking Red, Mountain Rose.

Sea salt–baked potato, Parmesan greens

The stuffed baked potato, that bastion of comfort eating, given a contemporary treatment.

> *enough for 2*
> large baking potatoes – 2
> butter or olive oil
> green salad leaves – 2 large handfuls
>
> **for the dressing**
> tarragon vinegar – a tablespoon
> Dijon mustard – a teaspoon
> an egg yolk
> olive oil – a scant ½ cup (100ml)
> grated Parmesan – 2 tablespoons
> lemon juice – 2 teaspoons

Preheat the oven to 400°F (200°C). Wet the potatoes, prick them with a fork, and roll them in flakes of sea salt, making certain that at least some stick to the skin. Bake them until tender; this can take anything from thirty-five minutes to an hour, depending on your potatoes.

To make the dressing, whisk the vinegar, mustard, egg yolk, and olive oil together with a little salt and black pepper, then beat in the grated cheese. Squeeze in the lemon juice, stir, and set aside for five minutes.

Serve the salt-baked potatoes, scooping off the top like a boiled egg and stirring in butter or olive oil as you wish. Once the potato flesh has been eaten, toss the salad leaves with the dressing and pile into the vacated potato skins. Eat salad, potato skins and all.

Baked potatoes, leeks, and fontina

I say fontina because that is what I had in the kitchen last time I made this—it's a fondue cheese that melts sublimely and doesn't overpower the leeks. But Taleggio, another milky Italian, would be just fine, too.

enough for 2
baking potatoes – 2, about 12 ounces (350g) each
leeks – 2 or 3
butter – a thick slice
fontina – 3 to 4 ounces (90 to 120g), coarsely grated, or Taleggio, cut into thin slices

Preheat the oven to 400°F (200°C). Scrub the potatoes, prick them with a fork or insert a metal skewer in them, then while they are still damp, dust them lightly with sea salt. Let sit to dry for a few minutes, then bake until the skin is crisp and the inside soft and fluffy—a matter of thirty-five minutes to an hour, depending on the potato variety.

Half an hour or so before you expect the potatoes to be ready, start cooking the leeks (it is worth remembering that baked potatoes are good natured, so a few minutes either way won't hurt). Split the leeks in half, wash them thoroughly, then cut them into finger-thick slices. Melt half the butter in a heavy pan, add the leeks, and let them cook slowly over low heat until they are soft and translucent. This will take longer than you might think, as much as fifteen or twenty minutes to soften them completely. An occasional stir will prevent them browning.

Split the potatoes in half and scoop the flesh into a bowl, then drop in the remaining butter and most of the cheese, and beat to a creamy mass with a wooden spoon or electric mixer. Taste and season with salt and black pepper. Pile back into the skins, dot the last of the cheese over, and return to the oven for a good fifteen minutes, until piping hot.

Baked potatoes, salt cod, and parsley

A beautiful marriage of textures, this: creamy salt cod purée and crisp potato skins. As baked potatoes go, this is a lot of work, and much washing up too, but the result is worth the trouble. Salt cod is not easy to track down; Spanish, Italian, and Portuguese markets and major supermarkets are your best bet.

The recipe makes rather too much filling, but it is not worth dealing with a smaller quantity of salt cod. There's no hardship anyway—simply keep the leftover purée in the fridge and eat it the next day with fingers of hot toast.

enough for 2
dried salt cod – 1 pound (500g)
large baking potatoes – 2
milk – ⅔ cup (150ml)
extra-virgin olive oil – ⅔ cup (150ml)
a large garlic clove
the juice of a lemon
parsley – a small bunch, chopped

Soak the salt cod in cold water for a good twenty-four hours, changing the water regularly.

Preheat the oven to 400°F (200°C). After scrubbing the potatoes well and pricking them here and there with a fork, put them in to bake. Once they have been baking for half an hour or so, drain the fish, put it in a deep pan, cover it with fresh cold water, then bring to a boil. When the water is bubbling, turn off the heat and cover the pan with a lid. Let it sit for fifteen minutes, then drain. Remove and discard the bones and skin. A messy job, and one of the few kitchen jobs for which I will put on a pair of rubber gloves. Put the salt cod into a food processor. Warm the milk (I use the steam nozzle on the coffee machine) and the olive oil separately.

Peel and coarsely chop the garlic and add it to the fish. Blitz, pouring in the milk and olive oil in a steady stream, letting the mixture whip to a sloppy cream.

Remove the potatoes from the oven, slit them open, and scoop out the flesh with a teaspoon, then add it to the salt cod. Blitz briefly to mix, then add the lemon juice, the chopped parsley leaves, and a few grinds of the pepper mill. Pile the purée into the potato skins and return to the hot oven for fifteen minutes.

Potato salads

There are two schools of thought about the perfect salad potato. Most agree that a waxy potato is best, as it holds its shape during cooking and slices neatly. The waxy texture ensures that the slices remain intact even when soaked with dressing. The other approach is to use a floury King Edward–style potato, boiled until its edges fray, then cut into crumbling slices, dressed with a robust oil-and-vinegar mixture while warm, and tossed with coarsely chopped green onions and parsley. Served with thickly sliced, fat-speckled salami and tiny, piquant cornichons, it provides a salad of hearty rusticity.

Yellow-fleshed potatoes that are waxy to the touch have always been popular in France and Scandinavia but only recently have they become easy to find in the UK. They are recognizable by their soaplike feel, and often by their oval or elongated shape. Rarely larger than a bantam's egg, they are at their most charming when the size of a large pebble.

* It is worth trying to dress the potatoes while they are still hot—they soak up the dressing more effectively.
* The decision about whether to skin potatoes meant for salad is a personal one. I like the rusticity of an unskinned potato salad. But there is also something very elegant about a salad made with skinned new potatoes.
* In this instance, vinegar seems a more suitable acid for a dressing than lemon juice.

Some excellent salad varieties

Amandine, Anya, Belle de Fontenay, Carlingford, Charlotte, International Kidney, Juliette, Lady Christl, Linzer Delikatess, Nicola, Pink Fir Apple, Ratte, Roseval, Royal Kidney, Rose Finn Apple, Adirondack Red, Fingerling Salad.

Linzer, and a perfect potato salad

Long, pale, and slim, the Linzer Delikatess is as elegant as a tuber could be. I found this Austrian variety at my usual market on a wet day in early July, and brought them home out of curiosity. The flesh was waxy and yellow, and held together well in salted boiling water. They were tender to the knife in ten minutes. Potatoes that keep their shape well in water tend to hold up when saturated with dressing, making them good for potato salads—in this case, a salad dressed with thick Spanish oil, mustard, and dill and tossed with chunks of peeled cucumber. We ate it with a fat, golden-skinned mackerel, smoked that morning by the fishmonger.

A salad of potatoes, mustard, and cucumber

At first rich, then intensely warm and piquant, this is a perfectly balanced salad for accompanying fish or maybe a grilled steak. It is just the job with freshly dressed crab or smoked trout or eel. The potatoes should be warm when you dress them, and eaten within twenty minutes or so, giving them time to soak up the flavors but not dry out. If you are dressing the salad in advance, I suggest you make a double quantity of dressing.

enough for 4
half a cucumber
new potatoes – 1 to 1½ pounds (500 to 750g)

for the dressing
superfine sugar – a good pinch (but no more)
white wine or cider vinegar – a tablespoon
Dijon mustard – a generous tablespoon
olive oil – 4 tablespoons
juniper berries – 6, lightly crushed
dill – 2 tablespoons, chopped

Peel the cucumber, halve it down its length, and remove the seeds with a teaspoon—they will only make the salad wet. Slice the cucumber into chunks about ¾ inch (2cm) thick. Sprinkle lightly with salt and let sit in a colander in the sink for about half an hour.

Bring a pan of water to a boil. Scrub the potatoes, thumbing off any flaky skin as you go. Salt the water, add the potatoes, and let them boil for about fifteen minutes, until they are tender when pierced with the tip of a knife. Drain them and briefly set aside.

While the potatoes are boiling, make the dressing. Put the sugar and vinegar in a small bowl and stir until the sugar has dissolved. Add some black pepper. Mix in the mustard, then gently whisk in the olive oil. Stir in the juniper berries, the cucumber, and the chopped dill and set aside.

Slice the warm potatoes, letting them fall into the dressing, then fold them together gently. Let sit for no more than twenty minutes, then serve.

A salad of potatoes, herring, and crème fraîche

A sweet-sharp salad with a creamy dressing. Avoid the temptation to overmix the salad, as the beets are inclined to send everything a very unfetching shade of marshmallow pink.

enough for 4 as a light main course
waxy potatoes – 10½ ounces (300g)
small cooked beets – 4
pickled herring fillets – 6
medium gherkins – 4
green onions – 4
dill – a small bunch
arugula leaves – 7 ounces (200g)

for the dressing
red wine vinegar – a tablespoon
olive oil – a tablespoon
smooth Dijon mustard – a teaspoon
crème fraîche – a scant ½ cup (100ml)
yogurt – a scant ½ cup (100g)

Scrub the potatoes and bring them to a boil in deep salted water. Let them simmer for fifteen minutes or so, until they are tender when pierced with the tip of a knife.

Peel the beets, cut them into thick wedges, and put them in a bowl. Remove the little wooden sticks that inevitably come with marinated herrings and cut each fillet into six chunks, then add to the beets but do not mix. Thickly slice the gherkins and add them to the beets and herring. Chop the green onions and the dill and add to the bowl. Rinse the arugula and check it over, removing any thick stalks or wilted leaves. Keep separate from the rest of the ingredients.

Drain the potatoes, then peel off their skins as soon as they are cool enough to hold. Don't let them get cold, though; you need to dress them while they are still warm. Cut each potato in half if they are very small, quarters if not, and add them to the mixing bowl.

Mix the vinegar and olive oil in a small bowl or jar with a fork and season with salt and black pepper and the mustard. Beat in the crème fraîche and yogurt. Gently fold the dressing into the rest of the ingredients in the bowl, stirring only lightly to avoid the beets sending everything pink. Divide the arugula among four plates and pile the potato salad on top.

Roast potato salad with rosemary and garlic

The idea of a potato salad usually involves slippery potatoes of the purest ivory, but an interesting take entails a much rougher texture brought about by roasting them before dressing.

enough for 4 as a side dish
new potatoes – 24
garlic – a bulb
olive oil
rosemary or thyme– a few sprigs

for the dressing
red wine vinegar – 2 tablespoons
smooth Dijon mustard – 2 tablespoons
olive oil – 5 tablespoons

Preheat the oven to 400°F (200°C). Scrub the potatoes thoroughly, then put them in an ovenproof dish or roasting pan. Break the garlic into cloves, but don't peel them. Add them to the potatoes. Drizzle over a little olive oil, then scatter with flakes of sea salt and the leaves from the rosemary or thyme sprigs. Bake for three-quarters of an hour to an hour, until they are puffed and golden and their insides are fluffy.

Pour the vinegar into a small jar with a lid and add the mustard, olive oil, and some salt and pepper. Shake it hard to give a thick dressing. You can use a little whisk if you prefer. When the potatoes come from the oven, press down hard on each one with the back of a spoon so that they crack open slightly, then pour over the mustard dressing. As you eat, press the soft garlic from its skin.

Gratins and baked dishes

I rather like the fact that cooks disagree about things. If we didn't, then cooking would be a much less interesting subject and in risk of atrophy. The traditional potato for a gratin, or dauphinois, is a yellow-fleshed, waxy variety that holds its shape, and yet I made my gratins with a floury potato for many years simply because I liked the fact that they collapsed into the creamy sauce. Boulangère likewise—I very much like the effect you get when potatoes collapse into meat stock.

Gratin dauphinois

enough for 6
waxy potatoes – about 2 pounds (1kg)
garlic – 2 large, juicy cloves
butter – just enough to butter the baking dish thickly
heavy cream – enough to cover the potatoes, about 2½ cups (600ml)

Preheat the oven to 325°F (160°C). Peel the potatoes and cut them into slices about ⅛ inch (3mm) thick. Cut the cloves of garlic in half and rub them round the inside of an ovenproof earthenware or enameled cast-iron dish. Smear the dish generously with butter. Lay the potato slices in the dish, orderly or hugger-mugger as the mood takes you, seasoning with salt and black pepper as you go.

Pour over the cream and slide the dish into the oven. Bake for an hour to an hour and a half, until the potatoes are virtually melting into the cream.

Some good things to put in your gratin

Smoked bacon Broil it first, then chop coarsely and scatter between the layers.
Smoked mackerel For which it is worth looking at my book *Real Food*.
Porcini Soak just a few dried mushrooms in water until soft, then tuck them in between the potatoes.
Cheese Grated Gruyère scattered over the top before baking will give a deliciously savory crust. Whether you think this already rich recipe needs more fat is another matter.
Anchovies Wiped of their salt or oil, anchovy fillets can be slipped in between the layers, Swedish style. The effect is more savory than fishy, and utterly delectable.

A potato supper

There is much comfort, warmth, solace, and satiety in a bowl of starch, especially in cold weather. This one has the benefit of stock too, providing either a simple supper or an accompaniment to a roast.

small, waxy potatoes – about 5 per person
a little peanut or light olive oil
a little butter for greasing the dish and a few knobs on top
bacon or pancetta – about 2 thin slices per person
sage leaves – 1 per person
stock – a good chicken one, but bouillon will do

Preheat the oven to 350°F (180°C). If the fine, pale skin doesn't bother you, there is no need to peel the potatoes, but you should give them a good rub with your thumb (I must say, I invariably peel mine, or at least scrape them well, but others think I am being persnickety). Whatever, you need to slice them no thicker than ⅛ inch (3mm). Warm enough oil to cover the bottom of a frying pan, then fry the sliced potatoes in it just long enough to color them lightly on both sides. Lift them out onto paper towels.

Generously butter a shallow baking dish or roasting pan. Cut the bacon into pieces about the size of a postage stamp. Layer the potatoes in the buttered dish, scattering the bacon, sage, and a grinding of salt and black pepper over them as you go. Dot the surface with a few little knobs of butter, then pour over enough stock to cover. Bake for about an hour, until the potatoes are soft enough to crush between your fingers.

Potatoes with dill and chicken stock

I am constantly on the lookout for potato dishes that will flatter a piece of meat or fish such as grilled mackerel, flash-fried lamb's liver, or some thick bacon slices. This is such a dish.

enough for 4 as a side dish
large baking potatoes – 2
dill leaves – a generous handful, roughly chopped
a large knob of butter
hot chicken or vegetable stock to cover – about 2 cups (500ml)

Preheat the oven to 400°F (200°C). Scrub the potatoes, peeling them only if you particularly wish to, then slice them thinly. Put them into a bowl and toss with salt, black pepper, and the dill.

Lightly butter a shallow baking dish. Layer the potatoes and their seasonings in the dish, then pour in enough stock to cover; the liquid should be just lapping at the top of the potatoes.

Bake for about fifty minutes, until the potato slices are truly tender and crusty on top.

A thin cake of potatoes and Parmesan

Potatoes cut thinly are not only good deep-fried but can be blissful when cooked with stock or butter until they are sodden and meltingly soft. I wanted a sliced potato dish that had the simplicity of *pommes à la boulangère* but something of the richness of its creamier cousin, *pommes à la dauphinoise*. This is what I have come up with: thinly sliced potatoes layered with garlic, butter, and grated Parmesan. Savory, melting, and, yes, rich, they are a near-perfect accompaniment for cold roast lamb or beef.

enough for 4
waxy potatoes – about 2 pounds (900g to 1kg)
butter – 9 tablespoons (125g)
garlic – 2 cloves
Parmesan – ¼ cup (30g), finely grated

Preheat the oven to 425°F (220°C). Peel the potatoes, then slice them thinly. I do this by hand but if you have a mandoline you can do it in a matter of seconds. The rounds should be so thin that you can almost see through them.

Melt the butter in a small pan. Peel the garlic, then crush it or, if you prefer, chop it finely. Smooth a little of the melted butter over the bottom of a shallow baking dish or a cast-iron frying pan and cover it with some of the potato slices, overlapping them slightly. Pour on a little more butter, then season with salt, garlic, black pepper, and a good dusting of Parmesan. Cover that with a further layer of potatoes, more seasoning, garlic, and Parmesan, then continue layering until you have used all the potatoes. Finish with butter and a light dusting of Parmesan.

Bake, pressing the cake down very firmly once or twice with a large spatula. After forty-five to fifty minutes, you should have a deep golden potato cake sizzling around its edges. Remove from the oven and let it sit to calm down for a few minutes before serving.

A winter dish of potatoes, onions, and melted cheese

enough for 4, with greens on the side
baking potatoes – 2 pounds (1kg)
a large onion
olive oil
Gruyère or other firm cheese – 5 ounces (150g), cut into small pieces
grated Parmesan – a small handful
greens, such as kale, spinach, or dark green cabbage – 4 large handfuls

Bring a large pan of water to a boil while you peel the potatoes and cut them as you would for boiling. Salt the water, add the potatoes, and let them simmer for fifteen to twenty minutes, until just tender enough to take the tip of a knife.

Preheat the oven to 350°F (180°C). As the potatoes are cooking, peel the onion, cut it in half and then into thick slices. Warm a little olive oil in a deep Dutch oven or other heavy pot over medium heat, add the onion, and let it soften and color lightly, stirring from time to time so that it does not brown.

When the potatoes are tender, drain them, then cut through each one (I do this while they are still in the pan) so that they are roughly bite sized. Add them to the onion pan—if they crumble a bit, that is all to the good—then toss them with the Gruyère. Grind over some salt and black pepper, then scatter with the grated Parmesan.

Bake for about thirty-five to forty minutes, until the cheese is melted and the potatoes and onion are golden. You can steam or boil the greens while this is happening, a few minutes before you expect the potatoes to be ready.

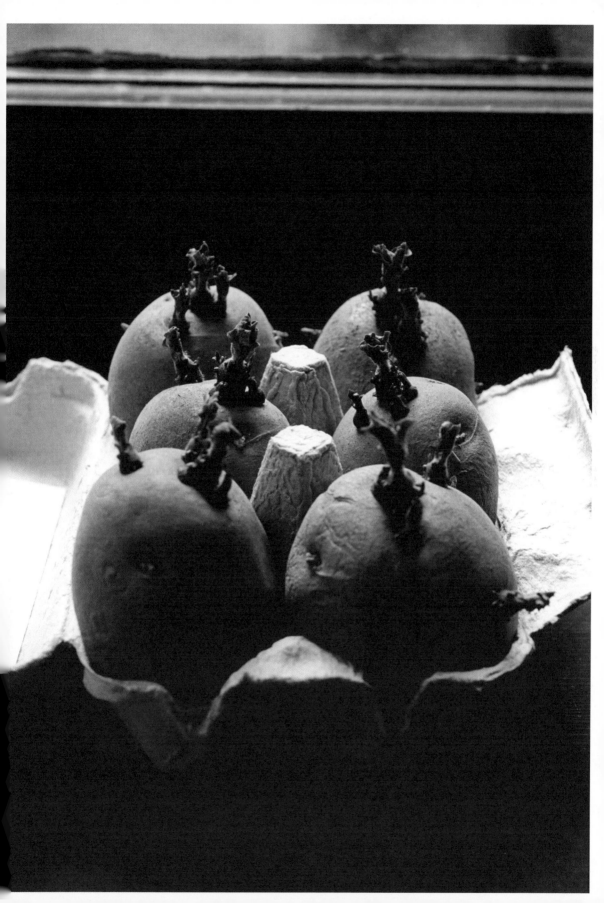

Herbed potato cake

This is my version of the Spanish omelette, being lighter, crisper, and more studded with herbs than the norm. The point here is that you can mix the herbs to suit your taste. Tarragon and mint are a must for me, but any of the more unusual herbs is worth using too: chopped sorrel leaves, salad burnet, lovage, or any of the lesser-known basils. Because the herbs are only lightly cooked in this recipe, their flavor will stay true.

enough for 6
waxy potatoes – 1⅔ pounds (800g)
green onions – 6
eggs – 3
all-purpose flour – a scant tablespoon
chopped parsley, mint, tarragon – 2 teaspoons (10g) each
olive oil

Grate the potatoes into a bowl, peeling them first if you wish. Finely slice the green onions into rounds and add them to the potatoes. Break the eggs and beat them lightly, then add them with the flour, chopped herbs, and a good seasoning of salt and pepper.

Warm a little olive oil in a 10-inch (24cm) nonstick frying pan. Add the potato mixture and spread it out so that it covers the bottom of the pan. Let it cook over medium heat for ten to fifteen minutes, until the underside is golden brown and the potato is tender. Meanwhile, preheat the broiler. Transfer the pan to the hot broiler and let brown. Cut into six wedges and serve.

Bubbles, squeaks, and rumbledethumps

Colcannon, rumbledethumps, *pyttipanna, biksemad, roupa velha*, and *stampot*—the local names used throughout Europe intrigue and delight but they all describe the same thing, a stir-up of potatoes and greens. In some cases, the two components are served freshly mixed; in others they are fried or baked to acquire a crust. Either way, this is good food at its most frugal. The ingredients may be cooked fresh or taken from yesterday's leftovers. *Roupa velha* is Portuguese for "old clothes."

* Irish colcannon is made from mashed potatoes and chopped, boiled kale. It is served unfried, in all its green and white purity.
* Rumbledethumps is a Scottish dish made with fried onions, cabbage, and mashed potatoes. After mixing, it is baked until golden.
* Bubble and squeak is generally shaped in rounds and fried in a pan, or left as one large cake, which looks splendid but is difficult to turn in the pan. Either way, the name comes from the sound it makes as it fries in the pan.

Cheese bubble and squeak

Two of these cheese-and-potato cakes are ample for a main course with maybe a spinach or chicory salad to follow.

> *makes 4, enough for 2*
> greens (purple spouting, Chinese broccoli, Savoy cabbage, etc.) –
>   7 ounces (200g)
> cooked potato – ¾ cup (200g) coarsely mashed
> goat cheese – 3½ ounces (100g)
> nutmeg
> all-purpose flour – a tablespoon, plus extra for coating
> a little olive oil

Wash the greens thoroughly, then cook in deep salted water until bright green and tender. Drain carefully and coarsely chop, discarding any tough stalks.

Mix the mashed potato with the greens, then cut up the goat cheese into small pieces and add to the potatoes and greens. Season generously with salt, black pepper, and, if you wish, a very little nutmeg. Stir in the flour.

Divide the mixture into fourths and shape each one into a rough patty 2½ to 3 inches (6 to 7.5cm) in diameter and about ¼ inch (6mm) thick. Put the patties on a floured plate, turning them once in the flour.

Get a thin layer of oil hot in a shallow, nonstick pan. Lower the patties into the oil and cook for about four minutes on each side, until golden and lightly crisp. Drain briefly on paper towels and serve.

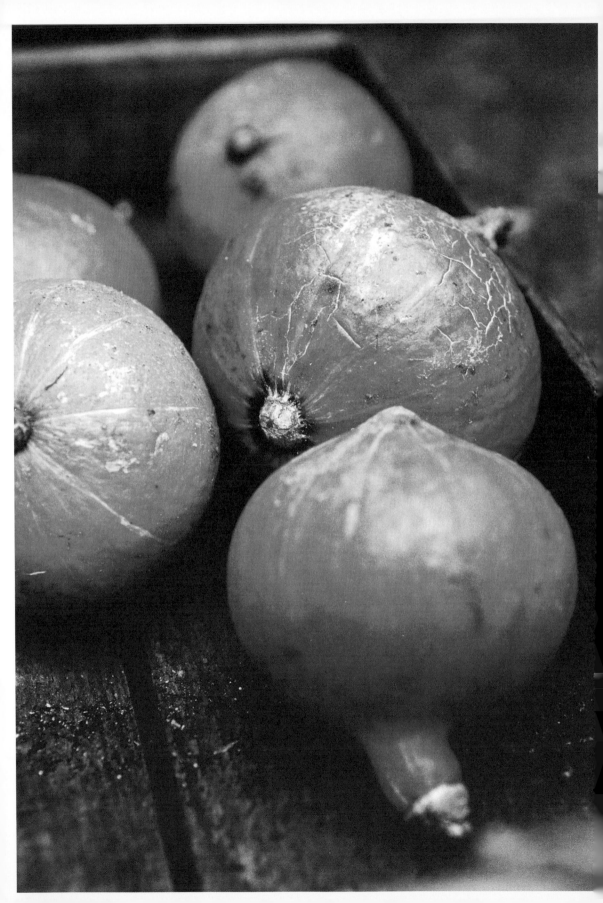

Pumpkin and
other winter squashes

Even as I write, in the slate gray light of a
December afternoon, there is a pumpkin in
the garden, shining orange bright among the
blackened leaves and tangled stems. A bowl of
soup waiting to happen.

Winter squashes are the hard-rinded, golden-
fleshed siblings of the more delicate green and
yellow summer varieties. They can be exotically
shaped like Aladdin's turban or as homely as
a cottage loaf. I call them sugar pumpkins, on
account of the intense sweetness of their flesh,
and revel in their somewhat sinister overtones.
A fat, round pumpkin is used both as a candlelit ghoul at Halloween and
as a fairytale stagecoach to whisk Cinderella to the ball. American and
French cooks have long appreciated them; in Britain the pumpkin still has
a stronger association with ghosts and goblins than it does with soup.

As summer slips into autumn, the pumpkin's skin, like that of all the
winter squashes, starts to harden. It will keep the sweet flesh in sound
enough condition until early spring—though whether it ends up as risotto
or a doorstop will depend on whether you can still get a knife through it.
They are a fruit really, but one that we use in soups, stews, curries, and as a
filling for ravioli.

I would grow a pumpkin even if it weren't edible. Few things are
more beautiful when morning fog swirls round the allotments on a damp
November dawn. But the real point of winter squash is the sweetness of
its flesh—only corn on the cob comes anywhere close. Their frugality
should not be underestimated. You can get a soup-stew of haricot beans,
late tomatoes, and cheese out of one for a cheap and filling supper. Half a
small one will make enough simple soup for four. A thick wedge is enough
per person as a side vegetable. I tuck chunks of mine under roast beef so the
sugary flesh picks up the deeply savory goo that collects under the meat.
Together they make a tantalizing forkful.

Everything from the enchanting, miniature Munchkin to the massive Atlantic Giant can be good to eat, though the flesh of some varieties can be more fibrous or watery than others. The blue-skinned pumpkins such as Crown Prince have the firmest flesh, which doesn't break up when steamed or roasted; the richest flavored are often the deepest orange. Any will make a satisfying, velvet-textured soup if added to softened onions, sweet spices, and a modicum of ripe chile.

To be honest, we didn't eat the first one. My best friend and I just hollowed out the interior with our hands and a bent kitchen spoon, gouged glaring eyes, and cut jagged teeth deep into its skin, then left the flesh in a plastic bag to rot. I must have been about ten. I am not sure we even knew the innards were edible. My family, slaves to the frozen pea, had never heard of pumpkin pie or soup. The giant squash, so enormous that two of us could barely lift it onto the garden wall, was there purely to add witchery to our Halloween revelry. Tired of roasting chestnuts, Dad put a glowing night-light in its belly, sending spooky shadows long into the night. A week later he took a spade to it, now a scene of appalling melancholy, and threw it on the compost heap with his prize dahlia tops that had been unexpectedly caught in the frost.

The plump, orange-skinned fruits are the ones most favored for Halloween lanterns, with skin firm enough to hold up against the heat of a candle. Rouge Vif d'Etamps and Mammoth are suitable subjects, as is Ghost Rider. Jack O'Lantern is, appropriately enough, the most reliable of all, having a tough, shiny orange skin that flickers spookily in the candlelight.

The winter squash is now as much a part of my cold-weather cooking as dried beans, fat apples, sweet onions, and cheap, bony cuts of meat. It is difficult to think of anything that is capable of bringing quite so much warmth, jollity, and good humor to the table on a frost-sparkling night. From September through to the last feeble weeks of February, squashes come at you in succession. Gold, pale blue, or deep green fruits, adding weight and cheer to your organic box, are at first a welcoming sight in a shopping bag of winter beige and brown. But just as one leaves the kitchen as a deep orange soup, a pebbly-topped crumble, or a cloud of buttery mash, another appears. Abundance turns to guilt. A single pumpkin in the vegetable rack will make you smile. Three of them and you feel they are laughing at you.

A pumpkin in the garden

The trailing vines of a pumpkin plant—hollow, fleshy, often spikily hairy—need a bit of space, so I encourage them up a climbing frame with pieces of twine loosely tied round their tendrils. With the exception of the heaviest varieties, it's a good way in for those with limited growing space.

The flowers, like squawking yellow birds at dawn, barely see the day through before they collapse. Male and female blossoms appear on the same plant, the female often discernible by the almost invisible immature fruit lurking behind the flower. Occasionally you need to get the paintbrush out and do a little pollinating yourself if they don't seem to be getting it on. It is a tender moment in the garden, taking pollen from one enormous open bloom to the next with the point of a soft brush.

As well as regular watering (every day at the height of summer), they like extra food in the form of liquid fertilizer. I do mine once every three weeks, as soon as the first fruits have set in late June to late September. You can almost hear them whispering thank you.

To encourage the plants to put their energy into ripening rather than climbing farther along the garden path, I pick out the growing tips once enough fruit have set. A large terra-cotta tile under each fruit will keep its skin clean and reflect the sun's warmth back to it.

I wait until the skin is hard before harvesting, then if they are to be kept for winter, I "cure" them in a sunny place for ten days or so. A window ledge indoors will do when the weather has turned wet, which it often has by then. Leaving a section of stalk attached to each fruit seems to help it keep. Makes them easier to carry, too. Store them in a cool place, well away from any chance of frost.

Picking a pumpkin or winter squash with a good length of stalk, letting it dry for a few days in the late autumn sun, and keeping it dry should ensure that it will last you through the winter. Those that aren't dried in this way tend to shrivel rather than keep. I have sometimes kept them so long that they have been known to require an occasional dusting. It's wise to store one in the vegetable rack; they are said to sweeten with age, like us. Until spring, that is, when the dense, flame-colored flesh seems to dry and the seeds and fibers coarsen. Even then they can be used for a soup.

A pumpkin diary

May 5 Planted the warty Marina di Chioggia, the flattened, vivid orange Rouge Vif d'Etamps, and the smoky blue Crown Prince, whose flesh is dense and the color of carrot soup. At the last minute I tuck in some Connecticut field pumpkin seeds too; they are apparently good for roasting. The seeds, possibly the largest you can plant next to fava beans, are soaked overnight, then go into small pots of light, peat-free compost in the cold frame. A windowsill will do. Planting this late, long after any fear of frost, means they germinate quickly. Earlier won't hurt if you can offer enough protection, but I have always found that late starters catch up. Like peas, they hate cold, wet soil.

The shoots usually appear within two weeks or so, sometimes less, and need a small, thin stake almost as soon as the relatively large first leaves open. I generally plant two to a small pot. Their root systems separate easily enough with a gentle tug on transfer to the garden.

June 8 The Connecticut field pumpkin has six good leaves, is about 8 inches (20cm) high, and ready to go out into the garden. I have had much success previously taking the young plants outside during the day for a week or two to harden them off. But they must come in at night. An early start is needed if they are to ripen fully by autumn. The pale yellow sap in the stems is nectar to a snail, so the young plants get a deep copper ring round them and a wide scattering of coffee grounds to irritate any approaching gastropod.

Mid-July The Rouge Vif d'Etamps are getting away, snaking out of their terra-cotta pot, their crisp, hairy stems dotted every inch (few centimeters) or so with tight, gracefully pointed buds and curling tendrils.

Late July Each morning there is a new, canary yellow flower singing its heart out. No signs of them setting fruit yet. The leaves have the diameter of dinner plates, and the thick, juicy stems drink as much water as I remember to give them.

August 18 Sometimes, if you stop peering hopefully on a daily basis, things happen of their own accord. I find the same principle works with the bathroom scales. Today I find several miniature fruits hiding under the larger leaves.

Late October The fruits are coloring nicely. The Connecticut squashes are full and round and the Vif d'Etamps has reached the end of the path; its skin is the color of a setting sun. The Marina di Chioggia, whose dark green, knobbly shell I was so looking forward to stroking, was lost to two young fox cubs, whose early-morning wrestling broke its tender stem.

November 14 The first frost last night turned the plants' leaves to slop, their stems a tangle of slime. I bring the fruits in, one to hack into pieces and turn into a glowing roast with butter and caramelized garlic; the others to sit in the scullery for a week or so until they are ready for winter storage.

Varieties

Crown Prince A pale, steel blue or gray skin, thick as they come, hides perhaps the most prized pumpkin flesh of all—firm, intense, and the deep saffron orange of a Thai monk's robe. A Crown Prince can last all winter in fine condition, and when you do finally decide to break through its hide and cook its deeply colored meat, you will find the close-textured flesh holds its shape like no other. To me, this is the perfect squash: a thing of quiet beauty whose flesh refuses to collapse into the sauce of a stew or coconut-rich laksa. The Crown Prince is well named.

Butternut* The squash du jour. The butternut is neat, shapely, and easy to carry home; its flesh is firm, not too sweet, and sports a thin skin that poses less of a danger to the cook and their knife than the larger varieties. Roasted with butter and herbs or blitzed to a grainy soup, the skin is edible. The real trump card here is the neat crater that appears once you have dug out the seeds and fibers; a hollow to hold just the right amount of melted mozzarella and pecorino; tomato and chile sauce; brown basmati and toasted pine nuts.

Ironbark Blue-black, heavily gnarled skin that is a challenge to break into. The tight, deep-ocher flesh keeps well. Giorgio Locatelli and the folks at Moro are fans.

Acorn Squash* The black-green ribs and furrows hide a soft lemon or canary-yellow flesh that is less sweet than it might be. The flesh can be described as watery or delicate, depending on your generosity of spirit, but kept until late January it will have firmed up and its sweetness will be more intense. A good one to roast—it takes barely forty minutes—maybe with a rice-based stuffing spiked with fat toasted cashews and thyme.

Onion Squash The onion variety has an unusual earthy quality and makes a firm, proudly standing mash. The color deepens with age, though this is not one of the best keeping varieties. It has a tendency to develop soft spots in storage. It is generally small enough to bring home without putting your back out.

Rouge Vif d'Etamps* It is difficult to think of anything that brings a bigger sense of fun into the garden. A squashed, vermilion globe whose tendrils wind themselves through the beans and over the low box hedges in a desperate attempt to get into the kitchen. I plant two of these each year and pick them around Halloween. They start life as two little leaves unfurling in the late spring sunshine and end up as soup for twenty or more.

Other varieties to consider: Marina di Chioggia* for its haunting appearance, like that of a giant toad; Turk's Turban* for its startling colors; Mammoth, which does what it says on the packet; and Buttercup,* sweet, small, and suitable for baking whole.

*Available from US seed sources.

A pumpkin in the kitchen

The French have an ancient soup-stew whose frugality ensures it falls under the modern label of "peasant cooking." They toast thick slices of bread, layer them with fried onions, garlic, and marjoram; blanched and skinned tomatoes; and thin slices of pumpkin. The dish is then topped up with water and olive oil and baked in a low oven for an hour or two. The lid is lifted for the last half hour to allow the soup to form a crust. They call it a *garbure catalane*, with a nod to its Spanish origins. I make a more robust version with chicken stock, softened onions, toasted sourdough bread, and both Gruyère and Parmesan cheeses. Sometimes I use Leicester and grated Berkswell cheese instead, to add a British fingerprint.

In the Rhône you might come across a *pain de courge*, a glowing egg yolk–yellow bread that is eaten toasted, like brioche. The Sicilians candy the biggest pumpkins in translucent slices to add to the pretty ricotta and marzipan dessert, *cassata*. Mantua, which carries the fruit as its city emblem, uses it as a stuffing for tortelli, sometimes mixed with the mustard pickle of the region. In Lombardy they may add a few crushed amaretti, endorsing the pumpkin's affinity for the almond. I buy these apricot-colored pillows from a local Italian deli, where they advise a heavy dusting of Parmesan to balance the marshmallow sweetness. In Emilia-Romagna, there is a habit of stirring a purée of the flesh into the dough for gnocchi (*di zucca*), which they boil and toss in melted butter before passing round the grated Parmesan.

Popular in Southeast Asia for coconut-laced broths and in America for a famous sweet, cinnamon-scented pie, for me pumpkins are nevertheless inseparable from the French countryside (where they also make a gratin of them with cream and crumbs), with abandoned farmhouses and decaying winter *potagers*, where a row of pumpkins firming up for winter storage is a familiar enough sight in the autumn. They also form, with beans and corn, the Holy Trinity of American country cooking, but their name, rather endearingly I feel, is from the French, *pompon*.

Putting the knife in—a word of caution

Sometimes the skin is so hard you feel the need for an axe. These old fruits are not called "ironbarks" for nothing. I cannot overemphasize the need for great care when breaking open your giant purchase, particularly if it has a smooth skin that might give it a tendency to slide. Put the creature down on the work surface, cut a thin slice from the base so it will stand firm, then peel by cutting downward toward the board. You can trim up any missed bits later. Slice in half and scoop out the seeds and fibers with a spoon or your fingers. You can toast the seeds if you feel the need for something to crunch between your teeth. You'll need some salt and a cold beer to go with them. Cut the deep orange meat into slices, chunks, dice, or whatever your recipe demands. Not that mine ever demand anything. They merely suggest.

The density and color of a squash's flesh dictates how your supper will turn out. Pale, easy-to-cut squash makes a sloppy mash and sometimes a weak soup. Dense, brightly colored flesh will produce a mash with backbone and a stew or curry whose principal ingredient hasn't melted into a slush—albeit a beautiful one. The harder your pumpkin is to cut, the sweeter and firmer its flesh will be and the more body and bite your supper will have. I don't despise the pale flesh of the acorn squash, but bake it instead, the heat of the oven concentrating its sometimes timid flavor.

Seasoning your pumpkin

If the traditional pairings are sweet, docile spices, the modern ones are hotter and more lively. The pumpkin is forever linked with fireworks: the bright reds and yellows of the spiky cactus dahlias with which it shares a patch in the garden; the soggy, blackened arugula you find next to it the day after Bonfire Night; the shock of the ripe chiles and lemongrass you can add to a pumpkin curry or a noodle-flecked soup for an autumn supper. How I look at it now is that the velvety sweetness of its flesh demands something upfront—the fireworks—to shake off the sugary notes: grated lemon or orange zest; shreds of crisp, almost burned bacon; toasted bread soaked with garlic butter; a loose tangle of frizzled ginger; chiles and more chiles. As you stir the big pan of soup on your stove, it is worth considering which you might use to add bite to its smooth, candied tone.

Citrus Lemon, lime, and especially orange will highlight the pumpkin's fruitiness. I add juice to soup or a roast and zest, dried peel, or lemongrass to a South Asian–style curry.

Bacon A few strips, crisp as ice, to a bowl of soup; larger pieces to a warm salad of baked butternut and parsley; hot fatback to a squash to be roasted.

Chile Crushed dried chipotles will lend a smoky layer to a thick soup; fresh orange and red, finely diced, should make a golden stew sing in the mouth.

Sweet spices Cinnamon and cloves for a pie; nutmeg for a gratin with cream and cheese.

Tomatoes Blend a handful into a soup to lift it from its sweet sleepiness; toss a few Gardener's Delight into a pumpkin bake so that they blacken in the heat.

Cheese Parmesan or Spenwood for stirring into soup; mozzarella and pecorino for melting in the hollow of a halved butternut.

Ginger Ground for a soup; grated in a curry; matchsticks to toss with a roast; deep-fried shreds on a plate of soup.

Rosemary For adding to the breadcrumbs of a crumble crust.

Sage For frying to a crisp and scattering over soup, or for lending its dusky notes to melted butter to pour over tortellini.

Almonds A handful, toasted, in a brown rice stuffing; a few added to the filling of a pasta cushion; a dash, no more, of Amaretto liqueur over a mound of mash.

And...

* The sweetness of the pumpkin and winter squash family works best with something very savory. I often marry slow-cooked sausages, whose skins have turned sticky, with sweet and fluffy pumpkin mash.

* Once a pumpkin has been cut, its storage time is substantially reduced. Rather than covering a wedge of it with plastic wrap, which encourages it to sweat, I store it in the fridge unwrapped, then just shave a wafer-thin slice off its edge and discard it each time I use it.

* I have never been convinced about winter squash with fish in the same way that I have about the delights of summer squash and zucchini. The extra sweetness is difficult to match with anything piscine. That said, prawns can work well enough with pumpkin in an Asian-style soup, as will scallops if you cook them on a hot grill so that a golden crust forms on the outside, then eat them with pumpkin purée.

* A pumpkin that sounds hollow when tapped will keep better than one where there is no sound at all.

* The really large members of the winter squash family can be intimidating. It is probably a good idea for new cooks to start with one of the smaller "onion" squash, which have much of the color and flavor of the big boys but are a jolly sight easier to handle.

A simple baked pumpkin

Preheat the oven to 400°F (200°C). Make a sloppy herb paste by mashing four large cloves of garlic with two tablespoons of chopped thyme and four of olive oil. Season with salt and black pepper. Cut 2 pounds (a kilo) of peeled pumpkin into small dice, add to a baking pan, and toss with the herb mixture. Bake for an hour or until the pumpkin is crisp outside and soft within.

It is worth mentioning that you can cook a whole pumpkin in the microwave in a matter of minutes.

A pumpkin pangrattato with rosemary and orange

Marrying textures and tastes to one another is one of the most satisfying pleasures of cooking: the soft with the crisp, the steamily hot with the icily cold, the spicy with the mint cool. I somehow had a feeling that crisp crumbs might work well with the soft, collapsing flesh of a squash. They do, but are more interesting when the crumbs are not packed on top like a crumble but lightly scattered over and between the pieces of squash.

> *enough for 4 as an accompaniment, 2 as a principal dish*
> pumpkin or butternut squash – 2 pounds (1kg)
> garlic – 3 cloves
> olive oil – 5 tablespoons, plus a tad more
> a mild red chile
> finely chopped rosemary leaves – a tablespoon
> the zest of half an orange
> coarsely chopped parsley leaves – a handful
> fresh white breadcrumbs – 4 handfuls
> butter – about 3 tablespoons (40g)

Preheat the oven to 350°F (180°C). Peel the squash, discarding the seeds and fibers, and cut the flesh into large, bite-sized pieces. Put the squash into a steamer basket or metal colander and steam over boiling water for fifteen to twenty minutes, until tender when pierced with the tip of a knife.

Peel and finely chop the garlic and put it into a shallow pan with the 5 tablespoons of olive oil over medium heat. Thinly slice the chile and add it to the pan with the rosemary and grated orange zest. The smell will be lightly aromatic. Add the parsley and breadcrumbs and stir briefly while they color lightly. They should be no darker than a pale gold.

Put the pumpkin in a shallow baking dish or roasting pan, salt and pepper it, then add the butter in small knobs. Sprinkle the breadcrumbs over and drizzle lightly with olive oil. Bake for thirty-five to forty minutes, until the crumbs are deep gold and the pumpkin is meltingly tender.

Sausage and a pumpkin mash

An hour after leaving Dijon, I was lost. A tangle of lanes, endless vineyards, and a low mist left me confused and desperately looking for a farm at which to ask for directions.

It wasn't the most poetic of farmyards, but there was dry mud and clean straw underfoot and tight bales of hay on which were perched a hundred or more fat, round pumpkins soaking up the late-afternoon sun like a group of ladies in a Beryl Cook painting. I whistled and called without reply; not even a dog barked. As I waited, the pumpkins seemed to be watching me, growing faintly malevolent in the fading golden light. I felt like a lost child in a haunting fairy tale. Whether it was the watching fruits or the deserted farm that spooked me, I got back in the car and left as fast as I could. Thirty years on, I think of them in an altogether friendlier light, but they are still what I want at Halloween and on Guy Fawkes' Night. I came up with this modern take on the classic sausage and mash a year or two ago in an attempt to pacify a herd of boisterous and hungry kids that descended on me one October. It worked.

enough for 4
pork sausages – 8 plump ones
seedy mustard – 2 tablespoons
smooth Dijon mustard – a tablespoon
runny honey – 3 heaping tablespoons
lemon juice – 2 tablespoons

for the mash
butternut, pumpkin, or other winter squash – 2 pounds (1kg)
a knob of butter (you really don't need much)

Preheat the oven to 400°F (200°C). Put the sausages in a baking pan large enough to take them in a single layer. If they overlap, they won't cook properly. In a bowl mix the mustards, honey, and lemon juice and stir well. Pour them over the sausages and toss gently. Bake for twenty-five to thirty minutes, rolling the sausages over in the honey and mustard mixture once or twice, so that they eventually take on a sticky, glossy coat.

For the mash: peel the squash, cut it in half lengthwise, and pull out the fibers. Cut the flesh into thick pieces and pile into a metal colander or steamer basket. Steam, covered, for about twenty minutes until tender.

Remove the squash from the heat, put it into the bowl of a stand mixer fitted with the paddle attachment, and mash with the butter and a little black pepper until thoroughly smooth. It is probably worth remembering that children generally hate lumps in food.

Divide the mash among four plates and pop the sausages on top.

A pan-cooked pumpkin with duck fat and garlic

January 2007. It is not especially cold, but has been raining nonstop for two days. Even the short dash from bus to front door leaves me soaked through and in need of some sort of carbohydrate and fat. Butter and beef dripping seem suddenly more appropriate than olive oil. Even more so the little bowl of duck fat I saved from last Sunday's roast. Perhaps it was the week before. No matter, it keeps for months. It is said that people used to rub this snow-white fat on their chest to ward off a cold. I prefer to take my duck dripping internally, and set about a simple layered potato dish with thyme and garlic. The addition of the pumpkin was a spur-of-the-moment thing. It works well, adding a sweet nuttiness to the recipe. I like it on its own too, with a sharp and vinegary green salad at its side. It is also a good side dish for meat of some sort and wonderful with cuts from yesterday's roast, just the thing for a cold roast chicken or duck leg.

enough for 4 as an accompaniment
potatoes – 4 medium-sized, floury or waxy
pumpkin – 1¼ pounds (600g)
duck fat – 3 lightly heaping tablespoons
a few sprigs of thyme or rosemary
a single clove of garlic, chopped

Peel the potatoes and pumpkin and slice them no thicker than a generous ⅛ inch (3mm). Melt the duck fat in a shallow, nonstick pan (I choose a cast-iron one, so well used it barely needs oiling), add the potato and pumpkin slices, neatly or hugger-mugger, seasoning them with salt, black pepper, thyme or rosemary leaves, and a little chopped garlic as you go. Have the heat on low and cover the pan with a lid. Cook the slices for about twenty-five to thirty minutes. As they start to soften, press them down with a spatula so they form a sort of cake that will be golden on the bottom, with slices of potato that are soft right through. I check them for tenderness by inserting a skewer right down through the center. If it goes in effortlessly, then they are done. Serve straight from the pan.

A warm pumpkin scone for a winter's afternoon

A warm scone is an object of extraordinary comfort, but even more so when it has potato in it. The farl, a slim scone of flour, butter, and mashed potato, is rarely seen nowadays and somehow all the more of a treat when it is. I have taken the idea and run with it, mashing steamed pumpkin into the hand-worked crumbs of flour and butter to make a bread that glows orange when you break it. Soft, warm, and floury, this is more than welcome for a Sunday breakfast in winter or a tea round the kitchen table.

Cooked initially in a frying pan and then finished in the oven, I love this with grilled Orkney bacon and slices of Cheddar sharp enough to make my lips smart—a fine contrast for the sweet, floury "scone" and its squishy center.

enough for 4
peeled and seeded pumpkin – 10½ ounces (300g)
all-purpose flour – 1 cup plus 2 tablespoons (140g)
baking soda – half a teaspoon
salt – half a teaspoon
butter – 5 tablespoons (70g)
an egg, beaten
warm milk – 6 tablespoons (90ml)
thyme leaves – 2 teaspoons
a little oil or butter

Cut the pumpkin into large chunks and steam until tender enough to mash. Preheat the oven to 400°F (200°C).

Mix the flour, baking soda, and salt in a large bowl. Cut the butter into small chunks and rub it in with your fingertips. You could do this in a food processor, but it hardly seems worth the washing up.

Crush the pumpkin with a potato masher, then beat in the egg, followed by the milk and thyme leaves. Scoop this into the flour mixture and mix well. Season with black pepper.

Warm a heavy, nonstick frying pan with a metal handle over low to medium heat. Melt a little oil or butter in it, then pile in the dough, and smooth it flat. Cook over low heat until the underside is pale gold.

Lightly oil a dinner plate. Loosen the underside of the scone with the help of a spatula. Put the plate over the top of the pan, then, holding the plate in place, tip the pan so that the scone falls onto the plate. Slide the scone back into the frying pan and cook the other side for four or five minutes. Put the pan in the oven for seven minutes, or until the scone is lightly set in the middle.

Turn the scone out of the pan and slice into thick wedges. Serve warm, with cheese or some grilled bacon.

Chickpeas with pumpkin, lemongrass, and cilantro

Sweet squashes marry well with the earthy flavor of beans and lentils. This is apparent in the dhal and pumpkin soup in *The Kitchen Diaries* and here in a more complex main dish that offers waves of chile heat with mild citrus and the dusty "old as time itself" taste of ground turmeric.

Dried (which is the only way most of us know them) chickpeas are the stars of the world's bean dishes, used to fill bellies everywhere from India to Egypt. Their character—knobbly, chewy, and virtually indestructible in the pot—makes them invaluable in slow-cooked dishes where you need to retain some texture.

Fresh chickpeas are bright emerald green and have an invigorating citrus note to them that is completely missing in the dried version. I saw some for the first time this year. I have long wanted to put lemongrass with chickpeas, partly to lift their spirits but also to return some of their lemony freshness to them (I use more lemon juice in my hummus than most as well). This recipe, which just happens to be suitable for vegans, does just that. Like many of those slow, bean-based dishes, it often tastes better the next day, when all the ingredients have had a chance to get acquainted.

enough for 4 to 6
dried chickpeas – 1 cup (200g), soaked in mineral water for several hours
onions – 2 medium
peanut oil – 2 tablespoons (plus a little more later)
garlic – 4 cloves
ginger – a thumb-sized piece
lemongrass – 3 large stalks
ground coriander – 2 teaspoons
ground turmeric – 2 teaspoons
green cardamom pods – 6
hot red chiles – 2
pumpkin – 1 pound (500g) peeled and seeded (about 2 pounds [1kg] unprepared weight)
vegetable stock – 1 cup (250ml)
coconut milk – 1¾ cups (400ml)
yellow mustard seeds – a tablespoon
cilantro leaves – a handful

to serve
cooked basmati rice for 4 to 6
limes – 2, halved

Drain the chickpeas and bring them to a boil in deep, unsalted water. Let them simmer for forty to fifty minutes, until tender.

Peel the onions and chop them quite finely. Pour the oil into a deep, heavy pot and add the onions, letting them cook over medium heat until soft and translucent. Meanwhile, peel the garlic and the ginger, remove any tough leaves from the lemongrass, then make all into a rough paste in a food processor. Stir into the softened onions and continue to cook. Add the ground coriander and turmeric, then lightly crush the seeds of the green cardamoms and seed and finely chop the fresh chiles before stirring them in. Keep the heat fairly low and on no account allow the ingredients to brown.

Chop the pumpkin into large chunks, though no larger than you would like to put in your mouth, then add to the pan, along with the drained cooked chickpeas and the stock. Bring to a boil, then decrease to a simmer and continue to cook at a gentle bubble until the pumpkin is tender. Stop as soon as the flesh is yielding to the tip of a knife; you don't want it to collapse.

Stir in the coconut milk and continue to simmer. Put a splash of oil into a nonstick pan and tip in the yellow mustard seeds. As soon as they start to pop, add them to the pumpkin together with the cilantro leaves. Serve with the rice and the lime halves, ready to squeeze over at the last minute.

A fry-up of pumpkin and apple to accompany a meaty supper

The fry-up has always appealed to me, in particular the bits that stay put at the bottom of the pan, the crusty scrapings that brown rather too much. I call them "the pan-stickings."

One of potato and duck fat is a deep-winter supper of immense pleasure; another of herb-speckled sausage meat and zucchini. This is robust cooking, crisp edged and flecked black and gold. It is not for those days when you want something genteel or elegant. This is the sort of supper to pile on a plate and eat with a cold beer.

The latest of my fry-ups is extraordinary in that two generally sweet ingredients come together to produce a deeply savory result. The key here is not to move the ingredients around the pan too much, letting them take on a sticky crust while allowing them to soften to a point where you can squash them with little or no pressure. The caraway seeds, which people tend to either love or hate, are entirely optional.

serves 4 as a side dish
a little butter
fatty bacon – 3 ounces (80g)
a medium onion
pumpkin flesh – about 1¼ pounds (650g)
apples, a dessert variety – 14 ounces (400g)
a lemon
caraway seeds – a pinch

Melt a slice of butter in a shallow pan, cut the bacon into short strips, and let them color lightly in the butter. Peel and coarsely chop the onion, add to the pan, and cook with the bacon until translucent but not browned. Cut the pumpkin flesh into manageable pieces and add to the pan, turning from time to time until golden in patches and almost tender.

Core and coarsely chop the apples, but don't peel them. Stir them into the pan and leave to putter gently until they are on the verge of collapse. Avoid stirring too much, which is likely to mash the softening pumpkin. Finely grate the zest from the lemon and add it to the pan with the juice, the caraway seeds, and a little salt.

You should end up with a pan of highly fragrant, tender pumpkin, onion, and apple on the verge of collapse. Serve alongside something meaty or, as I usually have it, as a main dish in its own right.

A new pumpkin laksa for a cold night

The first time I included pumpkin in a coconut-scented laksa was for a Bonfire Night supper in 2004 (see *The Kitchen Diaries*). The soup had to be sensational to make up for our distinct lack of fireworks (I think we wrote our names in the air with sparklers). Rich, sweet-sour, mouth-tinglingly hot, and yet curiously soothing, it had everything you need in a soup for a frosty night.

There is much pleasure to be had in the constant tweaking of a recipe to change not its essential character but its details. And so it has been with this soup. I have since gone on to remove the tomatoes or add some shredded greens as the mood and the state of the larder take me. Such improvisations, many made at the last minute, need to be done with care: you don't want too many flavors going on. Vietnamese soups such as this are traditionally ingredient rich but should never taste confused. By the same token, to simplify it too much would be to lose the soup's generosity and complexity and therefore its point.

The laksa appears complicated at first but in practice it is far from it. Once you understand the basics, the recipe falls into place and becomes something you can fiddle with to suit your own taste. The basic spice paste needs heat (ginger, garlic, tiny bird's eye chiles); the liquid needs body and sweetness (coconut milk, rich stock); the finish needs sourness and freshness (lime juice, mint, cilantro). The necessary saltiness comes from nam pla and tamari rather than salt itself. These notes in place, you can feel free to include noodles, tomatoes, greens, sweet vegetables, or meat as you wish. What matters is balance.

enough for 4
pumpkin, unskinned – 12 ounces (350g)
cilantro and mint leaves, to finish

for the spice paste
red bird's eye chiles – 3 or 4
garlic – 2 cloves
ginger – a thumb-sized lump
lemongrass – 2 plump stalks
cilantro stems – 5 or 6
cilantro leaves – a handful
sesame oil – 2 tablespoons

for the soup
chicken or vegetable stock – 2½ cups (600ml)
coconut milk – 1¾ cups (400ml)
nam pla (Thai fish sauce) – 2 tablespoons
tamari – 1 to 2 tablespoons, to taste
the juice of a lime
dried noodles – 3½ ounces (100g), cooked as it says on the packet,
    then drained

Peel and seed the pumpkin and cut the flesh into large chunks. Cook in a steamer or in a metal colander balanced over a pan of boiling water until tender. Remove from the heat.

For the spice paste, remove the stems from the chiles, peel the garlic, and peel and roughly chop the ginger and lemongrass. Put them all into a food processor with the cilantro stems and leaves and the sesame oil and blitz until you have a rough paste.

Get a large, deep pan hot and add the spice paste. Fry for a minute, then stir in the stock and coconut milk and bring to a boil. Let simmer for seven to ten minutes, then stir in the nam pla, tamari, lime juice, pumpkin, and the cooked and drained noodles. Simmer briefly, add the cilantro and mint leaves over the top, and serve in deep bowls.

Rutabaga

A creamy amber flushed with viridian, violet, and the flat maroon of dried blood, the rutabaga possesses a subtle and unusual beauty. What the Swedish call *kålrot* will make an incandescent mash, introduce a firm footing for a stew, and flatter both game and beef. Yet rarely is it treated with much respect.

Autumn is the rutabaga's moment of glory, when the roots are sweet, moist, and barely bigger than a clenched fist. A vegetable for when there is a fire in the grate and frost flowers on the windows. The fact that this is not a root at all, but the swollen stem base of a member of the cabbage family, means much to botanists and pedants but is of frankly little interest to the cook. To us in the hot seat, the rutabaga is firmly part of our useful family of "root vegetables."

Where some vegetables lose a little of their color on cooking, the rutabaga deepens to a translucent orange-yellow. In boiling water or steam, the rock-hard flesh softens to a loose, shimmering purée the color of a winter sunset. Enriched with butter and speckled with pepper, it shines brightly against a plate of dark, herby meatballs or thin strips of supersoft lamb's liver. Strange, then, that so many seem to end their days shriveling in a vegetable rack.

Rutabaga sponges up good flavors. It will suck up the burgundy juices of a beef stew or the spice of a lamb hotpot. I often cook mine in chicken stock before mashing, sometimes putting thyme and bay into the pot too, giving the golden purée a faintly savory edge.

My introduction to what the British call swede came in my early twenties. I had escaped from a testosterone-fueled kitchen in Yorkshire to the more tender charms of the bed-and-breakfast trade in Cornwall. I learned to make pasties like the Cornish, with crumbling pastry and a juicy filling of beef, potato, much pepper, and golden cubes of rutabaga. The marriage sprouted legs, and I included them in a winter pot of lamb shanks, with vivid parsley, given a freshness with salty-sour preserved lemons from the Middle East. It was in St. Ives that I also learned a fondness for mashed rutabagas (butter, pepper, a splash of gravy) with roast lamb to which you have added garlic and thyme in heroic quantities.

There is much confusion between rutabagas and turnips—the fact that rutabaga is also known as the Swedish turnip doesn't exactly help. In Scotland the rutabaga is most often known by the name turnip. When they talk of the delicious bashed "neeps," it is mashed rutabaga that arrives on your plate. But the differences are plain. Rutabagas are generally harvested when about the size of a grapefruit (a turnip bigger than a tennis ball is rarely worth eating). A rutabaga has several roots coming off its swollen stem (a turnip has just one). The rutabaga is creamy gold in color (though there is the odd white one) and they are always sold singly, rather than in a bunch like turnips.

But just as we think we have it all sorted, nature confounds us by producing a variety of golden turnips.

A rutabaga in the garden

It is said that the rutabaga grows more happily in a field than in a garden. My own space is small, and every inch of bare soil precious. Growing rutabagas, when they come with such reliability in the organic vegetable box, seems a poor use of valuable resources. Those with more space than I have might like to plant a short row for a steady winter supply.

I'm not sure there is a considerable difference in varieties of rutabaga in a culinary sense, but it is worth remembering that there are both yellow (preferred by the British and the Norwegians) and white (preferred by the Swedish). Allotment friends recommend Ruby for its sweetness and Magres for its resistance to mildew. (American Purple Top, a yellow variety, is a good US choice.)

The ground rules are the same as for cabbages: full sun, plus moisture-retentive, well-manured soil. A recipe that most of us can probably put to better use. Keen growers will sow the seed thinly in May, then thin the seedlings to a foot (30cm) or so apart. To prevent their roots splitting, they should be watered regularly when the plants are young.

Rutabagas sown in May and June will be ready from October onward. They will probably start to get woody toward early spring, but then who wants to eat even the most buttery mashed rutabaga when the sun is shining? Harvest as you need them from November, leaving them in the ground until the spring. Good luck with extracting a round rutabaga from frozen ground.

A rutabaga in the kitchen

A sloppy, amber mash of rutabaga will have a cooling effect when eaten alongside a plate of robustly spiced faggots (meatballs made of pork innards and belly) and their liverish gravy, a pie or stew with the almost rank flavors of pigeon or hare, or a supper of dark venison sausages. I will take it with pork, too, and in a beef stew, its liquid unthickened, where the vegetables can shine like beacons among the general beefiness. Salty bacon, in slices or boiled in a large piece, likes a pool of golden roots, too.

Rutabaga is at its most welcome in our house on a Saturday afternoon in deepest winter, the light fading, the trees standing bare. Then, as we think about making a supper that will warm and fulfill, the fat "roots" become an essential part of the backbone of vegetables that steadies a stew. I use slightly less rutabaga than carrot, celery, and onion, so that its flavor doesn't dominate—one handful to two of each of the others. The pot goes in the oven at about the time we are toasting crumpets, and will come out, a soul-enriching broth of lamb, golden roots, and collapsed potatoes, in time for supper.

I adore snow. I adore the quiet solace of stew. If the two come together, it creates a feeling of intense well-being and "all's-right."

Seasoning your rutabaga

The rutabaga's Christmas card list is not long:
Butter In any shape or form. When mashing, it is almost impossible to beat in too much.
Bacon The saltiness of smoked bacon or baked ham is good with the watery quality of mashed rutabaga.
Dill One of the few herbs really worth including.
Parsley The pairing of the root and this herb just seems right. They somehow belong together.
Lamb In a rich casserole.
Game As a mashed accompaniment to any game bird, the coolness of the rutabaga is a useful balance for the woodsy flavor of the meat.

And...

* The fact that the rutabaga is actually a member of the cabbage family (this is *Brassica napus*) becomes of interest once we are looking for things to cook it with. So bacon, pork, apples, and the like go rather well.
* When rutabaga is used alone, I have never managed to find a fish with which this root will work.
* Leaving them in the ground is probably the best way of keeping your rutabagas in good condition.
* If you like this vegetable, then join an organic-box delivery group. It is a safe bet that there will be one or two in each delivery in winter.

How to make the perfect mashed rutabaga

Rinse the rutabaga of its mud, then peel it. Cut the pale flesh into large chunks and pile into a steamer basket or metal colander. Place over a pan of boiling water and steam for twelve to fifteen minutes, then put into a bowl and crush with a potato masher. Fold in a slice of butter, some salt and black pepper, then beat hard with a wooden spoon.

A mash of roasted rutabaga (very good with roast beef)

Roasting intensifies the sweetness of the rutabaga. Peel and cut your roots into cubes, put them in a roasting pan with a thick slice of butter and some salt and black pepper, then cover with a piece of wax paper. Roast for twenty minutes or until the rutabaga has softened but not browned.

Remove from the oven and mash with a potato masher, incorporating more butter and black pepper as you need it.

Another good way with rutabaga

A recipe to tempt the "rutabagophobic."

Peel and cube 1 pound (500g) rutabaga. Melt 4 tablespoons (50g) butter in a deep saucepan with ¾ cup (200ml) water and a teaspoon of sugar. Drop the cubes into the pan with a couple of bay leaves and cover with a lid, shaking or turning them over from time to time. They will catch on the bottom of the pan if you don't. Test for tenderness after twenty minutes. They should emerge sweet, softly toothsome, and as translucent as a glowing candle. Use as a side dish.

A three-root mash

I'm not suggesting we should inflict anything on our family or friends that they won't eat, but there are worse ways of getting rid of an unwanted rutabaga than in this three-root mash. Works well with pretty much anything, even fish.

enough for 4
rutabaga – about 1½ pounds (750g)
carrots – 10½ ounces (300g)
potatoes – 10½ ounces (300g)
butter – about 3 tablespoons (40g)
nutmeg

Peel the rutabaga, carrots, and potatoes, chop them into large, similar-sized pieces, and bring them to a boil in lightly salted water. Decrease the heat as they reach a boil and let them simmer enthusiastically for about twenty-five minutes, until all are tender. One may be ready slightly before the others but it really doesn't matter here.

Drain, then crush with a potato masher. Introduce the butter and beat with a wooden spoon until fluffy. If you use an electric mixer, then go easy, taking care not to overmix and turn the mash "gluey." Season with black pepper and a brief grating of nutmeg.

Rutabaga "braised" with onion and stock

Even the smallest pinch of sugar will take any possible bitterness out of a rutabaga. The method that follows, of cooking the chopped vegetable with a small amount of butter and stock so that it takes on a deep, earthy richness, is one I use for carrots and turnips too. A very fine side order for roast chicken or something altogether more gamey.

enough for 4 as an accompaniment
a large rutabaga
a smallish onion, coarsely chopped
a small clove of garlic, crushed
butter – a walnut-sized lump
sugar – the merest pinch
enough chicken or vegetable stock or water to cover

Peel the rutabaga and cut it into large, fairly even chunks. Put it into a saucepan with the onion, garlic, butter, and sugar. Pour in enough stock or water just to cover the rutabaga and bring to a boil. Decrease the heat a little. Place a piece of wax paper or parchment paper over the top and then cover with a lid. Let simmer for twenty minutes or so, then lift the lid and boil vigorously until the liquid has almost evaporated. You should end up with butter-soft rutabaga on the point of collapse.

A good pasty recipe

There have been many highly original versions of the straightforward miner's lunch (if you couldn't come up to the surface for lunch, you took a warm pasty down with you, holding the thickly crimped edge with your grubby hands, then leaving it behind to appease the spirits of the mine) but I have rarely enjoyed one as much as those I have eaten in Cornwall.

My pasty is (categorically) not a Cornish pasty. I precook my filling, you see, which Cornish cooks would never do. I cook the meat and vegetables before wrapping them in the pastry crust purely because it results in a pasty whose filling is especially tender and giving. I also use a proportion of butter in the pastry too. The similarity between my pasty and a Cornish one is purely in the ingredients: beef, potato, onion, and rutabaga.

Chaucer was partial to a pasty—they appear in *The Canterbury Tales*, and in several of Shakespeare's plays, including *The Merry Wives of Windsor*, *All's Well That Ends Well*, and *Titus Andronicus*. We shall gloss over the small point that Titus uses Chiron and Demetrius's bodies rather than the more traditional beef skirt steak.

I do suggest you let the finished parcels rest for half an hour before baking, if you get the chance.

makes 6

for the pastry
lard – scant ½ cup (110g)
butter – ½ cup (115g)
bread flour – 3½ cups (450g)
an egg, beaten with a little milk, for brushing

for the filling
rutabaga – 7 ounces (200g)
potatoes – 14 ounces (400g)
onions – 2
butter – a thick slice
beef skirt steak – 1 pound (450g)

Freeze the lard and butter in one chunk each (wrapped in their paper) for a good hour, making them easier to grate.

Peel the rutabaga and potatoes, cut into ¾-inch (2cm) pieces, and bring to a boil in deep, lightly salted water. Simmer for ten to fifteen minutes, until almost tender, then drain. Peel and coarsely chop the onions, then let them soften in the butter in a shallow pan.

Grate the frozen lard and butter into the flour. This is most easily done if you keep the fats in their paper, dipping the cut edge into the flour every now and again to stop it sticking on the grater. Add a good half teaspoon of salt. Stir the fat into the flour along with enough cold water to make a firm but tender dough. I find about five or six tablespoons usually does it. Roll the dough into a ball and leave to rest in the fridge, wrapped in wax paper, for twenty minutes or so.

Meanwhile, cut the beef into small pieces, then, once the onions are soft, remove and add the beef to the hot pan. Let it color nicely on all sides, then remove and mix with the onions. Add a splash of water—or stock, if there is some around—to the pan, scrape at any stickings with a spatula, then pour this liquid over the meat. Add the drained rutabaga and potato. Season generously (my feeling is that the mixture should be really quite peppery). Preheat the oven to 400°F (200°C).

Divide the pastry into six equal pieces. Roll each lump into a disk about 7½ inches (18cm) in diameter, using a small plate as a template. Brush the edges with beaten egg and milk, then put a pile of the filling on each disk. Fold the dough over to make a semicircle, pressing hard to seal the edges. Crimp as you wish (a fork, a twist of the finger and thumb, a nice bit of braiding, as you fancy), then transfer to a baking sheet lined with parchment paper. Brush all over with beaten egg and milk. Cut a couple of steam holes in the top of each pasty to prevent them splitting. Bake for fifteen minutes, then decrease the heat to 350°F (180°C) and bake for forty-five minutes or so, until golden.

A rutabaga and cheese pasty

Modern pasty recipes, especially those in the more touristy enclaves of Britain's farthest southern county, stretch the recipe almost as far as Titus, swapping beef for pork, the rutabaga for apple, even daring to crimp the finished turnover on the top instead of at the side.

I make one without meat, in which I use goat cheese and thyme along with the usual starchy filling of potato and rutabaga. It is filling, yet somehow soft and gentle, too.

makes 6
the pastry recipe on page 490

for the filling
leeks – 2
butter – a thick slice
rutabaga – 7 ounces (200g)
potatoes – 14 ounces (400g)
the leaves of a bushy sprig of thyme, chopped
goat cheese – 8 ounces (250g)

Cut the leeks in half lengthwise, then into thin slices. Let soften in the butter in a small saucepan over medium heat. Placing a layer of wax paper over the top, then covering with a lid will encourage them to steam a little and stop them coloring too quickly.

Peel the rutabaga and the potatoes, dice them, and boil in salted water for ten minutes. Drain.

When the leeks are soft, mix them with the rutabaga and potatoes and season generously with black pepper and chopped thyme. Crumble in the goat cheese. Preheat the oven to 400°F (200°C).

Divide the pastry into six equal pieces. Roll each piece into a disk about 7½ inches (18cm) in diameter (I find a plate useful here). Brush the edges with beaten egg and milk, then put a pile of the filling on each disk. Fold the dough over to make a semicircle, sealing and crimping the edges tightly. Transfer to a baking sheet lined with parchment paper. Brush the pasties with beaten egg and milk, then pierce the crust of each pastry a couple of times to make steam holes. Bake for fifteen minutes, then decrease the heat to 350°F (180°C) and bake for forty-five minutes or so, until golden.

A baked cake of rutabaga and potato

Rutabaga's ability to sponge up liquid is shown to good effect when it is baked with butter and vegetable stock. When it is teamed up with potato and seasoned with garlic and a spot of mustard, it is as near to a main course as I feel you can safely get with this particular root.

enough for 4
potatoes – 1 pound (500g)
rutabaga – 1 pound (500g)
garlic – 4 cloves
butter – 7 tablespoons (85g)
Dijon mustard – 2 heaping teaspoons
thyme leaves – a teaspoon
vegetable stock – 6 tablespoons

Peel the potatoes, then cut them into very fine slices. A sharp knife is fine but if you have a mandoline (the vegetable slicer, that is, not the lutelike stringed instrument), use that. Whatever, your slices should be almost thin enough to see through. Do the same with the rutabaga, keeping the slices in cold water to prevent them browning.

Preheat the oven to 375°F (190°C). Peel and thinly slice the garlic. Over medium heat, melt the butter in a flameproof dish or sauté pan about 10 inches (25cm) in diameter. When it starts to bubble, decrease the heat and add the garlic. It needs to soften slightly without coloring—a matter of five minutes or so. Take the pan off the heat and stir in the mustard. Remove about two-thirds of the mustard and butter out of the pan and into a pitcher.

Drain the potato and rutabaga slices and pat them dry with paper towels or a clean kitchen towel. Put a third of the vegetables into the pan, layering them neatly or just chucking them in as the mood takes you, then drizzle them with some of the mustard butter in the pitcher. Season with the thyme leaves, pepper, and salt. Be quite generous with the salt. Repeat this twice, so that all the slices of vegetable are layered with the thyme and the mustard and garlic butter. Now pour the stock over the top.

Cover with a circle of wax paper or aluminum foil, pressing it down well on top of the cake. Bake for about an hour and ten minutes, until tender when pierced with the tip of a knife. Remove the foil, increase the heat to 425°F (220°C), and bake for a further ten minutes, until the top has colored and crisped a little.

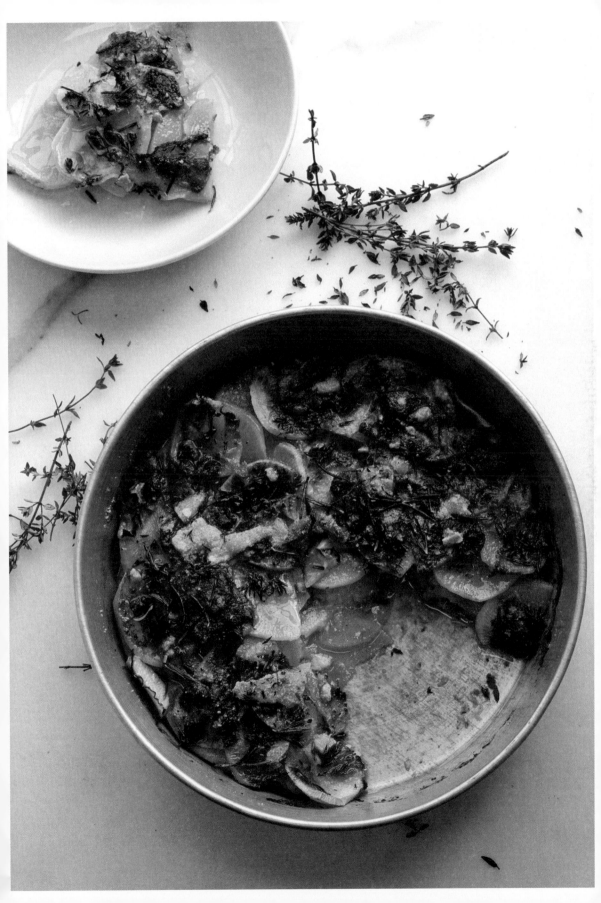

A slow roast of roots and herbs for when there is frost on the ground

Peel and chop up an assortment of rutabaga, parsnip, pumpkin or butternut squash, beets, and celery root. A squeeze of lemon on the celery root will stop it browning. Bring a large pan of water to a boil, add all the vegetables except the beets, and let them simmer for ten minutes. They should just take the tip of a knife. Drain.

Preheat the oven to 350°F (180°C). Warm plenty of butter (5 tablespoons [60g] to 4 pounds [2kg] of vegetables) in a roasting pan with a good glug of olive oil to stop it burning. Add the drained vegetables and the beets, turn them in the butter, then scatter with thyme leaves and a few whole, squashed garlic cloves. Roast for forty-five minutes to an hour, until the vegetables are soft inside, crisp and golden without. The initial boiling (you could steam them if you prefer) prevents them getting a hard outer skin as they roast.

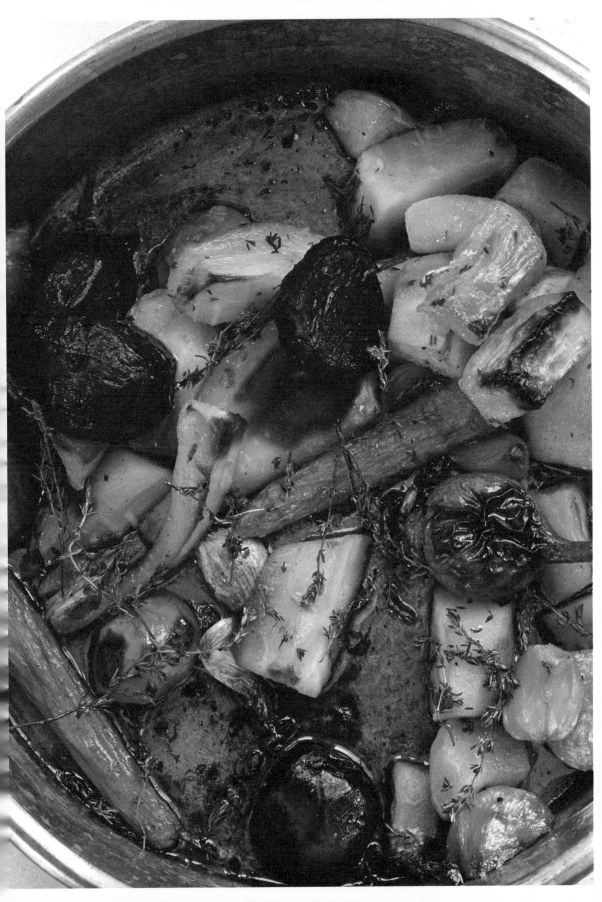

Baked rutabaga to accompany a meat dish

There are certain unfashionable meals I want to slap a preservation order on lest they disappear altogether. Faggots and gravy, traditional Midlands meatballs fashioned from pork innards and belly and wrapped in caul fat, is one such recipe (lardy cake—the name speaks for itself—is another). Pease pudding would be many people's chosen accompaniment; others probably a pile of minted fresh peas. To my mind, the faggot needs a cooling sidekick to soften the blow of the liver and onions. A mash of rutabaga is good, but also this rather more subtle approach.

enough for 4
a large rutabaga – about 1¼ pounds (650g), peeled weight
butter – 3 tablespoons (40g)
onions – 2 medium, thinly sliced
a large sprig of rosemary
chicken or vegetable stock to cover

Preheat the oven to 400°F (200°C). Cut the rutabaga into slices about ⅛ inch (3mm) thick. It is easier and safer to do this by first cutting a slice from one side to give a flat base as you cut.

Generously grease a baking dish or roasting pan with some of the butter. Lay the slices of rutabaga and onion in the dish, seasoning them with salt and black pepper, and strewing over the rosemary leaves as you go. Ladle over the stock so that it just about covers the vegetables—a matter of five or so ladlefuls—then dot on the rest of the butter.

Bake for an hour or so, turning the vegetables in the stock from time to time, until they are tender enough to crush between your fingers. Serve as a side dish, with some of the juices spooned over.

A dish of lamb shanks with preserved lemon and rutabaga

It's late March and green leaves as sharp as a dart are opening on the trees that shield this garden from the most bone chilling of the winter winds. The mornings are still crisp. You can see your breath. Stew weather. Unlike carrots, rutabaga becomes translucent when it cooks, making a casserole the glowing heart of the home.

enough for 4
onions – 2 large
olive oil – 3 tablespoons
lamb shanks – 4
all-purpose flour – 2 tablespoons
garlic – 3 cloves, thinly sliced
light stock (water will do) – 3 cups (750ml)
white vermouth or white wine – a scant ½ cup (100ml)
a large rutabaga
the juice of half a lemon
preserved lemons – 2
parsley – 4 bushy sprigs

Preheat the oven to 325°F (160°C). Peel the onions and slice them into thick segments. Warm the olive oil in a Dutch oven or other heavy pot and season the lamb shanks. Lightly brown the lamb all over in the hot oil, then lift it out and add the onions to the pan. Let them soften and turn a pale gold, then stir in the flour. Add the garlic, stock, and vermouth or white wine and bring to a boil. Peel the rutabaga and cut it into fat chunks about the size of a marshmallow. As soon as the liquid starts to boil, add the rutabaga, pushing the pieces under the gravy, then stir in the lemon juice, pushing the spent lemon shell among the rutabaga, plus a seasoning of salt and pepper. Return the lamb shanks to the pan. Cover with wax paper and then a lid and place in the oven for two hours, turning the shanks from time to time.

After an hour and a half's cooking, cut the preserved lemons in half and scrape out the pith. Chop the skin fairly finely. Remove the lamb from the oven, lift the lid, and push the chopped lemon down into the gravy. Cover once more and return to the oven for thirty minutes, until the lamb is easy to pull away from the bone and the rutabaga tender when pierced with the tip of a knife.

Remove the leaves from the parsley sprigs, chop coarsely, and stir into the gravy. Let sit, covered, for a few minutes to settle down, then check the seasoning and serve.

Salad leaves

In deepest summer, when all is quiet and, ideally, a heavy shower has just taken the edge off the heat, I like to put a single, perfect lettuce on the table together with a knife and a bottle of olive oil. You cut the crisp heart of the lettuce, still wet from the cold tap, into fourths and eat it as it is, with maybe just a little of the oil to gather in the folds of the leaves.

If the lettuce has long, crisp leaves I will sometimes use mayonnaise instead, thinned with a little cream or hot water until you can drizzle it slowly over the ice-crisp ribs. It may not be a lettuce in its purest sense. It may be a vast chicory such as Castelfranco, all pink and cream like a cabbage rose, or a mop head of green and white frisée, in which case I will use nothing but a squeeze of lemon juice.

There is something peaceful, almost sleep inducing, about a lettuce. The Latin name, *Lactuca,* is a reminder of the milky sap that appears from its stalk as you slice it. It was believed to control lust. I can see what they mean. Even at its crispest, a lettuce is gentle, calm, almost timid. The soporific effects are due to lactucin and lactucopicrin, which in small doses act as a sedative. Large amounts are said to have the opposite result, and lettuce was used as a sexual stimulant by the Egyptians. So, easy does it with the Little Gem.

We tend to take most salad leaves for granted, rarely affording them the respect they deserve. Flavor isn't really the point here. Texture and composition are almost more fundamental to what we are likely to call a good lettuce. Most of all, it must be fresh, almost more so than any other vegetable. When they are newly picked, with the dew still sitting in the waves and dimples of their leaves, you see these greens in a new light, a vegetable of the utmost tender, fragile beauty.

Lettuce loves cool weather, as somehow you might expect from its languid character, and will bolt if left growing in the sun. By bolt, I mean go to seed rather than run off. They prefer to grow in early or late summer rather than August, and in a slightly shaded place. Mine survive well enough under the medlar tree, the light filtered by the loose canopy of leaves. Sorrel grows here too, alongside cilantro, French parsley, Reine de Glace lettuce, and young green oakleaf.

I adore salad in all its forms, from the huge cups of iceberg to the red-tinged batavias and cheeky Tom Thumbs. Salad leaves are probably at their most romantic when the leaves are in the form of a full-blown rose, but the firmer varieties, with their longer, straighter leaves and snappable stems, are often the most useful. Anything with a rib crisp enough to scoop up hummus gets my vote. They take a dressing more happily than the very soft-fleshed varieties, which are inclined to become sodden once they meet the vinaigrette. Even a spoonful of dressing can dissolve some of the soft outer leaves of a young butterhead.

I feel slightly uncomfortable without a lettuce in the fridge, in much the same way I do without a lemon or a lump of craggy-edged Parmesan. I wouldn't feel much of a cook without the wherewithal to make salad.

The selection of salad leaves available to us in the markets has never been greater, and they go way beyond the simple green lettuce so dear to our hearts, with leaves of every shape, texture, and nuance you could imagine (I made a stunning salad from tiny bok choy and watercress leaves the other day). The point of sowing seed at home is not so much the joy of picking your own fat-hearted lettuce (though that can be a proud moment) but having the wherewithal to snip immature leaves as and when you need them.

The perennially useful, pleasingly brittle iceberg and the reliable Webb's Wonder have been joined by all the salad leaves we could ever have dreamed of. Red, slightly bitter ones for eating with cheese; long, thin rabbit ears for dressing with Caesar dressing; great waves large enough to hold a chile-spiked meatball; and mottled leaves to bring intrigue to a green salad. There are leaves the size of pancakes and others no bigger than a teaspoon. Some are sold still growing for us to keep alive on the window ledge.

Immature leaves, barely the size of a Chinese soupspoon, and micro-leaves as small as emeralds are the leaves du jour. I like them, they add charm and curiosity to a bowl of lettuce, but I find it hard to beat the quiet majesty of a simple, hearted lettuce. Micro-leaves pack a punch. Sunflower, pumpkin, radish, and sunflower seeds all produce shoots within a week or so of planting and leaves shortly after. They are cheap and straightforward to grow at home. I sprout them in a traditional salad sprouter but they will work on a thick layer of damp absorbent cotton or paper towels too. No matter that they are small; their flavors come in waves of spice and earth, as if to make up for their diminutive stature.

Salad leaves in the garden

I have more success with salad leaves than any other seeds. They germinate in days and grow happily in shallow compost. The difficulties arise once they are large enough to plant out in the garden, where they find themselves at the mercy of all that creeps and crawls in the veg patch.

Lettuce seeds germinate quickly, sometimes in less than a week, and can be grown on a windowsill if necessary. Depending on variety and size, they can be ready to pick in six weeks. Hearted lettuces will often take another month, depending on the weather.

As you might expect from such fragile shoots, lettuce can be capricious. A general rule is to keep it away from fierce heat, which makes it send up seed heads, and sow in spring, late summer and early autumn. It tends to arrive in packets containing hundreds or even thousands of seeds, and needs sowing with a careful hand to avoid clumps. The thinnings, barely the size of your little finger, can be eaten as a particularly tender salad ingredient.

I sow mine in fine compost in a shallow seed tray, water them well and leave in a cool, slightly shaded place to sprout. A covering of a plastic cloche or even the shade of a tree will help keep the worst of the sun off them. Within a week or two, they are up and form a mass of closely packed green leaves, the best of which can then be removed with a dibble or pencil and planted into larger pots or outside in a prepared bed. Only plant them straight outside if you have some slug and snail protection. Lettuce likes fine, free-draining soil without too many lumps. A sandy loam is ideal.

It is best not to overwater the seedlings, as it can result in mildew, particularly with the softer-leaved varieties. I rarely water mine more than two or three times a week. As they start to heart up, most varieties can get very thirsty—a lettuce is about 90 percent water—so it is worth increasing it to once a day. Too much rain is a problem for anything with very fragile leaves. Not only can it make the smaller leaves soggy (I have just lost a whole tray of unprotected seedlings during a day of torrential rain), but it encourages the slugs and snails to come out to play.

You can use virtually any container for growing a few young leaves. I find wooden seed trays lined with newspaper and filled with compost work very well, as do window boxes. The deep dimensions of the latter allow a more substantial root system, and therefore larger leaves. To be honest, anything will do, even old cans and polystyrene boxes.

Picking

There are two ways to approach picking your lettuces: either harvest the whole head in one swoop or carefully cut the outside leaves, leaving the smaller ones in place for later. New leaves will emerge within a week or two. This cut-and-come-again method works well with a mixture of leaves all sown in one box. I use a deep, wooden tray lined with plastic and filled with seed and cutting compost. My choice of leaves varies according to the time of year, but in early summer, as I write, it contains ruby chard, frisée, arugula, and oakleaf lettuces. Each leaf is harvested individually, cut just above the growing point. New leaves sprout to replace them within a few days.

Lettuce—the four characters

I think of lettuce as having four distinct leaf types: blousy and soft; crisp; long; and the loose, jagged ones. It is not a correct classification in either a horticultural or a culinary sense, but it helps me compose a more interesting salad and that is what matters.

Each type of leaf has its own virtues. Sometimes I want a simple plate of soft, buttery leaves; other times something crisp and icy. Mostly, I like a little of each, so I don't fall asleep halfway through my salad.

Soft leaves—the Peter Rabbit lettuces
Soft, tender butterhead lettuce is often maligned. With their tight, upward-facing leaves in a rosette formation, these are the lettuces of summers past.

Those that fit this description, such as red-blushed Quattro Stagioni, the aptly named Tom Thumb, and the milky-sapped Buttercrunch indeed have a sleepy quality. In the garden, I find their low-lying leaves are more attractive to slugs than the upright, crisper varieties. It is as if they are rolling out a carpet in welcome.

The leaves become waxier toward the heart and their softness seems somehow perfect for cold salmon on a blisteringly hot summer's day. They need a light dressing, so as not to make the fragile leaves "melt." You can doze off in the shade afterward. Squeeze them tenderly when you are shopping, to check for a decent heart.

Quattro Stagioni* (Marvel of the Four Seasons) Softish, bronze-tinted leaves with good flavor.
Buttercrunch* Quick to grow, softly crunchy leaves with a pale, tender heart.
May Queen* Lovely old-fashioned variety. Large, soft leaves with a hint of pink around the edges. Resembles an old cabbage rose.
Tom Thumb* Small, as you might expect, but with good flavor and fast

growth. Good for small gardens, as they take up half the space
of a big lettuce.

Also look out for the compact butterhead, Fortune, the soft, heavily
blistered leaves of Kagraner Sommer,* and Parella, with its ability to cope
with cold weather.

Crisp leaves—adding crunch to the salad bowl
Crisphead lettuces, such as Reine de Glace, Webb's Wonderful, and the
icebergs, have a firm heart and a clear, sweet, brightness to their leaves.
The heart is often white, and some have delightfully unruly edges. In the
garden they are mildly frost tolerant. In the kitchen they will take a punchy
dressing, or one thick with lemon and extra-virgin oil. A recently picked
one will keep for a week in the fridge, wrapped in newspaper or in a sealed
plastic bag.

Reine de Glace* Possibly my favorite lettuce. Crisp but somewhat spiky
leaves, good lettuce flavor, a little unobtrusive bitterness. Easy to grow.
Webb's Wonderful* Big, traditional salad lettuce with a pale, crisp heart.
Amorina Pink, frilly leaves, for late-spring planting. A little short on flavor
to my mind.
Bijou Glossy, blistered leaves the color of dried blood. A very beautiful
lettuce with a hint of bitterness. Cut and come again.
Salardin Pretty, frilled-edged lettuce with crisp, bright leaves. Stands
well in the garden without bolting.
Ice Queen Crisp, wavy, pointed leaves and a tight head. Good
summer lettuce.

Also look out for the tight-hearted early Great Lakes,* the waxy, quick-
growing Ice King, and Lakeland, a variety that works well in our climate,
producing more heart than outer leaves.

Long leaves—lettuce of the seven moons
Romaine, or as the British know it more bluntly, Cos, has been known as
Roman lettuce since the fourteenth century, when the Popes moved from
Rome to Avignon, bringing this long-leaved, tight-hearted lettuce with
them. The crunch is exhilarating, even eaten without dressing. It will take
anything you care to throw at it, even the rich egg-yolk-and-olive-oil Caesar
dressing, for which it is the only acceptable leaf. Little Gem, as useful as it is
ubiquitous, is a stunted version of Cos.

Lobjoits Sweet, long leaves and will heart up well if you water it well.
Little Gem* Sweet, pale lettuce with a firm, pointed heart. Barely bigger
than a head of chicory.

Freckles* Thin, pale green leaves with maroon mottling.
Chartwell Crunchy, sweet, and with an exceptional flavor.
Balloon* Large, red-brown leaves.
Pandero The red-leaved Little Gem.

Also keep an eye open for the magically named Lattuga delle Sette Lune, with its long, tightly packed leaves and faint ruby blotches. I have had much success with this beautiful Roman lettuce.

Loose leaves—canary tongues and oak leaves
Loosehead lettuces often have oakleaf-shaped leaves and a soft texture like silk underwear. They can liven up an everyday affair. I considered them overrated until I planted the canary-tongued Lingua di Canarino, which has the typically notched leaves but a little more crispness than its red-tinged cousins. The hand-sized outer leaves of the larger oakleaf varieties can be a little dull. Inside they are crisp and rather pretty. A few in a mixed leaf salad are interesting but I find they bore in quantity. The point is not to pick them as a whole head—although you can—but to pick the outer leaves a few at a time.

Lollo Bionda* Low on flavor but some find the pale, frilly leaves pretty in a salad. Doesn't form a heart.
Lollo Rosso* Ditto, but with even less enthusiasm.
Grenoble* French alpine lettuce with wavy, pink-tinged leaves. Can be frost tolerant, so worth a late-autumn planting.
Rubens Red* A crisp, emerald green and burgundy leaf that will also heart.
Salad Bowl* A green oakleaf type with a mild flavor. Don't overwater. A red version is available.

Also look out for Ashbrook, a crunchy, long-leaved variety, Batavia Blonde, which doesn't turn bitter in the heat and is good for summer growing, the very frilly Bergamo,* the vigorous Black Seeded Simpson,* and New Red Fire,* with a compact habit and lots of intense, burgundy red leaves.

*Available from US seed sources.

Other good leaves

Good King Henry Wide, pointed leaves like a shield and a flavor similar to spinach. A perennial that will withstand some shade.
Orache Growing up to six-plus feet (two meters) in height, these decorative annuals are mild, soft leaved, and rather beautiful. The red version is a delightful addition to the salad patch.

Sorrel My clump of sorrel grows under a tree, and the occasional lemony leaf in a spinach salad is both surprising and refreshing. It comes back year after year if you can get it established. Pick the outer leaves first. The shield-shaped buckler variety will grow happily in a pot for years. At least, mine has.

Mizuna Feathery, spiky, almost fernlike leaves that add bulk and visual interest to a bowl of salad. Sow right through the summer, picking the leaves when they are the length of your middle finger.

Corn salad Also known as mâche. It is almost impossible to kill this little plant. I pick the curiously soft and crunchy leaf by the whole rosette rather than individually, dropping them into a mixture of larger, stronger leaves. Possibly the mildest-tasting leaf of all.

Purslane Rounded, succulent leaves with a very mild flavor and crunchy texture.

Claytonia Also known as miner's lettuce. Pretty leaf, almost triangular in shape, with a delicate flowering shoot coming from its center. Mild, refreshing, and exceptionally delicate. It needs a light, sandy soil. Sow in summer for early spring picking, or in winter with cloche protection.

Landcress A good little plant this, providing dark, glossy, watercresslike leaves all winter. Almost impossible to kill, it gets very hot to the tongue in summer. Find it a moist corner in rich soil and its rounded leaves will see you through the coldest and most barren of months.

Arugula Also known as rocket. Throw in a few young arugula leaves and in one stroke you will have added exhilarating bitterness, mild heat, and interesting texture. While a bowl of lone arugula leaves is sometimes hard going—they can be spiky in the mouth—a few tucked among softer, more rounded leaves bring a little excitement.

A lettuce diary

May A cold, wet day in late May and I plant an assortment of lettuce seed in shallow wooden trays: Reine de Glace, a jagged-edged, crisphead variety that grows no matter how cold the weather is, and the ancient Lingua di Canarino, a loose-headed lettuce with bright green, heavily notched leaves like long, tender oak leaves. Neither variety bolts in hot weather.

June Lettuces dislike their roots being disturbed. Ideally you plant where they are to grow, but snails see off very young seedlings in my garden, so I transplant them when they are a little over 1¼ inches (3cm) high, holding them by the leaf rather than the fragile root. They sulk for a week, then, after a good rain, they settle and send up new leaves. Each lettuce is surrounded by a copper ring and some environmentally acceptable slug pellets.

July The loosehead varieties in the garden are sending up long plumes of acid-green leaves with wavy edges. The crisp hearts are in good leaf but have yet to plump up. My loathing of frills of any sort extends to lettuce. Lollo Rosso particularly offends. There is no escaping it this month, when it appears at every turn, even showing its face in my organic box. I feel I am being persecuted.

July 27 My ideal lettuce, the salad of a summer's afternoon dream, is a hearted variety, the stems crisp and full of sap, the leaves firm enough to stand on their backs like an open shell. Reine de Glace fits like a glove. The leaves are almost the size of the outer leaves of an iceberg but have a playful movement to them, like a surfer's wave. If you had to design the perfect mixture of softness and crunch, this would be it. They will stand up to a certain amount of heat, so I sow as late as July. This is the lettuce for that high-summer cold chicken salad, with white-tipped radishes, spanking-fresh green onions, cucumber, watercress, and creamy salad dressing.

August Traditionally a difficult time for any fragile leaf. The canary-tongued varieties are magnificent—tall, crisp leaved, and very beautifully formed. They are eating well, and strong enough of stature to take a dressing made of lemon juice, tarragon, and cream. They will see me through until the frosts.

And...

* Raised beds or plastic cloches are the most appropriate way of growing lettuce in the garden; box-lined hedges, which double as snail hotels, the least.
* If you grow under cloches, make sure your seedlings are well ventilated. Lettuces hate to swelter.
* Slugs and snails are the enemy. Do everything you can to discourage them except resorting to slug pellets without environmentally sound credentials.
* Some varieties can be grown outdoors even in winter; check on the package before planting.
* Both the seed and the plants like warm soil rather than hot.
* You can sow indoors from as early as January.
* An old fruit crate, lined with plastic and filled with seed compost, can be filled with several different varieties for picking throughout the summer.
* Pick single leaves regularly to encourage new growth, or leave the plant to form a large head.

Salad in the kitchen

Making salad is a daily ritual in our house. I can take all the time in the world over washing the leaves in ice-cold water—I use a large pottery bowl with a jade-green glaze, which flatters the leaves even as you wash them (why shouldn't washing vegetables be a pleasure?). Each leaf is unfolded tenderly, thoughtfully, and inspected for hidden aphids. Finding a slug in my salad is a horror I can live without. The leaves crisp slightly if the water is cold enough. It perks them up just as it would us.

I loathe kitchen clutter and unused gadgets, yet I wouldn't want to live without my salad spinner. Its centrifugal force dries the leaves without bruising them and that, to me, is essential. If I have to do without, then I put a piece of white, dimpled paper towel in the drained leaves and toss them gently. It soaks up an amazing amount of water. If you don't spin your lettuce, you will get soggy leaves and a diluted dressing.

You can cook with lettuce, watercress, and chicory but not with arugula (though it makes a good pesto) or with the very fragile mustard and cress. Lettuce braised with fava beans and olive oil is a light, soothing summer vegetable dish, and lettuce soup is a possibility, but I wouldn't get fancier than that.

A word about watercress

Watercress makes a famous soup and is exceptional as a flavoring for mayonnaise to serve with cold salmon—though to this cook it is never better than when seen in a fat, thick-stalked sprig, its leaves still glistening with water, tucked into a chicken salad or under a rare steak.

Watercress is the filling for my favorite sandwich. Thick white bread so fresh it is barely cool, unsalted butter so cold it makes holes in the bread, then watercress leaves and their thick stalks, the faintest snow of sea salt. You could add bacon if the fancy takes you, or cold chicken, or some thin slices of posh ham, or smoked salmon or eel, or layers of snow-white goat cheese, but I wouldn't. For me, a cool, lush green watercress sandwich eaten on a baking hot summer's afternoon, ranks higher than anything.

Due to its heat and slight spicy quality, this leaf is best added in small amounts to other, sweeter leaves. Yet a simple watercress salad with a mustardy dressing and a knife-sharp hit of red wine vinegar is just the thing for a supper of cold duck. A few slices of blood orange would be welcome too.

Putting a salad together

If there was a recipe that stood for everything I believe about good eating, it would be the quiet understatement that is a single variety of salad leaf in a simple bowl. Each leaf should be perfect, the dressing light and barely present, the whole effect one of generous simplicity.

More than baking bread or making a cake, rolling pastry or basting the roast, I am at my happiest in the kitchen when I am putting a salad together. Whether it is a single variety of leaf lightly dressed, or a more complex arrangement of leaves that flatter one another, the making of a salad is where kitchen craft crosses over into art.

There is much pleasure to be had in a bowl of leaves, herbs, and even flowers whose constituents have been chosen with great care. In early spring there might be a mixture of arugula, sorrel, and Treviso radicchio; in summer an inspired collection of everything you can find; then later, as the evenings shorten, a darker mix of burgundy and dense green leaves.

I make a salad specifically to fit the season. In spring, a mixture of the growing tips, bright and mild, a testament to rising sap; in summer an offering of full-blown lettuce, soft, tranquil, and pale; in winter a bowl of dark and sultry notes with a sting of bitterness from a member of the chicory family. This isn't always as deliberate as it sounds. Just buying or picking the leaves in season will often dictate the nature of your salad.

Salad leaves need to be rinsed. I do this in a large bowl of very cold water, unfurling and rinsing each leaf as I go. They are dried in a spinner, then piled into the salad bowl on top of the puddle of dressing. I then gently toss the salad with my hands, lightly coating each leaf with dressing.

I enjoy choosing which leaves to put in. Sometimes I am after a balance of soft, sweet, bitter, and crisp. Another day I might be looking for something especially gentle or hot. Matching certain leaves to what they are to accompany allows a certain amount of poetic license: bitter leaves with a pork chop; sweet leaves with cold poached fish; a bowl of exclusively mustardy leaves to go with cold, rose-colored beef. Then there is the day when you just get it wrong—too many earthy flavors together, a plethora of bitter leaves, a mild mixture that leaves you wanting. Even the mistakes can be interesting.

Leaves and their character

The flavor of salad leaves varies according to the age of the leaf and the time of year. Cold weather has a sweetening effect on bitter leaves; the more mature the leaf, the more pronounced its attributes will be.

Cool, mild, sweet These are what I use as a base on which to build. Bitter, hot, or spiky leaves stand out against a backdrop of any of the following: Little Gem, butterhead varieties, purslane, nabana (flowering Chinese cabbage), Chinese cabbage, mizuna, bok choy, tatsoi, texel (mustardlike Asian green), spinach, endive, corn salad (mâche), pea shoots.
Crisp Long, thin leaves tend to be crisper than fat, round ones. This includes the romaine family, iceberg, and fully mature Buttercrunch (a cross between soft butterhead and iceberg).
Bitter The chicories, including radicchio and endive (the endives are generally sweeter), arugula, and dandelion. The heart leaves, tucked away

in the middle of the plant, tend to be milder than the outer leaves.
The bitterness is more pronounced in hot weather and in older leaves.

Spiky A few jagged-edged leaves make an exciting contrast to the softer ones. More than a few is hard going and can tickle the throat. Choose from mizuna, arugula, frisée, and young dandelion.

Brightly colored The red leaves are good either as the occasional leaf in a mixture of cool greens or as a dominant theme. Their flavors tend to be more pungent than the green. Try amaranth, red perilla, beet leaves, red oakleaf, small ruby and rainbow chard leaves, radicchio, and the red and freckled lettuces.

Hot and spicy A few hot-to-the-tongue leaves to add to a bulk quantity of milder leaves: watercress, basil, mint (although generally cooling as a flavoring, the raw leaf is hot to the tongue, like a Polo mint), kale, mibuna, radish leaves, arugula, cress. Nasturtium leaves have a light, peppery quality.

Mustard flavor A small number of mustard-flavored leaves can work well in a salad destined to accompany pork or perhaps mackerel. You only need a few. Choose from gai lan, Green in Snow, giant red mustard, cress. They are all exceptionally easy to grow.

Earthy Kohlrabi, beet, and chard leaves.

Citrus Sorrel, purslane, buckler-leaf sorrel for adding freshness and exuberance.

Dressing your salad

A dressing is about balance and harmony, both of the ingredients within it and that of the dressing and the leaves. That said, it shouldn't be assumed that we must make a dressing at all. A good aromatic vinegar such as balsamic or sherry is often all you need, or a drizzle of olive oil or a squeeze of lemon. Arugula leaves, spiky, peppery, and vital, often get nothing more than salt and lemon at my table.

I rarely measure the ingredients for a salad dressing. In fact, whenever I do it never seems quite right. Ardent recipe followers will be devastated but good dressing is very much a case of intuition rather than doing what we are told. Sometimes the recipe is obvious, such as a sweeter dressing for bitter leaves. Other times you can just go as your appetite takes you.

The salt should be dissolved first in the vinegar or lemon juice. I find this mellows the acidity of the liquid. I then beat the oil in with a fork or a "doll's house" whisk I keep especially for the job. It is pleasing when the dressing emulsifies, as it coats the leaves more evenly, but I don't worry if it doesn't.

A mild Dijon mustard is worth adding for a thicker result, and in particular for a mild, leafy salad to accompany cold meats. It is also a good one to use with spinach.

A simple dressing for mild leaves

Dissolve a pinch of sea salt in the juice of half a lemon. Beat in a scant ½ cup (100ml) olive oil, then a little black pepper.

A classic dressing

Proportions vary, according to the exact qualities of the individual ingredients and to our personal taste, but it is generally accepted that a classic salad dressing will be about four parts fruity olive oil to one of red wine vinegar. A small shallot, finely chopped, is acceptable and should be added to the vinegar twenty minutes before the dressing is made, to give it time to mellow. Some like garlic in the recipe too, though not me. Well, occasionally in early summer, when the new, pink-flushed cloves appear.

Put a pinch of salt in a small bowl, then pour over the vinegar. Dissolve the salt by stirring, then whisk in the olive oil and a little black pepper.

A mustardy dressing

You really don't need much mustard, and it should be the mild Dijon variety if it isn't to overpower the leaves. A half teaspoon is enough, beaten into the vinegar of the classic dressing above just before the oil.

A lemon dressing for summer

Mix together a pinch of sea salt, a teaspoon of Dijon mustard, and the juice of half a lemon. Beat in ¾ cup (200ml) olive oil and a teaspoon of grated lemon zest. Let sit a few minutes for the ingredients to get to know one another.

A walnut oil dressing

The bitter endives particularly appreciate the creamy, nutty notes of walnut oil. Rather than using entirely walnut oil, which runs the risk of cloying, I use it half and half with either sunflower or a light, unpushy olive oil such as those from France.

Put a tablespoon of Dijon mustard in a small bowl with a pinch of sugar and three pinches of sea salt. Whisk in 2 tablespoons of lemon juice, then 3 of light olive oil, and 3 of walnut oil. Stir in a tablespoon of cold water and a little pepper. Some toasted walnut halves, scattered among the leaves like mushrooms in the autumn grass, would be appropriate and delicious.

A creamy dressing

Dijon mustard – 2 teaspoons
tarragon vinegar – 2 teaspoons
mild olive oil – 3 to 4 tablespoons
heavy or whipping cream – 2 to 3 tablespoons
flat-leaf parsley leaves – a handful

Mix the mustard, vinegar, and olive oil with a small whisk, then stir in the cream. Coarsely chop the parsley leaves and add them. Season with salt and black pepper. Pour the dressing onto the salad and toss gently.

A salad of lettuce, peas, and ham

enough for 4
cooked ham – 8 ounces (250g)
shelled fresh peas – 1¼ cups (180g)
white bread – 3 thin slices (75g)
a little oil
a large, soft-leaved lettuce
Berkswell or other deep-flavored, hard farmhouse cheese – 5 ounces
    (150g)
the creamy dressing, above

Shred the ham into large bite-sized pieces. You could use a knife for this if you wish, but I prefer the coarse texture of pieces torn by hand. Cook the peas briefly in deep, lightly salted water, then drain.

Tear the bread into small pieces, discarding the crusts as you go. Fry in a shallow layer of oil in a nonstick pan. As soon as they are nicely golden, remove to paper towels to drain. Salt them lightly.

While the bread is cooking, wash the lettuce, separate the leaves, tear them into manageable pieces, and put them in a serving bowl.

Take shavings of the cheese with a vegetable peeler and toss them into the lettuce leaves with the peas, golden bread, and shredded ham. Pour the dressing onto the salad and toss gently.

Cooking with salad leaves

There are odd occasions when you might want to put some heat under your salad leaves. Here are a few of them.

A soup of lettuce and peas

A good soup for a spring day, bright green and not too filling.

> *enough for 6*
> a large, round lettuce, about 14 ounces (400g)
> butter – a thick slice
> shallots – 2
> shelled peas – 3 cups (500g)
> chicken or vegetable stock, or water – 4 cups (a liter)
> mint – 3 bushy sprigs

Separate the lettuce leaves and wash them thoroughly. Even the smallest amount of grit will ruin the soup. Melt the butter in a deep saucepan over low to medium heat. Peel the shallots, slice them thinly, then let them soften in the butter. When they are tender but have yet to color, chop the lettuce up a bit and stir it into the butter. As soon as it has wilted, add the peas, stock, and mint leaves and bring to a boil. Decrease the heat, season with salt and black pepper, and let simmer for seven to ten minutes.

Remove the pan from the heat and purée the soup in a blender until smooth. Check the seasoning and serve hot.

A dish of lettuce for deepest summer

I ate this rather soothing way with lettuce twice last week, once for lunch, accompanied by a piece of salmon, the second time for supper, with nothing but a hunk of soft farmhouse bread, the sort with a dusting of white flour on top. Light, juicy, and clean tasting.

enough for 2 as a light meal, 4 as a side dish
medium lettuces – 2
butter – a thick slice
unsmoked bacon – 2½ ounces (75g), diced
small leeks – 2
shelled peas or fava beans – 1⅔ cups (250g)
vegetable stock – 1 cup (250ml)

Pull away and discard any tatty leaves from the lettuces, then cut each lettuce into quarters. Wash under cold running water to remove any trapped grit or aphids.

Melt the butter in a heavy-bottomed pan to which you have a lid. Add the diced bacon and let it stew in the butter for five minutes or so over medium heat. Meanwhile trim and wash the leeks and cut them into short pieces. Add them to the pan and continue cooking, stirring now and again, until they have started to soften.

Add the peas or fava beans, lettuce, and stock, add a seasoning of salt and black pepper, and bring to a boil. Turn it down as soon as it starts to bubble furiously, then cover with a tightly fitting lid. Let simmer for twenty minutes, by which time the lettuce will have sunk to four silky mounds and the liquid will have almost vanished.

Lift out the lettuce, leeks, peas, and bacon with a slotted spoon and place on a serving dish. If there is more than a ladleful of liquid in the pan, increase the heat and boil furiously to reduce it a little. Check the seasoning and pour it over the lettuce.

Spinach

Green, soothing, yet somehow vibrant, creamed spinach is something I could eat at every meal. I appreciate its calming, "there, there" quality with slices of warm ham, a pepper-crusted steak, a piece of grilled fish. Forget forks; the best way to get creamed spinach from plate to mouth is with a crisp and salty chip.

At the Saturday market, where I shop for stalks of broccoli no thicker than my little finger and beets pulled from the ground the morning before, there is often a wicker crate of spinach. Large leaves by today's standards, with stems thick enough to crunch, this is spinach that is as appropriate in a salad as it is in a soup, its large stems and leaves pert enough to stand up in your hand like a bunch of flowers.

When spinach is truly fresh, it squeaks as you rummage around in the pile, like the sound of wet Wellingtons on a rubber floor. I use this to gauge its freshness. Older leaves tend to relax, even flop, and don't talk to us as we pick them up. They are fine for soup. Sound, freshly picked leaves almost beg you to take them home.

There are two spinaches that really interest me: the coarse-leaved, easy-to-grow "perpetual" variety, which is botanically related to beets and Swiss chard, and the softer, tricky "true" spinach, *Spinacia oleracea*. Both are excellent in the kitchen, though true spinach is regarded as having the more refined flavor. True spinach is the one for salads, and can be picked very young; perpetual needs marginally longer cooking and is generally too tough for a salad.

Spinach is thought to have first been domesticated in Nepal, coming to Britain via Persia and Spain around the eleventh century. Many of the classic spinach recipes we use tend to be Indian or Italian, the latter influence coming, like so many other foods, from Catherine de Medici (could that woman eat or what?) and leaving us with such delights as eggs Florentine and all those intricate, layered bakes with cheese on top that are to this day labeled after her native city of Florence. *À la Florentine* always suggests something baked on a bed of the green stuff.

I have had a bumpy ride with this leaf, refusing to eat it until I was at least in double figures. My sister-in-law won me over by shrieking, "Ooooh, spinach!" on spotting a crate at the produce market. Her excitement (I had never seen anyone get excited over a vegetable before) was contagious and we took it straight home before the leaves had time to wilt. The speed at which the leaves arrived, in a generous emerald curl on the plate, was a revelation. A turning point too, if I think about it. Never before had I experienced a vegetable so tender, so green, so full of life.

Spinach in the garden

Both "true" spinach and the tougher "perpetual" spinach need cool, moist conditions and a chance of partial shade if they are to perform well. Perpetual is less fussy but both like plenty of moisture at their roots and prefer the soil to have been well manured before sowing. A dressing of pelleted chicken manure will go down well.

Most people sow the seed directly, as the seedlings are particularly fragile and difficult to transplant. The seeds will not germinate if the weather is too hot, so sow from midspring and again in early autumn, to keep you going through until the frosts. I sow generously, as the slugs are bound to get more than a few, and they are easier than carrots to thin out. In my experience the perpetual variety can be slow to germinate. Give it a good three or four weeks.

Plants need to be about 7½ inches (18cm) apart, in rows with 12 inches (30cm) between them. Mine are often a bit closer than that, due to lack of space. Plants too closely packed in can suffer from mildew. I have had most success using a plastic cloche at the early stages of growth, to protect them from slimy predators and gamboling fox cubs. Space permitting, you can make consecutive plantings during spring and autumn.

Whereas some of the food we grow will carry on regardless of the weather, spinach does like a lot of water. Failure to provide enough moisture will result in the plants running to seed. Of course, the more we water, the more we attract the attention of snails, who find little more to their taste than a freshly watered spinach leaf.

I have little room for spinach. I grow it more as an exercise to see how it behaves. Dominant is a reliable variety, bred for its true spinach flavor and disease resistance, and it has fared well enough on the cool, lightly shaded side of the garden. It's a magnet for greedy slugs, and the capacity for an entire row to shrink to a spoonful in the pan has ruled it out as a regular crop for me. There just isn't the space here.

I plant the spiky seeds straight into a bed on the cool side of the vegetable patch in early April, protect the seedlings as much as I can under cloches, and scatter organic slug pellets around the edges. Friends with more space than I have plant perpetual spinach in September, leaving the young plants to overwinter. They pick in early spring, but often complain that the results are not as good as their spring-planted crop. Although perpetual spinach is relatively hardy (after a decade of gardening, I am still surprised when any delicate leaves make it through the frost), anyone hoping to pick spinach in the depths of winter should probably try the coarser-leaved chard family.

Varieties

Spinach is ready for picking about twelve weeks after sowing.

Bordeaux* Soft, rather small leaves with purple-red stems. A very tender variety.
Medania* Smooth leaves, resistant to mildew, slow to bolt. A good one for midseason planting.
Giant Noble* Enormous thick leaves, but tender nonetheless.
Bloomsdale* Crumply, fleshy leaves with good flavor.
Dominant Soft, crinkly leaves with excellent flavor. Sarah Raven's favorite variety.
Perpetual Related to Swiss chard. Tough, lightly crinkled leaves that rarely bolt. Cut and come again.

*Available from US seed sources.

Spinach in the kitchen

I select spinach as much by feel as by eye. The smoother, waxier leaves are more appropriate for cooking than they are in a salad. Rub them gently between your thumb and forefinger; if they are pale and waxy with wide, smooth stems, then they are best in the pot. These coarser leaves tend to hold their volume a little better during cooking than the softer-leaved varieties.

Choosing spinach leaves for salad is easy. They will have a perkiness to them and an irresistible vitality. Their root ends tend to lose their pinkness as they age. It is never worth making a salad with anything but the freshest leaves. Even the smallest blemish will be exaggerated once it is in the bowl.

I dress and toss my salad as late as possible before eating. I sometimes put a puddle of dressing in the base of the bowl, the washed and dried leaves on top, and only toss the two as I eat. Spinach dressed too early has a habit of blackening.

You can make a salad with cooked spinach, too. I wilt the wet leaves in a shallow, tightly lidded pan, squeeze them almost dry, then toss with either lemon oil or a yogurt dressing. You can spend too much time untangling a mass of wilted and squeezed spinach, and a loose lump of leaves works well enough.

I am not sure you really "cook" spinach. It is more a case of showing it the pan. No other leaf eaten as a vegetable becomes tender so quickly—a matter of seconds rather than minutes.

The leaves need little or no water in the pan. They will often cook in the moisture that clings to the folds in the leaves after washing. I generally take them straight from sink to pan, dripping water along the counter as I go. Covered with a lid, that is all the liquid they need in which to steam, though they are less likely to stick to the pan if you pour in a film of water first. I find a pair of kitchen tongs invaluable here, for turning the spinach once, maybe twice, during cooking, each time replacing the lid so that the leaves soften in their own steam.

The only time the leaves get a long cooking is when they are being used as an integral layer in a baked dish—say, between chicken and sauce or between ground beef and pasta in a Florentine—or when they are simmered with potatoes in a stove-top Indian *saag aloo*. Although any cooking time longer than a few minutes is normally the death knell for fragile leaves, the cooked spinach survives by being protected by the layers of sauce, and can often emerge a startlingly bright green.

Spinach disappears in the pan. You stuff a green mountain of squeaking leaves into the pot, tucking in stray stalks as you squash down the lid, then four minutes later you lift out a squidgy bundle the size of your fist, maybe smaller. You press the water from it and your green mountain has shrunk to the size of a blackbird's egg. And that is what happens to it in the hands of gentle, watchful cooks. Heaven knows what someone who habitually overcooks their greens is left with.

The general advice is to keep it well away from large quantities of water. But you know what? If you dip your bunch of greens into a pasta pan of deep, angrily boiling water, hold it under with a slotted spoon for thirty seconds, then yank it out, there is less shrinkage, the color remains more vibrant, and the leaves cook more evenly. They relax in seconds rather than minutes (heat-soluble vitamins disappear just as quickly in steam as they do in water). The choice is up to us. When cooking spinach, it's the seconds that count, rather than the method.

Many people experience the famous "furry-teeth" effect when they have eaten up their spinach. This reaction—the effect of oxalic acid on your teeth—can be lessened by tossing your freshly cooked leaves in melted butter or cream. Curiously, oil doesn't seem to have the same effect. Another way to reduce the feeling is to squeeze a shot of lemon juice over the leaves. People make a bit of a fuss about it, but it is honestly not something that particularly bothers me.

Washing spinach

Grit tucks itself into every curl and fold of the spinach plant, particularly at the point where the stalk meets the root. Even the smallest speck can ruin a bowl of soup or a salad. Anyone who has had the teeth-jarring experience of crunching on a piece of grit will probably agree with me that it is worth taking almost obsessive care over washing spinach.

I have never found rinsing the leaves under running water particularly successful and tend to go with the dunking method instead. Washing your leaves in a sink or two of water can use more water than rinsing them under a running tap, so I fill my most capacious bowl and then pour the used water out in the garden.

To clean your leaves thoroughly, fill the sink or a very large bowl with cold water. The icier the water, the crisper the leaves will be. Add the spinach and gently swish the bunches around by their roots in the water. Let soak for ten minutes, during which time the trapped grit will gradually sink to the bottom.

Depending on how muddy your spinach is, you may need to repeat the process. Check each leaf individually—a very Zen moment—and gently shake them dry. Any destined for a salad will appreciate a ride in the salad spinner.

I am not a fan of the bagged, ready-rinsed salad leaf in general, and even less so of spinach. These round-ended leaves seem to have little going for them in terms of flavor or texture, and are less "spinachy" than the pointed, crinkly varieties. They also have a curious ability to collapse into a dead faint as soon as you tip them out of their bag.

Seasoning your spinach

Nutmeg The warm, musky notes of nutmeg are an essential part of creamed spinach, working with both the leaves and the cream.
Orange The refreshing quality of sweet oranges, and especially the dark-fleshed "blood" variety (often cringingly called "ruby" by the more prissy supermarkets), is a good foil for the mineral notes of the leaves.
Lemon Any bright-tasting citrus fruit will cut the earthier notes of spinach leaves and lift the true flavor a notch or two. Lemon oil (made with olive oil and fresh lemon juice), lemon zest and juice, and that of the lime all fit the bill, as does lemongrass.
Cream In soup, creamed vegetables and a dressing for wilted spinach.
Eggs Omelettes, soufflés, the classic *oeufs Florentine*, and eggs Benedict all show the two as a marriage made in heaven.
Anchovies The salty little fillets have an extraordinary affinity with spinach. Use them in moderate amounts as a salad ingredient, or in a dressing.

Bacon and pancetta Spinach and bacon salad is a classic, but the two can also meet up in a soup.

Parmesan Include in a dressing for the leaves or as a seasoning for any hot dish. Use to form a crust for a spinach gratin or soufflé.

Pine nuts Waxy, pointed nuts (the round-ended ones are considered inferior by aficionados) marry more successfully with this leaf than any other nuts (though walnuts can be good, too). When they are toasted, their warm, oily quality adds a welcome crunch to a spinach salad. I sometimes scatter them over a mound of the cooked leaves, too.

Mushrooms Spinach and mushroom salad and soup are famous but the best of all to my mind is when spinach and mushrooms are used as a stuffing for pancakes.

Garlic Some vegetables take to the whiff of garlic more happily than others. Zucchini, tomatoes, and eggplants love rubbing shoulders with a clove or two; less so green beans, fava beans, and beets. Spinach cannot get enough of the stuff.

Yogurt A blissful partnership.

And...

* The size of the leaf is no indication of its quality. Large leaves can be just as tender as those the length of your thumb.

* Washed leaves will keep in good condition for a couple of days in a sealed plastic bag in the vegetable crisper of the fridge. Pack them in while they are damp, but don't let water accumulate at the bottom of the bag or they will turn slimy.

* I often don't bother with salt when steaming spinach, but it can be added at the same time as you dress the cooked leaves with their melted butter, pan juices, or oil.

* Butter is the preferred cooking medium, softening the "furry-teeth" effect and muting the leaves' more strident mineral notes.

* Walnut and hazelnut oils make a more interesting dressing than olive for these leaves. Even more so if you involve lemon juice instead of vinegar.

Squeaking spinach, sizzling bacon

It's the first week of June, a gray sky threatening rain. I have bought true spinach home, the leaves pointed like the iron head of a prehistoric arrow. Tight little sprigs that stand up proud if you hold them at their pink base and crisp, water-rich stems that crunch when you break them.

It takes four washes to get the Herefordshire mud off them, plunging them over and over in deep water, each spent bowl of water poured over the garden. I have also bought some Ginger Pig long-back bacon, the slices so long they have to be doubled over in the pan.

No oil, just the hot fat from the frying pan and a splash of sherry vinegar poured over at the last minute. I put the leaves in a dish, then a splash of vinegar, the coarsely cut hot bacon, and the spitting fat. No salt or pepper, but a few cooked fava beans instead. Just everything tossed immediately while the fat is still hot and the spinach cold. Not so much a recipe as an assembly—crisp, juicy stalks crunch under the teeth with the hot, salty, fatty bacon.

Such a simple salad works because the sweet bacon mellows the clean acidity of the spinach and the sherry vinegar unites the two. The vinegar turns the two ingredients into a salad, like someone introducing two friends they know will get on.

I could have included capers, or seeded grapes or even some sliced avocado, or hand-torn croutons cooked in the bacon fat. But I didn't.

Spinach, orange, and feta

A favorite salad of mine is one where the spinach leaves are matched with oranges and feta. Lush, salty, refreshing, I use it to lift the spirits.

For each person, wash a good double handful of small, perfect spinach leaves. Peel and thickly slice a large orange, preferably a "blood" variety, catching as much of the juice as you can. Make a dressing with some of the juice, olive and walnut oil in equal amounts, and a little black pepper, but no salt. Toss the leaves and orange slices in the dressing, then crumble over the feta cheese, keeping the pieces quite large. Add a few sprouted seeds perhaps, or some torn bread, toasted.

Classic creamed spinach

The white sauce way. Yes, it's a drag to make white sauce, but what you end up with here is creamed spinach of extraordinary solace and luxury.

enough for 4
milk – 1¼ cups (300ml)
a small onion, peeled
a bay leaf
black peppercorns – 6
spinach – 2 pounds (1kg)
butter – 4 tablespoons (50g)
all-purpose flour – 6 tablespoons (50g)
heavy cream – 4 tablespoons
nutmeg

Put the milk in a saucepan with the onion, bay leaf, and black peppercorns. Bring to a boil, then decrease the heat to low and cook for ten minutes for the aromatics to do their stuff.

Discard the very toughest spinach stalks, then cook the leaves in a lidded pan with a film of water in the bottom. They should be tender in just a minute or two, maybe less. Drain and cool under cold running water, squeeze thoroughly but gently to remove most of the water, then chop finely.

Melt the butter in a heavy-bottomed nonstick saucepan, stir in the flour, and cook for a couple of minutes, stirring so that it doesn't burn. Whisk in the warm milk; you don't need the aromatics, they have done their work. When the sauce starts to thicken, decrease the heat to a low simmer and let it bubble gently for a good fifteen minutes. An occasional stir, taking care to get right in the corners, will prevent it burning.

Stir in the cream and chopped spinach, then finish with salt, pepper, and a fine grating of nutmeg.

A contemporary take on creamed spinach

Making creamed spinach without the traditional backbone of white sauce produces a quicker, greener, and slightly fresher-tasting result. It makes up in speed and greenness what it loses in nannying quality.

enough for 4
spinach – 2 pounds (1kg)
butter – 2 tablespoons (30g)
crème fraîche – 3 heaping tablespoons
nutmeg

Wash the spinach, pile it into a saucepan while it is still wet, cover with a lid, and steam for a minute or two until it has relaxed. It will need to be turned in the pan a couple of times. Remove, drain, squeeze as much as you can to remove the water, then put into a food processor with the butter and blitz until smooth. Now stir in the crème fraîche, some salt and pepper, and a little nutmeg.

A quick, hot spinach side dish

enough for 4 as a side dish
ginger – a thumb-sized piece
garlic – a single, plump clove
chiles – 2 small, hot red or green
vegetable oil – a glug or two
spinach – 1 pound (450g)
garam masala – a scant teaspoon
lemon juice – a squeeze

Peel the ginger, slice it, and reduce it to a sludge, either by chopping very, very finely or mincing it in a small food processor or grinder. Peel the garlic and mince or chop finely. Chop the chiles.

Get a wok or frying pan hot, pour in the oil, and when it shimmers add the minced ginger and garlic. Move the mixture quickly round the pan so it doesn't burn, then add the chopped chiles and the spinach, torn into large pieces (small leaves can be left whole).

Stir the spinach around the hot pan, letting it soften and collapse. There will be some liquid but it should almost evaporate as you continue; if it doesn't, increase the heat. Sprinkle in the garam masala, toss briefly, then add a little salt and freshen with a squeeze of lemon.

Salmon, steamed spinach, and a lemon salad

There is no fish I can think of that doesn't work with spinach. But where creamed spinach seems perfectly fine with a steak of halibut or haddock, the richer, oily fish such as salmon are more appropriately matched to the leaves in a simpler state.

A mouthful of lemon salad, at once breathtakingly sharp, is more than at home on the same fork as a piece of salmon or a bunch of meltingly soft spinach. Bring all three together and you have a dish of extraordinary vitality.

enough for 2
salmon – two 8- to 9-ounce (225 to 250g) pieces
olive oil
spinach – 1 pound (500g)

for the salad
lemons – 2
superfine sugar – 2 teaspoons
olive oil – 2 tablespoons
flat-leaf parsley – a small bunch
capers – a heaping tablespoon

Brush the salmon on both sides with olive oil, then season with salt. Get a nonstick frying pan hot. Place the fish, skin side down, in the pan and cook over medium heat for four or five minutes, until the skin has crisped. Turn, cover with a lid, and cook for a further five minutes or so, until the fish is lightly cooked through to the center.

Meanwhile, make the salad by cutting away the skin and white pith from the lemons with a sharp knife and slicing the lemons thinly. Put them into a bowl with the sugar, olive oil, and a good handful of parsley leaves, left whole. Add the capers and toss the salad gently. Let sit for a few minutes, during which time the sharpness of the lemon will mellow a little.

Wash the spinach thoroughly, then steam in a lidded pan for a minute or two, until tender. Drain.

Put the lemon salad and the spinach on warm plates and slide on the salmon.

A chicken, spinach, and pasta pie

A huge pie, lighter and (slightly) less trouble than a lasagne, this is as satisfying as winter food gets. Even with top-notch chicken and heavy cream, it is hardly an expensive supper, and it feeds four generously (some of us went back for seconds).

enough for 4
spaghetti – 12 ounces (350g)
mushrooms – 10½ ounces (300g)
olive oil – 3 tablespoons
butter – a thick slice
cooked chicken – 1 pound (500g; boned weight)
white wine – 2 glasses
heavy cream – 2 cups (450ml)
spinach – 7 ounces (200g)
Parmesan – 6½ ounces (190g), grated

Cook the spaghetti in deep, generously salted boiling water. Drain and set aside (a little olive oil will stop it sticking together). Preheat the oven to 350°F (180°C).

Cut the mushrooms into quarters. Warm the oil and butter in a deep pan and add the mushrooms, letting them color nicely here and there. Add the cooked chicken, cut into large pieces, and then pour in the wine. Bring to the boil, scraping away at the sticky remains on the bottom of the pan; they will add much flavor to the sauce. Pour the cream into the pan, bring back to a boil, and turn off the heat.

Wash the spinach and put it, still wet from rinsing, into a pan with a tight-fitting lid. Let it cook for a minute or two in its own steam, then drain, squeeze to remove excess water, and chop roughly.

Fold the cooked spaghetti, mushroom and chicken sauce, and spinach together, then stir in two-thirds of the grated Parmesan and some salt and black pepper and spoon into a large baking dish. Scatter the remaining cheese on top and bake for thirty-five minutes, until crisp and golden.

An Indian-inspired dish of spinach and potatoes

The classic Indian spinach dish *saag aloo*, where spinach and potatoes are added to spiced and softened onions, is often cooked a while longer than I would like it to be. Authentically, the spinach goes in before the potatoes, so that it makes an impromptu sauce. Delicious. But I sometimes make it less than classically, keeping the spinach almost whole and adding it last, so that it comes to the table singing brightly, more as an ingredient than a "sauce."

enough for 4 as a side dish, 2 as a main dish,
perhaps with warm Indian breads
potatoes – 1 pound (500g)
a large onion
vegetable oil or melted butter – 2 tablespoons
garlic – 2 fat cloves
a small green chile
ginger – a ¾-inch (2cm) lump
black mustard seeds – half a teaspoon
turmeric – half a teaspoon
spinach – 1 pound (450g)
the juice of half a lemon, probably less

Scrub the potatoes, cut them into large pieces, then either boil in deep, salted water or steam until tender. Drain and set aside.

Peel and finely slice the onion. Warm the vegetable oil or butter in a large pan, then add the onion and cook until soft and just starting to color. Finely chop the garlic, chile, and ginger and stir them in with the mustard seeds and turmeric. Continue cooking briefly, stirring the onion and spices regularly so they do not burn.

Add the cooked and drained potatoes and a wineglass of water. Bring to a boil and simmer for four or five minutes, until any "crustings" of onion and spices stuck on the pan have dissolved into the liquid. Increase the heat so that the liquid bubbles almost to nothing and the potatoes are starting to take on some of the color and flavor of the spices, then add the spinach— thoroughly washed and trimmed of its toughest stalks. Season generously with salt and a little ground black pepper.

Once the spinach has wilted and is bright green, check the seasoning, squeeze over a little lemon juice, and eat.

Spinach and mushroom gratin

The cream sauce of a vegetable gratin is something I like to eat with brown basmati rice, but barley, couscous, or quinoa would be just as suitable.

enough for 2 as a main dish with rice
chestnut mushrooms – 14 ounces (400g)
butter – a thick slice
olive oil
white wine – a small glass
heavy cream – 1¼ cups (300ml)
spinach – 14 ounces (400g)
Parmesan – 5 ounces (150g), grated

Preheat the oven to 350°F (180°C). Halve or quarter the mushrooms, depending on their size. Warm the butter and 2 tablespoons of oil in a deep pan and add the mushrooms, letting them color nicely here and there (expect to add more oil if they drink it all). Pour in the wine and bring to a boil. Continue to boil for a couple of minutes.

Pour the cream into the pan and let it come back to a boil, then simmer for two minutes. Turn off the heat. Wash the spinach and put it, still wet from rinsing, into a pan with a tight-fitting lid. Let the spinach cook for a minute or two in its own steam, then drain it and squeeze to remove excess water.

Reserve several tablespoons of the Parmesan. Fold together the mushrooms, drained spinach, salt and black pepper, and the rest of the grated Parmesan. Put into a shallow baking dish. Scatter the reserved cheese on top and bake for thirty-five minutes, until the top is crisp and golden.

A filling, carb-rich supper for a winter's evening

Early February, icy-cold day. I find great spinach in the shops but little to go with it. I grab a bag of those factory-made vacuum-packed gnocchi that always make me feel as if I have just eaten a duvet. With cream, blue cheese, and spinach, they have a rib-sticking quality that would keep out arctic cold, let alone a bit of urban chill. Sometimes I just need food like this.

enough for 2
vacuum-packed gnocchi – 1 pound (500g)
spinach leaves – 7 ounces (200g)
creamy Gorgonzola – 9 ounces (250g)
heavy cream – ¾ cup (200ml)
a little Parmesan or pecorino

Preheat the oven to 400°F (200°C). Bring a deep pan of water to a boil and salt it generously. Drop the gnocchi into the water and cook until they float to the surface—a matter of a few minutes. Drain and set aside.

Meanwhile, wash the spinach and remove the stalks. With the leaves still dripping wet, put them into a thick-bottomed pan set over medium heat and cover with a lid. The leaves will cook in their own steam in a matter of seconds. They are ready when they are completely wilted and bright emerald green. Remove them from the pan and let them cool briefly before wringing them dry. Now tear them up a little and put them, in lumps if that is how they are, into an ovenproof gratin dish or shallow baking dish. It should be large enough for the gnocchi to fit snugly in one layer. Cut the Gorgonzola into pieces and tuck in among the spinach, then scatter over the gnocchi.

Season with salt and black pepper, pour the cream over the lot—it won't quite cover everything, just sort of lap at the edges—then grate over a little Parmesan or pecorino, just enough so that you can see it. Bake until golden and bubbling—about thirty to thirty-five minutes. Serve piping hot.

Spinach, melted cheese, and lightly burned toast

Crisp toast, lightly burned at the edges, with a cargo of melting cheese is to my mind the ultimate snack. Spike it with mustard and I am probably at my happiest, but I do play around with the genre too: a layer of apple or homemade chutney under the cheese; a few bitter leaves of chicory or hot watercress on the side; a few capers, maybe.

Sometimes I take the recipe up a notch to give something that is more of a meal than a snack. Like when I trap a layer of cooked spinach between bread and cheese, or just mix the two together and give them a crust of toasted Parmesan. I could add that this is also a sound way of using bits of cheese that have accumulated in the fridge.

enough for 4
spinach – 9 ounces (250g)
English muffins – 4, or a short baguette or other toasting bread
crème fraîche – 5 tablespoons
smooth French mustard – a teaspoon
Taleggio or fontina – 3½ ounces (100g)
a little nutmeg
grated Parmesan

Wash the spinach leaves in plenty of cold running water and remove any coarse stems. Put the leaves, the water still clinging to them, into a thick-bottomed pan with a lid. Let the spinach steam for a minute or two, then remove it as soon as it is limp but still jewel bright. Cool it quickly under running water, squeeze the moisture from it with your hands, and set aside.

Toast the bread on both sides. If you are using muffins, split them by hand (to get a rough rather than knife-smooth surface) and toast them until pale gold.

Mix the drained spinach with the crème fraîche and mustard. Slice the cheese thinly and add it to the spinach with a good grinding of salt and black pepper. Grate over a very little nutmeg. I use no more than a mere three or four rubs across the fine teeth of the grater.

Pile the spinach onto the toasted bread, thickly to keep it juicy as it toasts, then dust it with grated Parmesan. Toast, on a baking sheet or grill pan, until the surface of the spinach and cheese starts to bubble, the Parmesan turning pale gold. Eat straightaway.

Tomatoes

We expect a lot of the tomato. *Lycopersicon esculentum* is not native to Britain. We do not have the ideal climate: too much rain, not enough scorching sun. They are fragile and do not travel well. Neither do we produce the olives and anchovies that seem so much a part of the fruit's soul. Even English basil, the tomato's inseparable seasoning, lacks the pepperiness of that grown in the Mediterranean. Yet for some reason, we expect to have the perfect tomato in our kitchen every day of the year. We import them thousands of miles, chill them, and then moan about their shortcomings. Surely we are expecting too much of a fruit that started out as a weed in South America.

The problem is the color. Red is the color of richness, ripeness, and sensuality. It is the color of the erotic. Scarlet is for anger and ecstasy, the color of love and lust (not for nothing is it the color of a Valentine's rose and a whore's lightbulb). Red signals a welcome and a warning. It is synonymous with Christmas and war. It is the color of blood. It is the color that probably has the greatest effect on our emotions. No wonder we expect so much of the tomato.

When a fruit is grown for flavor rather than its ability to travel without blemish, when it is given enough searing sun and not overfed and watered, it can add up to an intense experience. The way they are designed to burst in the mouth, to squirt their seeds and juice, to be both sharp and sweet at the same time, is what makes a lackluster tomato all the more frustrating.

Those I pick from my vegetable plot, their faces distorted with furrows and folds, often taste richer than the ones I buy at the markets. They respond to the wind and the brutal sun more favorably than those cosseted in the greenhouse. When people say tomatoes taste better in Italy, Spain, or France it is often because they have been grown outside. A tomato's character is enhanced by a rough life, a certain negligence, a gasping thirst, and the occasional drenching downpour. Pamper a tomato, overfeed it, overwater it, and you will get a Paris Hilton of a tomato. The rougher time it has, the more ugly its appearance, the more interesting it generally is.

I find the scent of a ripe tomato, especially that of its stem, faintly erotic. I always feel I have been "had" if there is no deep green, herbal smell to its stalk. I feel a fool for letting myself be seduced into buying. And yet that herbal scent is actually no guarantee of a richly flavored fruit, as anyone who has splashed out for tomatoes on the vine can testify. The plant and its smell can fool us.

Each time I pass them on my way up the garden, I rub their leaves and instantly sniff my fingers. It's a tender thing, and deeply appetizing in its intensity. As the months wear on, the habit becomes compulsive and I will occasionally break from my writing just to go out into the garden and stroke a leaf. By September it has become almost a perversion.

I devour them in the hand; eat them raw with olive oil, salt, and basil; grill them with oregano and garlic-rubbed bread; bake them with goat cheese; and occasionally simmer them as a sauce or soup. I marry them to the herbs of Southeast Asia and the dark spices of India. I simmer them lovingly into a purée, slice them into a sandwich, tuck them around the Sunday roast. It's a feast, a greedy, glorious feast.

But come the first frosts, I shut the door on the tomato. I have learned to live without them for the winter months. Occasionally I pick a few up, normally attached to their vine, hoping for just a shadow of that warm, peppery, herbal hit. Sometimes it is there, the ghost of a summer tomato you have grown for yourself. But more often than not I am disappointed and feel a fool.

A tomato in the garden

I have one precise memory of my father, still as clean and sharp as a pin, of him standing in his tobacco-scented greenhouse on a Sunday afternoon in late summer, pinching out the tops of his tomato plants with his finger and thumb—his way of encouraging them to direct their energies toward the swelling fruits. The smell of the discarded branches that filled the greenhouse, warm, green, and deeply aromatic, is possibly the best excuse I know for growing a tomato plant indoors. The scent is trapped in the humid greenhouse and you are engulfed by the very essence of deepest summer.

My father grew Moneymaker, the high-cropping, oh-so-perfectly-round fruit popular in the 1970s, which being in a greenhouse matured too quickly to develop the character of a fruit grown in the open air. The first I raised myself, balanced precariously on the stone windowsill of my first-floor flat, were the marble-sized Gardener's Delight, impervious to disease and almost impossible to kill. They were so refreshing in their sweet-sharpness that I picked as I watered. They never made it as far as the salad bowl.

Open to the rough slap of baking sun, rain, and the high winds that can hit this garden even in July, the fruit I plant now—Marmande, Costoluto Fiorentino, Green Zebra, and Sungold—brings along a certain expectation. I tend to be more attached to things I have grown myself than anything picked up at the markets. I develop a fondness for them, a certain wonder. My enjoyment may be heightened simply because I have had a hand in their upbringing (I am assuming one tends to like one's own offspring more than other people's).

The skin is a little thicker in outdoor-grown fruit but the flavor, like that of a free-range animal or bird left to cope with the elements, seems to have been cranked up a notch. If the sun has been relentless in July and August, the initial snap of sharpness will be backed up by a deep, mellow sweetness that requires neither salt nor pepper.

A tomato diary

Mid-April The plug plants from The Walled Garden have arrived by post, each stem barely the length of my little finger, with six long leaves attached, and ready to be potted on. I use an organic tomato compost, almost black and freckled with grit, which I buy mail order. The delicate plantlets go into tall plastic pots, one into each, and then into the cold frame. Before that I simply grew them on the windowsill, the pots tightly packed into a roasting tray lined with newspaper, where they fared just as well, if grew a little lankier than they do now. Anyone could do it.

May 4 I start to open the cold frame to the air during the day to give the plants a peek at what is to come.

Late May The plants have gone out into the garden, a good arm's length apart, each one supported by a thick bamboo pole to tie them to. They can grow to the height of a teenager. Snails love them, despite their hairy stems, so they are ringed with copper and labeled to make sure I don't forget which is which. For the last four years I have grown Marmande, partly for its gnarled beauty and its flesh that forms in furrows and folds to make an interesting shape on the plate. It is the tomato of the French street market, large enough to stuff and bake.

The most reliable is the large, heavily ribbed Costoluto Fiorentino, a classic variety from Florence. In my London garden, it is rarely ready until late August and will continue until the first frosts. The skins are usually tougher than those I have bought at grocer's shops in Italy, but the dense flesh slices as neatly as a raw steak, holding its seeds and glowing jelly. It is perfect for the classic tomato and mozzarella salad with olive oil and a handful of torn basil.

Late June The plants scattered around the garden appear to be biding their time. They look healthy enough but seem to be standing still, as if unsure what to make of all the rain. Other years have seen them in fruit by now.

Mid-July After sulking for weeks, all four varieties seem to have grown a good 8 inches (20cm) overnight. There are young fruits on the Marmande, already showing their characteristic ribs and nobbles. The leaves are covered in fine, white hairs, and just brushing past them emits waves of herbal fragrance on the morning air. I nip off the small shoots that grow at the axes between the stem and the horizontal branches. Left on, they sap the energy that the plant could put into producing fruit.

Late August Each morning I wake to find another Tigerella or Sungold has ripened. I like them best when they are still firm and slightly acidic. The larger fruit ripen slowly, the occasional one being removed if the clusters are too tightly packed. The bottom of the plant is browning but the upper leaves still produce their starlike flowers. Each fruit is treated like a precious egg, picked carefully and brought proudly into the kitchen. One or two of the plants have a bit of blight from the constant rain. I remove any brown, squishy fruit as soon as I spot them, and snip out any branches that are brown and soft. But the blight is almost inevitable toward the end of a wet season. Tragically, it can attack indoor-grown tomatoes too.

Late autumn In a good year, I am picking until the first frosts, by which time many plants will be thin, brown skeletons. At this point I pull the whole plant from the ground, shake off the soil, then hang it upside down indoors. Any stragglers will usually ripen.

Varieties

There are hundreds of varieties of tomato, from plums barely bigger than an almond to beefsteaks the size of a clenched fist. Some are red, pink, orange, yellow, purple, black, and even striped; some have thick skins, making them suitable for baking, others so thin they won't travel and need to be grown at home. Flavors vary from sharp and refreshingly sweet to the positively dull.

While some varieties thrive outside in our mixed climate, others need nurturing in a greenhouse. The following are those that have done well for me outside, have survived the occasional period of neglect and produced fruit to make this cook's heart sing.

Sungold* If you grow only one tomato, let this be the one. Sweet-sharp, small, golden fruit with masses of flavor. I grow it every year and it never fails to delight, even outdoors.

Gardener's Delight* Another cherry, but this time red. Probably the easiest to grow, it will never let you down.

Yellow Pear* A seventeenth-century variety with a mild flavor and much sugar. Vigorous and tough.

Green Zebra* Amber and green stripes, with crisp flesh and sharp, refreshing seeds. Gorgeous in a salad.

Costoluto Fiorentino* A large, ridged fruit that is happy outdoors. Rich flavor, almost herbal after a good amount of sunshine.

Marmande* A good cooking tomato this, and more than happy in our climate if we get a reasonable summer. Softly ridged, its thick skin means it is suitable for stuffing.

Auriga A large(ish), orange-fleshed variety that does well outside and looks very good in a salad with purple basil.

Brandywine* A knobbly, dark red and green variety with a spicy tomato flavor.

Black Krim* Dark and interesting-looking fruit with a very fine flavor.

Orange Santa Plum shaped but much smaller than Roma or San Marzano. A nicely sharp, rather cute addition to the garden.

*Available from US seed sources.

A tomato in the kitchen

The tomato plays less of a part in our traditional cooking than it does in the cuisines of Italy and Spain. You could trawl through old cookbooks and rarely come across a recipe that involved a cooked tomato. If we cook with them at all, it is mostly in recipes from other European countries—pizza, pasta sauces, slow casseroles, and soups. When we do, it is more often with the canned variety than with those fresh off the vine.

Cooking with fresh tomatoes can be a revelation to those who have been led along the canned tomato route. Cheap and convenient they undoubtedly are (and I would hate to be without a can or two), but canned tomatoes lack the sweet-sharp quality of a fresh one. They have a monotonous reliability that lacks spirit and vigor. I guess we like them because they always taste the same.

I have long used fresh tomatoes in curries to add a note of sweet acidity—and in braised oxtail and slow lamb stews. I add them to chicken sautés to simmer down to an impromptu sauce and bake them with bony cuts of lamb or with zucchini or eggplant. Slow cooked, they add a sharp richness to any dish.

It is rare, though, that cooked tomatoes are served as themselves. Occasionally they turn up stuffed with rice, onions, and golden raisins, in the Middle Eastern style or, as the Italians do, with rice, nutmeg, and Parmesan. Halved, grilled, and flecked with black pepper, they are part of the Great British Breakfast, the one that almost no one has any more. But the tomato is usually very much a member of the chorus rather than a star in its own right.

A cooked tom can be wonderful—a piquant, juice-filled orb of smoky, lip-puckering flavors. I roast mine with just a glug of olive oil and a few thyme leaves, until the skins char and split. I make an instant tomato sauce by crushing grilled or roast fruits with a fork and stirring in a little olive oil and torn basil. I tuck whole cherry tomatoes around the roast to break down into a rich sauce with the roasting juices.

A handful of mixed fruits in various sizes or shades, baked until they surrender their juices, makes a smart contrast to a ball of milkily soft buffalo mozzarella. Sliced, the little pear and cherry varieties add punch to a pizza, and can be tossed with linguine and basil. Their uses to the cook are almost endless.

Seasoning your tomatoes

Basil One of the most famous marriages of ingredients. Basil's warm, peppery notes have a profound effect on tomatoes, even more so when cool, milky mozzarella comes along to play.

Oregano The pizza herb. The musty notes work better in tomato sauces than in salads.

Salt Coarse, for teasing the sweetness out.

Cheese An age-old pairing. Any cheese, any tomato, it just works.

Anchovies The salty little fillets have an affinity with sweet, juicy tomatoes.

Olives In part, it is the saltiness of olives that makes them perfect for tomatoes, but they are linked in so many recipes that it is hard not to imagine them together. They form an ancient Mediterranean double act.

Thyme Tuck the odd sprig between the fruit as they bake.

And...

* Early-ripening tomatoes are often best for growing outside. Cherry varieties are particularly reliable.
* Grow bags are an excellent way to grow tomatoes for those with no garden. Tomato roots will happily grow horizontally if they cannot grow straight down.
* The key to a healthy plant is good ventilation. Try not to overcrowd them, and allow space for them to get plenty of air around them.
* A sunny spot is vital. They will take any amount of direct sunshine once they start fruiting.
* Blight is the biggest problem. It thrives in wet, humid summers. At the first sign of it, remove any infected leaves. It may not stop it, but it will slow down the spread.
* Feed plants with a good proprietary liquid food about every two weeks once the first fruit appears.
* The change from orange to red signifies the sweetening of the flesh within. If you like your tomatoes tart, pick them before they become deep crimson.
* Tomatoes hate fridges. Keep them in a cool room if you can. The cold affects both their flavor and their texture.
* To peel tomatoes, cut a small cross in the pointed end, dunk into boiling water for thirty seconds, then peel off the skin where it has started to split.
* Use the seeds and jelly from hollowed-out stuffed tomatoes in the stockpot.
* Ignore recipes that tell you to peel a tomato for salad. The skin would have to be very thick before this would be necessary.
* Bake tomatoes in a very hot oven. A cool one will make them watery.

A tomato for its own sake

You have found your tomato, sweetly ripe yet with a bite to it. It may still have the green shoulders of youth, or a few yellow freckles near its stalk. The seeded jelly inside will shine as you slice. As you have already resisted the temptation to eat it whole, you might like to slice it thinly, but no thinner than ¼ inch (6mm) thick. You lay the slices, overlapping, on a plate and drizzle olive oil over them, so that it falls in rivulets over the fruit. Fruity, peppery, green, or grassy, the choice is yours.

A little salt, barely noticeable, but no pepper this time. Just your tomato, oil, and a flick of sea salt.

A salad of bread and tomatoes

I have yet to have a panzanella that excites me. The name is so tempting, as is the sight of ripe tomatoes tossed with bread, herbs, and olive oil, but I have never found one that wasn't disappointing. At their best lackluster, at their worst slimy. One day I will find the glowing, basil-scented classic that so many people rave over.

My own version of this bread and tomato salad involves tossing pieces of garlic-rubbed toast with chopped red and orange tomatoes at the last minute, so that at least some of the bread stays crisp among the green oil and scarlet fruit. I chop up a mixture of tomatoes—red, orange, green, cherry, and pear shaped, even the odd beefsteak if it's very ripe—then put them and their juices into a bowl. I don't skin or seed, only twist out the herb-scented stalks, sniffing each one as I go.

I toast thin slices of sourdough loaf on the grill, until the centers are crisp and the outsides are black here and there. Pour olive oil—very green and fruity—over the tomatoes, toss in some torn basil leaves, and just a little wine vinegar. A clove of garlic, peeled and sliced as thin as tissue. Then a scattering of salt, and a twist of the pepper mill. I remove the toast from the grill, rub it with a cut clove of garlic, and tear it into pieces. The tomatoes and their juices are spooned into a deep dish, the toast tucked in, and then tossed, gently, briefly, before eating.

And with anchovies and basil

Slice your tomatoes in half and then into thick wedges. Toss them with olive oil and some torn basil leaves, then tuck in a few rinsed anchovy fillets. Pass round with a loaf for everyone to tear off as much as they need. The trick of this salad is to leave it for half an hour so that the anchovies and basil have time to season the juice.

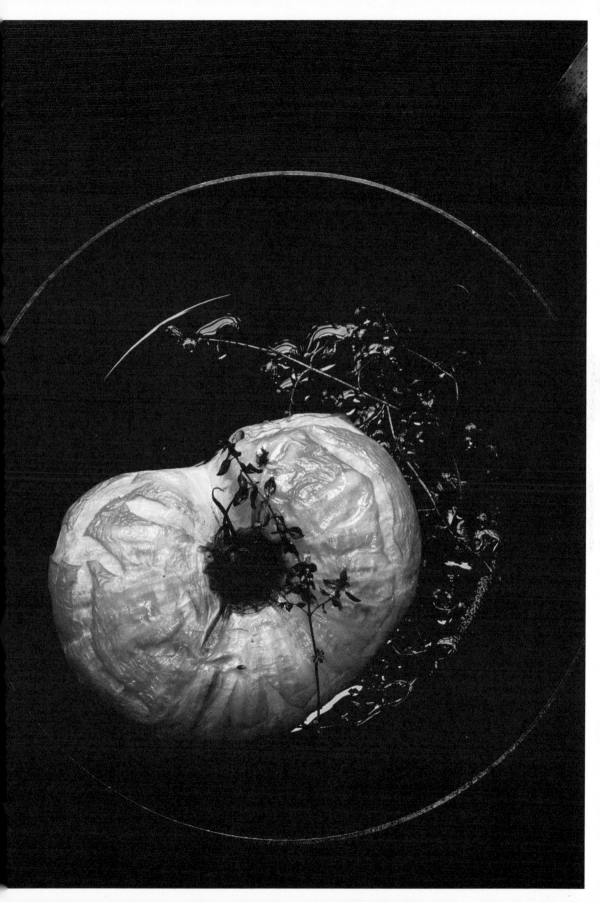

Roast cherry tomatoes

Put your tomatoes in a shallow roasting tin and drizzle olive oil over them. Grind over a little black pepper and add a few drops of balsamic vinegar. Toss them around in the dressing, then roast at 400°F (200°C) for about thirty minutes, until they are soft and oozing juices. Let them cool in their dish, so as not to waste a drop of their juice.

Baked tomatoes with cheese and thyme

The first time I made this, I discovered a wealth of delights: the way the tomato holds the little cheese like an eggcup holds an egg; the point at which the juice of the tomato and the melted cheese meet; and the subtle difference in smell and flavor depending on which cheese you use.

Two of these tomatoes are lunch for me if there is something else on the table—a couscous salad, perhaps, or some bread and salami. Others may want more.

enough for 2
large, ripe tomatoes – 4
olive oil
thyme – 4 or 5 bushy sprigs
fresh goat cheeses or other cheeses – 2 small

Preheat the oven to 350°F (180°C). Cut a thick slice from the top of each tomato. Using a teaspoon, scoop out enough of the seeds and flesh to make room for half a goat cheese (don't add the cheese yet). Put them snugly in an ovenproof baking dish, salt and pepper the inside, and add a teaspoon or so of olive oil to each one. Pull the leaves from the thyme and sprinkle them inside the tomatoes. Bake the tomatoes for twenty-five minutes, or until they are soft and lightly colored. Slice the cheeses in half if they are small, or in large pieces if they are larger than the diameter of the hollow. Whatever, just make the cheese fit into the tomatoes. Spoon a little oil from each tomato over the cheese, or add fresh oil if it has escaped, then return to the oven for ten minutes, until the cheese has melted.

A salad of roast tomatoes

A tomato's flavor intensifies in the heat of the oven. All its sweet-sharpness comes to the fore. I eat these warm, sprinkled with a little herb vinegar, sometimes sandwiched inside a crisp and chewy baguette.

enough for 4 as a side dish
medium tomatoes – 12
olive oil
thyme – 6 bushy sprigs
red wine vinegar

Preheat the oven to 400°F (200°C). Wipe the tomatoes and slice them in half across the middle. Put them, cut side up, in an ovenproof dish. Shake over a generous amount of good, though not expensive, olive oil and season with salt, coarsely ground black pepper, and the leaves from the thyme sprigs. Roast for about forty minutes, depending on the ripeness of your tomatoes, until they are puffed and tender. A few black edges will only add to their flavor.

As the tomatoes come from the oven, shake a little of the vinegar over them, then serve warm with crusty bread.

Slow-roast tomatoes with thyme and mozzarella

Late summer, the sun high, the vegetable patch is filled with slow-moving bees and tiny, piercing-blue butterflies. The day stands still, baking in the sunshine. The cats lie silently on the dusty stone terrace, too hot to move. It is the day for a lunch of melting softness. I wander into the kitchen on bare feet to roast tomatoes and break open a milky, silky buffalo mozzarella.

enough for 4
small to medium tomatoes – 16
olive oil
thyme leaves
buffalo mozzarella – 2 balls
basil – a small bunch

Preheat the oven to 325°F (160°C). Remove the stalks from the tomatoes and put the fruit into a small baking dish. They should fit snugly. Drizzle with olive oil and season with salt and black pepper. Pull the thyme leaves from their stalks and toss with the tomatoes and seasonings. Bake until they are truly soft and collapsing—a good hour or more. Pull the mozzarella in half. Put a half on each plate and season it with olive oil and torn basil leaves. Serve the roast tomatoes alongside.

Yellow tomatoes, grilled peppers

Grill a couple of red peppers until the skins blacken, then peel them. I find
the easiest way to do this is to put the still-hot peppers in a bowl and
cover with plastic wrap for ten minutes. This will help loosen their skins.

Once they are peeled, you will be left with soft, scarlet flesh, which
should be sliced into thick strips, then tossed with quartered yellow
tomatoes, olive oil, salt, and coarsely torn basil leaves. You could add
oregano, too, or cilantro if that is what is around. Let the salad sit for
a good twenty minutes before serving.

Parmesan tomatoes

A good savory little number this, fantastic with all manner of roasts and
grilled foods but equally worth making as a side dish for cool, almost liquid
mozzarella or a bowl of basmati rice flecked with torn herbs.

enough for 4 as a side dish
tomatoes – 1 pound (450g)
olive oil – 3 tablespoons
basil – a small bunch
Parmesan – 1½ ounces (40g), grated

Preheat the oven to 400°F (200°C). Cut the tomatoes in half and put them
into a bowl. Pour over the oil, then add a good grinding of black pepper and
a little salt. Tear the basil leaves and add them with the grated Parmesan.
Toss the ingredients gently together, then put them in an ovenproof baking
dish and bake for twenty-five to thirty minutes, until the tomatoes are soft
and the Parmesan is slightly crisp.

Roast beef with tomato gravy

Beef and tomatoes have enjoyed a long history together. Whether it's tomato ketchup on your burger or tomato paste in your beef casserole, the two have an established friendship.

Winter tomatoes—why do we buy them?—can add a surprising depth to gravy if they are roasted alongside the Sunday beef. I chuck them in with the onions and bay leaves that provide the background music for the gravy. The tomatoes sharpen up in the searing heat, their skin catches and burns, and they add a certain piquancy to the sweet onion and caked-on roasting juices. The winter tomato has at last found a point.

You may well want some roast potatoes to go with this. I usually boil them first for ten minutes, then drain and add to the roasting tin.

enough for 6
onions – 4
beef rib on the bone – 4 pounds (2kg)
a little oil or beef dripping
garlic – 6 cloves
tomatoes – 2
bay leaves – 3

for the gravy
all-purpose flour – 2 tablespoons
Madeira – a wineglass
stock – 2½ cups (600ml)
smooth Dijon mustard – a tablespoon
whole-grain mustard – a tablespoon or more to taste

Preheat the oven to 425°F (220°C). Peel the onions and boil them in unsalted water for fifteen minutes, then drain them. Smear the beef all over with oil or beef dripping, sea salt, and freshly ground pepper. Lay it in a roasting pan with the boiled onions, the whole, unpeeled garlic cloves, the tomatoes, and the bay leaves. Roast for twenty minutes. Decrease the oven temperature to 350°F (180°C) and continue roasting for a further ten minutes per pound (500g). When the beef is done, remove from its pan, then set it aside somewhere warm, lightly covered with aluminum foil to keep it warm while it rests and while you make the tomato gravy. (If you are roasting potatoes to accompany this, now is the time to take them out, put them in another dish, and continue roasting until crisp and golden.)

Squash the onions, tomatoes, and garlic in the pan with the back of a wooden spoon. Dust the flour on top and place the pan and its contents over medium heat, stirring almost constantly, until the flour browns a little. Pour in the Madeira and let it bubble a while, then add the stock and the mustards, stirring and scraping at the stuck-on roasting juices. Season, then leave to simmer, with the occasional stir, for ten to fifteen minutes (any longer and the gravy will lose much of its character). Check the seasoning and push through a coarse sieve into a warm pitcher—it really must be warm. Serve with the beef.

Seared beef, tomato salad

Most Asian markets carry Japanese nanami togarashi seasoning. It is a mixture of ground chile, orange peel, spices, and sesame seeds. For this beef salad, it is simply a question of rolling the beef in the seasoning and searing it quickly in a heavy pan. The beef is barely cooked and is eaten thinly sliced, like carpaccio. There will be some left over for tomorrow. I cannot think of a better accompaniment for it than a simple tomato salad.

enough for 4 as a light main dish
fillet of beef – 1 pound (500g)
olive oil
togarashi – 1 tablespoon

for the tomato salad
large, ripe tomatoes – 6
olive oil – 5 tablespoons (75ml)
red wine vinegar – 2 tablespoons
sugar – a pinch
cilantro leaves – a handful

Roll the fillet of beef in a little olive oil, then dust with the Japanese seasoning. Warm a couple of tablespoons of olive oil in a shallow pan and, once it starts to sizzle, brown the beef on all sides. Set aside to cool, then refrigerate for two hours.

Slice the tomatoes thinly and lay them on a serving plate. Make the dressing by mixing the olive oil, red wine vinegar, and a good pinch of sugar together, then stirring in the cilantro. Spoon the dressing over the tomatoes.

Remove the beef from the fridge and slice very, very thinly. It should be as thin as you can get it. Lay the slices on plates and serve with the tomato salad.

Baked tomatoes with chiles and coconut

How a dish smells is important. It whets the appetite, brings us to the table, and opens up a host of pleasures. With coconut, cardamom, and coriander, this simple dish of baked tomatoes is heady and aromatic. It curdles a bit, but no matter. You will need some rice or bread to go with it. Creamed coconut, a block of pure dried coconut, is available at Asian markets and online.

enough for 4
garlic – 2 cloves
a hot red chile or two
ginger – a thumb-sized piece
olive or peanut oil – 3 tablespoons
chile flakes – half a teaspoon
ground coriander – a teaspoon
ground turmeric – a teaspoon
cumin seeds – half a teaspoon
green cardamom pods – 6
moderately large tomatoes – 12
creamed coconut – 1¾ ounces (50g)
cilantro leaves – a handful

Peel and thinly slice the garlic. Halve the chiles and discard their seeds, then chop finely. Peel the ginger and slice it finely. It should be thin enough to see through. Warm the oil in a deep frying pan, then add the garlic, chile, and ginger, letting them soften but not color over medium heat.

Stir in the chile flakes, ground coriander, turmeric, and cumin seeds, then pop the cardamom seeds out of their husks, crush the seeds lightly, and stir them in. Once the spices have warmed through, chop four of the tomatoes, stir them into the spices, and pour in 1¼ cups (300ml) water. Bring to a boil, then slice each of the remaining tomatoes horizontally in half and lay them, cut side down, in the sauce. Cook for seven or eight minutes, until they are starting to soften. Turn each tomato over and continue to cook for a few minutes, until they are thoroughly tender.

Add the creamed coconut to the pan in small pieces, letting it dissolve into the sauce. A helpful stir with a teaspoon will work wonders here. From this point on, the sauce shouldn't boil, just simmer very gently until it is thick and the tomatoes are soft.

Once the tomatoes are tender to the point of collapse, they are ready. Scatter them with cilantro leaves and eat with a little rice or bread to mop them up.

A soup of tomatoes and crab

There is a small but distinguished group of seafood and tomato dishes, from the Provençal soups with their croûtes and brick-red rouille to Portuguese soup-stews reeking of garlic.

With those dishes as a starting point, I spent some time working on a soup of tomato and crab. After making several versions that were too thick and rich, I took the step of bringing chile and lemongrass into the proceedings to add a breath of freshness and vitality. This is a bright-tasting soup that sings with the sweet heat of chile and crustacean.

To add enough substance to treat it as a main dish (when this recipe will serve 3 or 4), I introduce a last-minute addition of bean shoots or maybe some shredded, very lightly cooked snow peas.

enough for 4 to 6
small green onions – 5
lemongrass – 3 stalks
olive oil – 2 tablespoons
a hot red chile
medium tomatoes – 4
chicken stock – 4 cups (a liter)
the juice of a small orange, or half a large one
mixed white and brown crabmeat – 1 pound (500g)
nam pla (Thai fish sauce) – a tablespoon
a lime, large and ripe
cilantro – a small bunch

Slice the green onions thinly, peel the outer leaves from the lemongrass, and cut the tender inner leaves into paper-thin slices. Warm the olive oil in a large, heavy-bottomed saucepan over medium heat, stir in the green onions and lemongrass, and let them soften without coloring. Seed and finely chop the chile, then add it to the pan.

Chop the tomatoes. You can peel and seed them if you wish but I really can't see the point. Stir them into the onions and let soften for a few minutes before pouring in the chicken stock and orange juice. Stir in the crabmeat, nam pla, and a little salt, bring to a boil, then decrease the heat immediately and let simmer for four or five minutes, stirring from time to time.

Squeeze in the lime juice. Coarsely chop a good handful of cilantro leaves and stir them in. Check the seasoning and serve piping hot.

A tomato salad with warm basil dressing

This colorful, big-flavored tomato salad is something you could eat alongside rose-pink cold roast beef, but it could easily make a more substantial candidate for a main course with the addition of a few croutons or some slices of olive oil–drenched toast. The colors are important here if the salad is to look lively—I usually use a mixture of tomatoes, including little pear-drop ones and yellow cherry tomatoes. I think it is worth adding that this is also good with cilantro instead of basil.

enough for 4 as a side salad
small shallots – 3
olive oil – scant ½ cup (100ml)
garlic – 2 cloves
flat-leaf parsley – 6 bushy sprigs
the juice of half a lemon
red wine vinegar – a tablespoon
anchovy fillets – 8
medium to large basil leaves – 20
small tomatoes – 25 to 30

Peel the shallots, chop them finely, and warm them in a shallow pan with the olive oil. Peel and finely slice the garlic and add it to the softening shallots. Remove the parsley leaves from their stalks and chop them coarsely. Stir them into the shallots with the lemon juice and red wine vinegar.

Rinse, dry, and coarsely chop the anchovies, tear up the basil leaves, and add both to the dressing. Taste and add a little black pepper if you think it needs it.

Cut the tomatoes in halves or quarters, depending on their size, dropping them into a mixing bowl as you go. Pour over the warm dressing (you should never get basil too hot), toss gently, and serve.

Turnips

I came rather late to the turnip. I had wriggled out of school dinners by living so close that I could walk home every day to eat. But once I had been moved to a school whose journey home through the country lanes took an hour or more, there was no choice but to queue up for stew and sponge. If the most eagerly swallowed dish was rhubarb crumble, with its soft, pebbly crust, the most difficult was turnip. It arrived at the table white and sour, a watery pulp as a side dish to leathery liver. A plate of hate. Yet it was served up with love and a smile, and lapped up by the rest of the local farming community. It just wasn't my thing.

Then I read, in a cookbook borrowed from the traveling library that pulled up once a month, that a woman called Elizabeth David cooked turnips with butter and superfine sugar until "the sauce turns brown and slightly sticky" and served them as an accompaniment to duck casserole with bacon and celery. Mrs. David pointed out that during their brief youth they cost "nearly as much as a hothouse peach." The mysterious woman with her foreign tastes got my curiosity up, though I am not sure I did anything about it.

Thirty years later, the arrival of the organic-box scheme in my neck of the woods brings lettuce so fresh its milky sap still sits on the cut stem, tomatoes whose stalks smell of warm spice, and carrots complete with their feathery tops. It also brings turnips. For months, I would lovingly place the new arrivals in the vegetable rack, sliding out last week's wizened bunch and sneaking them guiltily into the compost: "This week I will use you. I promise."

The turnip can be white, ivory, red, or golden. It can come with its shoulders brushed with lavender, moss green, or the hue of a wine stain. For a brief point in its life, it is small enough to hold in a bunch, like a posy. It can be cooked in butter and sherry, mashed with cream and butter, or given a glossy coat with sugar.

In the late 1800s, there were as many as fifty varieties listed, and the old names still intrigue: Long White Vertus, Vetch's Red Globe, Golden Ball or Orange Jelly, and Red-top Norfolk. Some have long, ratlike tails. In 1857 a seedsman said of Golden Ball, "A Cheshire variety of a handsome round form with a small top. The skin is pale orange, the flesh yellow and juicy, sweet and tender. When boiled, it almost acquires the consistency of jelly." Who could resist such a description?

The Romans knew the turnip, though hardly worshipped it, and part of its problems may stem from the fact that it has always been used as animal fodder. It has taken me most of my life to appreciate the turnip. To be charmed by its smooth skin, to be amused by the cheerful golden variety I get at the market, and to be happy to include it in my slow weekend cooking. There will always be a place in my kitchen for the turnip.

A turnip in the garden

Listen. I have never grown a turnip. I buy them from the farmers' market or the produce market when they are no bigger than a hen's egg. The ground space in an urban garden is precious and I find it wasteful not to use my few spare feet for growing something that is expensive or difficult to buy. And yet, if I had more room, I would grow a row or two of turnips. Just to taste, and let others taste, how good the freshly harvested ones can be.

The seed needs to go in where the vegetables are to grow—like carrots, they dislike being transplanted. Sow early and late, but not in high summer. They will need to end up a hand's width apart, so thin the seedlings as they get older. Friends tell me their turnips like a lot of water. You can do little with the green tops at this stage, bar chucking them in with green salad, but as they get toward eight or ten weeks old we can eat the green tops too, steamed for a minute or so. Unlike the rutabaga, the turnip won't stay in the ground over winter. They need to be pulled before the frosts.

Varieties

Orange Jelly* Also known as Golden Ball, a yellow-fleshed variety that I rate above all others for its tender flesh and mild flavor.
Snowball* Old variety, crisp and white. Good for grating raw.
Market Express Ready in six weeks or less. The one to grow if you want a sweet bunch of creamy white turnips only slightly bigger than a radish.
Purple-Topped Milan Crisp, mauve-shouldered white variety, popular for the last hundred years.

*Available from US seed sources.

A turnip in the kitchen

The older turnip appreciates a slowly ticking clock. Brought to tenderness in a stew deep with broth, simmered in chicken stock and mashed with a fork, baked slowly under a lid with sugar and sherry, the more mature turnip needs time if it is to get our interest.

Young specimens, barely bigger than a golf ball, can be cooked in half the time. These young turnips often have skins so thin they don't need peeling. They can be grated and tossed into a dressing or steamed and dressed with herb butter.

While I draw the line at saying every kitchen needs a turnip, I would suggest they are underused. Young and old alike are worth steaming, mashing, and buttering. They respond to a generous hand with the seasoning, and nothing good will come from being a tightwad with the butter.

As a vegetable with which to start a stew, the turnip provides a balance to the sweetness of the carrot, which alone justifies its place in the kitchen.

Seasoning your turnips

Orange Add grated zest or juice to the dressing of a raw turnip salad.
Sugar As valid a seasoning as salt and pepper for this vegetable.
Sherry Pour a little into a pan of butter-fried baby turnips.
Game Venison, mallard, pheasant, and squab will all benefit from a side dish of buttered roots.
Dill One of the few herbs that have any worthwhile effect here.
Bacon Add boiled and drained baby turnips to bacon that you have sautéed until golden.
Vinegar Sarah Raven has a lovely way with very young turnips, sweating them for five minutes in butter, then adding a little sugar and white wine vinegar before simmering them for a further ten. Very good with ham.

And...

* As a member of the cabbage family, the turnip likes a cool patch in the garden.
* You can store freshly dug turnips in the fridge if they are very small, in a box or bag in a cool place if they are larger than an orange. The larger ones will keep better than the small.
* Turnip greens make for good eating. Chop the washed leaves and thinner stalks, then cook in a very little water, as you might spinach. Toss with olive oil or melted butter and the merest squeeze of lemon juice.

Golden turnips with butter and sherry

First week of December 2007, cold and raining. The Fern Verrow stall at the market has a tray of golden turnips, the color of lavender honey and the size of Christmas baubles. I decided then and there to bake them in thick chunks with chicken stock and dill. I'm not sure where the dill idea comes from, other than the fact that it works with other root vegetables such as carrots, potatoes, and beets.

Once I get them home, it strikes me, perhaps rather later in life than it should, that a turnip might be better cooked without liquid. I cut each round root into six pieces from stalk to tip, put them in a heavy-bottomed pan with a thick slice of butter, a pinch of fudge-colored organic sugar, black-colored pepper, a splash of sherry, and some snipped dill. They sit over a low flame, covered with a puttering lid, until soft enough to crush between finger and thumb.

We eat them with a tray of faggots (meatballs of pork innards and belly) and gravy from the butcher. It could have been sausages. Sweet, earthy, warmly honeyed—I like the idea that something as mundane as a turnip could end up being unforgettable.

A little dish of sweet turnips

Drop tiny turnips into lightly salted boiling water and cook for ten minutes or so, until tender. Drain. Melt a thick slice of butter in a shallow pan and add the turnips and a spoonful of sugar. Cook over medium heat, shaking the pan from time to time, until the little orbs are glossy and sweet. The contrast between the sweet outer shell and slightly bitter turnip is astonishing with roast game birds.

Rabbit with bacon and turnips

Whereas most meats give us a choice of cooking on the bone or not, wild rabbit is one that really needs its bones if it is not to be dry. It is not the meatiest of choices, so you need to be generous with quantities here. Rabbit bones are small, and it's important to watch out for the tinier ones. The turnips in this provide all the carbs you need to soak up the sauce. It just needs some purple sprouting broccoli on the side.

enough for 3
wild rabbit (legs and saddle pieces) – 1¼ pounds (600g)
all-purpose flour
butter – 3 tablespoons (40g)
peanut oil
pancetta, in one piece – 7 ounces (200g)
small shallots – 6
turnips – 4 small to medium ones
dry Marsala – a scant ½ cup (100ml)
chicken or vegetable stock – 3¾ cups (900ml)
a little parsley
heavy cream – 4 tablespoons

Season the rabbit and dust it lightly with a little flour. Melt the butter in a little oil in a shallow pan over medium heat. Lightly brown the rabbit on all sides, then remove from the pan.

While the rabbit is browning, cut the pancetta into thick strips or cubes, then peel and chop the shallots. Once the rabbit is out, add the bacon and shallots to the pan and cook over fairly low heat until the shallots are soft but not colored. Cut the turnips into thick wedges and add them to the pan, together with 2 tablespoons of flour. Continue cooking briefly, then pour in the Marsala and stock. Bring to a boil, stirring gently.

Return the rabbit legs to the pan, but retain the saddle for the moment. Decrease the heat, cover with a lid, and let simmer for an hour and ten minutes, adding the saddle halfway through, until the meat is tender enough to slip from the bones with relative ease.

Coarsely chop the parsley and stir into the pan with the cream. Check the seasoning and serve.

A sweet and sticky casserole of duck with turnips and orange

As turnips do so well with orange, it is only a small step to use them with marmalade. Duck has this affinity too, so the three can come together successfully in a darkly sweet and rich casserole. Like duck à l'orange but sweeter and more suitable for a freezing winter's day.

The orange flavors here, from both fruit and bitter marmalade, should not dominate. The final flavor can be tweaked to your taste at the end with lemon juice or, better still, a bitter Seville orange.

Rice, pure and white, would be my first choice of accompaniment. If you start this dish the day before, you will have a better chance of removing most of the fat that floats to the surface.

enough for 3
peanut or vegetable oil
a large duck, cut into 6 pieces
smoked bacon – 8 ounces (250g)
onions – 2 medium to large
turnips – 4 smallish
ginger – a 1¼-inch (3cm) lump (about 1¾ ounces [50g])
light stock (or water at a push) – 4 cups (a liter)
the juice of 2 large, sweet oranges
bay leaves – 3
a stick of cinnamon
star anise – 2
marmalade – 2 to 3 tablespoons
the juice of a lemon or a Seville orange
rice, couscous, cracked wheat, or quinoa, to serve

Warm a very little oil in a Dutch oven or other heavy pot and lightly brown the duck in it, two or three pieces at a time. Drain them and set aside on paper towels. Cut the bacon into thick strips and add to the pan, letting them crisp lightly in the fat. Remove them and add to the duck. Meanwhile, peel and coarsely chop the onions.

Pour off all but 2 tablespoons of the fat from the pan, then add the onions and cook over medium to low heat, stirring occasionally. As the onions cook, peel the turnips, cut them into thick wedges, and add them to the pan. Cut the ginger into fine matchsticks, then add that too.

Once the onions have well and truly softened and are starting to turn pale gold, add the stock, orange juice, bay leaves, cinnamon stick, star anise, a generous grinding of salt, and some black pepper. Bring almost to a boil.

Return the duck pieces and bacon to the pan, decrease the heat to a slow simmer, and simmer for forty-five minutes to come slowly to tenderness.

Check the duck. It should be soft, but far from falling from its bones. Put the pan to one side and let it cool (if possible, you should leave it overnight). Scoop off as much fat as you can and discard. There will be quite a bit of this, and some is integral to the richness of the stew, so don't be too thorough about it. Just remove the excess.

Bring the pan back up to a simmer. Stir in the marmalade, then correct the seasoning with salt, pepper, and the juice of the lemon (or Seville orange, if you have one). The flavors should be warm, sweetly spiced, and with a comforting hint of marmalade.

Zucchini and
other summer squashes

The summer squashes, mild tasting, elegant, gently hued, are here from June until late autumn, when the hard-skinned winter varieties take over. Canary-yellow, green, and almost snow-white, they can be eaten skin, seeds, and all. Summer squashes appear in farmers' markets, allotments, and seed catalogues not just as the well-known long zucchini but as butter-yellow crooknecks, squat pattypans the shape of a Shaker pie, green golf-ball-sized Ronde de Nice, and, as the season takes its bow, plump, elephantine marrows.

Any tender-skinned variety can be used in place of the ubiquitous zucchini (so good when picked shiny and crisp from the plant), though the very small, round varieties may be a challenge to stuff. Try sheep's cheese and basil rather than ground meat. Their charm is in their quiet colors and gently bending shapes, and the pattypans, crimp edged like an apple tart, are heartbreakingly cute, but I would be hard-pressed to spot much of a difference in flavor.

What interest there is relies on the creamy taste of those picked very young, or the refreshing green quality of those cooked in olive oil with a final spritz of lemon. But we are not talking big flavors here; just the calm, nonconfrontational food that you might wish to eat on a summer's day in dappled shade. That thought alone is enough to have had me planting zucchini each spring for a decade, in pots, garden beds, and even on the compost heap.

It is curious that the British have taken up the French term *courgette* over the Italian *zucchini*. The latter is extraordinary—a lyrical word full of life and passion when said with an Italian accent, unlike the flaccid-sounding "courgette." I use the Italian at home when there is no one around to twitter about pretentiousness. My seeds come from Italy, as do the pots in which they germinate, the varieties themselves are Italian (Genovese, Romanesco, Bianco di Trieste) and I mostly cook them in the Roman manner, yet apparently I must give them the French name. What is more, as they are technically a fruit, but eaten as a vegetable, so too I swap the terms about to suit myself. Pedants will have a field day.

Lunchtime in Florence, a decade ago. We sit at a simple table set with a white cloth, thick plates, and tumblers for wineglasses. A dish is brought and placed in the center of the table, unasked for but gratefully accepted. The gift is two battered zucchini flowers, huge golden clouds the size of my hand and still hissing from the fryer. At their side sits half a lemon wrapped in frost-white cheesecloth.

We squeeze the lemon from on high and use a pinch of sea salt from the open saucer on the table. The batter shatters to send squirts of hot zucchini juice through our mouths. No garlic, no stuffing of Parmesan or ricotta, no herbs. Just a fragile (female) flower and its immature fruit encased in the lightest, crispiest, saltiest batter.

What followed was mostly pedestrian, but how could it not be, when the show had already been so successfully stolen? To this day, I have eaten very few zucchini in Italy that haven't been fried in some way, many in rustling slices on an earthenware dish, others cooked slowly in oil, always olive, with basil and garlic, or stuffed with the lightest ricotta and crisped in boiling oil.

My first encounter with a stuffed zucchini was in Greece, at a harborside restaurant without the help of a printed menu. Instead we wandered, stupefied by the searing heat, into the kitchen to point at whatever we liked the look of among an array of dented tin dishes of lukewarm, sleepy food. Zucchini lay slumped together stuffed with rice, raisins, oregano, and pine nuts, their filling jaundiced with saffron and finely mashed preserved lemons. Just as welcome was the sight of a sloppily tepid stew with eggplants, tomato, and onion that required little or no effort to eat.

Unlike spinach, broccoli, and tomatoes, the nutrient level of a zucchini is relatively low (the winter squashes have a rich supply of beta-carotene). Neither are they high on flavor, generally getting by with a little help from their friends, garlic, lemon, and tomato. Their popularity cannot be solely down to their ease of chopping. Yes, they stuff neatly enough, are refreshing in a crisp, tempura-style batter, and make a particularly fine fritter with salty cheese and dill (see *The Kitchen Diaries*), but will they stand up in their own right?

Those who dismiss the summer squashes, and there are many, might like to try a freshly picked crookneck, golden, or classic striped zucchini cooked lightly in olive oil until the flesh is translucent, seasoned with a generous pressing of a lemon, some sea salt, and a handful of torn basil leaves. Their charms will beguile even those who have previously written them off as all water (well, they are 90 percent). Moving on from the traditional rice stuffing and ratatouille-type melange, I offer a citrus-flavored salad, a basil- and tomato-scented quick supper, a sauté with bacon, and a hearty lentil filling for the larger specimens.

A zucchini in the garden

The squash family thrives on rich, moist soil and bright sunshine. Those grown on my compost heap, slightly shaded by a mirabelle plum tree, tend to produce more leaves than fruit. I have had as much success in pots as in the veg beds and conclude that the family is not fussy as long as you can keep it warm, well watered, and out of reach of slugs and snails who will, given the chance, feast on the fleshy stems like a panda on bamboo.

The flat, oval seed goes on its side into small pots of light compost no earlier than May. I keep it warm and slightly damp on a window ledge or outside in the cold frame until the young plants are a hand high, then carefully transplant them to a warm patch in the garden, a spadeful of muck dug in a week or two before (generous amounts of very well rotted manure will help the soil retain the essential moisture). You can also sow straight outdoors, but I find the snails tend to make a beeline for the downy-stemmed seedlings. The plants are ringed with coarse sand and a copper band to ward off the snails, and, if there is a spare one, a glass cloche to protect the young shoots from rain, wind, and clumsy fox cubs.

Squashes have a habit of sulking, then suddenly, when your back is turned, producing more fruits than you know what to do with. The pattypans are better behaved in this respect. I find that cutting any squash with a knife is preferable to tugging at them, which can easily weaken the stems of the main plant. Being soft skinned, they will not keep like the winter squashes, but a few days in the fridge will do little harm.

Each plant will contain both male and female flowers. Like birds, the cock flower has the more dramatic plumage. It is the larger male flower that is most suitable for stuffing, the smaller female one that produces the fruit. The male flower can be seen tied in bunches in Italian markets, like great golden throats. They are picked early, before they have time to fertilize the female flowers. Their job done, the male flowers flop, then shrivel.

Varieties

For ten years or more, I have grown Striato Pugliese, a bright green, striped zucchini with good flavor, and now and again, the delicate eau-de-nil, scallop-edged Peter Pan.

Gold Rush* An early, heavy-cropping zucchini-style squash with a crisp texture that some say is redolent of mushrooms.
Lebanese White Bush, White Egyptian* Beautiful, almost white variety, shaped like a small eggplant, this is the one for Middle Eastern dishes. Looks coolly elegant with mint.
Ronde de Nice* Bright green, round squash, good for stuffing (Sally Clarke has a sumptuous recipe with cream, porcini, and rosemary). Suitable for small gardens due to its compact habit.
Costata Romanesca* Heavily ridged, pale green fruits with good flavor (for a zucchini). Mine always produce a lot of male flowers of exceptional size, so ideal for stuffing. Generally sweeter than the dark green varieties.
Green (or Black) Milan Smooth, long, dark, and handsome.
Sweet Dumpling Tubby, cool mint green with darker stripes and freckles, this late-season squash is cute for stuffing. Harvest in October.

*Available from US seed sources.

The zucchini diaries

Mid-April Three Striato d'Italia plants arrive in the post. I have previously grown them from seed (follow the suggestions in the winter squash chapter on page 462) but this year I decided to try plug plants instead. Their juicy stems seem so fragile as I pot them up in rich compost in long, plastic pots. They settle in the cold frame, well watered.
Late May I plant them out, a tad later than I had hoped, in a bed that gets much sun. The plants are already top heavy and have to be supported with sticks. I put in seeds of Caserta and Cocozelle too, a variety that promises to be more of a marrow than a zucchini.
Early June I pop a spadeful of manure in the holes before lowering in half the plants. The others I transfer to a large terra-cotta pot, a backup I suppose, in case it turns out to be too soon to set them free in the garden.
Late June Suddenly the leaves seem to have grown to the size of sunflowers, their edges sharp and hairy. Like teenagers, watery vegetables seem to erupt into adulthood overnight. The flowers are profuse now, and the size of an outstretched palm. Some have no fruit underneath, but a couple of others have the first signs of a striped green zucchini plumping up under the vivid yellow flower.

July 15 I pick the first pair of zucchini. One is perfect, the other charmingly bent at the end. They are firmer and crisper than those from the markets and more brilliantly colored. We cook them in shallow Tuscan olive oil with nothing but salt and a squeeze of lemon.

August 2 The fruits are coming regularly now, each one taking about ten days to ripen. I pick them small, no larger than my index finger. Once every two weeks I give them a drink of liquid fertilizer, avoiding the leaves.

August 3 I am sitting on the back step gazing at Caserta in its wide terra-cotta pot. The marbled lime and acid green leaves jagged as the teeth of a saw; the flowers a rich saffron yellow. A rare plant, more decorative than d'Italia or Black Milan. Of its fruit, I know nothing yet.

August 25 Every time I open my eyes, another cheeky fruit is waving itself explicitly at anyone who passes.

October 5 Nothing but a marrow left, though the flowers are still coming, their deep-golden petals looking beautiful in the early autumn vegetable beds. None is frost hardy, and clearing away the soggy tangle of blackened stems one frosty December weekend is always strangely pleasing.

A zucchini in the kitchen

In an ideal world, the zucchini you buy at the market would come complete with its cheerful yellow flower. The blossoms, opening at dawn, last only a day, and in the relentless sun in my garden even less, collapsing in a soggy blob by nightfall. No wonder markets never have them for sale with their golden trumpet attached. Yet I have seen them sold that way on the canal boats in Venice and in small produce markets in the backstreets of Florence too. Occasionally they pop up at the farmers' market in Britain, a rare and showstopping find.

The shops here don't always treat what they sell with as much care as they do in Italy. The zucchini, with its stripes and speckles, dots and dashes, is a fragile fruit, its soft skin easily scarred by careless handling, yet they tend to be chucked around quite roughly in the markets. A recently picked zucchini has a gloss to it, and a clean, freshly cut, slightly hairy stalk. They look perky. There should be no scratches or blemishes. If you like the look of what you see, then squeeze it gently. If it is anything but firm, let it go. A flaccid zucchini is pointless. A recently picked one will keep well in the fridge, or in a cool place wrapped in newspaper, for up to a week. They lose their gloss as they age. A dull zucchini is an old zucchini. Inside, the seeds should be barely visible. Big seeds are a sure sign of aging vegetables.

Few zucchini are picked at a tender age, when they are barely the size of your index finger, but I think they should be. That is when they are probably at their best—glossy, toothsome, and with a mild, creamy flavor. Left too long on the plant or in the vegetable rack, they become dull, thick skinned, and woolly, but still edible enough if you scrape out the seeds with a teaspoon and bake the rest slowly with garlic and tomatoes.

The lone Great Dish in the zucchini's repertoire is *fiori di zucchini fritti*, the single flower dipped into very light batter (I make mine with fizzy mineral water) and deep-fried, then served with sea salt and a wedge of lemon. Often, they are stuffed with an almost ethereal filling of ricotta flavored with grated lemon zest and chopped basil. This is their moment of glory. But they are also fine when stewed with tomatoes and garlic, or stuffed with rice, pine nuts, and golden raisins, or part of a plate of roasted vegetables with garlic and thyme tucked among them.

You can bake a zucchini (with anchovy and breadcrumbs), stuff it (with ground veal, prosciutto, and Parmesan), or grate it, fresh from the garden, into a salad dressing. In the Trentino area of Italy, land of mushrooms and *tortelli di patate*—the crisp potato pancakes that accompany so many of the local dishes—they make thin slices of the fruit held in a fragile pancake of egg and grated Parmesan, known as *frittata di zucchini*. Note the habit of baking and frying. Nothing good will come from cooking any of this tribe in boiling water.

Zucchini share a species name, *Cucurbita pepo*, with summer squashes, winter squashes, and pumpkins. They are all made up of a large percentage of water, with mild flesh and, in the case of some of them, an edible skin when young. They are worth trying grated and tossed with hot olive oil, young thyme, and a squeeze of lemon. The dish takes just ten minutes, unless you grate too fast and need to hunt out a Band-Aid. I have found myself daydreaming while grating a large batch of zucchini.

While most summer squash will ripen in the languid, half-hearted warmth of a British summer, they need feverish heat in the kitchen if they are not to collapse into blandness. I prefer zucchini cut into finger-thick strips, like fat French fries, rather than rounds. Why? Because cut that way they retain a little more body and crispness.

For an ingredient with such a high percentage of moisture, the zucchini grills surprisingly well. Sliced into ribbonlike strips down its length, briefly salted, and rested in a colander to remove excess liquid, then patted dry and cooked over charcoal, it will take on a profound nuttiness. But it needs a good dressing of fruity olive oil, lemon, and fresh herbs. By which I probably mean basil.

The zucchini has long played a defining role in the Middle Eastern kitchen. Both sumptuous feasts and simple family dinners often include a dish of stuffed zucchini, limply tender, collapsing under the weight of their filling. Traditional stuffings, varying from family to family but often including tomatoes, green onions, and rice, are seasoned with mint, lemon, cinnamon, golden raisins, and sometimes sumac, the purplish lemony-flavored berries. In my book, this is food for the gods.

Seasoning the summer squashes

Basil For tearing up and scattering over crisply fried zucchini or for peppering up a tomato and zucchini fry-up.

Lemon Squeeze some over crisply fried slices of zucchini.

Garlic Because it just works.

Tomato For vegetable stews and thick, bean-speckled soups.

Golden raisins Strange one this, but the plump, golden dried fruits work well if included in a stuffing with pine nuts or tossed in a sauté with parsley and lemon juice.

Mint Toss with sliced zucchini before and after baking with olive oil. The dried herb works surprisingly well in stuffings.

Dill For including in cakes, salads, and pickles.

Olives and olive oil The saltiness of olives brings out all the sweetness in a zucchini. My own preference for cooking all summer squash is olive oil, while butter seems more appropriate to the winter varieties.

And...

* Sow the seeds on their sides. When sown flat, the water sits on their surface and they can rot.

* I get the best results when I am generous with the water and the manure.

* The yellow zucchini seem to have a softer skin than the green, and need gentler treatment in the pan. They tend to break up more easily.

* Unusual squashes don't always tell us whether they are thin-skinned summer varieties or thicker autumn ones. Tapping the bottom with your knuckles is a good clue. If it sounds hollow, then it is usually a "keeper." Silence means it's one that should be used quickly.

* The smaller the zucchini, the denser its flesh will be. It's the older specimens that have a loose, woolly texture.

* Deep-fried zucchini or their flowers make a refreshing first course with a little hollandaise or thinned garlic mayonnaise, but I often use them as an accompaniment to a lamb steak, or maybe a nice piece of beef rump. Deep-fried zucchini slices are sensational with steak béarnaise.

* Don't even think of freezing a glut of squashes. They lose all their magic. Make chutney instead. Better still, pass them round.

* As a rule, I find the round, crookneck, or pattypan summer squashes can be substituted for zucchini in any recipe. The flavor won't be exceptionally different but they can look very beautiful on the plate. The larger seeds present in some of the smaller pattypans are entirely edible. As the fruits get bigger, so do the seeds inside.

* All the summer squashes are good with fish. Lightly sautéed, zucchini are a suitably timid accompaniment to sea bass, haddock, and pollock.

Fruit and nut filling for baked zucchini

The ideal here would be the pale, plump zucchini varieties you find in Middle Eastern markets. I visit one near London's Edgware Road that even has them ready prepared, their seeds removed for stuffing, and packed into little plastic crates. If these torpedo-shaped squashes escape me, and they often do, then I use the ubiquitous type, halve them lengthwise and scatter the filling loosely over the top rather than making a clumsy attempt to stuff them.

The classic zucchini stuffings of the Middle East vary from family to family but usually include cooked rice or ground lamb, or occasionally walnuts, pine nuts, or hazelnuts, stirred into softened onion and then lightly seasoned with allspice, tomato paste, and parsley. The effect is a moist filling of elegance and pleasing predictability.

I sometimes want something more unusual. A stuffing that intrigues as much as it pleases.

enough for 4
a small to medium onion
olive oil
fresh white breadcrumbs – 1 cup (50g)
dried apricots – 1¾ ounces (50g)
pistachios – ⅓ cup (40g)
couscous – 1 cup (150g)
vegetable stock – 1 cup (250ml), boiling
thyme leaves – a tablespoon or so
the grated zest of a small lemon
parsley – a handful, chopped
zucchini – 8 medium to large

for the sauce
a small bunch of dill
a small clove of garlic
white wine vinegar – 2 tablespoons
olive oil – 3 tablespoons
yogurt – ¾ cup (200g)

Peel the onion, chop it finely, then let it soften with a little olive oil in a shallow pan over medium heat. Stir in the fresh breadcrumbs. Chop the dried apricots and the pistachios, then add them to the pan. Remove from the heat. Preheat the oven to 350°F (180°C).

Put the couscous in a heatproof bowl and pour over the boiling stock. Pour in a small glug of olive oil, then cover with a plate. Set aside for about ten minutes.

Add the thyme leaves, lemon zest, and chopped parsley to the breadcrumb mixture, then season thoroughly with salt and black pepper.

Once the couscous has soaked up all the liquid, stir it into the stuffing with a fork (this helps to keep the grains separate). Slit the zucchini in half from stem to tip and lay them snugly, cut side up, in a shallow ovenproof dish. Scatter the stuffing over the zucchini, cover the dish with aluminum foil or buttered parchment paper, and bake for twenty-five minutes.

While the zucchini bake, chop the dill, crush the garlic, and stir in the vinegar and olive oil. Beat in the yogurt with a small whisk or fork. Serve with the baked zucchini.

Zucchini on the grill

Young summer squashes of any sort grill rather well, but better if you salt them first, so that they relax rather than harden over the heat. As soon as they are lifted off the bars, I toss them in dressing, keeping them moist and silky. A side dish, and very good with mozzarella or feta.

enough for 2 to 4
courgettes – 4 medium
the zest and juice of a lemon
olive oil – 3 tablespoons
a small bunch of basil leaves

Wipe the zucchini and slice thinly along their length. I like to make them no thicker than ⅛ inch (3mm). Put them in a colander in the sink. Grind over a little salt and leave for half an hour. Prepare the grill. Once they are covered with little beads of moisture—as if they have broken out in a flop sweat—pat them dry and put the slices on the grill. Let them brown lightly in stripes on the underside, then turn them over and brown the other side.

Meanwhile, make the dressing. Grate the zest from the lemon into a mixing bowl. I do this finely and lightly, as any white pith will make the dressing bitter. Add the lemon juice, then beat in the olive oil with a fork or small hand whisk. Add a pinch of salt and black pepper. Coarsely tear the basil leaves, depending on their size—I like to leave small ones intact. Lightly crush them in the hand to release the oils, then add them to the dressing.

As each slice of zucchini becomes ready, drop it into the dressing and mix gently so that the slices become completely soaked. Set aside for ten minutes for the flavors to marry and the vegetables to soften slightly.

Spiced zucchini-and-carrot fritters

Small squashes deep-fry particularly well, offering a refreshing, almost juicy contrast to the ethereally crisp batter. This is one of those recipes—pancakes are another—that I tend to make when there are just two of us, and we can eat our sizzling fritters at the stove while the next one cooks. I find I get a much crisper result if I don't overcrowd the pan.

makes 6 or 8
a large carrot
a large leek
zucchini – 2
a large red chile, seeded
shredded cilantro leaves – a tablespoon
garlic – 2 cloves, chopped
self-rising flour – ¾ cup (100g)
baking soda – half a teaspoon
garam masala – 2 teaspoons
ice-cold water – about ⅔ cup (175ml)
oil for frying

for the chile sauce
plain yogurt – ⅔ cup (150g)
red and yellow chiles – 2 or 3 small, hot ones
cumin seeds – a teaspoon
cilantro leaves – a handful, roughly torn

Put the yogurt for the sauce into a bowl. Seed and finely chop the chiles, then stir them into the yogurt. Toast the cumin seeds in a dry nonstick pan, then, as they start to smell warm and dustily nutty, stir them into the sauce with the coarsely torn cilantro.

Cut the carrot and leek into fine strips about the length of your finger. Cut the zucchini and chile into very fine slices. Put all the vegetables and the cilantro and garlic into a bowl. Put the flour, baking soda, garam masala, and a generous amount of salt and pepper into another bowl, then beat in enough cold water to make a smooth but sticky batter. Add the vegetables and toss thoroughly.

Heat the oil in a deep pan. Carefully drop large tablespoons of the mixture into the hot oil, about four dollops at a time. Fry for three or four minutes, until they are puffed and golden. Serve hot, with the chile sauce.

A supper of zucchini, tomatoes, and basil

2008 saw not only my usual terra-cotta pots of Striato d'Italia on the back steps but also a trailing variety known as Caserta, a pale fruit the color of mint ice cream, with darker stripes. The light-skinned varieties such as Clarion, Di Faenza, and the almost ivory Lebanese White Bush look particularly delicate and summery when sautéed in butter and olive oil with a handful of herbs thrown in at the last moment, the scent of late summer hitting you as you spoon over the pan juices. Perhaps that should be swoon.

Squashes of every variety love a tomato. Occasionally you could argue they need it too. Late last summer, just as the beans were forming on the poles in the vegetable beds, I made a last-minute, rough-edged supper with little more than a few zucchini and a couple of tomatoes. It was done in fifteen minutes flat. There are many who would insist on skinning and seeding the tomatoes for this, but not only do I think it unnecessary here, it also means missing out on all their rich juices and scrunchy seeds.

> *enough for 4 as a side dish, 2 as a principal dish*
> zucchini – 5 medium
> olive oil – 3 tablespoons
> tomatoes – 4 medium to large
> basil leaves – a handful, torn
> lemon

Cut the zucchini into thick fingers. I think they work best about the size of thick, homemade French fries. Warm the oil in a deep pan and let the zucchini cook over medium heat for six to eight minutes or so, till they start to soften.

Chop the tomatoes roughly and add to the zucchini with the torn-up basil leaves, salt, pepper, and a good squeeze of lemon. Stir, cover with a loose-fitting lid, and let simmer for ten to twelve minutes, until the zucchini are totally tender and the tomatoes have cooked down to a basil-scented saucy slush. The colors should be bright, the zucchini softly yielding but not browned. Sponge up the sunny-tasting juices with bread.

A quick way with zucchini

This one is very useful when you need a vegetable in a hurry: you cut them into short pieces and toss them into a pan of hot olive oil, leave them to the tenderness fairy, then, when they are golden at the edges, season with lemon juice, salt, and black pepper. Add a scattering of hand-torn herb and you have a ten-minute vegetable dish of surprising freshness and refinement. A mound of brown rice at their side and you have supper, albeit one without protein.

A Thursday night supper

Thursdays are when we tend to make the best of a bad job, a supper prepared from whatever is left in the fridge (usually bacon or pancetta and a long-life vegetable of some sort). This is when we clear out the fridge before the Friday organic box and the Saturday trip to the market. While a winter rummage usually ends up as soup, a regular summer supper involves a hot frying pan, some smoked bacon, and a couple of zucchini.

I cut the bacon into cubes and let it cook with a little olive oil in a shallow pan. As the fat turns from white to gold, I dice a few zucchini and drop them in with a grinding of salt. An occasional stir, enough to stop them sticking but not so much that they fail to color, and then some salt. The dish is ready when the vegetables are tinged with gold, the bacon dark and smokily fragrant. I put it on a plate with a final drizzle from the olive oil bottle and some easily torn bread such as ciabatta. Sometimes I will add a few thyme leaves with the squash, a little rosemary at the beginning of cooking, or some basil at the end.

A lemon- and garlic-scented side dish

Middle Eastern cooking is flecked with the cool pepperiness of fresh mint. Italian, and especially Sicilian, cooks include mint with zucchini, often in tandem with garlic and lemon. I find mint invigorating with all summer squashes and often make a dish where they (pattypan is particularly suitable) are cooked in olive oil with mint and the merest hint of garlic. It is very good with grilled fish.

enough for 2
small zucchini – 14 ounces (400g)
garlic – 2 cloves
olive oil – 3 tablespoons
mint leaves – a good handful
flat-leaf parsley leaves – a small handful
the juice of half a lemon

Cut the zucchini in half lengthwise and then into short lengths. If they are real babies, you could simply halve them.

Peel the garlic and coarsely chop it. Warm the olive oil in a shallow pan. Add the chopped garlic, let it fry for a minute over medium heat, then add the zucchini. Let them cook in the oil, turning them occasionally, until they are lightly golden and tender. Add the whole mint leaves and parsley leaves. Increase the heat, pour in the lemon juice, and let it bubble briefly. Crumble over a little sea salt.

Zucchini and green lentils to accompany slices of dark and interesting ham

Green lentils and bacon has long been a salad worth making. I will occasionally fold in some shards of crisp, olive-oil-drenched toasted ciabatta or lots of whole parsley leaves. A couple of years ago I started moving the whole thing up a notch by putting the lentils against a few pieces of exquisite Spanish ham and adding a certain smokiness with wide slivers of zucchini, their edges blackened from the grill. This has become a late-summer lunch I can't get enough of.

enough for 4

for the salad
zucchini – 4 medium
small, dark green lentils – ¾ cup (150g)
olive oil – 2 tablespoons
parsley – a good handful, coarsely chopped
very thinly sliced jamon – 3½ ounces (100g)

for the dressing
red wine vinegar – a tablespoon
sherry vinegar – a tablespoon
olive oil – 4 tablespoons
a small clove of garlic, crushed
green onions – 4

Slice the zucchini into long, thin ribbons about the thickness of a piece of lasagne. Put them in a colander with a scattering of salt and set aside in the sink or on a plate for a good half hour, longer if you have it.

Cook the lentils in boiling, lightly salted water until tender but retaining a nutty bite. They are usually ready in fifteen to twenty minutes, but I start checking them after ten or so. I think it's essential that they keep their shape and don't soften. Drain them in a colander.

While the lentils are cooking, make the dressing by mixing the vinegars, the oil, and the crushed garlic together with a little salt and black pepper (I like to dissolve the salt in the vinegar first before adding the oil). Thinly slice the green onions and stir them into the dressing. As soon as the lentils are drained, toss them in the dressing and cover.

Mix the olive oil with the coarsely chopped parsley. Get the grill hot. If you prefer, a ridged grill pan will do.

Rinse the salt from the zucchini, pat them dry, then cook them on the hot grill until their flesh starts to soften and they have charred a pleasing golden brown here and there. As you remove each from the grill, toss it in the olive oil and parsley. Divide the lentils and zucchini among four plates, and eat with the ham.

A salad of raw zucchini, lemon, and toasted Parmesan

I was once rebuked for putting raw zucchini in a salad. Rather than tasteless, I found them to be nutty and pleasingly lactic. After having had my wrist slapped, I forgot about the idea for several years.

In the wet July of 2008, I spent a rare hot afternoon at Petersham Nurseries in Richmond, filling the car's trunk with wine-colored pelargoniums and pots of thyme for the back steps. Lunch was in the hands of Skye Gyngell, whose food I find tantalizing and delicately balanced. Her menu included a salad of raw zucchini. I felt vindicated. Perhaps I had been before my time. Skye had used zucchini the size of my little finger, sliced lengthwise and layered in a fragile pile with the vegetable's own flowers—eaten raw—and a dressing of basil oil and lemon zest. The real revelation was the pepperiness of the flowers and the extraordinary creaminess of the young zucchini. They had the quality of freshly picked wet walnuts, something they possess only when very young and fresh from the vine.

The accidental marrow

Marrow is a long, fat, green-and-white summer squash—rather like an overblown zucchini. The marrow is a handsome vegetable (one could say proud) and even more so when it appears at British harvest festivals propped against a jam jar of pink, red, and yellow dahlias. It looks good in the golden light of a church window on an autumn afternoon, rather less so in your own vegetable rack.

While I have never got into the whole show bench vegetable scene—the marrow was born to sport a rosette—it is fun to find them in the garden, lurking under the giant leaves like a beached tugboat. It is only as I try to cut through its shell with a not-so-sharp kitchen knife that I begin to regret the marrow's presence in the kitchen.

In the oven, the flesh softens to a buttery consistency, then collapses into a juicy slush. I like this for its refreshing quality, and for the delicate way it picks up the hint of garlic or tomato, tarragon or ginger that it is cooked with. Others feel the marrow's wateriness is a quality they can live without. The traditional English recipes involving ground meat in a coat of white sauce that one can trace back to the eighteenth century leave me cold, but once you bring in sweet-sharp tomatoes, young garlic, toasted pumpkin seeds, matchsticks of ginger, or a fistful of cilantro leaf and lemon, you are in for a pleasant surprise. The golden rule is to season well and bake but never boil.

I have never deliberately grown a marrow. In 2005 I grew several by accident, having overlooked a zucchini or two that grew like Topsy to give a zucchini suitable for cooking as a marrow. The two are botanically different, but an inflamed zucchini can be cooked as a marrow if it is not woolly inside, though it will lack the keeping quality of a true marrow.

Their names charm: Badger Cross, Tiger Cross, Green Bush. Their mottles and stripes have turned my organic box into a scene from a country show. I have eaten them baked with olive oil and butter (the marrow, for some reason, seems happier cooked with butter than olive oil, though I have no idea why), with corn and parsley, with lentils, basil, and peas, and yet I have never planted one. If there is ever a marrow in my kitchen it is by (happy) accident.

A lentil stuffing for a cheap supper

A marrow for supper will generally coincide with the leaves turning on the trees, the first early morning mists, new school uniform. Their bulk and their bargain-basement price ensure that they will make a cheap supper. For this, we love them. This filling—earthy, sloppy, and much nicer than ground meat—is good for pumpkin too.

> *enough for 4*
> small brown or green lentils (French lentils are perfect) – 1 cup (200g)
> a medium-sized marrow (or pumpkin)
> olive oil
> shallots – 2 large, or an onion
> garlic – 2 large cloves
> tomatoes – 6 medium, or 20 cherry tomatoes
> chile sauce, such as harissa
> green leaves, such as spinach or chard – 2 handfuls
> grated Parmesan – 2 tablespoons

Preheat the oven to 350°F (180°C). Bring a pan of water to a boil in which to cook the lentils. Add the lentils to the water and let simmer, I think rather vigorously, until you have tender lentils. On this occasion they should be soft rather than al dente.

Cut the marrow in half lengthwise but do not peel it; the rind will give it some support. Scoop out the core and put both halves into a roasting pan, then brush with olive oil and put in the preheated oven. Bake the marrow until tender and translucent—about twenty minutes—then remove from the oven. You could, alternatively, steam it.

Meanwhile, peel and slice the shallots and garlic and soften them in a saucepan with three tablespoons of olive oil. Chop the tomatoes, peeling them if they have tough skins (dunk the whole tomato into boiling water, then peel off the skin after a few seconds), and add them to the pan. Let them cook a while, till they are soft and mushy, then stir in your chile sauce. I use a couple of teaspoons of harissa here. The amount will depend on which chile sauce you have around and how hot you like your lentils to be. Remember that the marrow will soften the heat. Pour in just enough water (I use barely a cupful) to make a slushy sauce and be generous with the salt and black pepper.

Drain the cooked lentils, then stir them into the onion and chile sauce. Tear the spinach or chard leaves into small pieces and stir them into the lentils. Bring to the boil, then cover and let simmer over low heat until the greens are silky soft. Spoon the lentil mixture into the hollows in the marrow, scatter with the grated Parmesan, cover with aluminum foil or wax paper, and bake for twenty minutes.

Baked marrow, ground pork

A contemporary take on the ground meat–stuffed marrow. This economical supper stands or falls by the way the meat is cooked. The real flavor here comes from the caramelization of the sugars in the meat. To make the most of this, I have the oil at quite a high temperature as I add the meat, then resist the temptation to stir or turn the meat too soon. Continual movement will result in "wet" rather than crisp-edged, golden ground pork.

enough for 2 as a main dish

for the marrow
young marrow or large zucchini – 1½ pounds (750g)
garlic – 2 cloves, crushed
mint leaves – a handful
olive oil
the juice of half a lemon

for the pork
dill – a small handful
parsley – a small bunch
garlic – a couple of cloves
red chiles – 2 small, hot
olive oil
ground pork – 1 pound (450g)
the grated zest and juice of a lime

Halve the marrow and remove the seeds and fiber. I peel it only if the skin is particularly thick (if a fingernail lightly pressed against the skin fails to leave a wound, then it is unlikely ever to be tender enough to eat). Cut the flesh into thick chunks and toss in a roasting pan with the crushed garlic, mint leaves, a couple of generous glugs of olive oil, and the lemon juice. Set aside for an hour.

Preheat the oven to 350°F (180°C). Bake the marrow for forty-five minutes or so, until soft and tender. Coarsely chop the dill and its stems, the parsley leaves, and the garlic. Finely chop the chiles, removing the seeds if you like a milder effect.

To cook the pork, get a couple of tablespoons of olive oil smoking hot in a shallow pan, then add the meat. At this point, I don't turn or stir it, however tempting, till the underside has had a chance to color and crisp. Turn when you can to brown the other side. Add the dill, parsley, garlic, and chiles. Let the mixture cook over high heat, until all is fragrant, sizzling, and golden. Season generously with salt and black pepper, then stir in the lime juice and zest. Serve with the baked marrow.

A few other good things

This book is principally the story of my own vegetable patch and my own kitchen. One or two favorite vegetables, such as salsify, cardoons, and corn, are missing for the simple reason that I have never grown them and tend to leave them to the experts. In this short chapter of bits and pieces are some things that, for one or reason or another, have evaded me and my trowel and some, like radishes and cucumber, that only needed a few lines.

Globe artichokes

Handsome, huge, and utterly delectable as they are, this garden has consistently failed to please the globe artichoke, both the egg-sized purple Romanesco and the fuller-figured Green Globe.

Artichokes generally grow well in this climate, sometimes prolifically, their jagged, silver-green leaves forming majestic clumps. I have tried them in four out of six beds in my garden and even, in desperation, in large pots, but to no avail. This year, too late for full inclusion in this book, it looks as though I may have succeeded, with the current incumbents looking hale and hearty, happy in their place in (would you believe?) the rose bed.

Globe artichokes, with their sharp, sometimes prickly-edged "petals," are actually the plant's flower buds and will, if left, open up into showy mauve thistle heads. When picked young, their heads small and tight, they can be boiled and eaten in their entirety (they are splendid fried in batter at this point). A little later on, the globes can be boiled and presented whole, the petals plucked from the head and sucked clean of their flesh.

The real treasure—the soft, mild-flavored heart that makes up the base of the flower—lies hidden. This is found by removing all the petals and the inedible, hairy "choke" within. A soft gray-green in color, this tender heart is there for eating with vinaigrette or a buttery hollandaise sauce, or if exceptionally large, stuffed with breadcrumbs, lemon, and herbs.

I am disappointed not to be able to offer you a fuller account of this luxurious and highly prized vegetable. But every gardener, like every cook, meets their match. Mine, inexplicably, appears to be the artichoke.

Cucumber

Those with small gardens may have to forgo this one. The succulent, hairy-stemmed plants work best growing up a frame of twigs. Make it a strong one, as cucumbers can be heavy in quantity. A freshly cut cuke is a thing of joy and the flavor is often surprisingly intense. In many respects, they work best in a greenhouse, but they will grow happily outside during a hot summer. Find a sunny spot sheltered from the wind. If I had one foot of extra space I would grow a cane frame of cucumbers. They ask nothing from us save a strong support, lots of water, and a midseason feed with a drop of tomato fertilizer or liquid seaweed. They will reward us with small, firm fruits with an exceptional flavor.

Yes, I love this fruit thinly sliced with a crisp lettuce and chicken salad, grated and stirred into yogurt with fresh mint to cool down a spicy little meat patty, and even cooked slowly in butter to accompany a piece of white fish. But the best use I have come across is as a sandwich filling, held between two thick slices of the freshest white bread.

Try this: peel a medium cucumber, removing only the tough, outer part of the skin, leaving the outside still bright green. Slice thickly down its length and then cut each slice into small dice. Put in a colander in the sink, scatter salt over, and let sit for thirty minutes or so.

Put six heaping tablespoons of mayonnaise into a bowl and add half a teaspoon of smooth, mild mustard and a grinding of black pepper. Discard the roots and the toughest of the green shoots from a couple of green onions, then slice the rest into fine rings. Add to the mayonnaise with a teaspoon of capers and the coarsely chopped leaves from a bushy sprig of mint. Pat the cucumber dry and stir it into the mayonnaise, adding a drizzle of tarragon vinegar to brighten the flavors. Use as a dressing for smoked fish or as a sandwich filling.

Radishes

I grow the French Breakfast radish because of its sweet heat and pretty white tips but it is less successful than the all-red varieties—the ones that look like clowns' noses. There is no formal row of this member of the mustard family in my veg patch, just a few seeds sprinkled hugger-mugger among the other plants. They grow like Topsy in warm, light soil on the sunny side of the garden, and I have often eaten them within four weeks of planting. My first are sown even before the daffodils have finished flowering, the last in early September.

Radishes are ready to pick when you see their shoulders nudging through the surface of the soil. They are best eaten young and crisp, with cold, pale butter and a little saucer of sea salt flakes in which to dip them. Ignore any suggestions of cooking them; the writer is clearly deluded.

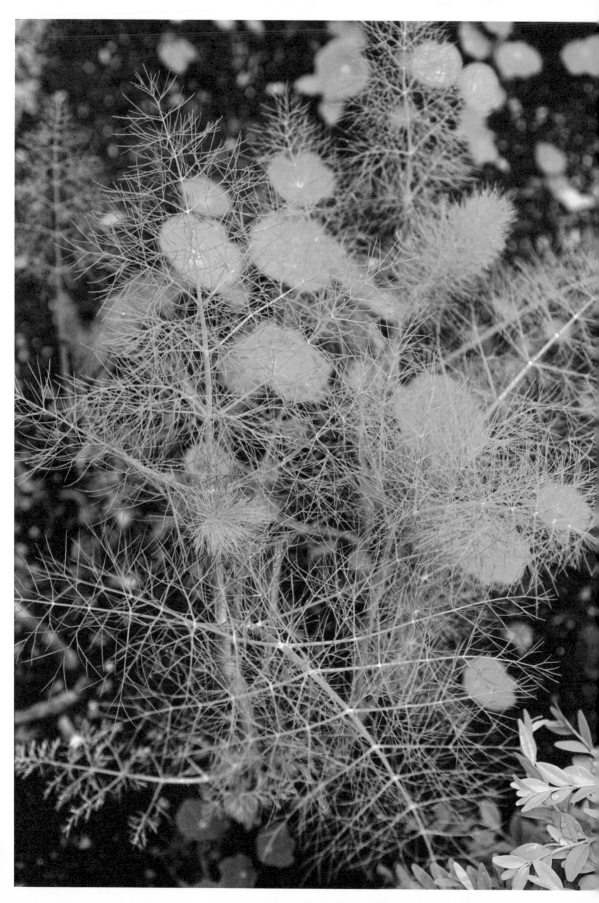

Try them sliced and dropped into yogurt with white wine vinegar, fresh mint or dill, and some salt. They need no pepper. They are in their element in a light lemon juice and olive oil dressing with masses of cilantro and mint leaves. A bright, knife-sharp salad for a sizzling-hot summer's day.

Green onions

Rarely is my fridge without a bunch of these elegant, mildly flavored alliums. While they are at their best perched in snow-white and green stripes atop a curl of crisp lettuce in an "English" salad, I also find them endlessly useful in the kitchen.

The white part is what we really want, but I add the coarser-textured green end to a stir-fry at the same time as the garlic. My enthusiasm for this immature onion has much to do with its ease of preparation—it needs no peeling. I have only grown this usually pain-free crop twice and have had less luck than I expected. They are generally easy—especially the gorgeous North Holland Blood Red and White Lisbon varieties—in a sunny, well-drained corner. You can sow the seed at any time from March to August. The plumper ones are good grilled and dressed with a splash of dark, mellow balsamic vinegar, or chopped and stirred into mashed potato.

Fennel

Once in a blue moon, I crave the hard white flesh and clean bite of a fennel bulb. It is usually on a needle-cold day, when the sky is gray-white and I want something with a steely crispness to go in a winter salad.

Fennel is hardly the most versatile of vegetables, and anise flavor at this intensity is not to everyone's taste. I appreciate fennel in paper-thin slices, so fine you can see through them. In a green salad to accompany smoked salmon or poached haddock, it shines in small amounts. Overused, even slightly, and it will dominate a dish and ruin your wine.

Growing in a garden or laid out on a trestle table at the market, the plants are astonishingly beautiful, with their fat white bulbs and mane of feathery leaves. In autumn, their smell is enticing. You can tuck thin wedges of fennel into a fish's belly as it bakes, or under the bones of a roasting rabbit.

Fennel is very fine on a crisp October day, each bulb cut in half lengthwise and cooked slowly in butter in a tightly covered heavy pan. Low heat and a splash of water will keep it from scorching and lessen its pushy character; a careful eye will ensure it emerges sweet and tender, its edges lightly caramelized, its scent like that of warm aniseed cookies. A lovely thing to eat with some thin slices of pork and their roasting juices.

About the author

Nigel Slater is the author of a collection of bestselling books including the classics *Real Fast Food, Appetite,* and the critically acclaimed *The Kitchen Diaries.* He has written a much-loved column for *The Observer* for seventeen years. His memoir, *Toast —The Story of a Boy's Hunger,* has won six major awards, including British Biography of the Year. Visit www.nigelslater.com.

Also by Nigel Slater

Eating for England
The Kitchen Diaries
Toast—The Story of a Boy's Hunger
Thirst
Appetite
Nigel Slater's Real Food
Real Cooking
The 30-Minute Cook
Real Fast Puddings
Real Fast Food

A note on the type

Claude Garamond (c. 1480–1561) cut type for the Parisian scholar-printer Robert Estienne in the first part of the sixteenth century, basing it on the type cut by Francesco Griffo for Venetian printer Aldus Manutius in 1495. Garamond refined his typeface in later versions, adding his own concepts as he developed his skills as a punchcutter.

Adobe Garamond, the type used in *Tender,* was designed by Robert Slimbach in 1989. The roman weights were based on the true Garamond, and the italics on those of punchcutter Robert Granjon. This font has been expanded to include small caps, titling caps, expert fonts, and swash caps, which were typical in the fifteenth and sixteenth centuries.

Revered British food writer Nigel Slater made a vow to himself on the eve of the new millennium—that he would transform his humble, forty-foot urban plot into a bountiful, edible vegetable garden. Over the next few years, he raised delicate, soft-leaved lettuces, eight varieties of potato, and violet-colored carrots, all behind his London home. Some fared well, some did not. But it was the process of growing, tending, and harvesting his own food that fundamentally changed him, as the produce he planted and nurtured became the cornerstone of his highly personal cooking style.

Tender is the lavishly illustrated chronicle of Slater's experiences with his homegrown vegetables, with his beloved garden, and in his kitchen. It's the story of a gentle cook, one who realizes how precious it is to bite into a freshly-picked, sun-ripened heirloom tomato straight off the vine.

Twenty-nine vegetables are explored and celebrated—what helps them thrive in the garden and how they work best in the kitchen. Each chapter offers charmingly homey recipes, such as **A Quick Way with Zucchini**, **A Contemporary Take on Creamed Spinach**, and **A Rich Dish of Sprouts and Cheese for a Very Cold Night**. Slater's sense of wonder at and reverence for the natural world is infectious, and his admiration for all manner of vegetables encourages us to explore lesser-known species and unsung varieties.

Slater is a renowned writer in his native England, cherished as much for his soaring prose as for his knowledge of food. And *Tender* is his opus—a book to sit with and savor as well as a trustworthy companion in the kitchen.